THE CATHOLIC CHURCH
IN SOUTH AFRICA

PATRICK RAYMUND GRIFFITH, O.P., D.D.

First Vicar Apostolic of the Cape of Good Hope (1837–62)

THE CATHOLIC CHURCH
IN SOUTH AFRICA

From its Origins to the Present Day

by

WILLIAM ERIC BROWN

M.C., D.D., M.A., B.Sc.

Edited by

MICHAEL DERRICK

P. J. KENEDY & SONS
NEW YORK

IMPRIMATUR
✠ DENIS E. HURLEY, O.M.I.
ARCHBISHOP OF DURBAN
DURBAN: APRIL 8, 1960

The Nihil obstat *and* Imprimatur *are a declaration that a book or pamphlet is considered to be free from doctrinal or moral error. It is not implied that those who have granted the* Nihil obstat *and* Imprimatur *agree with the contents, opinions or statements expressed.*

PRINTED IN GREAT BRITAIN

Such as it is, I offer this study to the archbishops and bishops of the Apostolic Delegation of Southern Africa, from whom I have received much kindness and unfailing patience with the delays caused by ill-health. But I would especially express my gratitude to Archbishop Lucas, S.V.D., who, when Apostolic Delegate to Southern Africa, bullied me into making the book. Only in that way, however, is he responsible for its many defects.

W. E. BROWN

CONTENTS

LIST OF ILLUSTRATIONS

LIST OF MAPS

PREFACE

WILLIAM ERIC BROWN, a priest of the archdiocese of Glasgow and the author of this book, spent the last eleven years of his life in South Africa and died there on 28 November 1957 at the age of sixty-four. He had retired to that country in 1946 in the hope of finding better health in a warmer climate, and spent his years there largely in the preparation of this work. At first he divided his time between Durban and Johannesburg, according to the season, and was able also to travel further afield; but latterly he was obliged to live in a sanatorium at Durban. Yet his intellect was never dimmed by suffering, and as his health declined so was he able to devote himself more exclusively to assembling the fruits of the researches which the South African bishops had asked him to undertake; until the last two years, when he was able to do little.

He was very well equipped for such work, having gone to South Africa with a reputation as an historian which was in itself sufficient guarantee that any history of the Church which he might undertake would be neither pedestrian nor parochial, but would be written against a broad and generous background of scholarship and culture. Born in Kent in 1893, he became a Catholic in 1919, one of those who had found the faith in the trenches of the First World War. His health had already been undermined on active service; he had had a distinguished war record, and held the Military Cross, but he had been both wounded and severely gassed, and it was from the consequences of the gas that eventually he died. His first inclination as a young man had not been towards history but towards the higher mathematics, in which he had gained a degree from the University of London before he went to France with the Royal Artillery, and it was a keen disappointment to him after the war when he was told that he had been away from mathematics too long to hope for a First in that discipline at Oxford. He took a First, at St John's College, where he was later elected an Honorary Fellow, but it was in history. In 1921 he went as a Lecturer in History to the University of Glasgow, where he became the close friend of Professor J. S. Phillimore, with whom in a short

space of years he raised to a high level the intellectual prestige of
the Catholic contribution to the life of the University.

In 1924 he resigned from the University to prepare for the
priesthood, and in September of that year he became a student
again, at St Edmund's College, Ware. He had been accepted for
the Archdiocese of Westminster, but Glasgow lost no time in
reclaiming him, inviting him to return after ordination as chaplain
to the Catholic students in the University there. He completed
his philosophy at Ware, writing at the same time a study of the
Scots martyr John Ogilvie, which was published in 1925; and in
1926 he went to the Scots College in Rome for his theology. In
Rome likewise he found time for research and writing, producing
a book on *The Achievement of the Middle Ages* and one on *Bishops*
for a series on " Pioneers of Christendom ". He corresponded
with learned societies, acquired the impressive title of Archivarius
et Palaeographus ex Ædibus Vaticanis, and took a leading part in the
preparation of the evidence for the beatification of John Ogilvie.
He was ordained priest at St John Lateran on Easter Sunday 1929,
and received his doctorate in the following summer.

Returning then to Glasgow, he took possession of the newly
established chaplaincy in Southpark Avenue which he occupied
for fifteen years, until he was obliged to retire to South Africa.
They were years which left a great and enduring mark; he gained
the devotion of great numbers of students, and his name will be
legendary among the Catholics of Glasgow and the West of Scotland
for many years to come. When he died it was written of him:

He saw from the very beginning that one man alone could not
directly influence five hundred students, but that if he could
grasp the natural leaders, the men and women of character, he
could influence the mass and the future. So he set out
deliberately to attract the best, and to them he literally poured
out his life. Patient and tenacious, he was at the disposal of any
student who cared to walk up the stairs and knock at the door of
his study. There during term time he spent endless hours,
talking and listening, explaining, exhorting, giving heedlessly
the riches of his mind, spending his small store of stamina.
Round him he gathered the cream of the Catholic body, and
Sunday nights at the chaplaincy became for many a student a
feast of reason, if not a flow of song, to be enjoyed in the present
and treasured in the memory.

Yet it was not really his learning nor his general culture that in the final analysis attracted the undergraduates and a host of friends. It was rather his tolerance, his kindness, his Christian charity that drew them. For he was above all a true priest, a living sacrifice after the model of his Master. To follow his vocation he had turned his back on the glittering prizes that were his for the taking, and he had converted his energies to winning souls, to sanctify the closed world of the University he knew so intimately. All the book-learning in the world will not bring a single soul to God unless it be consecrated to the service of the Almighty and warmed by divine grace. This conviction shone clearly through his weekly sermons to the students in the tiny chapel of the chaplaincy as he exhorted them to use their talents to the full for God's glory and not for empty prizes. It was the combination of a powerful intellect with radiant personal sanctity that gave him power over everyone who came within his charmed circle.

He continued his historical work in those years, lecturing on Church History at the archdiocesan seminary at Bearsden, and contributing the long section on " Christianity to the Edict of Milan " to the second volume of Edward Eyre's *European Civilization: Its Origin and Development* and the chapter on " The Reformation in Scotland " to the fourth.

It will be understood, then, that the Editor of this present volume approached his task with some temerity. Dr Brown left his studies in the history of the Church in South Africa without their final arrangement when he died, and they had to be prepared for the press. In particular there remained much duplication in the treatment of the same events under different chapter-headings. It proved necessary to re-plan the work, in a different series of chapters, but the Editor has not omitted any substantial part of Dr Brown's narrative within the scope of its title, and any omissions must be explained by the untimely death of its author. Yet Dr Brown did not write the kind of book which necessarily finds a place in the index for every important name. Nor did he use the simple chronological method in approaching his studies; it would probably have been impossible to do so; and while a broad chronological framework has been given to this book there are inevitably many occasions for returning to times and events to which reference has already been made.

Dr Brown's work began with the appointment of the first resident vicar apostolic at the Cape in 1837 and ended with the appointment of the first Apostolic Delegate in 1922. The Editor has added a prologue and an epilogue to indicate the main features of the earlier and the later history; but these make no claim to be based upon research, and cannot invite comparison with the main body of the work. Throughout his task the Editor has been greatly assisted by Father Howard St George, O.M.I., of Archbishop's House, Durban. He wishes also to express his gratitude for the kindness and patience shown by His Grace the Archbishop of Durban. Yet the Editor is well aware that it is not for him to make acknowledgements that might in any way give the impression that his work has been of anything more than a merely technical order.

MICHAEL DERRICK

Petersham, 1959

NOTE

Most nineteenth-century writers, generally without conscious insult, referred to the Africans as " Kaffirs." In this book, accordingly, that term occurs in quotations and references, although it has been avoided elsewhere.

Dr Brown frequently used the terms " Bantu " and " Natives." He left a note, however, expressing anxiety lest this should be misunderstood, and explaining that he was largely following the usage of his sources.

It may be of assistance to readers not acquainted with the African situation to know that " Bantu " (always a collective noun) is the name given to the indigenous race occupying most of Central and Southern Africa and comprising a great number of national or tribal groups, such as Zulus, Basutos and Xhosas.

PROLOGUE

THE Christian history of South Africa began exactly three hundred and fifty years before the first resident bishop arrived there, when, in 1487, King John II of Portugal sent two expeditions in search of the kingdom of Prester John, one by land and one by sea. The one which went by sea was commanded by Bartholomew Dias, who left Lisbon in August with two caravels and a supply-ship. Following the African coast southwards from the Congo, it passed on 8 December the farthest point that had been reached five years before by Diogo Cão, two hundred leagues south of the mouth of the Congo, and entered what Dias called, in honour of the day, the gulf of Santa Maria da Conceicão; it became known later on as Walvis Bay, the only good harbour in what is now South West Africa. There Dias erected one of his stone *padroes*, which he dedicated to Saint Philip; the remains of it were taken back to Lisbon in the nineteenth century. He sailed on, rounding the Cape without seeing it, passing what he called the Bahia dos Vaqueiros, the bay of cow-herds, now Mossel Bay, and dropping his anchor in Algoa Bay, where, off what is now Port Elizabeth, he landed on a rocky islet which he called the Ilheo da Santa Cruz, the Island of the Holy Cross. There he erected another of his *padroes*, which he dedicated to Saint Gregory, and there Mass was offered for the first time on the soil of South Africa.

After the Mass a council was held, Dias wanting to press on towards India and his men, exhausted and ill, wanting to return to Portugal. The decision was to go home; they followed the coast as far as the mouth of the Kowie or Great Fish river, and then turned, and on the homeward journey found the Cape, which they called the Cape of Storms, Cabo Tormentoso. By the end of the year the caravels were back in the Tagus; tradition says it was the Portuguese king who insisted that the Cape must be called Cabo de Bona Esperança, the Cape of Good Hope, since its discovery had at last given prospect of the sea-route to the Indies, although Duarte Pacheco says that Dias called it so from the first.

Ten years later Vasco da Gama left the Tagus and, after rounding the Cape, fulfilled the good hope and reached India. Men who had

I

sailed with Dias were in his crews, and *padroes* were in his holds.
Before he sailed the king had told him in a ceremonial allocution
that the voyage was intended firstly to spread the Christian Faith
and secondly to gain the riches of the East.   Vasco da Gama took
a most solemn oath on the banner of the Order of Christ that he
would carry that Faith wherever he went; nor has anyone since
gone to South Africa with more religious intention.   The night
before he sailed he spent in prayer in the Chapel of Our Lady of
Bethlehem, where the church of the Jeronimos now stands.   The
following morning began with High Mass, followed by a solemn
procession to the quay, with all the sailors carrying lighted candles
and a great crowd of people accompanying them and joining in the
responses of the litany.   When they reached the vessels in which
they were about to set out on what proved to be one of the most
momentous voyages in the history of the world, all those who were
to sail, officers and men, knelt for the general absolution and the
reading of the Bull in which the Pope granted a plenary indulgence
to those who might die on the voyage.   On 8 July they sailed;
early in November they landed in a bay west of the Cape which they
called Santa Helena, where they stayed for eight days; on 16
November they resumed their voyage; two days later they sighted
the Cape; on 22 November they rounded it, and on 25 November
they anchored in Mossel Bay, where they stayed for a fortnight,
sailing on the feast of the Immaculate Conception and sighting on
Christmas Day the land to which they accordingly gave the name
which it still bears, Tierra de Natal.

All this is part of the familiar and heroic history of the world.
Where Vasco da Gama had led other Portuguese voyagers followed.
The first church in South Africa was built by John da Nova in
Mossel Bay in 1501, the year before Vasco da Gama set out from
the Tagus for a second time.   For another generation to come the
high pitch of Portuguese enterprise in navigation was sustained;
yet the Cape was no more than a staging-point, and the records
tell nothing of any settlement there.   In 1510 the Viceroy of
India, Francisco de Almeida, was killed, with sixty-five of his men,
in a fight with the Hottentots when he landed at Table Bay on his
homeward voyage, and it is sometimes said that the Portuguese
avoided the Cape thereafter on that account.   Yet it is not easy
to understand why they should have done so; why they should not

in their greatest period have regarded the Cape on the contrary as a port of call as valuable as the English and Dutch and French later found it, where fresh meat and water and vegetables might be obtained. The loss of de Almeida was a disaster, but not a crushing one; many disasters were sustained in the great years of discovery, and the Portuguese did not show themselves in general deterred by hostile natives.

As the sixteenth century developed missionaries and merchants alike had the vision of India and the Far East constantly before their eyes, but the missionary achievement in Africa in that first half of the sixteenth century which ended with the arrival of St Francis Xavier in Japan was astonishing nevertheless. The king and queen of the Congo had been baptized even before the century began, and their kingdom remained Christian for a hundred years. Early in the sixteenth century the titular See of Utica, African and *in partibus infidelium*, was bestowed upon a prince of the Congo—the first African bishop south of the Sahara in the history of the Church.* In 1560 the Portuguese Jesuits undertook new missions on both the west and the east African coast, basing themselves on the island of Luanda in the west and on the Zambesi in the east. The Dominicans had already been on the Zambesi for fourteen years; and there, as on the Congo, a Christian African ruler was installed. The missionary endeavour in this part of Africa was much more considerable, and had much more far-reaching results, than later historians generally discovered whose task it was to peer behind the overlying history of the Dutch.† There is no evidence, it is true, of this endeavour penetrating overland to the Cape, but with such an abundant missionary zeal, such boundless enterprise simultaneously in three continents through a century and a half, it is clearly improbable that the Portuguese would have been frightened of the Hottentots on account of what happened to Almeida. When, midway through the seventeenth

* Leo X made him vicar apostolic of the Congo, but he died in Portugal and never set foot in Africa after his ordination to the priesthood.

† The leading authority is the late Father Sidney R. Welch (see Chapter XIV, II, *infra*). He was the author of the following works (published by Juta & Co., Cape Town): *Europe's Discovery of Southern Africa* (1953); *South Africa under King Manuel, 1495–1521* (1946); *South Africa under John III, 1521–1557* (1949); *South Africa under King Sebastian and the Cardinal, 1557–1580* (1949); *Portuguese Rule and the Spanish Crown in Africa, 1581–1640* (1950); and *Portuguese and Dutch in South Africa, 1641–1806 (1951)*.

century, the Calvinist Dutch hoisted their flag in Cape Town, Catholic priests were at once excluded with a rigid intolerance, and as early as 1660 a French bishop, wrecked in Table Bay, was forbidden to say Mass. Yet a quarter of a century later a party of Jesuits who were able to land because they were not only priests but also astronomers found the Catholic Church fairly well represented among the inhabitants of the Cape. The six astronomer-Jesuits of 1688 wrote:

Although we were engaged in observations day and night, they were not our only occupation. Hardly had we taken possession of our new observatory when the Catholics of this Colony, who are fairly numerous, got to hear of it and showed very great interest. . . . Those who could not express themselves otherwise, because we did not understand their language, knelt and kissed our hands. They drew their rosaries and medals from their necks to show us that they were Catholics. . . . Those who spoke French, Latin, Spanish and Portuguese made their confession. We visited the sick in their houses and in hospital. It was all we could do to console them in so short a time, seeing that they were not allowed to come on board to hear Mass, nor were we allowed to say it on shore.

That was in the year of the revocation of the Edict of Nantes; Huguenot refugees began to arrive in South Africa, the bitter enemies of the Catholic Church were reinforced, and it is doubtful whether the Mass was offered on South African soil for a hundred years thereafter.

Fully to understand that rigid exclusion it is necessary to recall that the decline of the maritime vigour of the Portuguese and the rise of the Dutch as a world-wide mercantile power had followed immediately upon the repression of the Netherlands by the Duke of Alva. The events which filled the Dutch with hatred for Catholic Spain were followed by the extension of Spanish rule to Portugal (1580–1640), so that the Dutch had even less inclination than before to distinguish between Spanish and Portuguese when they met them in South Africa or anywhere else. The "sea-beggars" who had brought about the rise of the Dutch Republic, rallying the northern provinces of the Netherlands and inviting the Prince of Orange to be their leader, were of the same blood as the Dutch sea-captains who as the seventeenth century advanced increasingly challenged the Portuguese, and the English as well, in Africa and the East.

The English East India Company had received its first charter in 1600 and the Dutch Company had been founded in the following year, and at first the two were natural partners united in fear of Spain. The first fleet which the English Company sent out, under Admiral Lancaster, spent seven weeks in Table Bay in 1601 while the men recovered from scurvy; it was not the first English fleet to anchor there, Admiral Raymond's expedition having called ten years before to take on fresh provisions. The English and Dutch companies made Table Bay a regular port of call, and neither was well disposed to any Portuguese they found. In 1619 the English Company invited the Dutch to join them in building a fort at the Cape; the Dutch declined, and in 1620 Captain Fitzherbert, in the first bid for exclusiveness, hoisted his flag on the Lion's Head and called it King James's Mount. But this was not an enterprise which endured; the Dutch challenge greatly increased during the civil war in England, and on 6 April 1652, four years after Spain had recognized the independence of the Netherlands, three Dutch vessels landed a garrison in Table Bay and Jan van Riebeek became the first Dutch Governor of the Cape; the flag was planted and the first decisive colonial foundation had at last been made, a hundred and fifty years after Vasco da Gama had anchored in Mossel Bay. It was fifteen years before de Ruyter sailed up the Medway and burned the ships at Chatham.

From the first the discipline of the Dutch Reformed Church was rigid at the Cape, and from the first no Catholic settlers were allowed there. Yet the Reformation never came near to making the Dutch at home into an exclusively Protestant people; nor had the rising against Spain been by any means an exclusively Protestant affair. In the Netherlands today more than a third of the people are Catholic; the proportion was almost exactly the same by the known statistics of a hundred years ago; the frontiers of the United Provinces of the Dutch Republic were very much the same after the Peace of Westphalia in the middle of the seventeenth century as they are today, and Catholics were a higher proportion then, before the long attrition had been carried far. It is tempting to wonder how far the history of South Africa might have been different, and whether the approach in these recent years to the critical problem of racial relationships might not have been different, if from the first the Dutch population in South Africa had been a true projection of the population in the Netherlands, with Catholics a minority of at least a third among the Boer farmers, numerous enough to establish a tradition in contrast to that which is in fact so deeply entrenched and which is grounded in Calvinist theology.

In 1795 the British occupied Cape Town to hold it against the French, and when the Dutch regained it in 1802 by the Peace of Amiens the Netherlands had become a Batavian Republic, with the Stadtholder in exile, the Orange Party in eclipse and the ideas of the French Revolution ascendant.   On 25 July 1804, the Commissioner-General of the Batavian Republic at the Cape, de Mist, published an ordinance promising religious toleration. " All religious societies which for the furtherance of virtue and good morals worshipped an Almighty Being " were to enjoy equal protection from the laws, and " no civil privileges were to be attached to any creed ".   At once three Catholic priests arrived from Holland, Joannes Lansink, Jacobus Nelissen and Lambertus Prinsen, and a room in the Castle was put at their disposal for use as a chapel, so that they could say Mass for the soldiers, many of whom were French.   Father Lansink was appointed prefect apostolic in 1805. In the autumn of that year, however, a British force under Major-General Sir David Baird was sent to recapture Cape Town, which surrendered on 10 January 1806.   Baird had the reputation of being a generous man, and his acts of severity were few; but he was a Scots Presbyterian who felt at one with the Calvinist Dutch where the Catholic Church was concerned, and he lost no time in expelling the three priests who had so recently arrived; the first Prefect Apostolic of the Cape died at sea on his way home.

Not until the British possession had been confirmed by the treaty of 1814 was the attempt made to find a successor to Father Lansink.   Then the initiative of the Vicar Apostolic of the London District, Bishop Poynter, led to the appointment of a Benedictine bishop, Dom Edward Bede Slater, who is reckoned to have been the first Vicar Apostolic of the Cape from the decree of Pope Pius VII in February 1818 until his death in 1832.   But the government in London forbade him to go there, so that, by a decree of the Congregation of Propaganda dated 21 January 1819, his appointment was extended to make him in addition the first Vicar Apostolic of Mauritius, and of Madagascar as well until 1829. He landed at Cape Town on his outward journey, on New Year's Day, 1820, but remained there only three weeks, sailing on to Mauritius and leaving in charge at Cape Town a certain Father Scully of whom more will be found in the pages that follow. It was in Father Scully's time, on 28 October 1822, that the foundation-stone was laid of a Catholic church in Harrington Street. " From beginning to end the building saw nothing but misfortunes; the materials used were bad, repairs had to be effected even before the building was completed, and finally, in the torrential storms of 1837, the church was destroyed and completely washed away ".* That was the year of the arrival of the third Vicar Apostolic to be appointed, the first to be appointed exclusively to the Cape; for the successor of Bishop Slater, another Benedictine, Dom William Placid Morris, had resided in Mauritius and never set foot on South African soil. But with the appointment of Bishop Griffith the history of the Catholic Church as a visible institution in South Africa begins.

* J. E. Brady, O.M.I., in *The Catholic Church and Southern Africa* (Cape Town, 1951).

Chapter I

BISHOP GRIFFITH

I. The Appointment

A T Maynooth College in County Kildare on 19 August 1837, eight years after the Catholic Emancipation Act had been passed at Westminster, Raymond Griffith, an Irish Dominican preparing for his episcopal consecration, commenced his journal:

> Received on Saturday 29 July three Bulls and two Papers of Privileges for the Cape of Good Hope. Of the three first, one removed the Cape from the Vicariate of Mauritius, the second appointed me Vicar Apostolic of the former, and the third elected me Bishop* of Palaeopolis in Turkey in Asia under the Archbishop of Ephesus.

Two sequences of events came together in that appointment. Early in 1837 a priest, John Brady, called at Cape Town on his way from Mauritius to Rome. There a group of Catholic laymen talked with him of their troubles, and he agreed to take to the Pope a petition which they had drawn up and signed, asking for the appointment of a pastor. It asserted that application had been made to the vicar apostolic in Mauritius, but that he had no priest to spare; that innumerable Catholics were going to alien ministers and marrying before them and having infants baptized by them; and that many were dying without the sacraments. The petition was signed by Dr O'Flinn; by Lieutenant-Colonel Christopher Bird, who had been secretary to the Governor; and by forty others, including four sergeants of the 98th Regiment, as well as the vice-consul of France. After consultations with the vicar apostolic in Mauritius, to whose ecclesiastical jurisdiction South Africa then belonged, the Holy See decided to form a new Vicariate of the Cape of Good Hope, coextensive with the political boundaries of the English colony, which included the island of St Helena. On the advice of Archbishop Murray, of Dublin, Raymond Griffith,

---

* I.e., titular bishop *in partibus.*

8

whom he had already recommended for the suggested vicariate of Madagascar,[1] was nominated.

The British Government provided the other sequence of events. From 1820 they had been prepared to pay an annual stipend of £200 to an accredited clergyman who would act as chaplain to the Roman Catholic community at the Cape. In the next fifteen years three had been appointed, and had left after bitter quarrels with the Catholic laymen who claimed, under the title of churchwardens, to administer the ecclesiastical property.* Litigation and memorials to the Governor from both parties were frequent, but despite this nuisance, or perhaps because of it, his secretary, Colonel Bell, wrote to the Under-Secretary of State in Whitehall on 27 March 1835 urging that the Roman Catholics of Cape Town were numerous and required a clergyman, and that the Governor should see that one was provided for them. Lord Glenelg, the Colonial Secretary, wrote to Archbishop Murray of Dublin asking him to arrange for a permanent chaplain and offering to pay the passage money as well as the stipend; and then, when Bishop Griffith had been appointed vicar apostolic, he wrote similarly to the Governor:

> I propose, therefore, to direct the issue of the customary allowance of £60 to Mr Griffith to defray the expense of his passage to the Cape, and you will, on your part, have the goodness to give directions for the payment to him of the annual stipend of £200† which was enjoyed by the Roman Catholic clergyman his predecessor.[2]

Recognition of the existence of a Catholic community at Cape Town and the duty of the public authority to provide financially for the priest who should serve it had indeed been an accepted principle of the English Governments long before the Emancipation Act of 1829. Sir David Baird, in expelling the three Dutch priests whom the Batavian Republic had sent out, acted on his own whim and authority, and apparently without informing London. Certainly Sir Rufane Donkin, who was acting Governor in 1821, made a grant of £75 a year to Father Scully, who was

---

* See pp. 21 sqq., infra.

† This stipend was paid until the death of Bishop Leonard in 1903. The Cape Parliament Act 5 of 1875 had provided for its continuance until the then incumbent should die or cease to hold office. Bishop Leonard was Vicar Apostolic of Cape Town from 1872.

there until 1824, and alluded to it, in the course of a controversy with Lord Charles Somerset, as an ordinary administrative measure. A salary was also paid without question both to Father Scully's successor, Father Wagenaar, and to Father Morel, O.P., during their stay as chaplains, and there was some ground for Lord Charles Somerset's reply in 1817 to a query of Bishop Poynter, the Vicar Apostolic of the London District, that a chaplain for the Roman Catholic community at the Cape would be welcomed; " all religious denominations ", it said, " are not only tolerated but entitled to equal privileges in the Colony according to the fundamental laws of the Batavian Republic, guaranteed to the inhabitants by the capitulation ".* It was not without irony that the Dutch should be cited as the champions of religious freedom. In fact the chief effect of the Emancipation Act in the colony was to remove the disabilities of Catholic laymen for office-holding. Even these had been for some time more often a dangerous threat; they were applied against Christopher Bird in 1824, but only because the spitefulness of an agitator happened to coincide with a dislike, on quite different grounds, conceived against Bird by Somerset.†

II. The Bishop Arrives

Raymond Griffith, whom the English Government thus accepted as chaplain to the scattered Roman Catholic community of the Cape Colony, estimated roughly as seven hundred, but whom the Holy See designated as vicar apostolic, was an Irish Dominican nearly forty years old. He had studied at San Clemente, the house of his order in Rome, and had won fame as a preacher. He had also served his people in Ireland during the cholera epidemics of 1831 and the following years.[3] After his consecration he spent four or five months collecting the funds and personnel which would be necessary for a vicar apostolic. His sister and his younger brother, Joseph, studying for the priesthood, would accompany him. So also would a fellow Dominican, Father Corcoran, and a Franciscan, Father Burke. Then he went to St Peter's College,

---

* A Spanish Dominican who stayed at the Cape during most of 1836 gained little command of English, and the Government would not pay him more than half the usual stipend.

† See p. 27, infra.

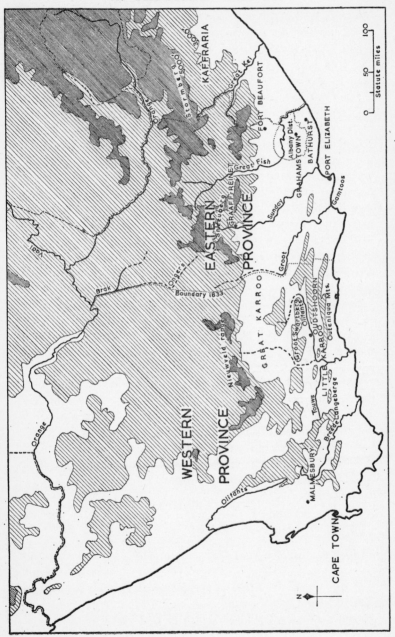

I. BISHOP GRIFFITH'S VICARIATE (SAVE FOR THE ISLAND OF ST HELENA)

Wexford, and persuaded three of the professors there and half a dozen students to join his vicariate later. With these arrangements made, Bishop Griffith travelled first to London, where he called on Lord Glenelg, and then to Plymouth, where his party were already assembled and whence they sailed for Cape Town in the *Comet*.

From Father Brady, who had helped in his appeal for funds in Dublin, and from Lord Glenelg, the new bishop probably learned something of the Catholics in his vicariate. The only hint given in his journal is his decision, before reaching Cape Town, to have nothing to do with those who called themselves churchwardens.[4] Either of his informants could have told him what a nuisance they had been, and in any case he probably associated the name with a movement for lay control in the Church, said to be a relic of the sentiments of the French Revolution.

The process of organizing a vicariate, and ultimately a diocese according to the Church's conception, out of these scattered quarrelsome Catholics, obviously depended to a large extent on the personality of Raymond Griffith. His journal shows him aware of his responsibility. On the voyage he studied two books on the powers and duty of a bishop, and after the first reading he commented: "I have no reason to plume myself on the character I have to exercise or the toil I have to endure".[5]

That extremely correct reflection is perhaps less revealing than the honesty of his record. Before settling down to episcopal questions he was going to read Homer, because " when at school I disliked Greek so much I didn't attend to the story ". In his boxes, however, there were copies of two popular novels, *Udolpho* and *Peter Simple*, and he finished these before turning to the *Iliad*. And his comments on books, as his choice of them, were far from conventional:

> I finished Homer today, or rather his *Iliad*, which is a splendid piece of rank nonsense: his Nestor an old hag in breeches; only one or two affecting passages in the whole and these at the end; the Greeks (if we believe him at least) were, in the palmy days of their glory and civilization, not a whit better than the negroes in the interior of Africa at the present day; nay, not half so merciful and human.

Or this on Bulwer's *England*, which he read afterwards:

There is much of the little boy in all his assumed manliness of criticism: he does not condescend to mention even Lingard, though Lingard catered so much to English bigotry in his history of England.[6]

It is a just criticism of Bulwer, and Lingard's letters show that the guess about his method was not altogether inaccurate.

Though the bishop spent two hours every day reciting the Dominican office with Father Corcoran in their cabin (unless they were exceptionally slow this must have included other exercises of prayer), he joined with the other passengers and the officers in backgammon or whist or cribbage every night except Sunday. And his sister caused him a lot of annoyance: at whist, " nothing can be worse or more infelicitous than Margaret's play "; at backgammon, " she is not always ' honest ' in the game ". The Scots might have called him forthright, but the English would say irascible. Certainly he was honest in recording his weaknesses. His earlier journey across England had been marked by valises or portmanteaux left behind in coach or boat or hotel, and recovered only after a lot of fuss; " I can never ", he wrote, " look after more than myself and one object at a time ".

With all this he managed to study the *Duty and Power of Bishops* before the party disembarked at Cape Town on Easter Saturday, 7 April 1838. Father Burke took lodgings for them all at 38 Castle Street, and the bishop arranged with the military authorities to say Mass the following day in the barracks. The next few weeks were spent in getting to know the government officials and the local conditions; and this was made easier because he immediately took to Christopher Bird, " a sensible, religious, well-meaning gentleman " who was now living in retirement in Castle Street. During these weeks, too, he learned more of the Catholics in Cape Town who formed the larger part of his charge, and whose affairs were tangled by quarrels and lawsuits made worse by the three years they had been without a priest at all.[7]

Immediately Raymond Griffith decided to accept as far as possible no responsibility for the past arrangements, to liquidate if he could the existing but ruined Church property, and to build up his own organization. This would take time; for the immediate present he arranged for the regular Sunday Mass, left his sister and brother and the two servants in charge of Father Corcoran, and with Father Burke took passages in the *Lord Saumarez*, a Jersey brig, for the five hundred mile voyage round the coast to Port Elizabeth, the extreme eastern end of his vicariate. His journal tells us several times how fearful he was of wrecks and storms and drowning, but the boat was the quickest way to reach the Catholics who were scattered in the garrisons and towns of the frontier of the Colony, and Bishop Griffith sailed on 24 June.

III. The Lie of the Land

The northern boundaries of Cape Colony varied somewhat with the political theories of Whitehall. Going east the frontier reached the Orange River beyond Colesburg but then turned south and finally ran along the Great Fish River. For more than a century the expansion of the population had been from Cape Town towards this Eastern area, and the farmers who settled there had become graziers rather than agriculturists. The change made it easier for them to satisfy their desire to live as planters, or seigneurs as one Dutch governor had described them. It also brought them into contact with the various Bantu groups who were moving south. With these they did some trade, but there were frequent cattle raids by the Africans and punitive expeditions by the farmers. The behaviour of the latter often differed from the policy of the officials in Cape Town (it was much the same state of affairs as obtained in South America when the Spaniards were colonizing), and the differences became more acute after British rule was established there in 1806. The farmers, mainly of Dutch or French Huguenot extraction, complained of the English habit of trying out first one policy and then another. After General Cradock drove the Kaffirs (as the Africans were called) back across the Fish River in 1812, the most consistent official aim was to establish that boundary and prevent any further expansion of the colony. At the same time the English assumed that all disputes could be satisfactorily solved by the principles of British justice, which the Bantu would naturally accept. The farmers knew this to be untrue, and in any case had no intention of treating with the Bantu as a sovereign foreign state; for them the only possible or desirable method was to teach the black man " proper respect " for the white man's power and authority. This tension had not been materially altered by the arrival of poor emigrants from England and Scotland. The home Government had sent over three thousand in 1820 and settled them in the Eastern district and so founded the towns of Albany and Bathurst. A little later Irish were similarly sent to Clanwilliam. Though these often became labourers for hire, some of them had, by the time of Griffith's arrival, managed to obtain large sheep farms or to engage in profitable trading with the Bantu across the river.

Their presence gave the English Government an additional excuse to impose the English law of evidence and the jury system on the old Roman-Dutch law of the country, and to make English the legal language. It is doubtful if the newcomers thought of this as a privilege, for they quickly learned the Dutch or Flemish patois which was spoken by the original farmers and was being called Afrikaans. And they learned too to share the colonists' view on the frontier question. Indeed, the Lieutenant-Governor at the time claimed that all the old Boers regretted their seizure of land from the Bantu, but the Colonists (i.e. the English settlers) taught them to regard the Bantu as irreclaimable savages.[8]

When Bishop Griffith arrived in the country, four years had elapsed since the British Government had emancipated all slaves in its dominions. But as the Act also bound the ex-slaves to compulsory apprenticeship for four years, it could be said that the system had only just come to an end. As elsewhere in the modern world, widely differing reports were made of it: some spoke of the familial and friendly relations of slaves and owners, others gave instances of vile cruelty; some slaves did become prosperous and engaged in trade and employed poor whites; the formation of the bastard people, Griquas and coloured, suggests that the farmers showed little respect for the human dignity or family rights of their chattels. It may be true that the Hottentots were materially better off in general as slaves than when they became hired labourers, and it has been claimed that the latter system was more profitable to the farmers. It was already common in the Eastern district before 1834, and only one-sixth of the forty thousand slaves emancipated came from that area.

The discontent of the farmers was not principally concerned with emancipation, or even with the monetary compensation, which was less than they expected, but with the laws, going back now ten years, which gave civil rights to the free Hottentot or Bushman and made him equal to the white citizens. The English reform of local administration was beginning to make the change effective, and the appointment of a separate Lieutenant-Governor for the Eastern district in 1820 brought government closer to the farms.[9] From 1834 onwards groups of families, related as a rule by blood as well as locality, sold their farms and trekked with their movable possessions to the country beyond the Orange river; and from there, in 1837, some had turned down to the eastern coast across the Drakensberg mountains.

When Bishop Griffith visited this part of his vicariate, then, he found it an area of large farms and small marketing centres— Port Elizabeth, he notes, had a total population, black and white, of less than two thousand, scarcely a tenth of the size of Cape Town. Everywhere there was the feeling of the frontier and the presence of troops, with Grahamstown as the chief garrison even more than the seat of the Lieutenant-Governor and civil administration. Frequently, too, he noted stories of the ill effects of recent ordinances, and particularly of the economic results of emancipation.

Curiously, however, there seems to have been little remark on the trekking of the last few years. It had affected, of course, only a small section of the population, and apparently the constitutional question, whether the emigrants had left their allegiance behind with their farms, was not seriously considered by their neighbours any more than by the Government. Their fortunes were being followed with interest at the moment of the bishop's arrival, for the *Comet* had just come from Delagoa Bay and brought the missionary Owen, " a thin, delicate, rather genteel man ", and the remnants of the English who had fled when the Zulu chief Dingane (or Dingaan) had massacred Retief and his companions. The captain " told me much about Dingaan and his people and the Boers who are six hundred families and will succeed against Dingaan and have called Port Natal Port Holland ".

IV. Reconnaissance

Port Elizabeth, the bishop wrote, " reminded us of Rock: 'tis built along the side of a hill, the houses generally white and roofed with tiles; has one long wide street and a few very short ones, consisting of a few houses; the huts of the Caffirs or Fingoes adjoin the town ". The bishop went by ox-wagon the twenty miles from Port Elizabeth to Uitenhage, and then to Grahamstown, which he found picturesque but uncomfortable. There he left a reluctant Father Burke—"who follows me like a shadow: I thought he had more spirit "—with £60 to establish a mission centre. Bathurst, Port Francis, Fort Beaufort and Somerset followed, and then Graaff Reinet, where he arrived on 22 August. This was an older settlement, and he found it " a beautiful town— houses neat, white-washed and thatched, seldom more than one storey, with a room and window over the centre of the front. The streets are planted with lemon and orange trees and are very regular. The water is conveyed by cart, clear and limpid, through the streets for purposes of irrigation."

He spent a week there and another at Beaufort before starting back by ox-cart for Cape Town.

Seemingly this was the most uncomfortable part of the journey, perhaps because he was tired. On 12 September:

> I shaved the first time for six days, and a sore job it was. I changed but could not think it the luxury Mr Burke used to designate it, who shaved and changed even in the ox-wagon from Uitenhage and annoyed me about comforts and clean shirts. I could bear to hear anybody talk of such things but a Franciscan minor observant who should wear no shirt *at all;* but poor B. never knew practically the rules or rigidities of his order, or he would never think of comforts and clean shirts, travelling by wagon in this colony. 'Tis absurd for a dandy to expect to be comfortable.[10]

Poor Father Burke!

By land, the bishop noted, " I have travelled in the colony some 1100 miles, quite enough for the rest of my life. It cost me 135 pounds, mere travelling charges."[11] The expense did not surprise him much, for he had had to pay 9s. per head per day to lodge and feed his party. Recently the cost of provisions had risen three or four hundred per cent. " The emigration of the Boers with their flocks from the colony, the payment of slave compensation money, and the apprehension of the land being untilled when the slave apprenticeship is over (just now) were the causes assigned for the monstrous rise of prices." His grouse was the £40 which the farmer charged him for the journey from Beaufort to Cape Town. But he could be as savage to himself as to Father Burke: "Like a fool I paid it, and like a fool have since regretted doing so".

During this reconnaissance of his field of work Bishop Griffith found the officers of the British regiments very willing to help him. As many of their soldiers were Irishmen (there were 301 Catholics in the 75th at Fort Beaufort) this was perhaps not surprising, but he met with the same friendliness from the civil authorities. It seems likely that he was a pleasing conversationalist and guest. His reading on the voyage out, his habit of making a note on the wine and the food and the cooking of each meal (though by preference and perhaps for his health he chose the simplest foods) are signs of a man who mixed easily with the world; and he was puzzled by poor Father Burke, who perhaps found it difficult, as we do, to grasp that the Catholic priest in a British Colony was accepted as part of the official world.

But the bishop had to discover this Catholic community for himself, and he regarded this as the chief business of his reconnaissance. First, of course, there were the Catholic soldiers, and his official position and friendliness with the commanding officers made this fairly easy. There were also a number of Irishmen— some sent over by the British Government in 1820, some time-expired soldiers, some deserters. Many were poor, but he noted of one McKenny that he was " the richest man in Grahamstown, a tanner, wine merchant, canteen keeper, money-lender, etc. ". After saying Mass at Somerset he persuaded twenty to sign a memorial asking for further Government assistance for a chaplain and a church-site, but remarked that some of them, " though having thousands of acres of land and very rich, could not sign their names, and these unfortunately were Irish ". Some of them had married Dutch wives, and when they were willing the bishop instructed them rapidly in the Catholic Faith and baptized them and their children. There were, too, a few English converts like Mr Slater, the attorney at Grahamstown; and several Alsatians, a few Italians and one Goanese at Port Elizabeth are also mentioned in the diary.

It is clear that his task was not always an easy one. Indeed, at the end of his first tour Raymond Griffith wrote despondently: " I have often smiled at my own and others' idea of the joy which a ministry coming here would excite in the breasts of the Catholics, for instead of any the least enthusiasm these people manifest the greatest indifference ". Though this critical attitude was natural perhaps to his schoolmaster-like temperament, it was rarely that he could write of those like the " red-haired man from Galway " whom he found at Port Elizabeth waiting to make his confession, or the Leahy of the same town " who has three children for baptism, a Dutch wife to be received and three older children (baptized by a Dutch minister) to receive oils ". Some were like the northern Irishman on the *Lord Saumarez* whom " I suspect to be a papist but he won't acknowledge it ". Others, like those of the 75th Regiment stationed at Fort Beaufort, had been eight years in the Colony without seeing a priest, and found it difficult to resume a sacramental life. Nor was the bishop without understanding even of those who had apostatized: " I think on the whole ", he wrote, " nay, I am sure, they have despaired of ever seeing priest again or Mass, and, wanting to have some religion to distinguish them from Hottentots, have joined the Dutch church ".[12] Then there was the problem which he met first at Beaufort Town. " I was instantly visited by an Irish papist, named MacMahon, from near Limerick, who told me a sad story of his own state and that of the only two other Catholics in this town—all three living in sin with black women."

The difficulty was not always as great as the modern feeling in South Africa would suggest. There was not a definite or universally accepted objection to intermarriage with native women. Andries Stockenstroom, the Swedish settler, had married a black.[13] The two sons of this marriage were white: one became Lieutenant-Governor of the Eastern District, the other a Civil Commissioner. Their sister, however, was a " perfect black ", and married to Mr Meintjies, the Civil Commissioner of Beaufort Town; and of his two daughters—who were present at the dinner party given to the bishop by their father—" one is white ", the bishop noted, " the other tawny (rather mulatto, real African) ".*

* This is the account which Bishop Griffith learned from some of his hosts and noted at the time. Sir Andries Stockenstroom, the Lieutenant-Governor, does not allude to the matter in his *Autiobiography*. He gives many details of his father's family, but none of his mother's. He says that at the age of seven or eight he was adopted into the family of a friend of his father at the

(*Footnote continued on page* 20

But there was little uniformity of social or religious custom in this matter. When the bishop was trying to deal with the concubinage at Beaufort he found

a strong desire here among the Free Blacks or liberated slaves to be baptized and married and become Christian (at any sacrifice), which the Presbyterian Colonist parson here will not do for them till they have gone to school for years, yet allows them in the meantime to live in concubinage and when compelled by the magistrate to marry them, he marries them without baptism though they desire it most anxiously. He wants men and women of sixty years old to go to school and learn psalm singing (the only religion they appear to me to be taught) and reading, and has some younger ones at it these ten years to no effect. Among these is the concubine of one of my unhappy three (a Prussian) who refuses to allow her three children (she has four) to be baptized by me, and her husband is wretch enough to allow her her way.[14]

MacMahon, however, promised to change his way of life. His wife was now dead, his only son away and his concubine anxious to become a Catholic. So after a few days' instruction she was to be received into the Church at Mass on the Sunday:

Mr Meintjies asked permission of me last night to attend [Mass], which I conceded. I had scarcely commenced explaining the Mass (which I must do in every strange place where it was never celebrated before) to the three or four of my own, when the whole male party of last night, six or eight, came in and remained with imperturbable patience till eleven, when I had done. After the Communion I preached on the Gospel and, after Mass, baptized at great length the black woman who has lived

Cape, but explains that his father had five more children to provide for. Of the latter the only other mention concerns his brother, who became a Civil Commissioner. All that is consistent with Bishop Griffith's story, but the latter would be, I understand, genetically impossible if we take " perfect black " strictly. But the bishop does not claim to have seen Mrs Meintjies herself. His own observation is limited to her two daughters, and the description " perfect black " for their mother must have been given to him, and could then, as now, be used to describe an obviously " coloured " person. I am inclined then to accept his statement as factual in this sense. In any case, the story as told to the bishop shows that racial intermarriage could be accepted then as socially possible, though remaining matter for gossip. The story may also account in part for the unpopularity of Andries Stockenstroom with the farmers, a fact which he admits but does not explain.

in sin with MacMahon. I had already received her promise, and believe it to be sincere, that she would no longer continue so to live. MacMahon promised the same and sleeps no longer under the same roof. She is 55 or 60 years of age and he can't be less than 50. Not content with this, however, I made them both renew the promises before all present, and where and when she did not understand an English word, the Civil Commissioner himself [Mr Meintjies] explained it in Dutch.[15]

At the end of his journey Bishop Griffith wrote in his diary that it was "quite enough for the rest of my life". But in the following year, and again in 1839, in 1841 and 1842, he went on the same mission, and until his health broke down such a trek to some outlying part of his vicariate was a regular occurrence. The practice was adopted by his successor at Cape Town, and by the rulers of the vicariates established later in the Eastern Province and in Natal. Like Bishop Griffith, they called it a " visitation ", but until about the year 1880 this canonical name is misleading. Their principal task on these journeys was not to inspect the work of the resident priest but to hunt out lay folk and those who, in Bishop Griffith's phrase, " ought to be papists ", to teach them the faith, to reconcile the apostates if need be, to call the isolated Catholic families to the sacraments, and so to encourage them to remain faithful till their bishop should visit them again or could send a priest to minister to them.

V. The " Churchwardens "

At Cape Town Bishop Griffith undertook a different task: to build up a local Catholic community of the traditional pattern with a continuous liturgical and sacramental habit. It did not take him long to piece together the Catholic history of the Cape Colony. A register of baptisms and marriages[16] shows names of many European origins, including a considerable number of Dutch, who still formed at this time the large majority of the population.[17] Though the practice of the Catholic religion had been forbidden by the Dutch rulers of the seventeenth and eighteenth centuries, and no colonists had been allowed to be registered as Catholics,[18] it seems probable that many of them held privately to the faith their families had professed in Holland. Certainly the revolutionary

Government of Batavia sent three priests to their Colony after they had obtained possession of it by the treaty of Amiens in 1801; Sir David Baird expelled them, as we have seen, in 1807. The bishop's own summary[19] shows how the story appeared to him:

I do not know that any missionary entered this Colony before 1802 or 1803. . . . There were in it, I have been told, three Dutch priests when Great Britain recovered the dominion of the country in 1806, but I have not been able to discover either tradition or monument that could attest the existence of any church or the traces of any ministry exercised by those men of God during the two or three years that they sojourned amongst my neophites.* Banished by the new possessors of the Cape, they returned to their own country about the time that followed the English occupation. From that period until 1820, that is to say during the space of fourteen years, there were neither apostles nor churches for our brethren, who must have become very numerous on account of a regiment of Frenchmen, Belgians and Germans, the greater part of whom settled in the Colony after having been discharged, and finally on account of the Catholic Army stationed in the country.

In 1819 and 1820 several Irish families transplanted here at the expense of the Government, and, scattered for the most part at 700 or 800 miles from the town, remained for a long time deprived of all spiritual succour for want of a pastor to visit them—for most of them nearly eighteen years elapsed before seeing a single priest. However, in 1820, a religious of the order of St Benedict, the Rev Father Cater [sic], came to reside in the chief town of the Colony. He was sent by his Lordship, the Vicar Apostolic of Mauritius and the Cape of Good Hope,† and, a few months after, the vicar apostolic landed himself, and seeing the plight of the Catholics moved his soul, and he left the Rev Father Scully, an Irishman, to discharge the duties of missionary. . . .

We learn that the Rev Father Scully obtained from the Municipality of the Cape in 1821 the site for the erection of a Catholic Temple. . . . To meet his engagements, Father Scully found the necessity of obtaining security from among his neophites, and thus was laid, without foreseeing it, the foundation

---

* Trace of these Dutch priests became so faint that Dr McCarthy denied their historicity in a public lecture in 1883; *Autobiography*, p. 394.

† Dom Bede Slater (here called Cater) was in fact himself the vicar apostolic, as has been noted in the Prologue, *supra*.

of all the quarrels and all the lawsuits that subsequently afflicted the congregation. . . . I leave in their oblivion the sad dissensions which are now existing and which are daily facing the priests.

On the 11 July 1824 Rev Father Scully quitted the Colony. He must have left it without regret, as he experienced in it nothing but affliction. His successor was a Dutch priest Theodore Haggener,* a man of talent, zeal and energy, who undertook to visit the Catholics established at Port Elizabeth, Uitenhage and Grahamstown, whilst the Rev Thomas Rishton administered the sacraments at the Cape of Good Hope. Shortly after, the dissensions of which I have spoken were revived with new violence, the post became untenable for the two ecclesiastics, one of whom, the Dutch priest, departed in the height of the tumult for his own country, and the other, the Rev Thomas Rishton, returned to England in 1835 with his health so impaired that he died shortly after in a convent of his order,† a victim of lay interference in spiritual affairs.

After their departure the congregation was without clergy until June 1836, when a Spanish Dominican, going from Europe to Manila, and obliged to stop at the Cape of Good Hope on account of his health, was entreated to exercise here the pastoral ministry. His sojourn was about a year, and he did all the good that could be expected from a priest unacquainted with the language used in the country and who addressed himself to minds led away by discord. . . .

The dissensions of the bishop's report were those of a group of laymen with the priests Scully, Wagenaar and Rishton. They had been recognized as a committee of churchwardens by the bishop in Mauritius and they claimed for themselves the temporal administration of the Church, leaving to the priest only capellanic or liturgical duties. Whatever might be said in theory this was historically a relic of the Josephism of the eighteenth century, which had been accepted and maintained as far as possible by Napoleon.‡ The

---

* I.e. Wagenaar.

† At Ampleforth.

‡ The language of eighteenth-century theism which was part of the same movement was common among many Catholics in these years. It is shown in Father Scully's appeal to other denominations to assist in his building fund, " because of our fellowship in worship of the same Divine Object, of our gratitude and our hopes, which the enlightened and liberal views of modern times have, I trust, so happily taught us to appreciate ".

practice had spread for a time to the United States, and there the Dominicans had resisted it strongly. Maybe Bishop Griffith had heard of that quarrel, since he was a Dominican; maybe he had been warned about the churchwardens from Rome or in London, since they had already taken their quarrels to the secular Government. But he does not give any hint of this in his diary. They appear at Cape Town as " five or six strange looking men who came on board and asked to see me: they announced themselves as churchwardens of the Catholic congregation." But already he had determined not to acknowledge them as wardens, " being self-appointed, soidisants, and unnecessary ".[20] When they wrote to him officially in the evening he sent Father Burke to tell them, " I'd hold no communication with them as wardens—I'll never recognize such officers ". This firm assertion of the norm of authority in the Catholic Church was successful, but for rather more than a year the bishop could not take for granted the entire loyalty of his people. In July, 1839, he found it worth noting that he got the full approval of a meeting of the congregation for a purchase he was making, of a site for a school church and presbytery, but (as he remarks) it was by the guidance of Colonel Bird and the support of Mr Begley and Mr Hurley. Nearly twenty years later he would write to the Vicar Apostolic of Natal:

> In answer to your question about ecclesiastical funds, my first job in the colony was to destroy a junta or committee of men who called themselves churchwardens and were foolishly established by the first Vicar Apostolic of Mauritius, to whom this colony first belonged. I had two or three meetings of the congregation when I commenced building the church, but committees I have had never, and I administered all the church funds myself. From the altar I announce the receipts of the money they gave for any public purpose and tell them how and for what it is spent.[21]

The dislike which Bishop Griffith showed for the churchwardens must have been strengthened by the financial muddle he found at Cape Town. The Burgher Senate had granted a plot of land to Father Scully in 1821, and he had built a small chapel on it, but had mortgaged the land to the Lombard Bank. The Supreme Court had declared this mortgage illegal and invalid, and some confused litigation had followed between the churchwardens and the curators

appointed by the court.[22]   To add to these troubles, the chapel had
fallen in during the severe rains of 1837, and the churchwardens,
who claimed custody of it, had done nothing for its repair.   By
the advice first of Colonel Bell, the secretary, and then of the
governor, Sir George Napier himself, Bishop Griffith applied in
terms of the 97th Ordinance for the ground and chapel to be
granted to him afresh, quit of all claims.   In this way he was able
to by-pass the curators and creditors and churchwardens, whose
memorial the governor ignored.

Freed now from the threat of an inherited legal debt, Bishop
Griffith used the money he had brought with him to buy for
£2,500 (on a 4 per cent mortgage) a large plot in Tanners Square
or Looyers Plein, together with a building called " the Museum ",
from Baron von Ludwig.   Here he set up his first church and transferred the school which he had already opened at the " old parsonage ", and it was for these transactions that he obtained the
full approval of the congregation on 24 July 1839.

In the establishment of his control and in his friendly contacts
with the governor, Bishop Griffith wrote gratefully of the help
of Colonel Bird.   This elderly layman (he was seventy years old
at the time) was the descendant of recusant English families who
had kept the faith throughout the two hundred years of persecution.
A fluent speaker of French and Italian, the army had taken him
from Dillon's regiment, in which he held a commission, to negotiate
with the Directory for the lives of French royalist nobles.   From
that he became a staff officer at the Cape during the first British
occupation, and then Assistant Military Secretary to the Duke of
York, the surprisingly competent Hanoverian who was in charge
at Whitehall in the early years of the century.   He refused a
military post under the Dublin Castle government because the
latter required the holder to take the oath designed to exclude
Catholics.   In Ireland, however, the British Government in practice
waived this requirement from those of its military officials who were
recusants, and from 1807 till 1824 with one short interval Christopher
Bird was on the staff of the Governor of Cape Colony.   It may
have been due to his faith, however, that he was passed over for the
chief secretaryship on one occasion, and obtained this post only
in 1818.   But the fine, intelligent, sensitive face of his miniature
portrait suggests a man who did not know the art of making his

way in the world. When a violent quarrel developed between Sir Rufane Shaw Donkin and Lord Charles Somerset, who had nominated Bird, the latter tried as a public servant to take no part in it, and Somerset, as often, lost his temper. An Irish settler named Parker, a bitter Orangeman, formally denounced Bird as a papist and Somerset allowed the anti-Catholic oath to be tendered to his chief secretary. Other wild allegations against him made by Somerset were refuted by Rufane Donkin and Sir Andries Stockenstroom, who were concerned in the matter. But when Bird refused the oath he was, quite legally, superseded and found himself without employment and impoverished. For this reason, probably, he continued to live at the Cape, teaching his children foreign languages and religion[23] and helping as far as he could the priests, Wagenaar (who received Mrs Bird into the Church) and Rishton, in their difficulties. He was so much a friend of the Dutch that they persuaded him to go to England to plead with the government against the devaluation of the local Dutch currency. But according to his son's memory the social relations of the family were almost wholly English. Bird preferred military men, and there was a large military and naval force at the Cape in those days and the officers brought their families with them. In addition there were Indian civil servants who came there for their holidays, while with some exceptions the Dutch were aloof by habits and language.

Christopher Bird left Cape Town in 1843 to spend his last years in Belgium, but for the first five difficult years of the new bishop he had been there to help in negotiations with the governor's world and to rally the Catholics to the episcopal plans. The grateful references to him in Bishop Griffith's diary and the friendship which he formed with Father Devereux are the only hints we have now of his Catholic action, unless the rather surprisingly English attitude of Cape Catholicism in the next hundred years was due partly to his influence.

VI. Public Relations

The Catholics in general accepted without question the conception of a society organized in Churches, each of which should receive monetary aid from the public authority which taxed them. It was not till the 'sixties that the idea of them as a voluntary and self-supporting body was put forward. And when Bishop Grimley expressed himself as privately of the opinion that they should so regard themselves he was taken to task by his more politically minded colleague Bishop Moran.*

The earlier attitude is well represented by the petition of Father Burke and the Catholics of Grahamstown to Lord Glenelg in 1839. They asked for an increase of salary for their pastor, a salary for his clerk, and funds towards the erection of a chapel, quoting the provisions for a Catholic clergy in New South Wales and the dependencies. Previous to 1828, they said, the Government had paid £100 to a priest at Grahamstown who left the frontier about that year. They therefore asked that the £1,000 which had accumulated in the previous ten years should be given for building their school and church.[24]

I have found no suggestion either in the communications of the government or in the diary of Bishop Griffith that his salary made him a servant of the state. The secular rulers merely recognized that within civil society Catholics formed a community desirous of the authority of a clergyman. They were prepared to treat with him as representative of that community. They had indeed made this clear in England when they preferred to negotiate with Bishop Milner rather than with the cisalpine committees of laymen who offered them what looked on paper more secure guarantees of loyalty. It had also been the practice in Ireland from the time of George II when the practical agreement with the bishops almost took on the nature of a concordat. It was therefore a system for which Bishop Griffith was fully prepared. And as it was still common form to believe that the revenues from taxation should be disbursed in the directions desired by the King's subjects, it followed as a corollary that the Government should make a contribution to the expenses of the clergyman accepted by the Catholics. The parallel present to their minds no doubt was the position of the acting Roman Catholic chaplain to regiments like the 27th who were stationed at the Cape when Griffith arrived and the 75th at Fort Beaufort—both largely Irish as far as non-commissioned officers and private soldiers were concerned. And they adopted a like

* Infra, pp. 127, sqq.

title—" chaplain to the Roman Catholic community "—as their official description.

Bishop Griffith had been ordained before the act for Catholic Emancipation became law in the United Kingdom, and accepted the attitude of the Government as a matter of course. He directed his efforts, as he wrote in his diary, to reclaiming " those who ought to be papists ". His reckoning, however, went beyond those who would have called themselves so. He found many who after marriage had joined the congregation to which their wives belonged, and he admitted to himself that some of them had really forgotten the faith of their childhood. " I am sure ", he wrote (correcting his first " on the whole I think "), " they have despaired of ever seeing a priest again or Mass, and, wanting to have some religion (to distinguish them from the Hottentots), have joined the Dutch Church ". All such he treated as rightfully potential members of his flock, and at Algoa Bay he extended the principle to include those whose parents were known to have been Catholics but who had not been taught their faith.

Presumably with the bishop's consent, Father Aidan Devereux applied the same rule in 1841. On his missionary journey of that year he sought out the farmers with Flemish and Brabant names because they had had Catholic parents or grandparents. For these he had obtained in Cape Town " with difficulty " some Dutch Catholic books, but these were unfortunately lost in the wreck of the ship by which they were sent to Algoa Bay.[25]

In strict logic, of course, this conception of their task could have led both missionaries on to appeal to all Europeans in the colony, since all had had Catholic ancestors. But the diary which Bishop Griffith kept for his first year and such letters of his as survived do not suggest to me that such a possibility crossed his mind. He accepted, I think, without much hesitation the title and position of chaplain to the Roman Catholic community, which irked his successor but which was the only one the Government recognized. But, as was natural to anyone accustomed to conditions in Ireland, England, or, indeed, anywhere in Europe, Bishop Griffith thought of his community as composed of families rather than individuals. Consequently, where a Catholic man had married a Protestant wife he strove for her conversion, and still more for the Catholic upbringing of the children. And it was perhaps natural to extend this as far as familial memory went and so to claim that those whose grandparents were Catholic " ought to be papists ".

This attitude of mind was common among priests of the eighteenth and early nineteenth century, particularly in countries where the Catholic Faith was legally proscribed and persecuted, because the quarrel of the reformation, simmering down, had led to this classification of families by religion. But even in the days when they most readily accepted the restriction of their apostolate, priests were ready to accept individuals into the Church. Gibbon and Boswell are well known and unhappy examples from the eighteenth century.

Bishop Griffith did not rigidly exclude such an individual approach. He related with evident pleasure the story told him by an Irish Protestant clergyman at Bathurst of the conversion of his mother-in-law, Mrs Frances Ford, whom he had advised, when she had become interested in theology, to " ask the Catholic priests: they can tell you more of that than we ". Accordingly she went to Father Wagenaar, the Dutch priest at Cape Town, and was instructed by him and received, with one of her daughters, into the Catholic Church. It may be that Father Wagenaar was an exceptional man—for the attitude of a *convertisseur* is partly temperamental, and he had already instructed the wife of Colonel Bird—or that the Dutch Catholic tradition was never so familial as the Irish and English, though their circumstances of persecution were similar. Certainly Bishop Griffith appears to have regarded the occurrence as surprising, and in all his own many conversations with Protestants recounted in his diary the subject of their religion does not occur—a silence which must surely be attributed in part to his manner or to his decision, which did not apparently lack vigour on other topics. But while he did not make or apparently seize opportunities to expound the Catholic Faith to Protestants in social intercourse, he was always willing—several instances occur in his account of the visitation—that they should come to his services, and he sometimes took account of their presence in his sermons, which were then especially long. In the second half of his episcopate he seems to have felt this duty more pressing. When he brought to St Mary's Cathedral the very able Dutch Dominican, Peter van Ewyk, he hoped that by his sermons in

Dutch Father van Ewyk would be able to convert some of those who came to St Mary's out of curiosity.   But there does not appear any record of success.

These few and restrained examples of direct Catholic propaganda—directed only to those who would come voluntarily to a Catholic church—were consistent with the bishop's position as one of the public authorities.   Such I think is the best description of his relation to the civil government.   He spoke for the Catholics and secured their fair proportion of the revenues and patronage. And Bishop Griffith made full use of this quasi-official standing. When he was planning to build a cathedral at Cape Town for his flock to worship in, as he began to do in November, 1838, immediately after his first visitation, he had easy and frequent access to the Governor, Sir George Napier, through Colonel Bell, the Colonial Secretary, with the excellent results that we have already seen.   He pressed further for a supply of stone and lime from Government quarries and the free services of convicts and soldiers. Though he was politely told that the latter could not legally be granted, he was given permission to quarry for stones where the Dutch Reformed Church had been allowed to do so.[26]

The quasi-official standing of the bishop was more evident when he visited the Eastern district of the Colony.   At Grahamstown he called on Colonel Peddie, the officer commanding the 72nd Regiment; his call was returned, and he was entertained in the mess.   He was similarly entertained at Somerset and Fort Beaufort obtaining information about the Catholics of the regiment art, of the neighbourhood.   He met with the same friendliness from the civil authorities.   Captain Stockenstroom, the Lieutenant-Governor—the son of Andries Stockenstroom—helped him in negotiations for obtaining a grant of land for a church at Port Elizabeth, and van Ryneveld, the Civil Commissioner at Graaf Reinet, gave him letters of introduction to the important people in the towns he was to visit.   So he was lodged at Beaufort Town by a half-pay officer named Baird, while Mr Meintjies, the Civil Commissioner and a brother-in-law of Captain Stockenstroom, gave a dinner in his honour, asking what the diary calls " the élite of Beaufort " to meet him.

The hospitality given him because of his office would scarcely allow a man of Bishop Griffith's social habit (if I read his diary

aright) to introduce the question of religious differences at table,
though on one occasion he did ask Baird to explain the attitude
of the local parson to the conversion of the coloured wives or
concubines of the settlers. But he was willing enough to use the
prestige of the magistrates to endorse the rules he made for his own
people.

Bishop Griffith did at times comment sharply on churlishness
when he met it, or on the forwardness of young women in his
company, but I think that there is no exception to the spirit of gratitude and understanding in the accounts of his meetings with army
or government officials. Probably it was a matter of temperament; and conversation, as is usual on these occasions, may well
have been made easier because he was, by his own recording, a
keen and understanding critic of food and drink—though his
digestion apparently imposed considerable abstention. He found
little difficulty in talking with Protestants, and Father McCarthy,
who knew him in the last years of his episcopate, says that his
greatest friend was William Porter, the Protestant Attorney-
General. Probably the same trait of character was in the mind of
Bishop Moran when he wrote in a private letter that Dr Griffith
"is respected at the Cape as an ecclesiastic, a gentleman and a
scholar".[27] Such a reputation is seldom won without affability
in social relations and a willingness to allow others to decline
religious topics.

VII. The Mercantile Academy

It was not only in his view of public authority that Bishop
Griffith approached the Protestant mind. At the end of 1838,
immediately after his return from the Eastern district, he opened a
Catholic school in Cape Town, first on the site of the old " parsonage " in Harrington Street and then, after a few months, in the
museum in Machtenburg Gardens which he had bought from Baron
von Ludwig. It was then that he was joined by the three members
of the staff at St Peter's College, Wexford, whom he had persuaded
to follow him: Father Aidan Devereux, who had been vice-rector
of the Irish College at Rome before becoming Professor of Latin
at St Peter's College; Father Brownrigg; and Mr Murphy, a

deacon already over thirty years old, whom Bishop Griffith ordained a few months after their arrival. The establishment of the school may, indeed, have been mainly due to Father Devereux; Bishop Moran, visiting some fifteen years later, referred to it as Devereux's school,[28] and Bishop Griffith himself described how this priest, during the bishop's absence on another visitation, pushed on the negotiations for the purchase of the museum and moved the school there as soon as possession was obtained.[29]

There was of course a centuries-old tradition of teaching by priests in Ireland and other Catholic countries, and as the Protestant Churches had only recently begun a corresponding practice (Scotland was an exception, and even there the dominie was seldom the minister) it was not unusual for Protestant parents to make use of the services of priests, as they did in England when the French Abbés came over during the revolution. Naturally they had to be assured of the kind of teaching, and I think Bishop Griffith must himself have drawn up the advertisement which he published (both in Dutch and English[30]) in the *Cape Directory Advertiser* for 1839. The Mercantile and Classical Academy, "under the immediate direction of the Right Reverend Dr Griffith, with the Reverend Aidan Devereux, late first professor of St Peter's College, Wexford, as Principal, the Reverend George Corcoran and Mr Joseph Griffith as assistants," offered an elaborate course in English, Greek, Latin, French and Italian, arithmetic, book-keeping, geometry, geography and the use of globes, history, elocution and composition. Then there comes the notice:

> While the strictest Christian morality will be enforced and the history of the Bible made a class-book, no works or expositions calculated to interfere with the peculiar tenets of any of the children will be introduced during school hours. The Roman Catholic Catechism will be taught to the Roman Catholic children every day immediately after the termination of school.

If I have rightly judged the bishop's outlook, these rules will have been kept. At the same time his sister opened a school for girls, but without promising so elaborate a curriculum.

The bishop himself taught in the boys' school at first, telling in a letter to Ireland of February, 1839,[31] how he went there every morning after breakfast "to teach A.B.C. etc.", and adding that at that time there were thirty pupils and that it was hard work to get them to conduct themselves properly. By June the numbers had risen to forty and they sadly needed an assistant teacher.[32]

It does not seem, however, that this academy succeeded as a bridge between the Catholics and the rest of the world in Cape Town. Not many years later Bishop Moran, a careful man, wrote that it caused several non-Catholic schools to be started in rivalry, so that the numbers under Father Devereux diminished. The standard of the curriculum, too, must have suffered when Father Corcoran was sent to Uitenhage in 1840 and Father Devereux to George in the following year. However, the advertisement for the Mercantile and Classical Academy in Machtenburg Gardens still appeared in the *Cape of Good Hope Almanack* for 1854,[33] and there were sixty boys on the roll when Bishop Grimley arrived in July, 1861. But he wrote in his diary that it was not " respectable "; there was one small schoolroom for boys and one teacher. Maybe it had not provoked the envy, and therefore had escaped the attacks, of others. Certainly Bishop Grimley's efforts at improvements were not liked, and the *Cape Argus* of 15 December, 1863, carried a letter with this passage:

> The Roman Catholics at the Cape were for many years under the supervision of an excellent bishop, of tolerant spirit, who endeavoured to make those within the pale of his Church do their duty as Christians without any proselytizing. . . . During this period the number of Roman Catholics was comparatively few. They have greatly increased in numbers during the last few years; and a new bishop has succeeded the unobtrusive good old prelate above alluded to . . . [There has been] a numerous importation of Irish Roman Catholic immigrants. . . . Protestants will pause before they send their children to be educated by the nuns and priests.

Within a year of the foundation of the school, the bishop had obtained leave to build a cathedral on the land he had purchased, had engaged a local architect named Spearman, had accepted what turned out to be the far too optimistic estimate of £5,000,* and was begging for funds from Protestants as well as Catholics and petitioning the civil government to make a grant, "because it is usual to distribute revenues to the tax-payers for public purposes".[34]

* It had cost £10,377 before its blessing.

On 21 August 1840 work was commenced on the foundations, and the foundation-stone was laid on 6 October 1841.

VIII. Foundations Laid

Raymond Griffith's first plan for the building of his vicariate seems clear. He would keep most of his priests in Cape Town, where the majority of the Catholics, as of the whole colony, were concentrated, and along with the ordinary pastoral work would found a reputable school and start work on a dignified cathedral church. On a smaller scale he may have hoped that similar work would be done at Grahamstown, the frontier capital, though it is clear that he had little confidence in the ability of Father Burke. Every year, however, he would go himself or send one of his priests on tour of the rest of the vicariate and so hold the scattered Catholics to their loyalty until he could establish parishes. The success which attended this plan is borne out by two figures for the Catholic population both of which came from the bishop. In one account, relating to 1839, he mentioned 700; in the other, which comes from 1841, he mentioned 2,500.[35] For the most part this indicates only the return to the sacraments of those who "ought to be papists" (the formal conversions from paganism and heresy during the period were 20 and 38 respectively), but it gives some indication of the work accomplished in those first two years.

Almost at once—certainly from the time of his second tour of the vicariate—the bishop modified this plan in order that work similar to that which he had started at Cape Town should commence in the other places. He sent the newly-ordained Father Murphy to help Father Burke at Grahamstown, and, as the latter died a week after his assistant's arrival, Father Murphy took charge. The following year, 1840, Father Corcoran went to Port Elizabeth, and early in 1841 Father Devereux went to George (at that time called Georgetown), because he had been suffering from rheumatism at the Cape. Each of them went to work on the model the bishop had established. A school of sorts for the children, a permanent church, were the first burdens to be undertaken by the Catholic community, while the priest was to seek out all who ought to be papists in the surrounding districts. Before 1839 was out the

Catholics of Grahamstown were applying to the governor of the
Cape for a grant to assist them in building their school,[36] and after
Devereux had been eighteen months at George he was able to report
to the bishop that he had organized a school for thirty children.[37]

For all this work Bishop Griffith was continually seeking for
priests, as far as his means allowed. Several more came from St
Peter's College, Wexford, which could indeed be regarded as a
parent of the Church in South Africa, for it provided three of the
bishops and half a dozen of the priests in the early days. But on
his rare journeys to Europe Bishop Griffith enlisted others whom
he came across—notably the Dutch Dominican Father van Ewyck.
For several years, too, he undertook the theological training of
those who had not commenced or had not completed their studies
but were willing to work in South Africa after ordination.

Meanwhile Bishop Griffith was often the only priest at Cape
Town to act as chaplain to the soldiers, the naval station, the
convicts, and as pastor of the city and district. In addition he had
to do a great deal of the teaching in the school, his only assistant
by then being his younger brother, whom he was also instructing
and training for the priesthood. Almost every year he had to
collect enough money to pay for another visitation of the vicariate,
and at the same time he went on with the plans for a cathedral,
with all the usual difficulties made by architects and contractors
who changed plans and found they had underestimated costs, and
he had to beg money from his acquaintances and friends in Ireland
so that he should not be compelled to accept a makeshift building.
Finance became a constant worry, and as late as 1853 he wrote to
Bishop Allard that he was "broke", and asked him to repay
promptly £48 he had spent on his behalf and instructions.[38] A
tradition among the Cape Town Catholics related by Alexander
Wilmot says that in the early days Miss Griffith had to be cook and
housekeeper as well as schoolmistress, and Joseph Griffith had to
clean the boots and answer the door as well as study theology and
teach in the Mercantile and Classical Academy.

The bishop had neither the health nor the flamboyant spirit
suitable to his task. At one time he wrote, "How sick I am of
this Colony—my complaint is becoming every day more in-
tolerable"; and somewhat later, "I have to write memorials to
the Government here and the Government in England: I have to

dispose, if possible, of the parsonage and old chapel ground to some advantage: I have to preach every evening and to fast till after preaching: I have to write to Rome and fifty letters. Besides in fact I have so many things to do that I know not where to begin." And after enumerating his troubles with people, " Then this abominable south-easter or *doctor* is blowing us out of our senses: it drives all the sand, gravel and even the stones of the street into our very eyes ".

The diary was written of course only for his own eyes. It purports to address his reflections to an unnamed lady whose brother and family had been his friends in Ireland but who would never see it. He relates his feelings quite simply, and tells of the tears he shed at the thought of being unlikely ever to return to his country or his friends. Something must be allowed for the Victorian honesty and lack of inhibition about the emotions; even so Raymond Griffith clearly found his work a burden, and almost hateful. Yet his portrait shows a man with the strong face of a capable headmaster, he clearly did his episcopal duty more than well, and he was a scholar who slowly built up a library that was worth at his death £2,000 in the opinion of his successor—himself a buyer of books. Everyone, Protestant and Catholic, seems to have remembered him as a friendly man, and he certainly sited and built a cathedral, which has the distinction of work of the early Pugin school and, consecrated in 1951, just a hundred years after he had blessed it, remains today, despite our present dislike of imitation gothic, the most imposing of the Catholic churches of Southern Africa.

Chapter II

BISHOP DEVEREUX

I. New Vicariates

IN 1846, five years before he blessed his new cathedral, Bishop Griffith sent Father Murphy to Rome to ask the Pope to divide the vicariate and to suggest that Aidan Devereux should be made vicar apostolic of the Eastern Province of the Cape. It is not difficult to guess two of his reasons. The tradition of the Catholic Church requires a bishop to be resident in his diocese and supposes that his presence should be at least frequently available to the faithful. The immediate contact of his government, the sacraments he administers, the liturgical ceremonies in which he acts are even more valuable in building up a new Catholic community than in continuing a long held tradition. But in the Cape Colony it was impossible for the bishop, for reasons of geography and finance and because of the work he had to do in Cape Town, to do more than visit the centres of the Eastern Province for a few days at intervals of at least a year.

A second reason arose from the Catholic tradition that a bishop should accept, as far as justice allows, the temporal outlook of his people. Economically and socially the life of the two Provinces, Eastern and Western, was different. The former was mainly pastoral, while in the latter agriculture and vine-growing and the industries of urban life were of long standing. The Eastern Province was a frontier area; a large proportion of its population were settlers, English, Scots, Irish and Germans, of the first generation, and they were conscious of the likelihood of attack by those they called " Kaffirs ", across their border, while they themselves often coveted the land those " Kaffirs " occupied. A year before Father Murphy's mission to Rome there had been a " war ",* for which the troops of Grahamstown were employed, and Father Murphy had won popularity as chaplain to the Irish troops. A deal of these difficulties were attributed in the Eastern Province to the

* Called the " War of the Axe ".

37

vacillating methods of the government at Cape Town, and for some
years there had been a demand for separate administration, the
justice of which was partly recognized by the appointment in 1836
of a Lieutenant-Governor for the Eastern Province. It would
clearly be difficult for a vicar apostolic in friendly relations with the
civil authorities at Cape Town and greatly helped by them, whose
people in the Western Province were not greatly affected by the
frontier situation, to change his outlook during his occasional
visitations to the Catholics of Beaufort, Somerset, Grahamstown
and Port Elizabeth.

It is clear that Raymond Griffith could have found ample work
for his half-dozen priests in the Western Province alone, but,
although he certainly did not view his task sentimentally, we can
exclude any selfish purpose of saving himself labour by sacrificing
Catholic mission work. Not only did he recommend his most
able assistant, Aidan Devereux, for the episcopal authority over the
Eastern Province, but he gave him, in Father Murphy and Father
Corcoran, his best two men, and in fact left himself with only
two newly ordained priests while four were taken over by the new
vicar apostolic.

Pius IX's Bull erecting the new vicariate was dated 30 July 1847.
Aidan Devereux was consecrated by Bishop Griffith at Cape Town,
and at the beginning of June 1848 he sailed for Europe, " to see the
Holy Father, to promote the interests of the mission, and to procure
priests, money, books and vestments ".[1] It may well be that
Bishop Griffith had this also in mind when he urged the division:
a new man could tap new sources and would be more likely to
succeed if he were appealing for his own work. But Bishop
Devereux had a further plan. When he found the Pope at Gaeta
(it was the year of revolution in Europe) he spoke to him on the
subject of Natal, and the Pope promised " to send a vicar apostolical
there at the earliest possible day ".[2] Nor was this a vague suggestion or promise. A few days later the Bishop met Cardinal
Franzoni at Naples[3], the Prefect of the Congregation of Propaganda,
the missionary department of the curia, and, despite the disorder
caused by the expulsion from Rome, the cardinal listened to and
accepted the suggestion that a religious order, preferably English-
speaking, should be asked to found a vicariate in the area pointed
out by Dr Devereux.

From the administrative practice of the Congregation of Propaganda under Cardinal Franzoni it is safe to conclude that Bishop Devereux had obtained and communicated the support of Bishop Griffith for his proposal. In 1846, certainly, some Catholic soldiers of the 45th stationed in Natal had given the bishop £4 as a contribution to his cathedral, but because he " meditated a church in Natal " he put the money aside until seven years later, when he sent it to the newly arrived vicar apostolic.[4]

The situation as far as it was known to Griffith and Devereux in 1848 was this.[5] A few parties of trekkers from the Eastern Province had established themselves in the lands east of the Drakensberg mountains and, after many vicissitudes, had compelled the Zulu tribes to keep north of the Tugela River and to accept the supremacy of the Boers. Durban, five hundred miles along the coast from Port Elizabeth, and Pietermaritzburg, sixty miles inland, were founded. The settlers were joined by others from the Eastern Province, a few merchants from Cape Town, or their representatives, and one or two Frenchmen from Mauritius. After many hesitations the British Government annexed this area to the Cape in 1844, and by letters patent of the following year gave it a Lieutenant-Governor and a separate administration. One of the early government surveyors was John Bird, the son of Colonel Bird, and like his father a great friend of Bishop Devereux.[6] Edward Chiappini, a merchant of Cape Town, who was in Natal on business for long periods in the 'forties, had been one of the " churchwardens " who met Bishop Griffith; and a Frenchman, Hippolyte Jargal, his business associate, was also a Catholic. A few of the sugar planters from Mauritius had already arrived, and the financial crisis on the island in 1847 was likely to bring many others.[7] With the Irish soldiers there was clearly the nucleus of a Catholic community in the colony.

In the same period one Boer group, emigrants from Cape Colony, had established themselves between the Orange and Vaal rivers and had founded Bloemfontein as their capital; two other groups had crossed the Vaal and made their headquarters at Pretoria and Potchefstroom respectively. They had regarded the land as their own by right of occupation, not admitting any sort of sovereignty to the sparse nomadic Bantu, who had used the area for occasional grazing. Inter-tribal wars had meanwhile formed more permanent and coherent groups among the latter. North of the Tugela, in what became known as Zululand, the chiefs Shaka and Dingane had welded their conquered enemies into a native state. The same was true of an area north of the River Limpopo and of what is now Bechuanaland, west of the Transvaal Boer Settlement. North of the Kei River, which formed the boundary of the Eastern Province of the Cape, there was another group of Bantu, mainly Pondos, with whom the colonists had almost continuous disputes concerning grazing lands and cattle raiding, but also a certain amount of trading. In Basutoland, the mountainous area south-west of the Drakensberg and extending to the fertile land bordering the Caledon river, and so contiguous with the Boer farms between the Orange and the Vaal, remnants of many tribes which had fled from Shaka and his Zulus had accepted, with some reluctance, the rule of a leader, Moshesh. Between them and the Boer farmers peace or a settled frontier had never been established, and the same was true of the relations of the Boers with the Griquas (or Bastards, a people of mixed descent) to the west of them. Whenever the Boers could establish a military supremacy, they treated their neighbours not as independent but as vassals, and required them to supply labour or to cede land on dictated terms. Rarely, however, did the Bantu accept the terms, agreed to by his chiefs after defeat, when they clashed, as in the circumstances they did, with his concepts of nomadic rights.

The British Government acted on principles which opposed one another. It was unwilling to annex more territory in Africa both because it would be unprofitable and because it could see no justification. It maintained the legal doctrine that natural born subjects, such as the emigrants from Cape Colony and their children, could not cast off their allegiance by departure and were responsible to it for any illegal acts they might commit. It held that the Boer system of compulsory apprenticeship for the Bantu was an invasion of the rights of the latter. Sometimes, therefore, the Governors at Cape Town had ignored the situation which obtained beyond the frontiers of the Colony, sometimes they had tried to treat with the Bantu tribes as though they were sovereign foreign states in which British subjects were trading or farming. As neither method brought peace to the frontier, they sometimes reluctantly proclaimed annexation, usually on the assumption either that the territory was uninhabited or that cession was made by the Bantu rulers. So Natal was made part of Cape Colony in 1845, and so the territory between the Orange and the Vaal was made the British Orange River Sovereignty in 1848, and the territory north of the Kei was made a protectorate in the same year.

Already a few Catholics had settled in these areas, and the British garrison sent to Bloemfontein included many Irish and was commanded by a Catholic, Major Donovan. Under British rule it would be easier for missionaries to approach the Bantu, among whom the Calvinist *Missions Evangeliques de Paris* and the Wesleyans were already at work.

These points—the movement of Catholics into an area beyond the Eastern Vicariate boundary, the opportunity of converting the pagan tribes, the advisability of English-speaking priests—were made by Bishop Devereux in his interview with Cardinal Franzoni at Naples. As the latter was to write later, the bishop pointed out the boundaries for the new vicariate which were adopted in the subsequent ' brief '. They were, according to Devereux, " Keya* on the west, the Portuguese possessions on the east, the tropics in the north "; though he added that the vicar apostolic, when appointed, would probably ask for a new division.[8]

In a written report made at Naples, or submitted soon afterwards, Bishop Devereux suggested that the work should be entrusted to the Fathers of the Society of Jesus, or to the recently formed Congregation of the Holy Ghost, and he made a point of visiting the General of the Jesuits at Lyons on the affairs of the mission.[9] The two religious orders suggested were unable to comply, and the Congregation of Propaganda then invited Bishop de Mazenod, founder and general of the Oblates of Mary Imaculate, to supply a vicar apostolic, priests and lay-brothers for the new territory; and the offer was accepted in April 1850.

Bishop Devereux did not cease to concern himself with the work. In October 1850 he sent Father Murphy to make a " visition " of Natal, like those Bishop Griffith had made before the Eastern Vicariate was formed. Father Murphy obtained from the government a plot for a church at Pietermaritzburg, the capital, and the promise of another at Durban;[10] he drew up a list of the Catholics

* I.e. the Kei river. The orientation is of course only roughly indicated.

he had discovered and left copies at the two towns; he made a general report on the prevalent vices among Catholics, and after his return to Grahamstown in May 1851 a French translation was sent to the *Oeuvre de la Propagation de la Foi* at Lyons, where it was given to the newly appointed vicar apostolic, Bishop Allard.[11] In October of the same year Bishop Devereux sent a Flemish priest, Father Hoenderwangers, to Bloemfontein to found a mission there and to visit as far as possible the scattered Catholics in the Orange River Sovereignty.

The successors of Bishop Devereux in the Eastern Vicariate claimed in their *Chronicon* that Natal and British Kaffraria were part of that vicariate until 1850.[12] Presumably they supposed that the technical civil extension of the Cape Colony to these areas (and the Sovereignty) carried with it the ecclesiastical jurisdiction. Bishop Devereux, however, made no such mistake. " My only right to send Father Murphy ", he wrote to Bishop Allard, " was a desire to do a work of charity and necessity."[13]

The principle on which he acted is clear. Looking beyond the borders of his own vicariate, he saw need and opportunity for Catholic missionary work for which his own resources were not adequate. He urged Rome, therefore, to entrust the territory to another bishop, with his own priests, and did what lay in his power to suggest and find willing and suitable men. Meanwhile, he tried to form a Catholic community ready for the new vicar apostolic as soon as he was appointed. It was simply an extension of the method which Bishop Griffith had employed for the eastern part of his vicariate in the early days, and it was to be used again and again in the years to come. So Bishop Leonard, the third Vicar Apostolic of Cape Town, arranged in 1874 for the setting up of the Central Prefecture under the Fathers of the African Missions of Lyons, to include the arid copper mining lands to the north-west with their Hottentot and coloured peoples of mixed descent. And when this attempt failed he called in the Oblates of St Francis de Sales, and as soon as they were established asked for, and obtained in 1884, the creation of the Orange River Prefecture. So also Bishop Jolivet of Natal (Allard's successor) urged the formation of the Kimberley vicariate in 1879, and suggested it should be entrusted to an Irishman because of the nationality of the Catholics of that area; and of a Transvaal vicariate, because it was politically separate from Natal, and its independence recognized by Britain; and of still a third vicariate between the Limpopo and the Zambesi which was passing under the control of the Chartered Company of Cecil Rhodes. Already in 1871 Bishop Ricards of the Eastern Vicariate had urged the general of the Jesuits to establish missionaries of his society on the Zambesi, and six years later obtained the promise of the Congregation of Propaganda to establish a new prefecture as soon as the Jesuits were ready. Presumably he still considered it part of his job to make provision for any part of Africa which might pass under British rule, and in fact the six Jesuit priests and five lay-brothers who went to work in the prefecture, which had been marked out by an Apostolic Rescript of February 1879, started from Grahamstown.

While each vicar apostolic then laboured chiefly for those of his own charge, and for the area where they were mostly to be found, he bore in mind the frontier of the Catholic advance either within his own boundaries or beyond them. Where lack of money and men, or the social and political circumstances, made it difficult for him, he asked the Holy See to establish a new vicariate, doing what he could meanwhile to prepare for its successful work. The result of that method can be seen in the foundation of the new circumscriptions: 1837, the Cape; 1847, the Eastern Vicariate of the Cape; 1850, Natal; 1874, the Central Prefecture; 1879, the Salisbury Mission, made into a prefecture in 1905; 1884, the Orange River Prefecture, which became a vicariate in 1898; 1886, Kimberley; 1889, Transvaal Prefecture, which became a vicariate in 1904; 1892, Windhoek; 1894, Basutoland; 1906, Northern Transvaal Mission, becoming a prefecture in 1910; 1909 Great Namaqualand; 1913, the Swaziland Mission. With these establishments Catholic communities had reached up to, and were in contact with, those of Portuguese East and West Africa, and the frontier phase had passed; later divisions were made not for these reasons but for the convenience and efficiency of ecclesiastical jurisdiction.

II. New Recruits

When Bishop Griffith urged the creation of new vicariates it is possible, but not likely, that he hoped for improvements on his

own method of work. Yet such in fact happened. Though
Aidan Devereux left his priests in the stations given them by Bishop
Griffith, and with the tasks of building a church and starting a
parochial school for Catholic children, he planned new developments at once. He brought out two students from Ireland and a
schoolmaster from London whom he employed immediately as
teachers. But in Europe in 1848–49 " to promote the interests of
his mission ", as he wrote in his *Chronicon,* he spoke of his anxiety
to raise the standard of education in South Africa and to break
down the prejudice and antiquated methods which encumbered it.[14]
In his opinion the other Christian bodies had not done so, though
they had started before the Catholics. He found the people he
wanted in the Assumptionist Sisters of the diocese of Paris, a newly
founded congregation which specialized in teaching, and persuaded their mother superior to let him take back to Grahamstown
three sisters and three postulants to work in his vicariate.

They had been founded only nine years before by the Abbé
Caubelot, an associate of Lamennais before his quarrel with the
Church, and from him they had learned to make full use of modern
knowledge and methods. Their leader, Sister Marie-Gertrude,
was certainly not one of the ordinary run of school-mistresses.
Josephine Amélie de Henningsen (as she was born) belonged by
family to the international aristocracy which had survived the
revolution. Brought up in the cultivated and diplomatic world
of Brussels until she was fifteen, she had taken part thereafter in the
literary and scientific pursuits popular in the London society of the
'thirties and 'forties. Like so many of the young ladies of society
of early Victorian days, she received a really good education,
following the public lectures of the great physicists and chemists of
the time, meeting Coleridge and Byron and hearing their opinions
on literature. While waiting for the bishop to collect the rest
of his party she was sent to London again, and made friends not
only with Nicholas Wiseman and John Henry Newman, but also,
through their introductions, with Manning, Allies and other
converts of the time. She likewise consulted without any hesitation such men as Lockhart and Humboldt when preparing for the
work in South Africa. Nor did her superiors forget that she would
also have to see to what is now called elementary education, and
they sent her to gain experience in the schools for the poor which

other congregations had founded in Paris. When she opened school for Bishop Devereux in Grahamstown she undoubtedly had an acquaintance with contemporary literary, scientific and religious opinion not likely to be met in other schools of the colony.[15]

There was, however, an initial difficulty: the other nuns could speak English only imperfectly. It was overcome by the generosity of an old lady whom we have already mentioned, Frances Ford, who helped Bishop Devereux as much as Colonel Bird had helped Bishop Griffith, though in different ways. She had been brought up as a unitarian in Kent, and had emigrated with her husband among the 1820 settlers to Cape Colony. There her daughter had married an Irish Protestant clergyman with whom the elderly widow discussed the doctrine of the Trinity.[16] To resolve her difficulties he had sent her to Father Wagenaar, who instructed both mother and another daughter, Janet, and received them into the Church. A son, John, and a third daughter, Elizabeth, were converted by Aidan Devereux during his first year at Cape Town, and the whole family became his friends.[17] They went to Grahamstown when he was appointed vicar apostolic, and the old lady, now nearly seventy, and her daughter Janet opened a " select school " for girls. One of the Assumptionist sisters described her at the time: "not tall but very straight . . . she learned to do everything, made shoes, taught piano playing, studied medicine and practised it . . . she could never see or take a joke . . . she never got rid of her Protestant dislike of images: even though she knelt before a statue, she never looked at it." This old and capable lady was generous enough to hand over her school to the newcomers, helped them with the teaching in the early days and taught the nuns English, ran a bazaar to provide funds and raised £300 for them.*

There would not of course be many nuns with the background of Sister Marie-Gertrude, and her exceptional qualities were soon recognized by both Catholics and Protestants in Grahamstown. But many of the other nuns sent out from Europe also brought to South Africa knowledge and ability to communicate it not normally found among the few lay people who were willing to undertake what has always been the poorly paid job of teacher. It was

---

* Another early school for girls was that kept at Graaf Reinet by the two sisters of Father van Caulewaert until their death in 1852.

one of the advantages which the Catholic Church possessed over other religious bodies that such people could be sent under obedience: "an English colony", Sister Marie-Gertrude said later, "was distasteful to me, the next thing to the Chinese missions. Since it was God's will I must accept. I have lived to see no country offer so much personal religious and political liberty as those under English rule."

The remark hints at the only difficulty, apart from the necessary finance, in bringing this culture to be domiciled in South Africa. It was in origin Parisian, and the mother-house and the Archbishop of Paris tried to make conditions which would preserve its French character, even asking their minister of foreign affairs to write to this effect to the governor of the Cape Colony. But they reckoned without the normal tendency of Catholic practice. After a few years Marie-Gertrude and some of her nuns preferred to stay in South Africa when their French superiors wanted to recall them. The Archbishop of Paris gave an ungracious consent, and the authorities in Rome empowered and advised Bishop Devereux to constitute them an independent diocesan congregation.

This first convent school in South Africa was so popular that many Protestants sent their children to the nuns. The Anglican Bishop Gray published a criticism of the school in the *Frontier Times*, at the end of 1850, though he subsequently explained that he meant no offence but was warning his own people against its influence. This, however, only came after a typically capable and indignant public reply of Bishop Devereux:

> Institutions similar to this are to be found in Smyrna and Alexandria, and the Sultan protects them in Constantinople. A branch of this very house was established about four months back in Richmond, Yorkshire, under the patronage of the Protestant Duke of Leeds. The insurrectionary mob who during the celebrated attack on Paris in 1848 had encamped in the nuns' garden in the Rue Chaillot, Champs Elysées, sent word to them not to be alarmed—that they would not molest them. Having stood the test of so many trials, I am sorry that they should have the misfortune to come under the ban of your Lordship.[18]

Along with the party of nuns, Bishop Devereux brought from Europe a subdeacon, James David Ricards, a past pupil of the St

Peter's, Wexford, where the bishop had once taught the classics, with two schoolmasters, Pierre Dubois and Jeremiah O'Riley, and a mechanic. The two schoolmasters went to Cape Town to be taught theology, in preparation for the priesthood, by Bishop Griffith, but that snuff-taking prelate[19] is said to have refused O'Riley because of his " filthy habit of smoking ".[20] The young man referred to himself afterwards as a catechist[21] and served the Church in that capacity as well as as a schoolmaster, and as the father of two priests, one of whom became a successor of Bishop Griffith.

III. " The Colonist "

Bishop Devereux's plan went beyond the recruitment of his clergy. At the end of 1850, soon after the ordination of James Ricards, he founded a weekly newspaper, *The Cape Colonist*. Its policy and business arrangements were presumably decided by discussion between the bishop and his assistants. It was published at Grahamstown. For a few weeks a local Catholic journalist, Frederick Barr, was the nominal editor and, one supposes, technical adviser. Certainly Father Ricards (he was ordained in 1851), who took over the practical editorship almost from the beginning, was a man of great powers of persuasion and appeal, and tradition has always regarded *The Colonist* (the title was shortened to this after a few numbers) as his paper. But at this time he was still very young and socially bashful, and it may well be that Bishop Devereux used the advice of Sister Marie-Gertrude, to whom the attitude which Nicholas Wiseman brought from Europe and tried to teach in England must have seemed the obvious one to adopt.

The newspaper gave accounts of European as well as colonial matters, and was referred to with pride later on by Catholics like the young lawyer Wilmot who became a member of the Legislative Council. But Bishop Devereux valued it chiefly, if we may judge from the references to it in his letters, as a means of answering attacks on the Catholic religion. Already in 1842, as a priest at George, he had noted in his diary that the Protestants made efforts to prevent the coloured population from coming near him; "they tell all sorts of stories about the Catholic religion, though ", he adds, " there are no insults to me personally ". He was far more sensitive than Bishop Griffith appears to have been to Protestant criticism, and perhaps he provoked it, for even those who admired his scholarship and courtly manners admitted his quick-tempered impulsiveness.[22] He hated, he told Bishop Allard when offering him space in *The Colonist* should he desire it, " the unpleasant and irksome job of writing on political subjects ";[23] but, he added, " since we established the Catholic journal these gentlemen [the Protestant ministers] are comparatively careful . . ."[24] With *The Colonist*, then, Bishop Devereux showed the Catholics of South Africa a new way in which they could publish the truth about their Faith. For him it was a matter of replying to attacks or correcting misunderstandings, but others, and especially his pupil Father Ricards, were to make their appeal to their fellow citizens on a wider scale.

The third innovation made by Bishop Devereux had been in his mind for some time. While still a priest at George he had noted in his diary that " the Dutch at Elephant River seem desirous of a Dutch priest because they are discontented with their minister ", and even earlier he had felt it " a great deficiency in not being able to speak or preach in Dutch ". This was common sense, for not only those whose families came originally from Holland but many of " the deserters from English regiments and others who flee their debts or punishments for crime " who were " scattered through the Orange River State "[25] were already using the Dutch patois, akin to Flemish, which was to be the basis of the Afrikaans language. So on his European tour the Bishop persuaded two Premonstratensians, de Sany and Hoenderwangers, and one secular priest, van Caulewaert, to come with him to his vicariate. At least the two Premonstratensian canons seem to have been popular enough with the Irish regiments, though there were naturally some language difficulties at first: Father de Sany left the reputation of a polished gentleman, but tradition also said that he concluded one of his sermons by saying: " At the last day the Lord will say to the wicked, ' hook it, ye blackguards ' ".[26]

It was, however, from the work of Father Hoenderwangers, said to be rough and ready, zealous and wanting in tact but full of kindness,[27] that the bishop expected most. In October 1851,[28] he sent him to Bloemfontein with £20 for himself and £20 to start building a church (and a further £10 during the year)[29] and recommendations to his Catholic friends, Major Donovan, who commanded the garrison, and John Ford, his convert who had married and settled in the newly established town. Major Donovan, the bishop thought, could protect the priest " against the violence of the Dutch ministers and their people ".[30] The arrangement seemed to work well. By the end of 1852 Donovan had obtained from the Government the title-deed for a large plot of land[31] and given it to Father Hoenderwangers. In the following year the English began to abandon the Sovereignty, and though Father Hoenderwangers said that " each village wants its own king and the heretics may confiscate Church property ",[32] he added that he feared nothing and was still optimistic when the new Boer Government was set up.[33] Already in July 1854 he was on amiable terms with them.[34] A year later he urged Bishop Allard to call on Mr Boshoff, the President of the new Orange River State, who was visiting Pietermaritzburg and assured him of a friendly reception.[35] Unfortunately the vicar apostolic " thought it would be imprudent to visit Mr Boshoff ".[36]

It is a little odd, perhaps, that Bishop Devereux, who was very popular with the soldiers of the British garrisons and liked to work with them, should have been the first to grasp the need for Dutch or Flemish speaking priests in South Africa. He was not, however, alone in the matter. Bishop Griffith brought the Dutch Dominican already mentioned, Father van Ewyck, to preach regularly in the new cathedral at Cape Town in 1852. Alexander Wilmot, who came to the colony from Scotland as a young law student at that time, had a story that the bishop found him wearing his habit at the Crystal Palace in London and said that he was the strangest exhibit there. It sounds like an authentic remark, but Wilmot adds that the people for whom the sermons were given were for the most part absent. It could be maintained, indeed, that the attempt to appeal to the Dutch-speaking population ended in failure. The successor to Bishop Devereux as vicar apostolic did not replace van Caulewaert and de Sany when they died, and when Hoenderwangers had both his legs broken in a wagon accident and went back to his monastery of Grimbergen, in 1869, Bishop Allard made no attempt to get another Flemish-speaking priest for the Orange River State.

There were probably many to whom the experiment was just one more example of Bishop Devereux's impulsive nature, which

even his admirers admitted. Certainly there were abundant
stories of the violent dislike which the Boers had for the Catholic
religion. In a way it was understandable. They had inherited
from their forebears—Huguenots and Hollander Protestants—
stories of their sufferings under papist rulers, stories often exaggerated and always unhistorical because omitting the violence of the
sixteenth-century revolts against the traditional order, but stories
which they accepted without question. It was not easy to see the
argument of Father Hoenderwangers that " Hollanders only hate
our religion because they never meet a Catholic priest ",[37] but
Bishop Devereux was intelligent enough to see that it was possibly
true, and optimistic enough to act on it.

The help which Bishop Griffith received from the official world
had shown one element in the attitude of Protestant society to the
Catholic Church. But there was this other and less pleasant one.
Aidan Devereux had reported from George in March 1841 that
the Dutch Calvinists and the descendants of the Huguenots were
bitter and had extraordinary notions of Catholicism; one of them
had told him fiercely that " a hundred years ago a Romish priest
passing through this country would be shot as readily as a wolf ".[38]
Though the clamour subsided after he had started a school, Father
Devereux often had to refer to it again, especially after he became
Vicar Apostolic of the Eastern District. In a letter of 26 June
1852, he complained that the Anglican Bishop Gray had destroyed
all the kindly feeling for the nuns shown hitherto by the Protestants
of Grahamstown.[39] A little later he told Bishop Allard, newly
arrived in Natal, that he was not surprised to hear of attacks by
Protestant ministers: " We hear them so often that we pay no
notice to them. And it has no effect on their flocks."[40] Naturally
the explanation suggests itself that Devereux provoked these outbursts himself. He did not, however, have that sort of reputation;
he was remembered as a kindly, dignified man. His letters to
Bishop Allard show him willing to help others and giving clear and
succinct advice, and Ricards, no bad judge, praised him as a theologian. Curiously, the priest who was said to preach controversial
sermons was the universally popular Father Murphy. But the nuns
in whose chapel he preached them found them very long, and
apparently dull.[41] Possibly this gives a hint of the explanation.

Bishop Devereux was an able and wide-awake man, and it was

not surprising that those who believed it their duty to hinder the work of the Catholic Church should be aroused to action by him. Their material of war was already present in the traditions which Dutch Calvinists and French Huguenots had brought from Europe, of the sufferings of their ancestors in the sixteenth and seventeenth centuries: the massacre of St Bartholomew, Alva's rule in the Netherlands, the dragonnades of Louis XIV. Historically these accounts were often inaccurate and always unbalanced, but they were respectable and rested on some basis of fact. But they were supplemented by gross inventions of the Maria Monk type, revelations, supposed to be made by escaped nuns, of contemporary Catholic immorality and sadism. Such stories now began to be repeated in talk and sermons and printed in the local newspapers as well as in books. It was to counter these allegations[42] that Devereux founded *The Cape Colonist*.

There was first of all the direct answer to the scurrilous allegations. This was not difficult, because they had been made without evidence, and the authors in many cases had been condemned in the civil courts of other countries or publicly exposed in the press. Even the historical charges could be discredited fairly easily, for polemic of that type always exaggerates and so contradicts the documentary sources and the statements of the learned of its own party. Controversy of this sort, however, is not enough. Few who were not Catholics would be disposed to read it, and many would not be in a position to weigh the evidence. For them it is necessary to show on other grounds that Catholics are intelligent people with a reasonable viewpoint in public affairs. Convinced of this, they will be ready to listen to the Catholic case with regard to events of the past.

For this reason *The Colonist* discussed the political situation of South Africa, and put forward, presumably with Bishop Devereux's approval, the cause of Grahamstown and the frontier, asking for a resident governor and attacking the policy of Sir Harry Smith at Cape Town.[43] In his editorials of this time Ricards advocated representative government for the colony, urged the claims of the Eastern Province to its own resident Governor, favoured separation from the Bantu territories, and opposed the abandonment of the Orange River Sovereignty by the home government and the view popular in London, where *The Times* was urging the abandon-

ment of the whole of South Africa and the retention of the naval
station at Simonstown alone, that the colonists should be left to their
own devices. At the same time he defended them against the
charges made at Exeter Hall, of cruelty to the Bantu, and pointed
out that it was the Hottentots who claimed to be treating the
English as the Israelites had treated the Amorites. Though he did
not accept *The Tablet's* suggestion of a Roman wall and ditch
against " Kaffirs ", he urged a separation of territory as the best
method of keeping peace. This vigorous editorial policy made the
paper popular; despite the small numbers of the Catholics, the loss
on the first year was only £100, and by the third there was a small
profit. It eventually ceased publication in 1859, when it was sold
to John Quinn, one of its compositors, who transformed it into
The Fort Beaufort Advocate.*

It was in the framework of such discussions, reasonably conducted
and with a strict regard for facts, that *The Colonist* carried the
Catholic's answer to the stories of St Bartholomew, the Inquisition,
and the Gunpowder Plot, and to the scurrilities of the Maria Monk
type. And as Bishop Devereux wrote of his opponents to the
Vicar Apostolic of Natal, "since we established the Catholic
journal, these gentlemen are comparatively careful ".[44]

The historical defence which Ricards published in *The Colonist*
could no doubt have been made by Bishop Griffith, for the latter
was well versed in history. But he would have made it only to his
friends in government circles. In the sheets of *The Colonist* it
reached a wider public of non-Catholics—for the paper was paying
for itself after three years, and continued to do so.

More important, perhaps, was the effect on Catholic laymen.
They were shown that the charges against the action of the Church,
contemporary or in the past, could be discussed reasonably, and
convincingly in public, and that this was the best method of dealing
with them. It could even be said that such answers are the reasonable demands the world makes of Catholics taking part in public
life. Whether they like it or not, they are credited with some of

---

* The statement that Father Ricards sold it because he was too busy with
other projects probably comes from J. C. O'Riley who came to South
Africa and remained his friend. Certainly he was engaged in founding a
seminary for the vicariate in addition to his pastoral work. But the demise
of the paper may not be unconnected with the appointment of Dr Moran as
vicar apostolic.

the prestige, influence, and formed policy which the Church exercises in different countries; and they are regarded as holding the tradition which formed the Europe of the Christian nations. If they want to disown all this they must do so positively and are not respected for separating themselves from their birthright. Taking their birthright for granted, they must naturally be prepared to show that it has been beneficial in the long run to mankind, and therefore to explain or refute what is alleged against it.

Certainly from the days of *The Colonist* this attitude was accepted by Catholics. Either by public lecture or pamphlet or periodical, the history and contemporary policy of the Church have been continuously defended in South Africa. The literary work was largely undertaken by priests like Father O'Haire and Monsignor Kolbe, but the many laymen in public life—Justice Dwyer, Sir Thomas Upington, Christopher Bird, Charles Coghlan—made no secret of their faith; and some of them—Wilmot is I think the name of greatest honour—wrote and lectured vigorously to defend it.

It has to be recognized that Bishop Devereux, who died in 1854, made no adequate provision for the permanence of the works he inaugurated. He had hoped that the Assumptionist nuns would obtain more recruits from Paris and at the same time would become a South African institute. The Archbishop of Paris and the mother general wanted to maintain the French character of the order, and tried to recall them when this was being lost. The original agreement did not really cover the situation, and, to settle the dispute, the Congregation of Propaganda advised Bishop Devereux to accept those nuns who were willing to stay as a diocesan order of the Eastern Vicariate. The solution was accepted, but a number of the nuns went back to the mother-house in Paris, and for many years the new education which Devereux had hoped for was on a very restricted scale.[45]

Perhaps Bishop Devereux himself would not have thought his method needed apology. He had nearly killed himself by his devotion to cholera victims in Ireland as a young man. He had sacrificed academic ease to join Bishop Griffith in Africa. He had ruined his health at Cape Town by attending to Catholic sailors on ships putting into the port.[46] A man so ready to throw himself into the work he had chosen could plead also that the conditions of the colony were too insecure to worry about the future. His vicariate was constantly on the look-out for tribal raids and even wars; on one occasion he turned the church at Grahamstown into a fortress, and Mother Marie-Gertrude led her nuns and their children into safety armed with a cavalry sabre which, she boasted, she had learned to use in her youthful days. To do his work in those conditions, Bishop Devereux may well have thought that the most prudent course was to start as many good works as he could with the men and money he had, and to leave developments to the days when the frontier had settled down.

Chapter III

BISHOP GRIMLEY

I. The Lean Years

IN the fifteen years following the trek of the Boer farmers in 1836 the white population of the Cape Colony became richer and doubled its numbers. But this was followed for a like period by lean years. The British Government settled two thousand Germans, veterans of the Crimean war and their families, in the Eastern Province, but those who emigrated, chiefly to Australia, were more numerous. South Africa was no longer thought of as a land of promise. Political unrest added to the economic depression. The British Government had planned in the late 'forties to use it as a place for the settlement of convicts, many of whom would have been Irish political prisoners. There was an immediate outcry, in which all sections of the white population were at one, and the project was dropped. But that was the only occasion which united the Western and Eastern Provinces. The latter were very conscious of the pressure of the Bantu and had suffered often from their raids; they were in full agreement with the forward policy of Sir Harry Smith, who had annexed British Kaffraria in 1848. But there was little sympathy for them in the Cape Colony, and they pressed, therefore, for a completely separate government. The instructions of Whitehall, with whom all decisions of the policy rested, had changed every few years. There were Victorian statesmen who took quite seriously their obligations to impose fair dealing with regard to the Bantu and to promote their civilization. The complaints of Exeter Hall, repeated year after year, insisted that the colony did not intend to co-operate, and Exeter Hall was not only the mouthpiece of the London Missionary Society and many Protestant bodies. It was in close contact with many of the capable men who were building the English civil service and preparing the memoranda on which statesmen acted. The successors of Sir Harry Smith were told to withdraw troops behind the Orange River, and by 1853 the independence of the farm republics to the north was recognized. What they did to the Bantu tribes they found was their own business. Nor was the public opinion in London opposed to this policy.

There are four sources of information by which to reconstruct a picture of the Catholic community during these hard times. *The Life and Times of the Rt. Rev. James David Ricards* was published at Cape Town in 1908 by the Hon. Alexander Wilmot. The author had come to the colony in 1853 after some training in a Scots law office. He was a member, and probably the heir, of the old Catholic line of the Earls of Rochester, and in addition to his public service as a member of the Legislative Council he lectured and wrote on the antiquities of Rhodesia, earning a fellowship of the Geographical Society. By training and practice he is a good witness, but he wrote thirty years and more after the period of this chapter and, perhaps because of his qualifications, he only relates a few incidents which affected the life of his subject before Ricards became the Vicar Apostolic of the Eastern Vicariate.

The second book has a lengthy title: *Recollections of Twelve Years' Residence (as a Missionary Priest), viz., from July 1863 to June, 1875, in the Western District of the Cape of Good Hope, South Africa, Selected Chiefly from his Diary by the Rev. James O'Haire.* This priest certainly wrote in such a vivid style as to suggest that he had a diary before him. And much of what he says dovetails with information supplied by others. But the " chiefly " of the title is a warning, and the picture in his mind which would determine the colours, and even the selection, of incidents was that of a man after he had left the scene. He has certainly omitted some things which would tell against the perfect agreement between himself and his bishop.

There is, thirdly, the manuscript continuation of Devereux's *Chronicon* of the Eastern Vicariate, written by his successor, Bishop Moran. It covers the years 1857 to 1869, with a preliminary note (though written later) on the earlier history of the vicariate. Almost the whole of it is in the third person; only for two pages (out of more than fifty) does the bishop forget this discipline, and then he apologizes and returns to the impersonal style. Naturally enough such an account is factual, but save for those few pages, where he dreads the proposal of the British Government to leave the frontier unguarded, insecure and open to Zulu invasion, it is colourless.

Thomas Grimley was the second vicar apostolic of the Western Vicariate of the Cape. He had been a canon of the Metropolitan Chapter of Dublin and, on the recommendation of his archbishop, was named coadjutor to Bishop Griffith when the latter was stricken with paralysis in 1861. His manuscript diary of his journey to the Vatican Council in 1870 and his manuscript "history" of his episcopate form our fourth source. The "history" has as its subtitle "autobiography" and this is a more accurate description. In fact these manuscripts are a series of notes written almost immediately after the events recorded, and are concerned often with the reflection and emotions of the writer in regard to those events.

The sense of a failing mission recurs again and again. Within seven months of his arrival at Cape Town one hundred Catholics had left for Australia.[1] In November 1863 he notes that 140 Catholics have emigrated to New Zealand: "What will become of my flock? . . . Deus me adjuvet". A year later he was writing to one of his priests whom he had sent to America to try to raise funds. This Father O'Reilly had collected only £150, not enough for his own fare home, and had suggested that he should send this by post but stay himself permanently in the United States. Bishop Grimley wrote:[2] "We have had innumerable insolvencies". Then emigration to New Zealand increased. "I have lost between four and five hundred Catholics, which has decimated my congregation. The cross is my portion in this foreign land." So he accepted the suggestion; he would lose one of his priests but he would be able to pay off a little of his debt.

Nor was the spiritual life of the flock which remained such as a bishop would desire. Father O'Haire, writing some years afterwards and writing perhaps to edify, leaves the impression of a ready response to his apostolic labours. But Bishop Grimley noted in 1864 that out of his estimated eight thousand Catholics only a quarter had made their Easter communion. Though the estimate was probably exaggerated, including those who ought to be papists in the bishop's reckoning of families, a detailed visitation of one area by Father Quaid reported that 40 per cent refused to make their "Easters". Three years later the bishop himself found six Catholics and six or seven "perverts" at Worcester, but none would come to the sacraments. And in 1869 the optimistic O'Haire had to report that the Catholics at Paarl were disgraceful; drunkenness and wife-beating were their habitual crimes. There and at Malmesbury, where conditions were " goodish ", he had admitted fifty-two to their Easter duties, but there were as many more yet to be admitted.

It is probable that the willingness of Father O'Reilly to stay in America in 1865 and the return of Father Quaid to Ireland in the following year, though " he was a good priest ",[3] were due to the conditions of work in the vicariate. After three years spent in collecting a congregation at Malmesbury, and after a flamboyant opening of the church he had built,* poor Father O'Haire had to go to Oudtshoorn because there were a hundred and fifty Catholics there, and Malmesbury was left without a priest.

Without more priests and, therefore, more money, the situation seemed hopeless, and Bishop Moran of the Eastern Vicariate accepted and acted on that conclusion. He wrote to his colleague on 3 May 1864:[4]

I am in receipt of your letter, from which I perceive you are discouraged at the prospects of your vicariate. But there is no use in this. It is impossible for either of us to make much progress without more priests and greater pecuniary means. I suppose that by this time the Holy See is aware of this. Such being the case, it is clear that nothing more can be expected from us than to work along in a reasonable way with the staff and means at our disposal. Let us then do our duty, which means a fair share of work, and then rest content. If after this souls perish, we shall not be accountable. As many of my priests are growing old and delicate, and my pecuniary means small, and as I see little prospect of help for many years, I have made up my mind to abandon the idea of distant missions, permanent and temporary; *Nemo tenetur ad impossibilia.* Many Catholics leave the neighbourhood of priests without sufficient necessity. Surely in our circumstances we are not called upon to follow them. . . . My experience is that more is done . . . by the priests keeping close to their several missions and homes than by running about after a few people. . . . Another thing . . . never to establish a mission at a greater distance from another mission than a day's ride. . . . I mean about eighty miles, for such a distance can be travelled in a day in an emergency.

* He brought up the choir from Cape Town Cathedral and welcomed the bishop with a salvo of cannon.

The standard of work which Bishop Moran adopted was not an easy one; an eighty-mile ride, even only in an emergency, is pretty hard going for a fit man, and would be exhausting for a priest growing old and delicate. But the scheme was obviously a sensible and level-headed restriction of work to the means available.

Bishop Grimley, however, could not be persuaded to adopt it. In the Western Vicariate the priests must try to reach every Catholic, no matter what it cost in physical labour. Two years after this letter Father O'Haire, reporting on his tour of the district of Oudtshoorn, noted that he had covered 2,500 miles to accomplish it. Even the wild district in the north-west of the vicariate, Namaqualand and Bushmanland up to the mouth of the Orange River, must have its regular visitation because there were a few scattered Catholics working in the copper mines, or in the convict settlement or amongst the itinerant traders. Father Meagher was sent there in 1861–2, Father Quaid in 1863. At the end of that year the mining company gave two *erven* of land at Springbok for a church, and in 1865 Bishop Grimley went there himself to lay the foundation of a church dedicated to St Columbanus. The following year he persuaded the company to give him £50 for this church, and in 1867 and 1869 he spent three months visiting the territory, though well aware that there were only about a hundred Catholics in the whole of Namaqualand and Bushmanland.[5]

II. *A Journey through Namaqualand*

These "visitations" were a recurring incident in the life of the priests and vicars apostolic in the thirty years after Bishop Griffith arrived. They could be called a normal activity of Catholic life, for they brought priest and people together. As the number of priests increased in later years they became less frequent, and with improvement in conditions of travel less arduous. It is difficult, in fact, to recover a concrete picture of the earlier visitation, but Bishop Grimley's note of his third journey through Namaqualand in 1869 will perhaps serve this purpose:

April 8th. Today I left Table Bay on board the cutter *Klipper*. I was accompanied by my young catechist, George Kearns, who for economical purposes was termed my servant, although he fared nearly as well as his master. The sea was rough, but the wind favourable. We were only one day and two nights

on sea. I was sick, George was worse. On Saturday morning,
10 April, I landed at Hondeklip Bay. The miserable aspect of
the scene, the knowledge I had that there were only a few
Catholics, who could not extend aid to me, the wretchedness
of the inhabitants, cast a shadow over my spirit, for I had no
place to turn my steps to—there was no hotel except a house
unsuited to me. Poor Mrs Nicholson was there, it was true, but
how uncertain are human things; a few years ago well-to-do,
now possessing nothing. My blood chilled at the thought of
thriving myself on people so fallen into poverty. This was
only a passing feeling; God did not abandon me, but provided
for my little wants. A poor missioner travelling in Namaqualand must submit to many inconveniences. My great difficulty
was how I was to get to Springbok, where I would be in the
centre of my work, but where to get a cart I knew not, to pay
for one I was really unable. I wrote to parties to aid me.

In the Bay I found the following Catholics: Mrs Nicholson
and her two very young daughters, Harry and Mrs Strisky and
three daughters, Mrs Turner, servant at Pilkingtons, Dorche, a
Damara servant at Nicholsons. (Catholics at Hondeklip, 10.)
Mrs. Nicholson, Harry and Dorche approached Holy Communion. Mrs Turner is living where she ought not. I begged
of her to leave her place.

On the 11 April I baptized Johnson's child (since dead). On
that day I said Mass, and had only George at Holy Communion.
I am obliged to remain at Hondeklip for nine days. The
weather being very foggy, and my residence being a wooden
house admitting free ventilation, I caught a severe cold.

12 *April.* I baptized *sub conditione* Caroline Nicholson. This
child when in danger of death had been baptized by Dorche.
I enquired of this poor Damara girl what words she had used
when pouring the water; she said "I baktize".

While in the Bay I had Mass each morning and Rosary each
evening at Mrs Nicholson's. Trials surround me at Hondeklip.
All my little flock were not as they ought to have been. In
order to rescue Nicholson's two sons from heresy I offered to
educate them free of all expense at St Joseph's Academy. Prejudice and blind bigotry prevented his consenting. May God
look upon those boys, who were baptized in holy faith. At
last a cart came to the Bay for me, many thanks to John Shaw—
he is a brick.

19 *April*. I left Hondeklip today. As there was no room in the cart I had to leave faithful George behind me. I reached that night Kekokiez. Matters at Kekokiez wore a sombre aspect. After the day's fasting, the supper table did not groan under the luxuries of the season, but as fasting is good, may my soul have the benefit of the transaction. The night was cold, and being put to sleep in a room in which there was thorough ventilation, I felt for days after the effects of too much fresh air. Had the Proprietor viewed the advantages of his institution from the same standpoint as I did, I am persuaded his charge would have been more moderate.

20 *April*. I started for Mr Fletcher's, a kind-hearted Presbyterian, who gave me what I much needed, a good breakfast. May God convert him.

After leaving Fletcher's, I proceeded to the convict station at Buffalo River, having made arrangements for a return visit. I left for Springbok, where I arrived at 11 o'clock at night. I stopped at Maloney's hotel, where every attention was paid me. I got a large room sufficiently spacious to accommodate my little flock for devotional purposes.

At and near Springbok I found the following Catholics:— Mr and Mrs Maloney, Mrs and John Crowley and their two children, Charles Crowley, John Shaw, Joseph Cardinal, Edward Barry, Olivera, brother and four children, Tom Daniels, Mr Dominicus (Clerk at Talbots)—Number of Catholics at Springbok, 18. Of these, the following made their Easter duty: Mr and Mrs Maloney, Mr and Mrs John Crowley, and John Crowley. Edward Barry and Olivera went to confession. I did not see Tom Daniels, of Dancekraal, nor Olivera's brother. I exhorted all I saw to approach the Sacraments. Some followed my advice, others would not. I told them that my hands would be free of their blood.

22 *April, Thursday*. I learned today the sad intelligence of the accident that befell my dear young priest—the Rev. Patrick Dunne of Simonstown.

25 *April*. I baptized today Maria Suzanna, daughter of John Olivera, this evening in the real presence of Jesus Christ under the Adorable Sacrament. Many Protestants attended.

26 April. I baptized Maria Magdalena Hayes, wife of John Hayes of Augenis, Bushmanland, also his infant daughter Catherine. Catholics at Augenis, 9.

Today, I married at Springbok Margaret Dunne and Michael Clanchy. Margaret's laughing powers were sadly taxed during the sacred ceremony.

John Hayes informed me there is a Mrs Coetzee, a Catholic living in Bushmanland about two days from him. She has one or more children, Catholic. I could not see her.

27 April. I started for Spektakel, and was accompanied by Mr Cardinal and George. Our steeds were so serious in their general appearance that we had no apprehensions of a " runaway ". We off-saddled at Modderfontein, and enjoyed Mrs Woodfield's generosity. We proceeded at Spektakel, which we reached at 7 o'clock p.m. The following day I visited the Catholics wherever I could find them.

The following Catholics are at Spektakel:—John Regan, Edward Thomas, living with a woman, James Scott, not married, Mr and Thomas Smith and five children, Hugh Quinn, married to a Dutch woman who exhibited good dispositions towards the Catholic faith, John Fitzgerald, living with another man's wife, Mrs O'Toole, living in adultery with Dick Hart. Dick said he was a Catholic, but I doubt it. Catholics living at Spektakel, 16. Of all, only John Regan went to his Easter Communion.

28 April. I married at Spektakel William Smith to Eliza Cloote.

The Catholics at Spektakel are morally in a wretched condition, except John Regan, who at our departure asked for a little holy water, as he had nothing else there " to drive the devil away ". May God hasten to send a priest to this perishing flock. I went about the mat huts and did all I could to induce the Catholics to abandon vice. I stopped at Spektakel two nights and a day.

I baptized Mrs Smith and five children, and three children of John Fitzgerald.

29 April. I left Spektakel and visited Modderfontein, the residence of Mr Woodfield, Superintendent-General of the Mines. Mr Woodfield was very kind to me, and invited me to spend a few days there. Duties prevented my acceptation.

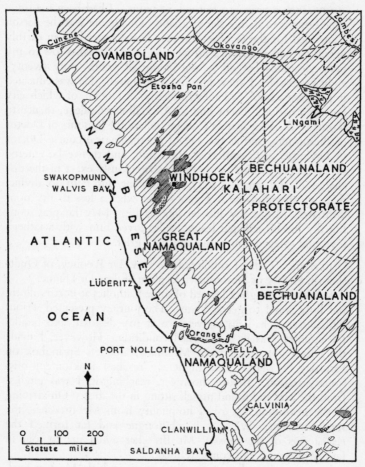

2. NAMAQUALAND AND OVAMBOLAND

Then he told me of what he had seen in the papers by that day's post of the accident to my priest Dr Dunne. What a shock I got. My heart became steeped in sorrow. I could not realize such an event—such a priest, so learned, so pious. I had been for some time hoping to divide the vicariate. Dr Dunne was the person I intended for the George district. Now, instead of an earthly mitre, he had received a crown of glory. What a loss to my poor vicariate—cut off in the bloom of youth, only twenty-eight years old. I knew him in his boyhood. He was educated in my own school, St Paul's Academy, of Dublin, of which city he was a native. I sent him to All Hallows College, thence to Rome to the Propaganda College, where the honours of Doctor of Philosophy, and at the end of his theological course Doctor of Divinity, were conferred upon him, and thence he entered on his sacred mission, so holy, so scrupulously exact in the discharge of the smallest duty, so prudent, his faith so divine, that one thought—he is a saint. But what a loss to my poor vicariate. Might my life be like to his. May he pray continually for his afflicted bishop, who loved him with a father's love, and grieved him with a mother's grief.

30 *April.* Today I appointed the Rev. Dr Rooney, of Oudtshoorn, Rector of Simonstown in place of dear Dr Dunne.

While at Springbok I heard of some Catholics at Port Nolloth, but how was I to get at them? The journey presented serious difficulties. I had no conveyance at my disposal, and besides the country was in a disturbed condition. However, I made the effort, got a cart from Mr Shaw, and left Springbok on Saturday, 1 May. That night we reached Kokfontein missionary station. Before, however, reaching it, I was pitched from the cart and found myself sitting in the dust. On arriving at the institution we asked hospitality from Mr Breecher, the superintendent. We got it; biltongue and fat formed the *magna pars* of the repast. Mr Breecher asked me to join in family prayers. I of course refused.

I was conducted to a small room in which Mr Cardinal, George and myself were to spend the night. Next day being Sunday, I got up early that I might make preparations for Holy Mass. The question arose, where would I say Mass? Would Mr Breecher permit the greatest rite of the Romish religion to be performed in the Rhenish Missionary Institution? I went to him and spoke as gently as I could, asking permission. He told me he was the house pastor, and also a bishop. I expressed my astonishment, as I had not been before aware of the dignity to which he had been elevated. I begged to remark that the office of a priest was to offer sacrifice, but I was not aware that he either offered sacrifice or had authority to do so. Mr Breecher is a man of the strongest prejudice against the Catholic Church. He attacked the Pope's supremacy, and, having misquoted Scripture, I had to correct him. With prejudice and ignorance combined, they form a formidable barrier to conversion. I however obtained my request to have Mass in our miserable bedroom. He allowed us a table and two candlesticks. I then celebrated the sacrifice in the Kokfontein Institution. After Mass I left for the convict station at Nomads. There was no Catholic there.

I then proceeded to Oograbis. After night, our cart man, not knowing the route, drove us into a sandy labyrinth from which we did not know how to extricate ourselves. At last my drooping spirits were cheered by the barking somewhere of a dog. I concluded where there was a dog there was likely a house. The driver went in the direction of the barking, and after some time made his appearance accompanied by two black men, who accompanied us to Oograbis, where we were received as hospitably as circumstances permitted by Mr Fielding, a Catholic at Oograbis, and Mr Flynn (Fielding's clerk), and William Carroll, the blacksmith. I met at Oograbis my acquaintances Mr and Mrs Todd, who treated me very kindly.

On the following morning I left for Port Nolloth. The road is sandy, and hence we did not arrive until 7 o'clock. I was kindly received by Mr Dryer, a Protestant. I got a room for myself and George; next day I went about seeking after my flock. I found John Burns and wife, John Linde, Charles Perigot. John Burns went to Holy Communion. His wife is an imbecile. John Linde is living with a woman. Charles Perigot is living with a married woman. Alas. Alas. I begged of him to leave her.

I celebrated Mass in Mr Dryer's house on the 5 May, the first Mass that was ever celebrated in Port Nolloth. Port Nolloth has now about ten houses. I think it will yet become a place of some importance, as the bay is far superior to that of Hondeklip. After Mass I left for Oograbis, reached that same evening, heard confessions, and, next day being the feast of the Ascension of Our Lord, I celebrated Mass in Oograbis. Flynn and Carroll went to Holy Communion. After Mass we left for Nomads. Long before we could reach our destination the dark shades of a cold winter's evening gathered around us. We were a considerable distance from Nomads, we were doubtful if we were on the right road, we could not see a few yards before us, and we became painfully convinced that we had missed the path. We turned back some hundreds of yards and changed our route. Slowly we moved on. There was no moonlight to brighten our weary path, even black clouds concealed from us the very stars. The wind began to howl in the mountains, and then the rain fell heavily. We had an open cart, and hence no protection from the storm. There was no tree under whose branches we might recline. There was no house or hut, however miserable, to afford us shelter, and to add to our sad condition the horses were worn out, and utterly unable to draw us out of the mountainside. I had to walk. I put my cloak around me, and walked before the horses. The rain falling in abundance soon saturated my cloak, my trousers and coat. The water flowed into my very boots. I walked wearily along. Occasionally from the darkness of the night and the unevenness of the road, I would strike rather roughly against George, who kept very closely by me. When we reached the top of the hill I was so exhausted that I had to await the arrival of the cart, and, holding on, walked after. At last we reached Nomads. I directed my steps towards Mr Fletcher's mat house. When near the house I fell prostrate on the earth. I soon arose, and found myself at the low entrance to Sandy's habitation—poor Sandy Fletcher, a Scotch Presbyterian, but a most kind-hearted man. I asked Fletcher at once for a trouser, saying that the life of a bishop was in his hands. He opened his box and took out a large, bright coloured trouser. I pronounced it first-class, and soon had it on. I then asked for a coat and boots. He handed me a large, coarse white coat, and boots, the leather of which never saw the tanner's yard. I looked at myself and said, " Well, if the Pope saw me now!" All the time the rain was falling, and dropping through the worn mats. I closed one large aperture by fastening against it a dried fish. Oh, that night I shall never forget. A fire was kindled in the middle of the hut. Yet we were far from comfortable, for the wind was rushing through the old mats. Mr Fletcher proposed that I should go to bed, that is, get into his bed, which consisted of two skins. I was asked if I would have a nightcap. I gladly accepted it to preserve my head from the breeze and rain. Sandy produced a large red woollen cap which, from its appearance, had seen many years of service. I put it on. Thus in trousers, coat and cap, I turned in between the two skins, and would have been fairly comfortable were it not for the rain falling on my face, but was, however, exhausted with fatigue, and, waking in the night, saw George and Cardinal asleep. I expected a severe cold would have been the consequence of this wretched and memorable night, but thanks to my good God, who always protects the missioner, I did not experience the slightest bad effect.

On the following morning I left for Kokfontein, where I met Mr Breecher. After a few words' conversation, I parted with the prayer, " May God convert you ". We proceeded on our journey to Springbok, where we arrived at about midnight. Next day, Saturday, I left for Buffalo River convict station. As we could not leave Springbok before 1 o'clock p.m., we did not arrive before 10 o'clock. At the convict station I was hospitably received by Mr Dallas, the Superintendent. The next morning I celebrated Mass in the head overseer's quarters. Three Catholics refused, I was told, to go to Mass. On Sunday evening I had rosary and instruction, followed by confessions. There are thirteen Catholic constables. The following did not approach sacraments: Alexander Donohue, Van Heeren, Harrington and Lybert.

I found at the station the following Catholics: Michael Chancy, Head Overseer, Margaret Chancy, his wife, Patrick Cancraffy, Thomas McCluskey, John Thornton, Patrick, Margaret, Mary, Eliza and Michael Kinsella, John Smith, Van Heeren, Matthew Troy, James Fitzsimmons, Patrick Harrington, John Smith, Henry Marshall, Lybert, Alexander Donohue—in all 19 Catholics.

Constable Joseph O'Connor wished to be baptized, but he was not sufficiently instructed. On Monday morning I commenced Mass at half-past five o'clock. The lightning was flashing and the thunder pealing the entire morning. I had the consolation of administering the holy communion to ten constables and two women. McCluskey, without any suggestion whatever on my part, presented to me on the part of the constables a present of £8 2s. 6d.

After leaving the station, I proceeded to Mr Fletcher's, the government surveyor, on the most important business of finding out an eligible site in Bushmanland for a Catholic missionary institution. Mr Fletcher is a Scotch Presbyterian, and hence very canny. I laid open my plans, informing him the government was aware of my intentions and very friendly disposed towards me. He assured me he would wish to see me succeed, and that he could state from his fifteen years' experience that the Protestant institutions did no good for the natives. He said he alone knew the watercourses in Bushmanland, that I might calculate on his aid, and he was sure I would get plenty of water. He would recommend some place between Heipe, Augenis, Ougrabip, Klein Windhoek, Eendop, selected from 60 miles east and west, and 160 north and south. Mr Fletcher remarked that this selection would bring our missioners within reach of the tribes beyond the river. May God for his own greater glory and the salvation of souls bless this great work. I place this glorious undertaking under the protection of St Joseph, the spouse of our Holy Mother. No work placed under St Joseph ever yet failed, neither shall this.

After leaving Mr Fletcher's place, I proceeded to Rietfontein, where I baptized George, the infant son of Anton Abler. I heard the confessions of Mr and Mrs Abler. I reached Hondeklip late that same night.

13 *May*. I baptized today the son of James Hayes, of Kenrup.

14 *May*. This morning I had at Holy Communion, Mrs and Elizabeth Nagel, Mr and Mrs Strisky, and Dorche, Mrs Nicholson's servant. After Mass I confirmed Mrs and Elizabeth Nagel and Dorche, the Damara girl.

As far as I could ascertain, the entire number of Catholics in Namaqualand and Bushmanland is 197.

15 *May, Saturday*. After Mass I embarked on board the *Klipper* for Table Bay, which, after a pleasant passage of four days, I reached on the 19 May.

III. *Practical Problems*

1. SCHOOLS

There was work for the bishop at Cape Town as well as in the outlying districts of his vicariate. On his first arrival Bishop Grimley remarked that " there were no respectable male or female schools ". They had decayed badly during the last long illness of his predecessor, and, though there were still sixty boys and fifty girls on the roll, the buildings were poor.

He " saw the necessity at once of raising the standard of Catholic education ", and a sermon on the subject brought in £105. The real difficulty was suitable teachers. For the girls he found an admirable solution because his vicar general, Monsignor McMahon, persuaded the Irish Dominican nuns of Cabra, near Dublin, to send some sisters to the Cape in 1863, not only to take over the girls' day school but to found a boarding school as well. In this community there was also a remarkable person, Mother Dympna, with a flair for teaching the deaf and dumb, who in 1874 opened a school for their work which was later called the Grimley Institute.

When Bishop Grimley failed to persuade the Christian Brothers to start a school for boys he set up, in January 1864, what he called a Josephian Institute. This was a school conducted by two laymen, Mr Mahon and Mr McLaughlin, but they had to promise to follow a religious rule drawn up by the bishop. Only by an entry of the following September do we learn that McLaughlin was really a priest named McCafferty, who had turned up in Cape Town in 1863 and was living as a layman and of unsatisfactory life. Apparently Bishop Grimley had hoped that his religious rule would make him a suitable schoolmaster. After six months he had " taken to drink " and, letting it be known that he was a priest, had collected a party of Catholic supporters in his refusal of the bishop's rule. " To get rid of him quietly I paid £25 for his passage to New Zealand. He left yesterday, and may he never come back."[6] The following January the other schoolmaster left Cape Town furtively, without giving notice, and apparently with the police in pursuit.[7]

It was not only the teachers who were unsuitable. In 1861 Grimley noted that, though there were then sixty boys and fifty girls on the roll of the old school in Machtenburg Gardens, the buildings were poor and there were in fact " no respectable male or female schools ".[8] And the conditions at Grahamstown, Port Elizabeth and Uitenhage were much the same. There were Catholic free schools in each town, but, according to Bishop Moran, they were miserable.[9]

The foolish optimism of that Josephian institute was, however, only an attempt to make do until the proper equipment could be obtained. The only two Catholic boys' schools of any size in South Africa were the academy at Cape Town and St Aidan's

seminary which Father Ricards had started at Grahamstown for
Bishop Moran in 1858, but which was also hampered by lack of
teachers, despite the versatility of its principal. But Bishop
Grimley was continuing his appeals to the teaching orders, and in
1867 he brought out five Marist Brothers, technically laymen in
temporary religious vows but in fact members of a well-organized
and far-flung society devoted entirely to teaching boys, and
charged them to found and run two elementary schools for boys.
They obtained from the bishop a clear-drawn contract, and the
new establishment was a success from its start. At least one feature
of that success was due to Grimley's intervention. He saw that it
was necessary in the conditions of the Cape for the school to accept
boarders, but the Marists protested that their rule did not allow
them to do so. The bishop immediately obtained from Pius IX
a dispensation from the rule. He installed them in what was for
those days a spacious school building; and so, before the 'seventies
began, the Catholic system of education by the religious orders had
entered, for both boys and girls, into the cultural formation of
South Africa. And when Sir Philip Wodehouse, the governor,
laid the foundation-stone of the Marists' school in 1868, the *Cape
Argus*, which had attacked Bishop Grimley's educational policy a
few years earlier, reported: " The gratifying fact that these new
schools would be thoroughly undenominational was also stated ".[10]

2. FINANCE

The bishop's difficulties were almost entirely due to poverty.
Three or four times the autobiography gives a summary of the
annual return to the civil government, and this always shows a
deficit of rather more than £2,500. Against this must be put the
grant obtained yearly from the French Society for the Propagation
of the Faith, usually 22,000 francs. It is not surprising, then, that
Bishop Grimley, wanting to find £1,500 every year over and above
his ordinary sources, and wanting to develop his pastoral work,
should try every possible means of increasing his income. Sometimes he was foolish. Following the practice of his predecessor
he brought a Belgian priest named Kums to the Cape and sent him
up country where he would meet the Hollanders. Father Kums
returned after a week producing nothing but some military meta-
phors about masked batteries and lines of Sebastopol, so the

bishop authorized him " to collect in Belgium " for the vicariate. Unsuccessful in this, Kums sent word that he was going to Rome to ask for a formal authorization. Immediately Bishop Grimley took alarm, for he had sent his vicar general to Rome on a similar errand the previous year. He wrote to Father Kums withdrawing his authorization and telling him to find himself a place in Europe. But the next year he was writing to all and sundry to disown the priest, for the latter had already obtained £139 from the Roman congregation on the strength of Grimley's letter. Apparently he used this for expenses; and in a second letter the bishop charges him with misappropriation and with using forged letters. To his diary he confided, " May God give me grace to say with Holy Job, the Lord giveth and the Lord taketh away: blessed be the name of the Lord ". But it was after all his own fault, for he also gives the text of his own authorization:

> Nous déléguons le Rev. F. T. M. J. Kums, missionaire apostolique, afin de recueiller des fidèles, tout ecclesiastiques que laiques, des aumônes et des subsides pour ériger des missions parmi les Hollandais de ce pays, qui depuis plus de deux siècles suivent l'hérésie de Calvin.

He certainly needed the money, but the terms were very broad for a questor, and scarcely canonical.

It is easier perhaps to sympathize with the bishop in his attempt to get money from the Government. Every occasion was urged. The garrison soldiers came to Mass, so in 1862 he obtained a guinea a week for this service. He wanted to arrange Mass for the convicts, so he asked, unsuccessfully, the superintendent to give £15 for a chalice. Despite his failure he continued of course his pastoral work with the convicts on Robben Island and at the two Government hospitals, but in 1865 he was again asking the Government to make him a grant for this work. Two years later he memorialized the governor for £50 for the priest attending Robben Island infirmary, and this time the matter was put before Parliament.

Not all of these efforts were wasted labour. By 1864 he had secured grants from the Cape Colony Government for £520, and they remained at this figure to the end of his episcopate. He persuaded the Colony Mine Company to give him the site of the church at Springbok and £50—he had urged them " on commercial

principles" to help him support a priest in Namaqualand. And
after some impassioned correspondence he obtained from Whitehall a very reasonable allowance for the chaplain at St Helena.

The annual deficit of £1,500, after reckoning the Government
subsidies and the normal church collections and the grant from the
Society for the Propagation of the Faith, was a constant nightmare
to Bishop Grimley. "To be candid," he wrote to Father O'Reilly,
in 1865, "I undertook works which I am not able now to pay for.
The foundation of Malmesbury was laid three years ago. Since
then I was unable to lay a stone upon a stone. I am now raising
the building, but will have to go in debt for £500". Nor was his
distress softened by the thought that a cathedral had been built in
Port Elizabeth free of debt. But this had been done by the exertions
of one priest, Monsignor Murphy, who had already raised the
money for another church and who, from his own savings, was
able to buy a property for the convent and school of the Dominican
nuns.[11] The Eastern Vicariate was also poor; Bishop Moran
could not afford the passage money to go to the Vatican Council.
But very sensibly he left the business of raising money to the priest
who was skilled at it, and did not embark on a multitude of schemes
together.

The lamentations of Bishop Grimley about his debts were perhaps a necessary spur to keep the financial difficulties constantly
before him. By special appeals, by sermons and speeches, through
his friends in Ireland, he managed to find most of the money, and
when his successor, John Leonard, a businesslike man, took over
the vicariate, he noted that the total debt was only £2,200, and
that £800 of this had been incurred since Bishop Grimley's death.[12]
It was not a great deal, considering the schools and churches founded
during his vicariate. Perhaps he had not grasped sufficiently that
the development of Catholic centres would normally more than
repay the loans incurred by their founding; but he could scarcely
be expected to understand in the middle of the nineteenth century
the doctrine of the unbalanced budget.

It is not a reflection on any clergyman that he should beg for the
good works he has to do. But what seems odd to the English habit
of mind is that Bishop Grimley, with his very real difficulties about
money, should have spent so much on collecting church ornaments.
When he wrote to James O'Haire, then a clerical student, "I am

become a beggar on a great scale ", he mentioned beads and medals and relics, vestments and chalices, as well as a little library for the use of the mission.[13]   In 1864 he was particularly doleful: " Yesterday 102 left this vicariate, 60 or 70 a few months ago.   Many are preparing to follow, it is said all the Irish in Cape Town—and then *actum est de Catholica religione* in this part of the world." But, he added, " I shall labour to the last and hope against hope ", and said that he had accordingly contracted for a marble altar, reredos, tesellated pavement, concrete steps and sedilia for £300.   Of the great issues debated and defined at the Vatican Council which he attended, of the relations of reason and faith, of the infallibility of the Roman pontiff, he wrote little in his diary.   But he noted how he obtained 300 lire from Prince Massimi for a statue of St Joseph, how the Princess Odescalchi gave him a mitre, how some nuns gave him a monstrance and a thurible; and how he asked Monsignor Capel to find him a bell for his cathedral and the interview with the Marquess of Bute, " who did not restrict me in price or size of bell.   May God bless him."

Dr Thomas Grimley, it must be said, did much to deserve the reputation which the Catholic clergyman was given by the nineteenth century, of always looking for gifts.   And on one occasion at least he was somewhat cavalier in his treatment of them.   On his journey to Rome immediately after his appointment he called on Napoleon III and, as the bishop of St Helena, asked for and obtained 5,000 francs for the church on that island.[14]   In 1864, he noted in his autobiography that he had built a house for the priest of Oudtshoorn with the £200 that Napoleon III had given him. " I thought it better ", he observed, but was careful that the register of Oudtshoorn should record its debt to St Helena.[15]

There is, I think, an explanation of this clerical attitude.   The previous hundred years had seen the spoliation of the Catholic Church by the civil governments all over Europe, and the wealth which the clergy had administered for the maintenance of worship and for works of charity was now in the hands of laymen and devoted to other purposes than those for which it had been given. The compensation given was absurdly unequal to the robbery, and was treated as a salary conceded by the state.   It was scarcely surprising that some of those trained in the seminaries of the clergy, where these facts were known and not hidden by the official histories and catchwords, should regard it as their right to recover for the Church some part of what had been taken and to administer it as they wished. There is, indeed, no such proposition in the moral theology approved by the Church—which always allows such historical bygones to pass into limbo—but the memory would remain, unconsciously perhaps, in the minds of those formed by the older generation of priests.

In this connection the opening sentence of Bishop Grimley's autobiography is not without point. " From my earliest infancy ", he wrote, " I entertained a predilection for the ecclesiastical state." This purposed clericalism showed itself in his assumption that all the world ought to help him to rebuild a dignified Catholic worship, and that, as a bishop, he could decide the better way to use their contributions. But it did not modify in any way his readiness to rebuke what he regarded as wrongdoing on the part of the powerful; in the very interview when he first asked Napoleon III for a contribution, and before he had come to the point, he took occasion to tell the Emperor: " Latterly, I must say, your Majesty has descended in the estimation of Irishmen ".[16]

The same seminary tradition probably accounts for the ejaculatory prayers which round off the entries in his autobiography and which make it so different from the sardonic comments Bishop Griffith committed to paper. (Just as his portrait shows an almost typical ecclesiastical face, while his predecessor looks like a judge, or maybe a headmaster of the old school.) But the pious reflections came quite naturally to Thomas Grimley. They occur even more frequently in letters to his intimate friends like O'Haire, where they are mingled with much good sense; they occur, too, in his letters to public authorities, even in the factual returns he had to make to the Congregation of Propaganda, where they must have caused Cardinal Barnabò some surprise.

But it would be a foolish prejudice to suppose that this habit made the bishop difficult in social life, or unattractive. After two years' experience of the memorials about extra grants, and not long after a letter in the *Cape Argus* had attacked his proselytizing spirit,[17] the committee of the Civil Service club sent the auditor-general to invite the bishop to become a member. He replied that he was in debt and could not afford to join; perhaps after a year or two he might be allowed to do so, and in any case he would never forget their kindness.[18] It is said that Catholics are very generous towards their priests, whatever their faults, and this attitude may have survived even in the hard conditions of Cape Colony in the 'sixties. But it surely showed a special liking for their bishop when, after all the collections he had imposed on them, they presented him with £351 to enable him to go to the Vatican Council.[19] Bishop Moran, as we have seen, could not afford the journey.

The ejaculatory prayers were in all probability the natural and reasonable and religious relief of the tension of this highly-strung, emotional man as he rushed at every fence on his course. And such a man can be a really intimate friend, as Bishop Grimley certainly was to Father James O'Haire. He could scold him unmercifully.[20] On one occasion it was a rebuke for lecturing on the temporal power (of the papacy); " it's too strong ", the Bishop wrote, " for Mossel Bay prejudice " (where it had been given). Father O'Haire noted shortly afterwards that he gave the lecture at Fraserburg, and the whole population turned out to hear it at five shillings a head;[21] he raised the charge to 7s. 6d. at Victoria West shortly afterwards, and still had a packed hall.

This theme of moderation recurs again and again in the bishop's affectionate letters. But he was quite humbly ready to tell of his own failure to keep this impossible counsel. On one of his visitations he had found the Protestants friendly and " so preached on the unity of the true Church. I did not attack any sect. I merely proved my own proposition." Yet as soon as the word " Luther " occurred one of the audience walked out. " It is strange that, unconsciously, I fear I have done much harm. The Protestants I am sure would not come again."[22]

IV. Bishop Grimley as Apologist

Bishop Grimley held firmly to the view that the publicizing of Catholic doctrine would do no good if it created bitterness in the minds of others. The title of one of his lectures, " The Harmony of Sciences and Christianity ", indicates his own attitude and desire in the matter. And he was obviously worried lest Father O'Haire, the only one of his priests who was gifted at this work, the apostolate of the public lecture, should fail to practise the counsel. At the

beginning of 1866 he wrote to him, following a newspaper report
of a lecture, "Don't pitch into the Protestants. . . . You don't
know this Colony yet. Keep to your moral discourses, win the
Protestants by the beauty of your morality."[23] It is likely that the
bishop was using the word " moral " in a somewhat special sense in
this case—many mid-Victorian writers did so—or it may be that he
saw other points and characteristics of the lectures than were noted
by the reporters.   Later in the same year he repeated the instruction:
" Our grand principle must be never to compromise an iota of our
faith, yet never given unnecessary offence. We catch neither flies
nor men with a bitter ingredient."[24] When Father O'Haire
addressed an open letter to the Anglican Bishop Gray, the bishop
described it as " telling ", but " injurious "; and he instructed
Father O'Haire " not to write to the newspapers until we get one of
our own ".[25]

Worse happened two years later. A Catholic explorer, John
Chapman, joined the Freemasons and the fact became public
knowledge. O'Haire expostulated with him by letter, which the
Freemasons then published in a pamphlet called *The Priest and
the Freemason*. A few months later Chapman fell ill in the diamond
fields, called for a priest, and was reconciled before death by Father
Le Bihan, O.M.I.; though the Freemasons insisted on burying him
with their rites, the Protestant minister at whose house he was
staying sent this information to Father O'Haire, who printed it in
his Recollections.[26] But when *The Priest and the Freemason* was
first published Bishop Grimley was alarmed. " Your letter to
John Chapman ", he wrote, " is in everybody's hands. It was a
most unfortunate letter; it has raised a storm which will, I believe,
do immense harm, although, I know well, unintentional on your
part. Oh, that you had never written it!"[27]

It is clear that Bishop Grimley and Father O'Haire regarded their
lectures as of importance in building the Catholic community of
South Africa. Their opinion may of course have been touched
with vanity, but it was not simple conceit. And men who have to
spend as much physical energy in their work as these two did in
their visitations usually underrate the chiefly intellectual effort and
effect of a discourse. Many of these lectures were repeated in the
villages and towns of those visitations. The whole scattered

Catholic population was persuaded to some view on a topic of general interest by men whom they respected and who were certainly eloquent by the standards of that time and place. And according to the secular press, as also by the box-office returns, a considerable number of the Protestant population came to hear these lectures; persuaded or not, they picked up something of what Catholicism meant. In St Mary's Cathedral at Cape Town the Governor-General and the official world—" the élite of Cape Town society ", as Father O'Haire called it—were often present to hear the bishop.

The newspapers of the time tell the same tale. When Bishop Grimley preached at the opening of Father O'Haire's church at Malmesbury the *Advertiser and Mail* of 30 September, 1865, told its readers that " Protestants of every denomination attended both at the opening and evening services ", and that " all who heard the right reverend preacher were both delighted and edified ".

The full text of these popular addresses has not survived, but, as with all oratory, it is probable that their success was due in part to the temperament and enthusiasm, the friendliness, of the speakers. Certainly their diaries show them always ready and desirous to explain the Catholic religion to any who can be persuaded to listen, and in all cases to make its practices public.

They showed this spirit as they went about the work of " visitation " which was inherited from Bishop Griffith and faithfully continued by them. On one occasion, hearing a navvy use some Voltairean remarks, O'Haire, who was passing, " gently corrected him ".[28] In this case the result was surprising, for the navvy, " with diabolical rage, threatened me with a carving knife at my breast ". The argument did not develop on syllogistic lines, for George Kearns, a student who was accompanying O'Haire, seized another knife and said he " would steep it in the navvy's heart's blood ". The Voltairean ran away, and Father O'Haire seems to have been satisfied.

Bishop Grimley often urged sweetness and gentleness on his zealous priests; although he could be severe at times, as with the Lutheran missionary at Kokfontein. After a visit from President Brand of the Orange River Sovereignty the Bishop found him a very liberal man and not bigoted against Catholics,[29] and similarly noted after meeting the Anglican Bishop Gray, with whom he had had a controversy, "he seems in *bona fide* ".[30] Father O'Haire, whose verbal disputes were conducted much more bitterly, thought that "goodwill binds class to class, nation to nation, and creed to creed at the Cape ".[31] Opinions in the opposite sense, however, could be quoted from the diaries, and it would seem that both these men were so mercurial that they were ready to generalize from the latest incident of this experience. Such a temperament makes their evidence very suspect when it goes beyond particular events, but it suggests that they reacted very quickly to an audience, and so established early the friendly relations which are the foundation of good oratory. The very practical and near-cynical Monsignor McMahon, though he could comment on O'Haire, "I think he will soon leave off physic if he has to pay for it ", also wrote: "He draws all sorts . . . he is worth a shipload ".

The suggestion of a friendly understanding of Catholic achievement is, I think, the keynote of the rather bald summaries we have of Bishop Grimley's lectures. There was one on Sacred Music, given first as a preliminary to a concert in St Mary's Cathedral. It reads like a catalogue. The heroes of old, even Achilles, were all musicians. The art has an honoured place in the Old Testament and was used only for worship. The angelic sons of the morning, Moses, Mary the Prophetess, King David and Solomon and the Macchabees practised it. The Christians made full use of it according to Pliny, Lucian, St Ignatius and St Cyprian. A short description of the Ambrosian chant and then of the Gregorian chant followed, with references to its English exponents from Alfred the Great to the time of the Oxford degree in music established in the reign of King John! Maybe there were some valuable reflections on each of the instances quoted, though time could not have allowed for many, and, as O'Haire remarked,[32] the bishop was not himself a musician. But the purpose seems plain—to suggest that the Catholic Church had preserved a religious practice of the Old Testament and had handed it down as developed by those whom all venerated as Fathers of the Church. Of slight apologetic value, one might think, but it was the sort of thing that Nicholas Wiseman had introduced in England some twenty years earlier, and it had played its part in breaking down prejudice.

The only part of this lecture which O'Haire reports *verbatim* is the peroration, with its final sentence as the concert was about to

begin: " I have done. Let the heavenly art speak for itself. "
This type of rhetoric does, perhaps, or did, depend on a final
passage of flamboyant character to leave the desired impression.
Certainly Bishop Grimley attached importance to it: he preserved
in his diary the words which brought his lecture on " Literature in
the Middle Ages " to its conclusion:

> Woman, thou partner of man's toil, thou sharer in his fate,
> thou ornament of society, it is to the Catholic Church—the
> Church of the Middle Ages—that you owe the elevated position
> you hold in the world.[33]

From O'Haire's summary of the lecture as given at Oudtshoorn
—its first appearance was in St Mary's, Cape Town, in 1864, when
the selling of seats made £75—it was mainly a statement of the
writings and discoveries of the Middle Ages (and the renaissance,
treated as their continuation). The scholastics, the crusades,
printing, the universities, Guido d'Arezzo, the mariner's compass,
the invention of spectacles and gunpowder, gothic architecture:
such is O'Haire's list: was it his jumbled memory, or did he get
the bishop's notes?

It is possible that this mere statement of examples of the variety
of Catholic culture, accurate as far as it went but without analysis
or order, was the best way to convince an untrained audience that
the Church could be valuable to them. There is more argument
in another lecture, on " The Inspiration of the Scriptures ", which
Bishop Grimley gave several times. The occasion of its first
delivery was a violent and public controversy on the subject among
the Protestants of Cape Town.[34] A summary printed in the *Cape
Argus*[35] shows him to have started with reliable quotations from the
Christian writers of the first centuries, accepted of course by
Anglicans as well as Catholics, to set out the doctrine. The
teaching of the divines of the Church of England followed, both
to show their agreement and to indicate the difficulty they necessarily found in the question: how can we tell which books are
inspired, or what writings constitute the Sacred Scriptures? The only
solution not concealing a logical fallacy was, the lecturer maintained, an appeal to the tradition of the Church. Its authority
could be established by using the gospels as historical evidence;
from that proved authority we could learn which books formed

the canon of Scripture and were inspired. The necessary place which tradition had in the Christian system, its preservation unchanged in the Catholic Church: all this was suggested rather than controversially maintained. The Anglicans, holding to Christian belief, found a problem difficult of solution; in Catholic theology the problem did not exist. Such was the impression which the lecture gave, and the *Argus* reported it as " a very able lecture, listened to with breathless attention by a numerous audience ". The bishop concluded by assuring his audience that he had attacked no denomination.

It reminds one again of Nicholas Wiseman's approach to the English: you find intellectual difficulties in Christianity which become moral problems for you; you will find that they are solved if you will add to your belief precisely those doctrines of the Catholic Church which you rejected when you separated from it. And it may be that there is a connection with the fact that Grimley was making his theological studies in Ireland when Wiseman's articles and lectures were disturbing the minds of John Henry Newman and many others.

Several of the other lectures reported at different times in the newspapers of the Cape tried, whatever their title, to present a picture of life in Europe which was at one in the profession of the Catholic Faith; and this of course was implicit in the lectures on monasticism which Father O'Haire gave and Bishop Grimley prepared for publication. They were clearly an outcome of the historical school of Görres and Montalembert; they often exaggerated the importance of the Church in mediaeval culture and the obedience and even the respect which was paid to it; the picture was in fact still romanticized. But they did presuppose in every example that the Church was not a voluntary society dependent on the state and subject to its government; that it was in fact older than any of the existing kingdoms or empires, and of itself was capable of fashioning social life. Just as the earlier lecture had claimed implicitly that the Catholic Church was unique among the bodies which accepted the Christian Scriptures, so these others claimed that she was unique in being independent of all secular governments and cultures.

It is always difficult to discover afterwards what makes the spoken word popular, but the Catholic attitude implied in these repeated lectures must surely have been grasped by some of the audience. And this must have been especially the case with the Catholics who attended.   That it caused them no surprise or alarm shows indeed that the doctrine was part of normal Catholic tradition.   But in the first half of the century it had been minimized, and Catholics were beginning to think of their religion as the peculiar privilege or burden of the families which had inherited it.   Bishop Griffith had written quite naturally of those who ought to be papists, alluding to a tiny minority of the population.   When he made his voyage from England he had retired each day to his cabin to say the divine office with his fellow Dominican, but he had not even sought out those of the crew whom he was told were Catholics. When Grimley came out from Europe he had offered Mass on board ship and had said the rosary daily and publicly in both the first and second class saloons.   When O'Haire came out a year or so later, when he had only just been ordained, he boasted that the officers, crew and passengers sometimes attended the instructions he gave to the four Catholics aboard.[36]   And now in their lecturing campaign they were at least hinting the claim of the Church that all men and women, and not merely those of a few families, ought to be papists.

Bishop Grimley died a few days after his return from the Vatican Council.   Father O'Haire left South Africa to return to Ireland a few years later; his health was not good, and perhaps he was insufficiently appreciated by Bishop Leonard, who wrote: " Father O'Haire's intentions are good, but he is reckless with money.   He is not prudent, but is a hard-working and zealous priest."[37]   His memorial is the church of St Francis de Sales which he built at Malmesbury, the solemn opening of which was long remembered. Catholics from Cape Town left by omnibus on the Saturday morning.   When Bishop Grimley arrived a Mr Kennedy fired twenty-one shots (the royal salute) from his cannon in the church grounds.   "The inhabitants", the bishop wrote in his diary, " were startled and perhaps alarmed at the whole proceeding." But the *Advertiser and Mail* gave the function two columns on 30 September 1865.   "The choir of St Mary's Cathedral ", they said, " so long famed for transcendent musical talent, lent its valuable assistance on the auspicious occasion."   And the sermon by the bishop on this occasion, as we have already seen, was not passed over.

The Eastern Vicariate also had its lecturer-priest in Father Ricards who became popular for his readings of Dickens and Lever and Moore, and for his talks on physics and chemistry, which would not normally lead by a swift path to the marks of the true Church. When he became vicar apostolic, in 1871, he continued the practice, though his subject-matter became more directly religious as he grew older. After the death of Bishop Grimley and the departure of Father O'Haire the work was continued by Father McCarthy and Father Kolbe. Of the next generation Dr Sidney Welch in the Cape Province, Dr Sormany in Natal and Father Cox in the Transvaal also played their part as lecturers, but the fashion was exhausted or dying out by the time the first world war began. But for fifty years most of the centres of population in South Africa had many opportunities of hearing intelligent and informed Catholics thinking aloud. To the extent that those opportunities were used the Church became not merely the visible society of its text books but audible to the surrounding world.

Chapter IV

CAPE COLONY: 1870–1900

I. Introductory

BISHOP GRIMLEY left a manuscript diary of his attendance at the Vatican Council in 1870. He was wholeheartedly in favour of the definition of papal infallibility, as being the accepted traditional belief of the Catholics of South Africa, and entered his name at one stage to speak in this sense, making a few notes of his argument.[1] He withdrew his name from the list, however, and the diary gives, in fact, no information about the tension between the various groups. It has little general interest save its record that many who knew Pius IX believed him to be a saint and expected therefore his future canonization.[2]

He bought Theiner's edition of Baronius, we learn, and arranged to buy the fifty-four volumes of the Bollandists for the episcopal library. But he had often to complain of his health, especially of a bronchitis contracted when visiting his mother's grave in Ireland. The voyage back to South Africa did not cure him, and he died a few weeks after landing in Cape Town. Two years later another Irish priest, John Leonard, who had acted as Bishop Grimley's agent in Ireland and had there collected money for his vicariate, was appointed to succeed him.

Meanwhile there had been a change of direction in the Eastern Vicariate. Before the Vatican Council Bishop Moran had been transferred to the see of Dunedin, in New Zealand. While they were in Rome, he and Bishops Allard and Grimley had recommended[3] that Dr Ricards, the rector of the seminary at Grahamstown, former editor of *The Colonist* and well-known and popular in Cape Colony as a lecturer, should be made vicar apostolic, and he was so appointed the following year. In 1873 Bishop Allard was asked to send in his resignation, and in his place as vicar apostolic of Natal was sent the forty-eight-year-old Charles Jolivet, O.M.I., who had had several years' experience as a parish priest in Liverpool.

When these three men, Ricards, Leonard and Jolivet, were appointed the fortunes of the Catholic Church in South Africa were by no means promising. We have already quoted Bishop Moran's downright letter on the conditions of his vicariate.* At the Vatican Council Bishop Grimley had reported that ten years before the Catholics of his vicariate had been more numerous than now; that this had come about not by apostasy but by emigration to America and New Zealand; that the decrease in public works and in commerce especially affected Catholics, and that this would continue. It seems impossible now to check the accounts statistically. The figures given at various times in the records are estimates of the number " who should be papists ", and this varies with the standard adopted. But the consensus of men so different in temperament as Bishop Moran, Bishop Grimley and Bishop Allard makes it clear that the Catholic missionary effort in South Africa was almost exhausted in the early 'seventies.

The situation, however, was already changing when they left the scene. With the discovery of diamonds in Griqualand at the end of the 'sixties, and of gold in the Transvaal some ten years later, entirely new centres of population grew up around Kimberley and on the Witwatersrand, and wealth in the form of money became available on a large scale. The greater demand for the crops and commerce of the rest of the country brought much development, not least in railroads and other forms of transport. Between 1875 and 1891 the white population, excluding the diamond-digging and gold-mining areas, rose from 375,000 to 630,000 and, with some slight vicissitudes, this was accompanied by an increasing general prosperity which continued till the Anglo-Boer war at the turn of the century.

The change, economic and demographic, was an opportunity for the Catholics as for others. Their numbers increased, though at a slightly lower rate than that of the total population. They were 2·8 per cent of that total in 1875, and in 1891 (for the same area) they were 2·4 per cent. To a considerable extent they had been and remained more urban than rural; in the latter year the census

* p. 58, supra.

showed them to number 9·6 per cent in Port Elizabeth, 5 per cent in the Cape District. Roughly this proportion seems to have been true also of the diamond-digging areas (4·78 per cent of the population of Kimberley was Catholic), and probably of the Witwatersrand as well.[4] As far as provinces were concerned, the Eastern Province of the Cape led with nearly 8,000 white Catholics, the Western and Central Prefectures had over 6,000, the Orange River State 2,500 and Natal only 600. A few years later the Catholic numbers in Johannesburg were estimated at 4,000.[5]

With the increase in material prosperity churches and resident priests were multiplied. It was most noticeable in the old vicariate of Natal, from which the prefectures of the Transvaal and Basutoland, as well as the vicariate of Kimberley, were formed during this period. It had been the least developed area as far as Catholic institutions were concerned when Bishop Jolivet was appointed to rule it in 1876. According to a report in the *Natal Mercury* of 1899, he had by then built ninety churches and chapels, and although the buildings of the Trappist missionaries in Natal and East Griqualand and the Oblates in Basutoland fall to be subtracted from the figure, the centres of Catholic worship for the mainly white population had so increased that it was possible to think of the vicariate in terms of parishes. In the Eastern and Western Cape the building of new churches was also frequently recorded, so that by the end of the century a Catholic in South Africa (outside Namaqualand and Bechuanaland) was no longer normally dependent on the annual visit of an itinerant priest or bishop. He could usually, though sometimes only with difficulty, assist at Sunday Mass and know his parish priest. The system of Catholic life which had obtained in most of Europe for some eight hundred years, and the working of which priests and people understood by tradition, was taking root to South Africa. It is likely enough that the weekly following of the Church's liturgical seasons, the sermons which would contain so much matter of common form, the collections for and buying of this or that statue or altar, would become so customary as to be unremarked, but the Catholic habit, gathering up, though unconsciously, all the past of Christendom, was probably the source of the other activities of the Catholic community during these years.

II. Leading Laymen

The history of the Church in South Africa now begins to include what has since been called Catholic Action, the work of laymen in public life. In some of the small towns which the era of prosperity brought into being one or other of them, by the chance of fortune or ability or both, took a leading place. John Gately, a soldier of the 60th Rifles, took his discharge in South Africa in preference to the commissioned rank which was offered him. He settled in the township of East London, then built on the western bank of the Buffalo River, and traded as a forwarding agent for the last thirty years and more of the century. In time he became practically the head of the small community, a justice of the peace, twice mayor. Throughout his career he lived publicly as a practising Catholic. Until a church was built Mass was said in his house every quarter, but otherwise he travelled the forty miles to King William's Town every Sunday. He refused to attend the services of other religions even in his official capacity. Nor would he go to public dinners on a Friday; there was no fun, he said, in looking on while others feasted. In his case, and in others like him, Catholicism was asserting itself as a social discipline, even in small matters, independent of secular customs. It was fortunate for the Church that he won a reputation for strict integrity as an official; there was never a suggestion that he gained financially by his public work and his friends could claim, at his death, that none of the town improvements he planned and carried through benefited the neighbourhood of his own house.[6]

John Bird, of Pietermaritzburg, the son of that Colonel Bird who had been secretary to the Cape government and had welcomed Bishop Griffith on his first arrival in the colony, is best known for his historical work, *Annals of Natal*, published in two substantial volumes and indispensable for research into the Voortrekker period. He worked at the survey of Natal for the government from 1851. Eight years later he was recommended for the post of Treasurer-General, but was passed over by Whitehall. Not till 1876, and after doing the actual work for some years, did he receive the appointment, and constant insomnia made him resign almost immediately. In a memoir left for his son he said quite frankly that (like his father before him) he was not given the promotion he knew he deserved—but he wrote without bitterness and without blaming anyone.

After resigning the treasurership he was made an acting judge of the Native Court. In this post he found himself dealing with divorce actions. After consultation with Bishop Allard he adopted the principle: the first marriage of a native is valid, and no Catholic judge could presume to break it, but subsequent unions could be decided according to native law. Fortunately, he wrote, only three or four suits for divorce from the first wife came before him, and these he did not grant; but his refusal meant an appeal to the secretary for native affairs (technically to the supreme chief, an inexpensive affair for the natives), so it was not necessary for him to make the matter one of religious principle. Towards the end of 1879, however, a Christian native brought an action for divorce and was entitled to it by the code of native law. John Bird sought to get it heard before another judge but it was technically difficult: " it was then evident ", he wrote, " I had no longer a right to subject suitors to undue delay and legal expense ". Accordingly he resigned his post. Apparently it was common knowledge that he did so for a religious principle, but he refused to make any public explanation. " It is always odious ", he wrote, " unless it can be useful, to advert to religious differences."

In his reticence (and indeed in his whole make-up) he kept that tradition of English Catholicism which was fashioned during the centuries of the penal laws and to which its admirers have given the rather curious adjective, sober. It is very doubtful whether, in South Africa or elsewhere, the tradition has been attractive to others than the families trained in it; nor is it clear that John Bird was morally bound to take the action he did. But like Gately he recognized his religion as determinant of his public conduct, and so helped to show what Catholicism demands. Conscious of this standard, he was able to resist the pressure of public opinion.

Another prominent Catholic was John Patrick Fitzgerald, F.R.S., who held an almost official position in King William's Town, which was the capital of British Kaffraria. When practising as a doctor in New Zealand he had met Sir George Grey, and when the latter became Governor of the Cape it was probably by his recommendation that the Colonial Office urged Dr. Fitzgerald to go to the newly-established British territory. Almost at once he chose a fine site for a hospital, advised on its plan and superintended its construction. Many of the features of Grey Hospital, as it was named—the large bricked-in reservoir under the quadrangle for the catchment of rain, the roof cistern to which the water could be pumped, as well as the general lay-out—are probably due to him. He was especially proud of his system of dry-earth closets, which made sanitary hygiene possible in the days before waterborne sewage. But in his lifetime his fame rested on his skill as a surgeon, particularly for cataract and lithotomy, and from 1856, when he came to South Africa, until he retired in 1891, he was probably the best known doctor of the colony. Throughout those years he was the leading Catholic of the town, and a great friend and helper of the Dominican convent where his daughters were educated.

Even in the Calvinist republics laymen were able to work openly for the Catholic faith. The O'Donoghues, father and son, persuaded President Pretorius in 1870 to secure the repeal of the enactment of the *Grondwet* which made the saying of the Mass illegal, and their influence with him was still referred to in the press a quarter of a century afterwards.[7] In the Cape Province there were several Catholic laymen taking a prominent place in public life. Justice Fitzpatrick and Justice Dwyer on the bench, Thomas Upington as an eloquent Attorney General (he had come from Ireland with Bishop Devereux as a clerical student) were well-known figures.

These were of Irish descent. Colonel Schermbrucker was a German from the Rhineland and had been a lieutenant in the Prussian army. Like so many of his class in the nineteenth century —and how unlike the picture of them in English literature! — he was able to turn his hand to many trades. After serving with the German legion in the Crimean war, he came out with the party settled by the British government along the banks of the Buffalo River. There he made his living in turn as a butcher, an auctioneer, a charcoal burner, an editor of a newspaper, as a colonel of irregular horse in the Frontier Wars, to become finally a member of the legislative assembly, an ardent worker for responsible government and a minister of the Crown in the Sprigg administration of 1874. In 1889 he was commissioner of public works in the Cape government. In public life he won considerable praise for his promotion of afforestation in the Colony, and he remained always, first in the

Eastern province and later in Cape Town, one of the leading Catholic laymen.[8]

Alexander Wilmot, of whom we have already spoken, became a member of the legislature, and was proud of his success in restricting legally the sale of intoxicants to the Bantu. In the 'nineties he was a frequent advocate of the idea of an Afrikaner nation under the English Crown, but he was better known for his studies on the ruins of an ancient civilization in Mashonaland.

Charles Coghlan, the son-in-law of Colonel Schermbrucker and later Prime Minister of Southern Rhodesia, was a lawyer of Kimberley, and became mayor of that town shortly before and during the Anglo-Boer war. These men were always ready to take part with their fellow Catholics in public meetings; Gately and Wilmot certainly helped Bishop Ricards with financial advice and in the raising of loans; Schermbrucker occasionally and Wilmot often wrote for the *Catholic Magazine*, which became in the 'nineties the expression of cultured Catholic opinion. Each of them followed his own path in politics, so that no question arose of a Catholic interest or party. That concept, assumed as a matter of course under the old system of Colonial Administration, had no place in the theory of responsible government which was accepted in the 'seventies at the Cape, and the attitude of these Catholic laymen undoubtedly helped to prevent religion from becoming a political issue. But the gain was not so obvious in the field of education. To treat that as a matter of politics alone was in fact to make public education, for which all paid, a training in the outlook of the Protestant majority, more effective because it was often done without awareness. But a public man who accepted the new theory of representative government was scarcely in a position to argue successfully that Catholic taxpayers had a right to ask from the public revenue a Catholic education for their children. Certainly these Catholic laymen in public life failed to do so.

The priests everywhere were fully occupied these years in building up their congregations and often, as part of that work, in building churches and schools or improving them. Probably Father Kenelm Vaughan had this in mind when he reported after a tour of the country in 1892 that he was surprised by the amount and vigour of Catholic activities everywhere.[9] But it was seldom that their individual labours made an impression on the general culture. The local press recognized the beauty of Father Fagan's new church at King William's Town, and the Cape Director of Education the excellence of the school buildings designed and erected by Father Rooney at Knysna. Generally speaking, however, the first effect of the development of parishes was to create a Catholic enclave which monopolized the time and work of the priest for his own people.

III. *The Western Vicariate: Bishop Leonard*

Bishop John Leonard was vicar apostolic of the Western Cape during the last quarter of the nineteenth century, and some pages that he added to his predecessor's diary, together with copies of many of his letters and notes for the years 1879–89, have survived to illustrate the spirit of his rule. He had acted as agent and collector of donations in Ireland for Bishop Grimley, and the finance of the vicariate was a recurrent and evidently important occupation of his mind. The collection of money must take up much of the time of a vicar apostolic who depends in large part on voluntary gifts of individuals or societies; both Bishop Grimley and Bishop Ricards worried themselves and many other people with the matter.

A large proportion of the records of the Church in South Africa during these years, indeed, were concerned with money, and an ill-disposed and superficial critic could write of it as a commercial enterprise. The characteristic is not of course peculiar to the time or place; it could be found in the archives of any mediaeval diocese, and was not unknown to the apostolic age, as St Paul's letters tell us.

To measure the importance of the record by its quantity is misleading. With the money-economy every human society has invented for itself there comes the need for registration and for preserving the same in archives. But the relative importance of finance has to be estimated on other data. In the case of commercial enterprises the purpose is to obtain the maximum profit, and all money transactions are simplified by that fact. The business of the vicars apostolic, however, was to establish Catholic institutions, and, though these should be self-supporting in the long run, by the charity of all concerned, their value could not be reckoned in terms of money profit.

Even so, different attitudes were possible in regard to the initial stages, which usually meant raising a loan. Bishop Ricards, and Bishop Grimley still more, thought of it as a nuisance and worried desperately about the difficulties and about the losses if the enterprise failed. Ricards' explanations about his methods and those of his subordinates suggest almost a feeling of guilt, as though money were an evil even if necessary. Bishop Jolivet seems seldom to have considered financial matters seriously. The works he embarked on were desirable for the Church, and he raised the money in any way open to him, though it might sometimes leave a headache for his superiors in Rome or for his successor.

To judge by what he wrote, John Leonard accepted finance as one of his duties, a part of the Catholic work of a vicar apostolic, and therefore set himself quietly and calmly and successfully to pay off one debt as a preliminary to incurring another. His first entry at the end of Bishop Grimley's autobiography is an analysis of the deficit on the vicariate and its revenues. Five pages later he notes that the debt on his arrival was £2,000 and that he used his own capital (£500) to reduce it. Five years later, when he opened the church and convent and school in Somerset Road, Cape Town, which were the memorial of his predecessor, he gave an abstract of the vicariate accounts to his people, pointing out that all save £300 of that original debt had now been paid, but that a new loan had been necessary for the buildings and further commitments would have to be made for other good works.

The careful accounting called for constant money-raising efforts on the part of his clergy. Sometimes, as in 1879, he sent Father Colgan to England, Ireland and America on a begging tour with letters stating his needs, but he was watchful of his progress and recalled him when he was unsuccessful. Nor did the bishop spare himself the unpleasant task. In 1881 the building fund for Somerset Road was still short by £700, so he sent a personal letter to the wealthier Catholics asking them to promise subscriptions, to be spread over the next two years. Judge Dwyer sent £5, so the bishop asked for an interview and put a note of it among his letters. He opened the attack by mentioning that some comparatively poor Catholics had given £200. The judge pointed out that he was not a member of the vicariate (his home was in the Eastern Cape, though his work brought him to Cape Town) and that he could not subscribe to everything. However, he promised £50

over the two years and asked the bishop if that was not good.
" Well ", he was answered, " I cannot say it is". " Then I will
give you nothing ", said the judge, " you know what troubles I
have been put to by the British government and the Catholic
attorney general".   To this the bishop countered: "I am not
responsible for what they do to you and it is not fair that I should
be punished ".[10]

Unfortunately there is no record of what contribution the judge
finally agreed to, but he certainly remained a friend and a leader
among the Catholic laymen. With so forthright a bishop, sure of
the usefulness of his projects and ready to ask for what they needed,
it does not come as a surprise to find a note that in the last eight
years (i.e. since Bishop Leonard's arrival in Cape Town) the
Catholics had raised fully £16,000, besides the ordinary collections
for the maintenance of the churches.

The calm, vigorous control which Bishop Leonard kept on the
finance of his vicariate had one important result. The building of
new churches, the establishment of orphanages and schools and
other charitable works were accomplished without making the
bishop a nervous wreck, as happened in the Eastern Vicariate, and
without causing worry to his clergy and laity, or encouraging them
to launch out on madcap schemes. But the frame of mind which
made it possible for Bishop Leonard to do this work could not but
affect his relations with others and his judgment of them. Among
his earliest notes on arriving at Cape Town in September 1873, is
that Father O'Haire, then administrator of the cathedral, had spent
£800 on very expensive furniture and alterations to the house and
convent since the death of Bishop Grimley, and had done so
without even reporting either to the new vicar apostolic or to his
vicar general. He had also sent notes to people in Cape Town
which read like appeals for offerings, despite a prohibition of any
such thing by the bishop. Worst of all, he kept no accounts but
put the bills in a drawer, paying them off whenever he had sufficient
funds.[11] It is not surprising to find at the end of O'Haire's *Recollections* that he was sent to Malmesbury at the end of September
in the hope that his health would be restored and was allowed to
go home to Ireland in the following June.[12] Even in his annoyance
Bishop Leonard was just to that flamboyant but energetic man.
" Father O'Haire's intentions ", he wrote, " are good, but he is

reckless with money." And again: "He is not prudent, but he is a hardworking and zealous priest ".[13]

The same characteristics appear in an incident a few years later. The priests at the cathedral were Fathers McCarthy, McAuliffe and Corboy. One day the bishop received a note from them: they respectfully submitted that their present allowance of £35 per annum was inadequate and that the funds of St Mary's (the cathedral) should enable the bishop to allow them £60; "this", they added, "considerably affects our mutual relations". Along with this the bishop transcribed his reply in his letter-book:

> I cannot afford to do so without reducing the staff. So Father Corboy (the junior) can go next week (I explained the position to him before he came), and then I can pay Fathers McAuliffe and McCarthy £50 each. If you prefer a division of the dues (i.e. fees for marriages and so on) I agree but shall claim my share as bishop. It would be better for you in future to write to me individually and not jointly.[14]

He was understating his own case; when Father Corboy offered himself five years before for work in the vicariate the bishop had written that he guaranteed £25 per annum with board and lodging, £75 if the priest was provided with a house but supported himself, and £100 if nothing was provided for him.[15] Shortly after asking for his "rise" Father Corboy entered the Jesuit novitiate, and later became a very successful rector of the Society's training centre at Dunbrody. But the bishop evidently accepted the argument for an increase of stipend, and after this incident he kept it at £50 for those who lived with him and £100 for those who were provided with a house but had to feed themselves.

It is very likely that some of his clergy thought John Leonard too much of an accountant in his dealings with them. Certainly he insisted that money matters must be handled with care and exactitude, but it is clear that he did not treat it as the only important thing in life. His attitude to finance is one form of his respect for method and law in all his dealings. From the beginning of his episcopate he brought to the notice of his people the positive laws of the Church which had been little respected in the past owing to the circumstances of the colony. So at one time he wrote very firmly to a leading Catholic magistrate whose family were taking part in dances of which the Church disapproved; he published a pastoral letter stating the Church's dislike of marriages between Catholics and those of other religions; he firmly refused the sacraments to a Catholic girl who was married in an Anglican church—at that time canonically valid but illicit—and blamed her parents for being present.[16] He took care to observe the law himself; three warnings were published at Mass, and on the following Sunday a notice was read from the altars that this marriage was in consequence "illicit, sinful and sacrilegious, though valid and binding". But in no instance did Bishop Leonard forget that he was dealing with human beings, who might be genuinely mistaken and in any case were capable of repentance and reconciliation. So the clergy were warned that their general instructions on "mixed" marriages were to be made "mildly, with no denouncing";[17] the bishop argued with the peccant bride so paternally that within a year she made a written declaration of her sorrow and her wish to repair the scandal caused;[18] and the dancing magistrate became the chief organizer of funds for one of the bishop's building schemes.

A good example of John Leonard's discipline, and also of his humanity, occurred in 1886. The Salvation Army had started its work at George and attracted many to its revivalist meetings. Father Kittenbusch, the parish priest, was worried because a leading Catholic, a Dr Clarke, had attended them and a number of children and the poorer people had followed; could he make examples? The bishop's reply was that children were not to be excluded either from school or the sacraments for this reason, nor were grown-up people simply for having gone to the meetings. But they were not to be given the sacraments unless they promised to keep away from the meetings in future; and it might be well to defer the sacraments to those who had gone after being given a personal warning.

An instance of the steady development which could be expected under such a vicar apostolic is recorded in a letter of 6 October 1885 acknowledging a gift of 40,000 francs (£1,600) from the *Oeuvre de la Propagation de la Foi*, the French society which acted as Maecenas to the Catholic Church in South Africa throughout the nineteenth century. Bishop Leonard gives some details of the work of that year. He has built a new school at Mossel Bay and explains that it is absolutely necessary for the health of the children and the priest who has had to teach four and a half hours a day in a little stuffy room, in addition of course to his other pastoral work. He is also building a new church and presbytery at Rondebosch and using the old church as a school, because the government has often urged him to improve the old school buildings where it has been impossible to separate the boys and girls. Then he goes on to give some statistics. He has twenty-one priests, of whom two are South African born, and twenty churches and chapels. There is one boarding school for boys and another for girls, thirty-one parochial schools managed by ten priests; one orphanage and one home for the aged poor, both run by Sisters of Nazareth; and there is one school for deaf mutes, conducted by Dominican sisters. He draws attention to only one increase of Catholic life: the number of communions has risen from 13,343 to 23,354 in the last three years.[19] But comparing his detail with that which he noted when he came to the Cape rather more than ten years earlier,[20] there were now five more priests, eight more churches, and eighteen more parochial schools.

John Leonard did not look on this work with any complacency. At the end of 1884, after copying the statistics from the *Cape of Good Hope Blue Book*, he made a note: " The Catholic Church is advancing steadily but also too slowly ". Nor was his own work confined to the direction of building and its finances. When he came to Cape Town the northern part of his vicariate, around Oudtshoorn, had just been transferred to the Lyons African Mission, an arrangement made by his predecessor. These fathers did not settle down to the work, were full of complaints, and resigned the task after a few years. Yet John Leonard so managed them that they remained on friendly and grateful terms with him personally, and with him alone, working under his direction as administrator until he was able to replace them. At the same time he brought the Oblates of St Francis de Sales to Namaqualand, showed them their work in visitations, and taught them how to deal with government officials and laws which were strange to them. Another care which occasioned frequent letters was that of securing that the young men he sent to be trained for the priesthood in Europe should spend a year after ordination learning German or Hollands so that they might be able to serve those who were not English-speaking; and on more than one occasion he tried to secure Catholic books in Dutch for the same purpose.[21]

A great deal of John Leonard's work had necessarily to be done by correspondence, because his health became bad soon after his arrival, and early in 1886 his medical advisers forbade him to attempt the visitation of his diocese.[22] He made no attempt, therefore, to follow Bishop Grimley's example of public speaking, but he founded a lending library for Catholic people[23] and encouraged two of his priests, Father McCarthy and Dr Kolbe, to lecture, and was sufficiently interested himself to include in his papers good résumés of two of their efforts.[22]

The letters I have quoted or cited seem to show John Leonard as a capable methodical bishop, hard working within the limits which ill-health imposed. It came as a surprise to read an opinion formed by two very different men who knew him well. John Maria Simon was the first Oblate of St Francis de Sales sent to work in Namaqualand, where he later became vicar apostolic. He was vivaciously French, unable when he arrived to speak any other language, and one of his necessary tasks was to extract as much financial aid as he could from the careful Bishop Leonard, a quiet Irishman insistent all the time that Simon should observe all the local civil regulations, alien though they might be to his experience. Yet when Bishop Leonard came to spend a fortnight with him in this wild country in 1884, after noting the bishop's feeble health, though he was only fifty-four years old, Simon described him as prayerful, recollected and saintly. And Alexander Wilmot in 1910 wrote for the Catholic Magazine some notes on the ecclesiastics he had known since coming to South Africa in 1853. Bishop Griffith was retiring and a great reader; Bishop Ricards was a great controversialist, but, years before his death, his nerves gave way entirely and he became sad and sorrowful; Bishop Grimley thought of nothing else but his work; and of John Leonard he wrote: " He always seemed to me to be a saint ".[25]

Because of that rare judgment made by two intelligent but very different men who knew the bishop well it was worth looking through the letter-books more carefully. There are maybe two places which perhaps demand such an explanation. In 1886 Anthony Gaughren was appointed to the new vicariate of Kimberley, and Bishop Leonard wrote him a letter of congratulation and good wishes. His name, the bishop said, was one of those he had submitted to Rome twelve months earlier when he had asked for a coadjutor. Then he added some simple direct spiritual advice:

Look on your appointment as the will of God: be faithful to the graces and inspirations which will be poured down upon you: pray fervently for guidance in all your actions, even in what may appear trivial and almost nothing more than routine work, and leave the issue to God, and all will go well with you although you are coming to a strange land. You will find your flock truly generous and obedient and your life, I hope, as happy as you can expect in this vale of tears."[26]

If that was John Leonard's own rule of life, it reads singularly like a " little way " for bishops very similar to that which his contemporary Thérèse was following at Lisieux.

He seems to have put it into practice not much more than a month before he wrote that letter. Rome had chosen John Rooney, a priest of the vicariate, to be coadjutor, and Bishop Leonard called a meeting of six of his leading priests to suggest that they prepare an address of welcome to the new bishop on his consecration. Dr Colgan, the vicar-general, had never worked easily with John Rooney: " that man loves to make mysteries " had been his comment on one occasion.[27] But now he refused to take the chair at the meeting, complained that he had not been consulted about the coadjutor, and said plainly that it would have been desirable to bring in a stranger. Bishop Leonard pointed out that there was no precedent for consulting the clergy, that he had in fact named two others who were strangers, along with John Rooney, but that the Holy See had chosen the latter.[28] The vicar-general was not content with that explanation, and wrote to his bishop to say that he would bring the matter before a higher tribunal. There is not the slightest doubt of the canonical correctness of the procedure, and Bishop Leonard might well have employed ecclesiastical discipline against the irate vicar-general. Instead of that he wrote him a dignified but kindly protest for bringing charges against his own bishop without warning, and in

the presence of other priests. As for further action, he reminded
Dr Colgan that " we are both bound by charity ", but that he had
entire freedom to appeal to the Congregation of Propaganda or to
the Holy Father. And when Dr Colgan, still vicar-general, asked
for a priest to prepare his complaint, the bishop sent him this
assistance.[29]

That firm but kindly treatment even of gross stupidity may well
have come from the inner saintliness which impressed Father
Simon and Alexander Wilmot. It probably characterized his
rule and brought his plans to successful issue even more than his
prudent care of the finances.

Though needing and using his coadjutor for the visitations and
the routine work, John Leonard remained vicar apostolic till his
death in 1908, when he was almost eighty, and his letters show that
the other bishops were still asking his advice on all important
matters. Meanwhile the Catholic life of his own vicariate was
vigorous. The institute of the Salesian fathers at Cape Town
developed into what would now be called a school of vocational
training in various trades. The work of the St Vincent de Paul
Society for the relief of the poor spread through all the parishes.
In 1896 a Catholic Young Men's Association was formed, and two
years later a vigorous debating society. University extension
lectures organized by and among Catholics in the city had an
average weekly attendance of seventy-two in 1892, and of these
twenty-two passed the examination which gave them the second-
class certificate as school teachers. Three years later an even
more ambitious scheme of lectures was running. This activity
seems to have been the work of the priests Fathers McCarthy,
Kolbe, Kelly, O'Riley and Welch and a few laymen, who also did
most of the writing for the *Catholic Magazine* which began publication in 1891. Bishop Leonard remained in the background, and
his feebleness of health gave him every excuse to do so. But we
should probably be correct to relate the harmony of the development to his calm and just mind.

Especially does this seem true of the difficult war years of the end
of the century. Before 1879 the general trend of the Catholic
lectures and writing seems to have favoured the formation of an
Afrikaner nation (it was the theme of some of Wilmot's speeches)

and to have been very critical of the stupidities of English govern-ments. But when the quarrel between Whitehall and the Trans-vaal republic developed and Sir Alfred Milner came to the Cape as governor, opinion was divided. Dr Kolbe followed the commander-in-chief and lieutenant-governor, Sir William Butler,* in holding that there was not reasonable cause for war, though Paul Kruger had been stupid and unjust. Most of the other leading Catholic priests and laymen were convinced by Milner's presentation of his case. As most, if not all, of these Catholic publicists were well able and accustomed to state their views in pungent and forthright phrases, it is a real tribute to their charity that they avoided any unforgivable remarks. But in such a case it is usual to find that the influence of the bishop counts for much, and though there is no positive written evidence it seems likely that John Leonard did much to control events so that, after the war, the team could work together as before.

IV. The Eastern Vicariate

1. BISHOP MORAN

In the last quarter of the nineteenth century the scattered Catholics of large areas of South Africa were still without organization, and in other areas the organization was undeveloped. The main task of the vicars apostolic remained. They were not merely chaplains, as the civil government regarded them, to bring the sacraments to faithful already present, but bishops to found churches which would call into existence the Catholic way of life. The personal work, in its failures as well as its successes, was still the most important part of the history of the Church during this period.

Among the vicars apostolic of that period James David Ricards of the Eastern Vicariate was the senior. He had come to South Africa, as we have already seen, with Dr Devereux, from St Peter's College, Wexford. At that time, in 1849, he was a deacon, and while he was completing his studies for the priesthood the bishop set him, as also we have already seen, to edit *The Colonist*, which he did with much distinction and success from 1851 to 1859.

---

* Lieut.-General Sir William Francis Butler, G.C.B. (1838-1910), was himself a Catholic. His *Autobiography* was published in London in 1911. He was a brother-in-law of Alice Meynell.

When Dr Devereux died, in 1854, Bishop Griffith appointed Father Ricards to be his delegate as administrator of the Eastern Vicariate and many expected him to be appointed to succeed, despite his youthfulness (he was twenty-nine).* His former teacher, Father Murphy, and another older priest complained to Rome that he was not strict enough and, though they were told politely not to be silly,† another former teacher of Ricards at St Peter's, Wexford, Dr Moran, was at length named vicar apostolic in 1856.‡

The new bishop soon let it be known that he was strongly opposed to the demand for representative government in the colony—a policy which Father Ricards had long supported, though perhaps, as Alexander Wilmot suggested in his *Life of Ricards*, without much real interest or enthusiasm—holding (and it was a weighty argument) that as the white population was a small minority the type of rule proposed could not seriously be called representative, or urged on that ground. He thought that justice could be better administered in a community of several races by officials of the Crown than by representatives of one section. In 1857 Ricards was sent to gather together Catholic congregations among the German settlers on the banks of the Buffalo River and in the military stations on the frontier and in British Kaffraria, a work which made editorship impossible. The following year, when the bishop sold *The Colonist* as a going concern to a Catholic layman, Father Ricards was instructed to found a Catholic school and seminary for priests in Grahamstown. This was his chief work for the next dozen years; but at the same time he had made himself a reputation, with the bishop's approval, as a lecturer on the scientific subjects then so popular, and by his public readings. There are frequent and very laudatory references to his eloquence in the secular press of these years, and indeed to the end of his life.

---

* Ricards' friend O'Riley said that it was only because of his youth that he was not appointed.

† Their chief complaint was that Father Ricards had permitted two nuns to ride horses when that exercise was recommended for them by the physicians. The Congregation of Propaganda pointed out that St Teresa of Avila had ridden a mule regularly, and asked what objection there could be to the practice.

‡ Ricards seems always to have worked under his former schoolmasters: Bishop Devereux was one, Father Murphy was another. If Moran had not actually taught him, he had been one of the senior students when Ricards first went to St Peter's.

Bishop Moran was a canonist, and his ambition seems to have been to organize what he regarded as the normal working of a diocese—the administration of the sacraments, parish schools for Catholic children, a seminary for training priests—as well as his resources allowed. Indeed, a letter of his to Bishop Grimley* explicitly stated this view, and renounced any attempts to break out of this routine. In 1857 he noted in the *Chronicon* that there were Catholic free schools for boys at Grahamstown, Port Elizabeth, Uitenhage, Alice and Graaf Reinet, although in the last two places the only teacher was the local priest. In 1867 he brought out Irish Dominican sisters from Sion Hill, Dublin, to Port Elizabeth and in the following year they opened two schools for girls, one fee-paying and the other free. It was perhaps characteristic of Moran that in the *Chronicon* he spoke of his own work always in the third person.

Although *The Colonist* came to an end, Bishop Moran was himself ready on occasion to become a pamphleteer. Thus in 1860 a Wesleyan minister, W. Sergeant, published *A Check to Popery*, and Bishop Moran replied with *The Checker Check-mated*. The warfare by pamphlets reminiscent in their titles of seventeenth-century England continued. In 1868 Ricards came to the support of his bishop with *The Check-mater and his Critic*, the subject of which was the doctrine of St Cyprian. The approach of Ricards was changing with experience. Instead of concentrating on answering charges he now set out the patristic doctrine to show that the Catholic Church was the true continuator of received Christian truth, and therefore enjoyed all the rights of possession. It was a far more positive appeal to non-Catholic culture, and Ricards was to develop it in several books after he succeeded Bishop Moran.

2. BISHOP RICARDS

In April, 1870, Moran was appointed to Dunedin, and James Ricards succeeded him as Vicar Apostolic of the Eastern District in 1871. The new bishop wrote one page of the *Chronicon* in the old way, but then he broke into the first person and so continued; till paralysis struck him down in September 1893 he was incessantly engaged, personally and not merely *ex officio*, in plans and schemes

* Quoted, p. 58, *supra*.

and negotiations which often resulted in new works for the strengthening of Catholic life in South Africa.

For four years his *Chronicon* shows a round of episcopal functions, blessings of churches, blessings of bells, confirmations, preaching missions, presiding at meetings of Catholic societies and giving public lectures. His biographer Wilmot noted that he loved ceremonies, but all the time he was collecting a fund to promote larger works, even making a *quête*—with the permission of the vicar apostolic of Natal—in the diamond fields. In 1875 he had amassed a fund of between three and four thousand pounds and sailed to Europe to seek the help of the religious orders with which he had already been in touch by letter.

From this first trip he brought back three secular priests, four nuns and three ecclesiastical students for his vicariate. But he had also persuaded the provincial of the Society of Jesus in England to take over St Aidan's College as a school and to continue the training there of his few students for the priesthood. There was a sensibly drawn contract between the vicar apostolic and the Society, providing for all likely contingencies, including the withdrawal of the fathers should they wish it. The present-day St Aidan's, staffed by the Society of Jesus, admitting only Catholic boys (the admission of ecclesiastical students was abandoned after a few years) dates from this agreement. At the same time Bishop Ricards persuaded the Jesuit provincial to send out two Hollander fathers to take over the mission of the Graaf Reinet district, where a knowledge of their language was almost indispensable for a priest.

Among the merchants of Port Elizabeth was a German Catholic, Max Anton Fraundorfer, a native of Augsburg. Through his introductions Bishop Ricards in 1875 met Herr Miller, a leading layman of that city, and the Archbishop of Munich, who promised help for the Eastern Vicariate from the Ludwig Missionary Association.[30] It seems likely that the plan of bringing German sisters to the colony was then conceived, but the convent of King William's Town has a tradition that the suggestion came originally from the government.[31] Soon after his return from Europe Bishop Ricards began negotiations with the government for a grant of land in King William's Town for a convent and school. Father Fagan, the parish priest, began to collect money for building, and Fraundorfer negotiated for the bishop with the Dominican nuns of

Augsburg, who had a teaching tradition of several centuries. Again a simple contract was drawn up. Six qualified and experienced sisters were to be sent. The bishop was to provide the convent building and grounds and to lend the passage money, and he promised to do all he could for them should their school fail to pay its way. There was an initial difficulty due to the ignorance of English on the part of the sisters, but they borrowed one of the best teachers from the Assumptionist convent at Grahamstown and soon became proficient. After about a year, during which time, as the nuns noted in their archives, the bishop kept them going with the proceeds of his lectures and pamphlets, the school was self-supporting. It might well be so, for it offered pupils a worth-while curriculum. It is scarcely surprising that they soon attracted numbers of Protestant as well as Catholic pupils. In 1879, two years after the foundation, Dr Langham Dale, the Director of Education for Cape Colony, recognized the convent as a training school for teachers for the third-class certificate, and from 1883 their public (free) school was given a state grant. Two years later the nuns opened a school for deaf children and one for natives. In 1891 they bought a farm at Izeli, seven miles from King William's Town, and with the help of native catechists supplied by the Jesuit fathers from Keilands started an industrial school for the Bantu. Already, however, as the number of nuns increased, some coming from Germany, some from Ireland, some from South Africa, they were going far beyond the King William's Town area. In 1883 they opened a school at East London, in 1894 a convent at Graaf Reinet, and later a school for coloured children.

Though coming originally from a Dominican convent, the Sisters were by canon law a quasi-diocesan congregation and Bishop Ricards was their ecclesiastical superior, though he had agreed not to interfere with their rules.[32] The question became important when, in 1889, first the prefect apostolic of the Transvaal and then the vicar apostolic of Natal asked them to establish convents in those territories. With some difficulty they obtained the necessary permission from Bishop Ricards, and in 1889 the establishments at Potchefstroom and Oakford were made. Very soon afterwards the latter became a congregation separate from that of King William's Town.

V. Approach to the Africans

1. THE TRAPPISTS COME TO DUNBRODY

On his first visit to Europe as a bishop, James Ricards was working at a plan to evangelize the Bantu of his vicariate. In 1876 he noted in his *Chronicon* that the idea had been in his mind for twenty years. Probably its remote author was Bishop Devereux, to whose memory he was devoted and who had so strongly urged at Rome the erection of the Natal vicariate to work primarily for the Zulus. The problems must have recurred to Father Ricards in 1866 when he visited Bishop Allard in Basutoland and made friends with him; on his return he lectured on the work of the Oblates, and when he became administrator he allowed one of them, Father Hidien, to solicit alms for his work throughout the Eastern Vicariate.[33]

Having become vicar apostolic it was possible for the planning to become more concrete. On his way to Europe, presumably, he learned of the work of the Trappist monks in Algeria, and of their agricultural colonies. Such an institution, it seemed to him, would overcome the difficulties which the Oblates had found in preaching to the Zulus, and, to a less extent, in Basutoland; the missionaries would bring the advantages of material civilization and so obtain more easily a hearing for their religion, and at the same time would have the means of subsistence for themselves. While in Rome he talked over the project with Bishop Allard, who had resigned his vicariate in Natal by this time and who agreed most cordially (according to Ricards) that it would be the best way with the Bantu.

The argument put before Bishop Allard, and in the following years before British governors and officials, was probably the one which Bishop Ricards developed in his book, written in 1879, called *The Catholic Church and the Kaffir*. He claimed (as he had done in *The Colonist*) that the Thembu people had been impossibly difficult neighbours for the colonists of the frontier. It was a stupidity on the part of the home government, and especially of Lord Glenelg, to listen to those who represented "the spirited defensive struggles of the Colonists as barbarous outrages on Kaffirs". The efforts of various governors to keep the whites and blacks separated had failed, and Benjamin d'Urban's plan of controlling native chiefs by British magistrates was repudiated by Whitehall. The Frontier Wars of 1846, 1850 and 1877 had been caused by these blunders.

Nor had the missionary work of Protestants been of much use. Though many of those engaged in it had been men of integrity and every good quality, most of them had come to acknowledge that their work—through their schools and teaching—had not succeeded, and the natives had fallen back into the carnalities of paganism. Though Bishop Ricards admitted that there was not sufficient evidence, he recorded the general opinion of the farmers that the raw native was preferable to the " converted ".

A few weeks after his return from Europe, Bishop Ricards had selected the site in Kaffraria where he wanted to plant his Trappists, and during the following two years he had several meetings with the Colonial Secretary, the Director of Education and the Governor, at all of which he tried to persuade them that land should be given for this purpose. In every case he came away with the conviction of their approval, but always with a warning of some difficulty. At one time the government could not act unless the Bantu expressed a wish for the monks to come; at another Mr Solomon might oppose, in the Legislative Assembly, a grant for religious purposes.[34] At last the bishop obtained for £2,000 a tract of bush land at Dunbrody and mortgaged it to Fraundorfer.

At this time his plan was to persuade Irish or French Trappists to come, and in 1879 he took ship for Europe again, having arranged to meet the General Council of abbots and priors at Sept Fons in France. After he had explained his plan and the urgency of the work to them the Prior of Maria Stern, in Bosnia, Franz Pfanner, offered to make the attempt. The bishop went on to Rome and explained his Trappist project to Cardinal Simeoni, of the Congregation of Propaganda, and to Pope Leo XIII. Having obtained the necessary permissions from them he went on to Augsburg, where in a day's negotiations, with Fraundorfer as interpreter (the bishop was no linguist and did not speak German), he " arranged everything ".[35]

The first necessary condition was that the bishop should lend the prior £2,000 to pay off a debt on the abbey of Maria Stern; Prior Franz gave him a receipt for the money and Fraundorfer arranged for the payment. Otherwise there seems to have been no written contract, but the bishop promised to pay the passages of twenty-five monks, to provide on loan the agricultural machinery for the settlement, and to feed the community at Dunbrody until they had cultivated the land. In the event he had to pay passages of a party of thirty-two monks, and a layman in addition. During the early part of 1880 he was busy trying to collect the passage money; the Duke of Norfolk gave him £500, and he collected £50 in Glasgow, £74 in Liverpool and a further sum in Ireland. Lord Kimberley at the Colonial office would not give him an official letter of approval for fear of a Protestant outcry, but he promised to protect the monks against any injustice in South Africa, and it was presumably because of his goodwill that some months later the Cape Government gave £112 towards the passage money.

2. DUNBRODY TO MARIANNHILL

In August 1880 the monks were installed at Dunbrody, and for two years and more there was a tussle between the bishop and the prior. The latter had his own plan; the Trappists should build a suitable monastery first, during which time their bills for food and equipment would be met by the vicariate. The bishop, on the other hand, supposed that the monks would begin by cultivating the ground until they could feed themselves, and he would then transfer the property to them and they could build at their own expense. Prior Franz continued with his plan despite the renewed protests of the bishop. By November, as he noted, he had spent £1,672 on them since their arrival, and he would not be responsible for anything more save necessary provisions. The prior agreed to go on building at his own expense, but insisted that he must be allowed to bring out still more monks, and that the bishop must pay their passages and upkeep. This we know from the prior's note of 1888.[36] He undoubtedly went beyond the terms of the original agreement, but the bishop made no protest at the time. The prior called his second proposal a new contract, but no written record of it has been found.[37] It is almost impossible to suppose that the bishop agreed to it, because the expense of it for him would have been as great as that of going on with the building. It looks as though the prior, having decided in his own mind that this was the only possible way of continuing the project, and persuaded that it must continue, regarded it as binding: a somewhat curious concept of contracts, perhaps, but it showed at least a grasp of the practical needs of the original plan. By May 1881, the bishop was warning tradesmen that he would not pay for things ordered by the prior.

There were further difficulties because some of the monks complained that their superior was too severe and strict in his interpretation of their rule, but after a visitation of the monastery made through an interpreter the bishop was convinced that the general feeling was one of loyalty to the prior; he sent the four complaining Trappists back to Europe. It may be that their accounts decided Prior Franz four months later, in June 1881, to go to Europe to "clear his name of calumny". He told the bishop that he would stay six months and collect money for the foundation.

At this point apparently the bishop brought up the matter of the £2,000 loan, which must be repaid, he said, before the property could be transferred to Trappist ownership. To his surprise the prior considered this a matter for the General Chapter of his order, to whom he said it had been mentioned. The dispute ran apparently over all their differences, especially over the neglect of farming for buildings, and, according to the bishop, it ended with a slight apology from the prior.[38] The latter delayed his return to Europe for a year. The bishop tried to persuade the government to give the Trappists a farm in Tembuland, on the frontier, but was told that no decision could be made until that area had been proclaimed an imperial territory. He then wrote to the General Chapter of the Trappists putting his case, and received a reply in October 1881, saying that Prior Franz agreed to take over the feeding of the community in September 1882 and offered to pay £200 per annum for ten years from that date. The bishop asked for repayment twice as fast, and promised transfer of the property when it was completed. Meanwhile, he would help with the provision of food in return for control of the expenditure.

A solution to the dispute came with apparent suddenness in 1882. On 24 July Bishop Ricards noted "a letter from Bishop Jolivet that he is willing to receive the Trappists and allow them to make a foundation, my rights being secured". It is tempting to suppose that Prior Franz, who had left for Europe in 1881, had either visited

Natal or had written to its vicar apostolic. But he makes no mention of this in his own short account written some five years later.* It is possible that the suggestion was made, after his departure, by his sub-prior, Father Joseph. But in view of Father Franz's strong rule and Father Joseph's timidity it is unlikely. Bishop Ricards' *Chronicon* mentions that the monks were looking for a more suitable site when their prior went to Europe, and I am inclined to think that Bishop Ricards may have consulted his brother bishop himself. Certainly Bishop Jolivet made no difficulties, but tried to hurry a decision by recommending a site for the Trappists at Indwe, near Umtata. The unfortunate Father Joseph naturally tried to delay matters until his superior's return. Before accepting Bishop Jolivet's offer he must look round the country in the Natal vicariate. In September, however, Bishop Ricards had arranged with the Jesuits at Grahamstown to take over Dunbrody as it stood, mortgaged to Fraundorfer.

Father Joseph promptly claimed that the buildings and equipment which belonged to the Trappists were worth £5,000; but an official valuer, called in by the bishop, fixed them at £1,500. Against this the bishop could show that the vicariate had spent some £3,000 for the support of the monks, but he was willing to waive that provided that they now went to Natal. Last of all, in October, Father Joseph produced a letter from his prior forbidding him to leave Dunbrody without permission from Rome. But the bishop insisted, a letter eventually arrived from the prior, who was then touring Germany to collect funds and monks and novices—as he was doing most successfully—instructing those at Dunbrody to pack up and sail for the port of Natal, and, after a friendly farewell meeting with the bishop, a party of twenty-five monks, led by Father Joseph, sailed on 24 November. Three days later they were camping on the Bluff near Durban and received the formal permission of Bishop Jolivet to make a settlement in his vicariate, but at their own expense.

The only outstanding dispute now was the loan of £2,000, for which Prior Franz still denied liability. Bishop Ricards had already sent the whole correspondence between himself and the

* In writing of the origins of Mariannhill he alluded often to the unsuitability of the soil at Dunbrody as one reason for the move to Natal. It would not be correct to suggest that the move was simply a sequel to the disagreements with Bishop Ricards.

Trappists to the Cardinal Prefect of Propaganda, asking that the Archbishop of Munich and the Bishop of Augsburg should arbitrate.[39] The enquiry dragged on till 1889, when it was decided in favour of the bishop, but he was advised to forgo his claim for interest and to accept repayment of the capital by instalments. He did so, but reluctantly.[40]

Though this enterprise, the most grandiose of Bishop Ricards' plans, and to which he had given all his enthusiasm, failed as far as his own vicariate was concerned, he did not lose interest in the Trappists. News of their success in Natal was noted with pleasure in his *Chronicon*, and when Prior Franz was slow in sending his defence to Rome about the loan, Bishop Ricards asked the vicar apostolic of Natal to give him friendly warning lest the authorities should regard the delay as contumacious. And on his side Prior Franz only said, in his account of Dunbrody, that the bishop stopped helping them for lack of money.

But for all the good sense and temper which both showed in the dispute, this venture was a big failure as far as Bishop Ricards was concerned. It is not difficult to see at least some of the reasons. Probably the conduct of negotiations at all stages through an interpreter caused some of the misunderstandings about what was promised by either party, and made it more desirable than usual to have a written contract. But the bishop possessed exactly that charm which makes the eloquence of a lecturer. Whether he was talking with government officials or with the superiors of religious orders, he persuaded them to give verbal approval to his projects as he explained them. The secular officials, however, always withdrew behind the hedge of procedure before they made a decision, and the Provincial of the English Jesuits and the Mother Superior of the Augsburg Dominicans asked for formal agreements. Unfortunately Prior Franz was clearly an impulsive man. He had made his original offer to come mainly on the bishop's description of the African opportunity, without knowing what the land was like or what the episcopal resources were. At the second meeting in Augsburg—in the course of a day—he supposed apparently that the bishop could afford to support his community while he built the monastery according to his own plans. And the fact that the bishop so readily undertook to finance his £2,000 Bosnian debt probably confirmed him in this view.

Nor was Bishop Ricards less impulsive. Apparently he bought Dunbrody when he found the delays of the civil authorities too much for his patience, and he did so before he had obtained either a promise or even a half promise from the Trappists to undertake the work. And he supposed that his plan of cultivating the land first and building a monastery afterwards was so obviously wise that he did not enquire either into the views of Prior Franz or even into the traditions of Trappist foundations.

Perhaps such risks had to be taken in pioneer work, and perhaps the same can be said for the bishop's method of finance. He relied on his personal ability to collect the necessary funds once the Trappists had promised to come. There were some grounds for his optimism. In 1888 he made a note in the *Chronicon* that since 1870 he had collected from various sources £36,724; about half of this went to the upkeep of his mission stations, and about a third on his new foundation; the expenditure of £2,000 on his European travels could reasonably be called overhead expenses, and the support of his own *mensa* worked out at about £175 a year.[41] But while schools for Europeans like St Aidan's and the convent at King William's Town were likely to succeed financially and would soon repay their loans and so enable the bishop to start on a new scheme, a little thought would have shown that this was not true of a monastery whose work was to teach the Bantu the way of European agriculture. Even had Prior Franz cultivated enough land to feed his monks a considerable capital sum would have been necessary for buildings; when the Trappists came to Dunbrody the prior believed that the vicariate could and would provide it; at Mariannhill he knew he must do so himself, and he collected it in Europe.

But Bishop Ricards did not collect the funds before he embarked on his projects. Like Bishop Grimley he borrowed money, and he worried about it much less than Grimley did, athough he worried quite a lot. In regard to his Catholic missions he was wise in this respect; the prosperity of his people was increasing, and a Catholic congregation could be relied on to increase, and then to repay what had been spent to provide a pastor and a church. In the early days too, according to the entries in the *Chronicon*, the vicar apostolic was often able to borrow free of interest from well-to-do Catholics. But as the extent of his indebtedness and the scale of his expenditure grew he had to pay as much as 7 per cent annual interest,[42] and when he tried in 1886 to raise a loan of £2,700 the Guardian Company refused to offer more than £2,100. For this particular need Alexander Wilmot finally gave him an endorsement which was accepted.[43] To add to his troubles, the zest for building is easily communicated and the practice of borrowing imitated. Monsignor Murphy, his old schoolmaster, had saved and collected the money for the fine church at Port Elizabeth and for the land for the Dominican convent there. Father Fagan, who had worked in a grocery business before becoming a priest, had been economical in getting the site and buildings for the convent at King William's Town. But when Father O'Brien handed over the parish of Port Elizabeth in 1881 the bishop found he had a debt of £888 and thought it entirely unreasonable. Just before that time he had built a house for the Marist Brothers whom he had brought to the vicariate and was paying 7 per cent on the mortgage. They were anxious to open a novitiate at Uitenhage, and in 1886 Father O'Brien, without the bishop's permission, borrowed the necessary money for them. In 1887 the bishop had to remind the Superior of the Marists that the cost of establishing them had been altogether £4,825. Their profits from school fees were not anything like enough to pay the interest and to establish a sinking fund; in the meanwhile the vicariate had to bear the burden.

These responsibilities did not exhaust James Ricards' energy. While he was in Rome in 1879 he took up the matter of the land beyond the Limpopo to which Bishop Grimley had directed the attention of the Congregation of Propaganda. But Bishop Ricards pressed a practical proposal of entrusting it to the Jesuit fathers whom he was bringing to his own vicariate. Apparently he considered (as indeed his friend Bishop Allard had thought) that the Natal vicariate did not extend beyond the Transvaal—or perhaps he was acting as the senior vicar apostolic of South Africa. The Congregation, however, consulted Bishop Jolivet of Natal, who expressed his willingness to hand over the territory, nominally in his charge, to the English Province of the Society of Jesus. In consequence a mission of fathers set out from Grahamstown in 1879 and St Aidan's College remained for some years their base of operations. In a year or so a party of Dominican nuns, some from

King William's Town, some from the Cape, went north to found a school and later (instructed by Dr Jameson) a hospital, chiefly for the British, in Mashonaland.

And while he was busy with all these enterprises Bishop Ricards managed to find time not only for his lectures but also to write, and to have published, in 1883–5 three more books—*Luther and his Work, Catholic Christianity and Modern Unbelief* and *Aletheia*. The first named probably required most study, although it was based on the work of Döllinger, but the other two are well and closely argued, and *Catholic Christianity*, of which at least four impressions sold, is interesting and easy to read.

VI. The Apologetic of Bishop Ricards

While still a young priest under Bishop Devereux, and editor of *The Colonist*, Ricards enjoyed the reputation of being the best preacher in South Africa. R. W. Murray, the founder of the *Cape Argus*, praised him as a journalist, scholar and divine, and was finally brought into the Catholic Church by his explanations of Christian doctrine.[44] At the same time his lectures on scientific subjects—his father, a doctor, had given him that formation and he remained an enthusiastic amateur of chemistry all his days—were in demand; and not less his "readings", particularly of Dickens and Lever. One of the Grahamstown newspapers said that laughter held both her sides when he gave the trial scene from Pickwick.

After he was appointed vicar apostolic he began a direct appeal to the outside world with the publication of *The Church and the Kaffir* in 1879, *Catholic Christianity and Modern Unbelief* in 1884, and *Aletheia* in 1885. It seems that the change of approach was deliberately chosen, because, in the author's opinion, the religious climate had altered. In a pastoral of 1876 he observed that, whereas the Cape had been Britain's "pet Protestant colony" forty years earlier, "Catholic institutions are now held in respect throughout the province by all whose respect is worth having". It was time to set out in full what Newman called "the Catholic System".

The Church and the Kaffir is interesting chiefly as an analysis of the difficulties of the situation in the province between the whites and the natives, and its suggestion as to the method of overcoming them by governmental action. But it was persuasive as apologetic because it showed the Catholic bishop ready to understand and state the varieties of native customs, neither romanticizing them nor despising them; to appreciate the grounds for the opinion of the colonists and such factual basis as could justify it; and to recognize the failure of the Protestant missionaries' effort (recognized indeed by themselves) without impugning their good faith or integrity. It was very different from the rhetoric of Exeter Hall which seemed to sway the English governments. And then the Catholic proposals were set out not on theoretical grounds but because they had already succeeded in the somewhat similar situation of North Africa, and the bishop announced that he would bring the Trappists, whose work there was praised, to undertake a like task in the Kei River area.

In this work Bishop Ricards showed clearly his sense of the need to understand the mind of his reader and allow for it. In the other two works, just mentioned, which are directly apologetic, this is obvious even from the style. The terse sentences of the preface to *Catholic Christianity* are of a different culture from the rhetoric and perorations of Bishop Grimley. Maybe Ricards owed his advantage to the fact of never having taught in the ecclesiastical seminaries of the English-speaking world, where a flamboyant style, imitative chiefly of the faults of seventeenth-century prose, long persisted. Certainly Wilmot and the local newspapers said again and again that Ricards lectured differently from the others, from Devereux, Grimley, Murphy, Moran; and all those had been seminary professors. Anyway, the choice was deliberate on the author's part. In the preface to *Aletheia* he admired and praised the work of Moody, Sankey and Spurgeon, the great nonconformist preachers, because, " though they often miss the majestic truth ", they do avoid " a pulpit twang and the rhythm peculiarly its own ".

He adopted a similar rule in his method of argument. There were in his day, he said, abundant works of instruction and devotion in English, so that theological students were much more favoured in his than in the previous generation. " There was never an age when the well disposed body of English-speaking Catholics . . . were better instructed than at present."[45] But unfortunately the books were not written in the spirit and taste of the times, so that works brimful of learning and piety made little impression, even on Catholics. Quoting St Bernard's "We must take people as they are, not as we wish them", he set himself to argue in the discursive way which his own age had adopted. In *Catholic Christianity* he started with the concrete religious life of the Catholic, and showed how it depends on doctrines, and how these are beyond human invention or explanation and relate the Catholic to a God-revealing truth. So he contrived to show his readers, from knowledge that they could check, what the Catholic meant by the mysteries of religion; and at the same time he avoided definitions, dear indeed to seminary professors and perhaps to all of donnish mind but always suggesting to Protestants that the author treats of terms rather than things.

It should perhaps be counted as a merit in a discursive book that its argument cannot be summarized in a syllogism. But to indicate his purpose Bishop Ricards adopted the old style of sub-title—the more modest forerunner of the publisher's blurb. That of *Catholic Christianity* ran:

A plain and brief statement of *The Real Doctrines of the Roman Catholic Church*, as opposed to those falsely attributed to her by Christians who reject her authority and by unbelievers in Revelation; that thus *A Contrast* may be easily drawn between the "Faith once delivered to the Saints" and the conflicting theories and scientific guesses of the present age; and serving as a *Refutation* to the assaults of modern infidelity.

The first impression was therefore of a clear explanation of the Catholic doctrines which were currently denied, of the glories of Mary and particularly of her Immaculate Conception, of merit and justification, of atonement and the Blessed Sacrament. The bishop brought out the misunderstanding of these doctrines by Protestants, and how these doctrines do have practical effects in the life of Catholics, their attitude to education, marriage, vocations. But he avoided generally any derision of Protestant views, and insisted that actual graces, interior as well as exterior, are given outside the Church. So he excused in large measure the attacks which he repelled: "I cannot help liking", he wrote "the expression of strong and earnest feelings against the Church—or rather against what they believe of it; with Dr Johnson, I like a strong hater".

JAMES DAVID RICARDS, D.D.
Third Vicar Apostolic of the Eastern Districts of the
Cape of Good Hope (1871–91)

JEAN MARIE SIMON, O.S.F.S., D.D.
Prefect Apostolic of Namaqualand
Consecrated 21st September 1898, died 21st November 1932

But though he could reasonably claim that the book was scarcely polemical, the argument was one to insinuate itself into the reader's mind. Each of the Catholic doctrines was shown to lead the believer's thought back to the Incarnation, to enable him more consistently and completely, and with greater variety of action, to make Christ the physical centre of his adoration. As Ricards wrote in the preface, the doctrines of the Church " spring from a right understanding of God in the flesh ".

The force of this contention lay in the implied corollary: those who rejected these doctrines were closing paths by which men could approach Christ and so were weakening the hold of Christ on their loyalty. It was the loss of belief in the divinity of Christ and all that it implies which men of that generation called infidelity. The danger of it was a recurrent note in all Newman's sermons and writings, both before and after his submission to the Catholic Church. The very intelligent Anglican Bishop Colenso of Natal had said that in fifty years' time the world would be divided into two sections only—Free Thought and Roman Catholicism; and, as one reviewer pointed out, Dr Ricards had come to the same conclusion.

A modern reader might doubt whether the last claim of the title-page, that of " serving as a Refutation to the assaults of modern infidelity ", could be maintained. Here and there, as in dealing with the evolution of religion, *Catholic Christianity* showed the attack to have no historical foundation. But the discursive method itself prevented the author from ever assembling and analysing the enemy's arguments as a whole. Perhaps he would have said that it was guerilla warfare and must be dealt with piecemeal. The merit of *Catholic Christianity* lay elsewhere. It showed the Faith as a coherent system of knowledge and behaviour, given by revelation and great enough to embrace and transform the whole life of mankind, personal and social; and the author did this by concrete examples. The debate of his time, he claimed, was no longer the dispute about points of learning, as in France in the eighteenth century. " The Voltaireans ", he wrote in his introduction, " were wits and scholars . . . but things are quite different now." He had to deal with those who would ignore and make men ignore the whole fact of Christianity—" the great discovery of the age is agnosticism "—and this would lead to a way of life altogether less desirable than that created by Christianity. With a political insight which was not common Bishop Ricards pointed out in his introduction that the maintenance of order no longer depended on the conscience of the people accepting authority but on " the power of the law supported by bayonets ". The administrative states which were the succession states of the French Revolution were already on the way to becoming the police states of the twentieth century, and " for this reason the infidelity that is corrupting the masses of the chief towns of Europe causes no alarm, and therefore it has advanced unchecked ".

Bishop Ricards himself was aware that *Catholic Christianity* did not answer all the difficulties which would occur to the unbeliever. He posted the manuscript to the printer on 21 July 1884, and by 18 November he had finished another book, *Aletheia*, to answer the chief of them: " The Outspoken Truth ", the title page calls it, " on the all-important question of Divine Authoritative Teaching ". The Christian side in the great debate, he pointed out in the introduction to this, asks a man to give his assent to dogmas he does not understand. Even simple but important matters like eternal life and retribution are presented as mysteries bound up with the nature of God, and the teachers themselves do not profess fully to understand these mysteries. On what grounds do they allege the divine authority which alone would justify their claim? Or, to put what is substantially the same question as it then occurred to most men, given that the gospels contain a divine message, how are we to know its meaning? If there were no authorized interpreter we should be bound, he contended, to take the most rationalistic meaning; that is, the meaning which human reason by itself would come to. As a matter of historical fact, on all the great issues men have arrived at opposite and sometimes contradictory conclusions from the texts. By that method the Trinitarian was no better off, as regards Divine Faith, than his learned Unitarian opponent; either was trusting to his own power (a fallible power) of interpretation. Those then who, outside the Church, held to Catholic doctrines, were urging what was a matter of opinion, and should say so. The various Christian bodies did, in fact, insist on their own tradition in the matter; and Ricards cited the decision of a Wesleyan Synod in England as requiring their members to follow such a rule. And, going back into history, it was clear that they followed Catholic tradition in all those doctrines they held in common with the Church. The only way of escaping from these difficulties was to claim, as the Catholic Church did, to be the infallible interpreter of the divine message. And since the matter of greatest moment for man is that he should accept God's word, and therefore must know what it is, the argument could be put more strongly: " The great point is this: without an infallible teacher there cannot be imagined such a thing as divine calm and unwavering faith ".

The Catholic Church claimed infallibility for herself, and was therefore consistent in requiring acceptance of her beliefs. Those who expressly repudiated infallibility for themselves and for others had deprived themselves logically of the right to teach religion at all. " The choice is between revelation not guessed by private judgment but determined by the everlasting Church: and on the other hand there is the religion of humanity."[46]

It was the argument which Dryden had set out in *The Hind and he Panther*, and it would be temerarious to dispute with Dryden. But Ricards pointed out a qualification which should be added to the thesis. After quoting Newman, " There is no medium in true philosophy between Atheism and Catholicity ", he wrote:

> I do not for a moment mean that there may not be, outside the Catholic fold, a pious faith, a well-meaning and trusting faith: but I maintain that, except in Catholic principles, there can be no reasonable or logical faith.[47]

In the sentence of Newman, then, the word philosophy must be emphasized, because in fact many good faithful people have found a medium for themselves. " Nay, more ", he went on, " they may positively reject Catholic doctrines as a whole, and yet believe in certain dogmas with real faith; because, as most eminent Catholic theologians teach, the infallible authority of the Church does not necessarily enter into the essence of an act of faith."[48]

After this philosophic defence it is surprising to find that Ricards did not consider that he had yet stated the Catholic doctrine of infallibility. And yet he had the right of it. He had shown that anybody using documentary sources such as the Scriptures must logically claim to possess an organ of authoritative interpretation;

it would be an obvious need in the case of a school of philosophy or of a traditional law, and in so important a matter as religion the authority must claim to be undeceived and undeceiving. But this only proves that our human reason postulates infallibility. So Archbishop Whately, the Anglican Archbishop of Dublin, argued that Roman Catholics formulated the doctrine to explain a function found to be practically necessary.

Against that suggestion Bishop Ricards appealed to the doctrine of infallibility in the Catholic tradition. This, he showed, did not start from the function of interpretation but from the Gospel promise of the assistance of the Holy Ghost, the guide who cannot lead the Church astray. The doctrine itself was one of the truths revealed by Jesus Christ, and describes a supernatural gift added to the powers of the human mind. The philosophical argument, of Dryden or Newman, showed, as did all such arguments, that one of the functions of this gift was reasonable and desirable. But the nature of that gift could be discovered only from revelation and there also must proof of its existence be sought. Nor was there, Ricards insisted, any *petitio principii* in the argument. He had shown the Church's presentation of doctrine to be coherent because infallibility was claimed as part of it; he could show (but in this small book there was not space to set out the evidence) that there were sound motives for accepting the divine warrant claimed by the Church. All that was a process of reason treating the Scriptures and other documents merely as authentically historical:

> Reason does its part as far as reason can go: it leads us, as it were, to the feet of God by the motives of credibility which it furnishes, and then God himself speaks through his appointed guides. The supernatural accomplishes what is beyond the power of the natural man, however highly gifted.

From this position it was easy for Bishop Ricards to draw out the doctrine of papal infallibility (and in this he showed how deeply he had reflected on St Cyprian):

> The successors of St Peter form, like the apostle himself, the centre of unity in the Church. . . . And as Catholic unity rests on the visible unity of Faith, on the oneness of the visible external profession made by believers, the Pope is the centre of

the external profession of the Catholic Faith. If the Pope could fall into error in his external profession of the Faith, the foundation of unity in the Church would necessarily fail.

Most readers would agree that *Aletheia* is more carefully and subtly argued than *Catholic Christianity*. In the former the author considered and overcame the real weakness of Dryden's argument in *The Hind and the Panther* (and of many modern works of Catholic apologetic): that the human desirability of an infallible Church does not prove that God created it. And by stressing the real nature of infallibility, the assistance of the Holy Ghost, he was able to explain and defend the development of Christian doctrine, and in particular the definition of the dogma of the Immaculate Conception. But despite this superiority there was only one edition of *Aletheia* to four of *Catholic Christianity*. Since the importance of the books to the history of the Church in South Africa rests on their diffusion, on the fact that their arguments were repeated in sermons and instructions and conversations, it is well to bear this fact in mind. The reason for it is not far to seek. Ricards estimated clearly enough the method of attack of the infidelity of his day. Quoting Manning, he wrote that from Locke to Whately Englishmen accepted Christian doctrine in so far as their reason could see a good analogy for it—the argument that it was *conveniens*. But now they either accepted some of it by the human tradition of the religious body they belonged to or refused to believe what reason could not prove and so became for the most part agnostic.

In this way the question of certitude, and so of infallibility, becomes logically important. But Ricards mistakenly made the further deduction that it had become the main part of apologetics. The virulence of the agnosticism of his day, and ever since, was its power to make men overlook the importance of Christian doctrine and therefore its relevance to themselves. They would not be ready to consider the certitude of Catholic dogma unless they were made first to grasp its vital meaning. It was psychologically necessary to put before men the theme of *Catholic Christianity* before they would be ready to be instructed in the *Aletheia*. But Catholic apologists would always be tempted to hurry on to the question of infallibility just because, to those already possessed of the faith, it was the crucial argument.

VII. *Consolidation under Bishop Strobino*

The strain of work and worry eventually proved too much for the nerves of Bishop Ricards. Wilmot in his biography dates the first breakdown to 1881 and implies that the lectures in these later years lacked their earlier sparkle. Certainly the bishop admits in the *Chronicon* that in 1886 he was feeling depressed in mind and that his doctor had told him he must go on a sea voyage. The subsequent trip to Europe seems to have been as fully occupied with business as the earlier ones, and a year or so after his return he was making arrangements for the foundation of Nazareth House in Port Elizabeth and planning to re-start a diocesan seminary at St Aidan's as part of the Jesuit school.

But the financial position was not better on his return. By this time, too, it had become known, and a committee of laymen made suggestions and criticisms. The bishop insisted firmly but kindly that it was his business, but when the clergy asked him to appoint consultors to advise him on money matters he agreed. His health was not improved, and in 1890 he thought death was so near that he left sealed instructions for the coadjutor he had asked Rome to appoint.[49] In an episcopate of less than twenty years he had established St Aidan's College for boys under the Jesuits and the Marist schools at Port Elizabeth and Uitenhage and the school of the De La Salle Brothers at King William's Town; for girls he had founded the King William's Town convent, the Nazareth House Orphanage and another Dominican convent school at Port Elizabeth, and schools for Europeans and for coloureds had been formed from these in East London, Uitenhage and other places both within and outside the vicariate. He had been the chief mover in sending the Jesuit mission to the Zambesi territory, and, though the Trappist monastery he had planned had failed, the monks brought to South Africa were already doing their work for the Zulu in Natal. Nor had the Dunbrody scheme failed altogether; the Jesuit fathers had started several missions for Bantu and an industrial school. All this Bishop Ricards had accomplished, in addition to forming some half-dozen new parishes in the vicariate; and by his lectures he had won the goodwill and admiration of those outside the Church, while his books had provided Catholics with a well reasoned defence of their faith in the language of the cultural world

of his day. It was a reasonably good return to have gained for
the expenditure of his health and the straitened, but not ruined,
finances of his vicariate.

But in May, 1891, there arrived a letter, dated 25 April, from the
Congregation of Propaganda, criticizing the bishops for the deficiency in numbers and zeal of their clergy, the slow rate of conversions, the frequency of mixed marriages, and the condition of
Catholic schools. Apparently it was based on the returns which
had been sent in from vicariates and prefectures. The bishops and
prefects apostolic met at Grahamstown in November and each
prepared his answer. That of Bishop Ricards insisted on the
difficult conditions of the country, the lack of funds and of response
to his appeals for priests in Europe; but he claimed that his priests
were zealous and that his schools were so good that they were
popular with Protestants.[50]

From the last entries which Bishop Ricards made in the *Chronicon*
it seems clear that the charge, almost of negligence, came to him
as a surprise. For a man in ill-health, a bundle of nerves, who had
spent his energy abundantly and generously, it must have been a
bitter blow. Fortunately his request for a coadjutor had been
granted, and one of his priests, Peter Strobino, was consecrated
during the bishops' meeting at Grahamstown. Thereafter Dr
Ricards seems to have done little; sometimes he gave his consent
to measures the coadjutor asked for, but often he delayed them;[51]
in September, 1893, he had a stroke, and the following November
he died.

When the Congregation of Propaganda told Bishop Ricards
to submit his suggestions for a coadjutor he sent in only one name—
Peter Strobino, an Italian in his middle thirties, a very competent
but sickly man who had been working in the vicariate for some
ten years and had accompanied the bishop to Europe as secretary
in 1886. The other vicars apostolic, and the clergy generally,
seem to have been pleased with the subsequent appointment.[52]
Bishop Ricards must have known Father Strobino's views, and
perhaps it shows a consciousness of his own failings and a largeness
of mind that he recommended so strongly a man who wanted to
do just those things which he himself had neglected or thought
unimportant. For Bishop Strobino promptly started to enquire

into the quality of the work of the priests and of the schools and to recommend measures for its improvement. He found indeed that the rather vague criticisms of the Congregation of Propaganda had a considerable basis in fact, and the Roman " letter " no doubt helped him to insist on some reforms.

In 1891 Bishop Strobino gave his conclusions in the *Chronicon*: there were only eight serviceable priests in the vicariate, for three were in delicate health and could not work, three others were so ill that they could do little work, and one was *in multis deficiens*. There were rebellious nuns in the convents at Port Elizabeth and Grahamstown, King William's Town and Uitenhage, and there were troubles connected with the recent foundations at Potchefstroom and Klerksdorp. In three cases he attributed the trouble to the prioresses. " The Marist Brothers ", he wrote, " don't seem up to the work." He set about his reforms with vigour, beginning with missions in all parishes, preached by the Jesuit fathers.

Letter after letter was sent to the Congregation of Propaganda, asking for substantial help in money and for priests. Bishop Strobino asked Father Cullen, a Jesuit, " to beat up " the seminaries in Ireland to find volunteers for work in South Africa. Meanwhile he found three lads in the vicariate who wanted to become priests and arranged for them to be trained in Italy, paying the expenses of their passages out of his own pocket. A letter to the brother-general of the Marists[53] urging him to make the schools more efficient, to prepare the boys for public examinations and to insist on greater kindness to the boys, was effective, and a visitor-general was sent out to reorganize the work of the Marist institutions. The three negligent prioresses were removed from office under episcopal pressure, but constitutionally. By strict economy the interest on all loans was paid, and £1,000 was saved in a year.

Like all reformers, Bishop Strobino was impatient. The vicar apostolic delayed over some suggested measures, especially those which would impose stricter discipline on the priests, and in 1893 the coadjutor asked the Cardinal Prefect of Propaganda to write to Bishop Ricards urging stronger action. In the following year Bishop Strobino became vicar apostolic himself, and had by this time raised the number of secular priests to sixteen, though he reckoned four of them to be broken in health; he had, however, a promise of three German priests and one Irishman. More important, perhaps, he found that his priests, whom he met in two conferences, were well disposed to co-operate with him in regard to their parish work. That year all the priests attended a full three days' retreat. For the first time Bishop Strobino could write in the *Chronicon* that the outlook was brighter; he had now eighteen secular priests, of whom only three were in delicate health, and a Jesuit and a Trappist were doing parish work for him on loan; he had three students in Italy and four in Ireland.[54]

Even before he felt certain of this improvement he was planning and beginning other work. He told his priests that as soon as their number was increased he wanted to start churches for natives in all centres. Only a few of the secular clergy were interested, but he persuaded the Jesuit fathers and the King William's Town Dominican nuns to start native schools which would be run by the sisters in all the Keilands territory.

The other plan was the result of his convictions that " our nuns are not up to present (modern) required efficiency in teaching and organizing schools ". He proposed, therefore, " to obtain from home a first-class lady teacher who will train the sisters and organize the schools for them, the convents to pay all the expenses ".[55] And he succeeded; in October, 1894, Miss Constance Fox arrived from England to spend six months at King William's Town, six at Port Elizabeth, six at Grahamstown, with the task of " improving the tone of our convent schools ".

From early in that year the doctors warned Bishop Strobino that both his lungs and his liver were diseased. They wanted him to live at Graaf Reinet, and he tried for a while to organize his vicariate from there, but found it almost impossible. After suggesting his own retirement, and asking at least for a coadjutor, he struggled on for two years, living in a jacket of plaster of paris and kept going with morphia. But he kept control of his affairs, and indeed it was during this mortal illness that he persuaded the nuns to accept Miss Fox's supervision, and arranged for the Keilands mission schools. When he died in 1896 he had made Bishop Ricards' great projects viable and permanent.

Chapter V

CHURCH, STATE AND SCHOOLS: I

I. Conditions of Aid

THE Catholic schools of the Cape Province, as we have seen, always welcomed Protestant or Jewish children. Their position was logical enough. Since the days of scholasticism Catholics had distinguished between natural knowledge, which could be acquired and imparted by training the reasoning faculties, and knowledge by revelation obtained only by faith. True, the formation of morals is also a part of education, but practically all men in the first half of the nineteenth century believed that the Christian system was so reasonably desirable that it could be taught without invoking revealed dogma. The Catholics therefore saw no difficulty in providing an education for the children of Protestant parents, and were not conscious of any proselytism in doing so. The large number of Protestant and Jewish parents who continued the practice of sending their children to Catholic schools shows that the bargain was kept.

But the protests of the Anglican, Wesleyan, Baptist and Dutch Reformed ministers, frequently renewed, were not caused merely by jealousy of the success of Catholic schools. From the time of their formation in the sixteenth century the new religious bodies, particularly those with a Calvinist strain, had lost or rejected the firm distinction between natural and revealed knowledge. They had always assumed and taught that the Catholic religion could be seen to be untrue and idolatrous by anyone using his untrammelled reason. As a corollary they held that a Catholic educator must have a deformed mind, and must impart that twist to his pupils or leave them, in part at least, in the darkness of ignorance. In particular the training he gave would prevent children from seeing what the Protestants claimed to be the obvious sense of the Scriptures.

The principle had its corollaries too in the education of the

124

Protestant schools. It was assumed that the reasonableness of the sixteenth-century rejection of the authority of the Church, the duty of working out and abiding by one's own interpretation of the Scriptures, the superfluity of a sacrificing priesthood, were, if not self-evident, at least the conclusions of every well-educated man. It should not therefore have been surprising that they would call an education undenominational which presupposed these and other basic tenets of Protestantism, and would claim that it should include the Scriptures so understood. But it was also not surprising that the Catholic Church would insist as strongly as possible that such an education would imperil the faith of Catholic children.

The difference between the two positions then (or now) was not strictly one of consistency. If the distinction between natural and revealed knowledge is valid, then Bishop Grimley was strictly logical in claiming in 1863 that the Marist schools were undenominational but in saying also that Catholic parents should avoid sending their children to other schools even if these were called undenominational. If the Protestant doctrines are patent to reason alone then the ministers were logical to attack the convent schools. But for those who were impatient of logical analysis Bishop Grimley was being unreasonable; he wanted Protestant parents to send their children to his schools but would not allow Catholic parents a similar liberty of choice. A letter in the *Cape Argus* of 15 December 1863, after comparing him unfavourably with " the unobtrusive good old prelate whom he has succeeded ", said his views were " no direct concern of Protestants . . . but Protestants will pause before they send their children to be educated by nuns or priests ".

The mutual suspicion of educational methods between Catholics and Protestants, therefore, was a result of the historic positions of the revolt in the sixteenth century, and it is not surprising that it continued throughout the development of the Catholic Church in South Africa. But in the 'sixties the civil government became involved. In the first half of the nineteenth century education, like farming and trade, was provided by private persons. The executive, or ultimately the English Colonial Secretary, was expected to distribute to them for this civilizing work some part of the revenue taken in taxation. And it was on this ground that the Catholics appealed to them for assistance in paying the fares of nun teachers to come to the colony, and for building the schools. Nor were grants refused in principle; in 1817, long before Catholic Emancipation, Lord Charles Somerset had assured Bishop Poynter, one of the English vicars apostolic, that all denominations at the Cape were entitled to equal privileges. Though Catholics did complain that the grants they received were on a much smaller scale *per capita* than those of the Anglicans, the system could easily have been adjusted and adequate education provided by it for all children.

The Dutch Reformed Church, also, like the Catholics and the Anglicans, founded schools for its own local congregations. The government of a colony was naturally more political in attitude than this European tradition of voluntary education, and in the days of the Batavian Republic Governor de Mist had planned to take control of all education at the Cape. Before he had time to do anything in the matter the colony was ceded to the British; and Lord Charles Somerset founded a number of government schools, largely, perhaps, for the purpose of making English the dominant language. The first half of the nineteenth century, moreover, saw the movement towards the administrative state of today begin to take shape. Instead of supervising the work of private citizens and corporations by laws and the distribution of public revenue, the executive formed a civil service to direct in detail and finally to supply what became known as social services. One of the early steps in this development of the modern state was the treatment of education as a matter of public policy. The impetus was probably given by James Stephen and his associates in England, and it came to Cape Colony when Sir John Herschel recommended that a government servant be superintendent of all schools. Dr James Rose-Innes was accordingly appointed in 1839 to be Director of Education at the Cape; and two years later schools directly under the control of the state were established. At the same time, at Dr Rose-Innes' proposal, 50 per cent grants were offered to all "mission" schools which would accept the conditions which he laid down, one of these being that the Bible, and only the Bible, should be used for the daily religious instruction. It was thought that the contentious question of religious instruction was being cleverly evaded, giving uniformity of treatment without favouring the claims of any one "denomination". For Calvinists such as those of the Dutch Reformed Kerk this was wholly acceptable, since they held the Bible to be the sole and sufficient source of religious knowledge and its Calvinistic meaning to be obvious; and as they formed the large majority they could rely on most teachers expounding it in their sense. Though less welcome to Anglicans, the arrangement was tolerable to them.

To a professed agnostic like James Stephen or to the members of the Clapham sect whence he derived, and presumably to Dr Rose-Innes, it was self-evident impartiality. They did not see that it assumed in fact the Calvinist position in the religious quarrel—which was also, on this issue, that of the Anglican communion of the time. The Catholics refused for twenty years to accept it, and were therefore ineligible for the grant.

Meanwhile, Dr Dale had succeeded Rose-Innes. He was a man of wide sympathies, and was really desirous to promote sound education. Bishop Grimley, in the Western vicariate, thought it possible to negotiate with him, but Bishop Moran, in the Eastern, put very forcibly the traditional Catholic standpoint in a letter he wrote to Bishop Grimley on 23 June 1863:

I can sympathize with you in your difficulties on the subject of education, for our difficulties arising from this source have been enormous. In fact I have turned schoolmaster myself, and so have all my priests. We all teach school, first because we have not the means of paying schoolmasters, and second to save our children from the danger of perversion of Protestant schools. Well, as far as I am concerned, I am prepared to persevere in this course rather than accept aid from the government on the condition of reading any portion of the Bible as a school book. The principle is a Protestant one, and is intended to undermine the teaching authority of the Church. Besides, it is most injurious to pupils. Every man acquainted with the working of this Protestant principle must be convinced that neither the dogmas of faith nor the principles of morality are taught under such a system. I know it well. Considerable numbers of Protestant children have come from time to time to our schools after having been for years in Protestant schools, and I can assure you that after having read their Bible daily, they were found without exception to be utterly ignorant not only of the history of the Bible, but also of the essential truths—I mean the primary mysteries—whereas on the other hand they were quite satisfied they had fulfilled every duty by the mere fact of having read the Bible, and filled with the pride of their right to form their own opinions, provided always they did not learn Catholicity, but should there be any leaning in this direction, then the right of judging was not to be even tolerated. Our own children, taught according to the Catholic religion, to the amazement of the Protestants, are always found to be thoroughly instructed not only in the history of the Bible, but also in the dogmas and moral principles of religion. Consequently, as far as I am concerned, I never will do anything calculated directly or indirectly to sanction apparently a principle which I believe, and which I know from experience, to be destructive to religion.

My dear Lord, believe me, this Protestant principle, after its direct antagonism to the teaching authority of the Church, is not more than a cloak for idleness. It is much less laborious to make the children read a portion of the scriptures and commit to memory a few texts of scripture, which as a rule they apply in a nonsensical manner, than to catechize them daily. Neither the government nor the legislature has any right to impose upon us any such condition as the daily reading of the Bible as a school book as indispensable to our obtaining our just share of the education grant. Such a condition is a tyrannical interference with religious liberty, and is unheard of under Catholic governments in reference to their Protestant subjects. I would advise you, then, to insist upon your right, and refuse to abate one jot of your principles on the subject of genuine education. In this matter I firmly believe it is the executive that is entirely to blame. They have the power to change the minute of which we complain, and I have not the least doubt that the country would applaud them if they did so. My experience convinces me that the Parliament wishes to do justice to all religious bodies, and that it would sanction any system handled by the executive with that end in view. I can hardly say that I am acquainted with any of the members. I know Mr Wood, Mr Slater and Mr Godlonton a little, but only a little, but from my limited acquaintance with them I have arrived at the conviction that they, so far from opposing us, would help to see justice done in this matter of education. Were such a system proposed, I am convinced that Parliament would sanction it at once. Is not Dale capable of dealing with this question? And if he is not, why does he not resign his place?

The reason for this expostulation was that Bishop Grimley was already negotiating with the new Superintendent of Education, Dr Langham Dale, who had succeeded Rose-Innes in 1859, to find an interpretation of the minute on religious instruction which would enable the Catholic schools to qualify for the government grant. On 17 June, before he had received Bishop Moran's letter, Bishop Grimley had written to Dr Dale:

My dear Dr Dale,

I am very anxious to understand thoroughly the full meaning of the condition which heretofore has been the obstacle to Catholics accepting governmental aid for schools in this colony.

Firstly, with regard to the limitation of religious instruction to the sacred scriptures, am I to understand from the term " sacred scriptures " any edition, e.g. the Douay, so that in the event of my accepting the grant, would I be free to use the Douay edition?

Secondly, in giving religious instruction in the sacred scriptures, am I to understand that the teacher is not allowed to offer any doctrinal or other explanation, but merely listen to the pupils read?

Thirdly, am I to understand that each pupil is to have a copy of the scriptures for his or her perusal during the time allowed for religious instruction?

Fourthly, would I be obliged to see that the pupils should read the entire Scripture, or would I fulfil the requirements of the condition by reading any portion of the sacred volume I might judge most useful for my pupils? By the term " entire Scripture " you understand me to mean to read daily a certain portion until the entire Old and New Testaments should be read through.

Fifthly, would I fulfil the condition of giving religious instruction in the sacred scriptures by giving catechetical instruction, which I believe to be founded on and flowing from the sacred volume?

As I believe a clear explanation of the above queries would be necessary for me before I take the steps I may deem conducive to removing certain obstacles, may I presume on your kindness to furnish me with such.

Whatever the purpose of those who had drawn the rule Bishop

Grimley had found an ingenious way of making it possible for Catholics to use it. And Dr Dale was certainly willing to allow this course, for his reply was as follows:

My Lord,

I have the honour to acknowledge your letter of the 17th instant requesting me to give a clear explanation of certain queries regarding religious instruction in schools receiving aid from the government, so that you may understand thoroughly the full meaning of the condition which heretofore has been the obstacle to Catholics accepting government aid for their schools in this colony.

Firstly. In regard to the limitation of religious instruction to the sacred scriptures, you enquire whether you are to understand from the term " sacred scriptures " any edition, e.g. Douay. The version known as the authorized version is usually read in schools conducted in the English language, but both Dutch and Kaffir versions are used in others at the discretion of the managers. I consider, therefore, that you would be free to use the Douay edition if you thought fit.

Secondly. You ask whether in giving religious instruction in the sacred scriptures the teacher is allowed to offer any doctrinal or other explanation or merely to listen to the reading of the pupils. I consider that such explanations must be given, chiefly of a verbal character, as the text or passage may require, to enable the reader to understand its meaning.

Thirdly. I do not consider it necessary that each pupil should have a copy of the Scriptures for his or her perusal during the time set apart for religious instruction. The following arrangement is that which was proposed by my predecessor, and is still observed in the schools:

RELIGIOUS INSTRUCTION:

In regard to religious instruction, I recommend that it form the first exercise of the morning school, and that during that exercise the pupils be thrown into three divisions, the first to consist of those who can read—they are to be occupied in repeating texts of scriptures simultaneously in order to their being committed to memory, texts to be selected by the master and taught by a monitor. The second division to consist of those who can read imperfectly—they will be occupied in reading with a monitor or an usher the parables and miracles of our Saviour. The third division to consist of those that cannot read correctly or with ease. They will construct a Bible class and will be engaged under a master for scriptural reading.

Fourthly. I consider the course of Scripture reading referred to under the fourth paragraph is to be *referred* to by the principal of the school.

Fifthly. Catechetical instruction within the ordinary school hours is excluded.[1]

In another letter to Bishop Grimley Dr Dale suggested that it would be better to get some general principle about religious education into which the Catholic practice could be fitted, but that this would require parliamentary sanction. He urged therefore that an approach should be made to that body.

The outcome of these negotiations was that the Catholic schools received a grant, but by privilege, and smaller than would have been given to a comparable " undenominational " school. They were allowed, however, to interpret Scripture in their own way, though not to impose it on their Protestant pupils. On these lines the Catholic schools of Cape Colony developed; separate classes in religion were provided for Catholics and Protestants, the syllabus for the latter being submitted to the director of education, and with a parents' option to keep their children from the instruction. On the whole, it was the solution which Bishop Grimley regarded as sufficiently satisfactory, and Catholics generally were pleased with it in the early days.

There was little difference between the attitudes of Bishop Moran and of Dr Langham Dale. The former took the old view of the colonial government, that it should use the revenue to help the separate interests which made up the community, in this case the religious groups, to give education to their children according to their parents' faith. Dr Dale held that it was the function of the government " to exercise its influence, legitimately and wisely, not in aiming at an absolute authority but in removing hindrances".[2] Principal Malherbe summarizes it:

The Government thus makes use of every existing agency and encourages such efforts by means of state aid, but in no case does it take the initial step in providing educational facilities, however great the need in any particular place.[3]

Such a system fitted naturally to the idea of the government as representative of all the interests or traditions which made up the community, irrespective of their present numerical strength. Even when this conception changed to that of responsible government, where the administration was supposed to be directed by the majority vote at the last election, it was not essential that the educational system should be altered. It could be regarded as outside the issues put to the electorate, and the schools of the traditional religious groups could all be assisted ; as in fact happened later in Holland and in Scotland. But to many the principle of responsible government implied that the administration chosen by the electorate was the only representative of the country and so must have complete control of all the social services it subsidized. These, therefore, must be uniform for all, and religious education, as one of them, must be undenominational.

Both views were defended in the debates of the assembly. The findings of the Watermeyer Government Commission in 1863 would seemingly have extended financial assistance on the pound-for-pound basis to all schools. But the schedule to the Education Act of 1865 restricted this to undenominational public schools, while allowing grants-in-aid to church schools on a lower scale and for teachers' salaries only.

The era of responsible government in South Africa began with this system of " undenominational " public schools as its norm, Catholic and other religious schools being privileged exceptions because of past history. The assumption that the electorate were really agreed on the main questions of social order, which underlies the theory of responsible government, was held to include the nature of education. So the tendency has always been to larger relative expenditure on the public schools and the treatment of grants to denominational schools as a questionable privilege. The fallacy of the reasoning lies of course in the word " undenominational ". It was taken to mean acceptable to all Christians even if regarded by them as inadequate; a sort of basic religion like basic English. In fact the religious instruction of the public schools was necessarily a denial of the Catholic doctrine of the Christian Church, and could also easily become offensive to other Christian bodies. Where a large majority belonged to one creed, say the Calvinists, it might easily reflect their doctrines; where secularism became

common in the teaching profession it might easily become rationalistic. But for most people the religious outlook of school becomes
that of social life, and as these public schools grew and multiplied
under responsible government the need for the Catholic Church
to declare her own religious attitude publicly became more and
more important.

Generally speaking the Catholics did not pay attention to the
point which Bishop Moran had put so strongly in 1863. Acceptance of their position as a privileged or exceptional one, with a
special interpretation of Bible-instruction, was a tacit admission
that the public or government schools were essentially Protestant,
even though called undenominational. Naturally enough the
Dutch Reformed Church, the Baptists, the Wesleyans and most
Anglicans could accept "undenominational" religious teaching
because it did not clash with their own beliefs concerning the use
and meaning of the Scriptures; and so they could qualify for the
larger grants given to such schools.

II. Development

During the next generation the Catholic community proved
itself worthy of the assistance it received in promoting the education
of South African children. Besides a large increase in mission
schools, the Marist Brothers made foundations in Cape Town,
Uitenhage and Port Elizabeth. The seminary of St Aidan's,
Grahamstown, was transferred to the Society of Jesus and became
under their control a large high school. Among other educational
centres Bishop Gaughren founded St Leo's College at Clocolan,
near Basutoland, with priests as teachers. This school closed
when the Anglo-Boer war started, and the boys were transferred
to St Charles's, in Pietermaritzburg, which itself closed in 1912,
to re-open in 1914 under the Marist Brothers. A new order, the
Salesians, were brought to Cape Town to open an industrial school
where boys were trained in various trades while completing their
literary education. Mother Dympna of the Irish Dominicans, with
a Miss Lyne, founded her institute for the deaf and dumb in Cape-
town, and the German Dominican nuns introduced a new (oral)
method for the deaf at King William's Town. The Irish

Dominicans of Cape Town built and staffed new High Schools at Rondebosch, Wynberg (Springfield), Port Elizabeth and Uitenhage, and taught in (public) mission schools in the peninsula and at Marymount and elsewhere in the Eastern Province. In 1877 and 1883 Bishop Ricards and Father Fagan brought the German Dominican nuns from Augsburg to King William's Town and East London and established high schools for girls in those towns. During this period too Catholic educational work was extended into the new provinces and states to the north. By 1893 Oakford, Pietermaritzburg and Newcastle in Natal, Bloemfontein in the Orange River Sovereignty, Pretoria, Potchefstroom and Johannesburg in the Transvaal, and Salisbury in the Chartered Company's territory which was to become Rhodesia, all had Catholic high schools.

In nearly every case, when a foundation was first made the vicar apostolic had to advance the money for the site and buildings, to pay for the passage of the teaching brothers and sisters and sometimes to guarantee the upkeep. These expenses, or part of them, were often refunded over a term of years by the religious order and the money, raised by loan or subscription, was in that sense used again in this development of education. But even so it was a heavy burden on a very small community whose resources, and therefore credit with money-lending banks and societies, were not large. In 1891 Bishop Ricards calculated that his Eastern Vicariate had collected £123,000 during the past forty-one years for these purposes.

For the bishops and the Catholic parents who sent their children to the Catholic schools the overriding consideration was that they gave an intellectual formation in which a detailed knowledge and practice of the Catholic religion found its due place. Many parents who were not Catholics thought that the training they gave, even separated from formal religious teaching, was worth paying for. Possibly they recognized half-consciously that the Catholic religious orders brought to South Africa, through their traditions and through individual teachers, some part of that imponderable European culture which had French, German, and Spanish elements in it as well as Irish and English. Nor was praise lacking from the government officials. Dr Muir's report of 1893 on the public examinations had, as on previous occasions, some good words for the instruction given by the Catholic schools. Even in the Transvaal, which had previously refused to assist the Marist Brothers' College because their teachers (though some were Dutch) were not Protestant, President Kruger gave them financial aid in the last three years of his rule.[4]

The exception to this approval came from the Congregation of Propaganda in Rome. After examining the reports of development in South Africa, the congregation, as we have seen, sent the vicars apostolic a number of criticisms, and one of these was that they had not organized schools in the manner or the extent incumbent on them.[5] The bishops did not accept the rebuke without protest, legitimately pointing out that their schools were so good that they were popular with Protestant parents. The well-informed did, however, recognize a need for considerable improvement. Father FitzHenry, of the Eastern Vicariate, commenting on the official *Analysis of Public Examinations*, claimed that Catholic schools on the whole had lost no ground in the last twenty years—but this was rather faint praise; and he went on to urge that children should be left longer at these schools in future.[6] In 1908 Dr Kolbe was to use the standard of twenty years earlier as a minimum beneath which it was disgraceful to fall.[7]

The determination of Bishop Strobino to raise the level of instruction was characteristic of much Catholic activity in the ensuing quarter of a century. The teaching orders already established, Dominican and Holy Family, Holy Cross and Loreto nuns, the Marist Brothers, the Oblates of Mary Immaculate, made many new foundations as the Catholic community increased. But this could almost be called a routine growth, given their popularity with parents; and it is a clear advantage of education by religious orders that their own superiors are ready and sometimes anxious to co-operate with the local bishop after the first school has been successfully launched. This development, however, was not sufficient to meet the demand for education, and some new orders with a reputation as teachers of youth were brought in; the Irish Christian Brothers came to Kimberley, the De La Salle Brothers to King William's Town and later to East London, the Brothers of Charity to Pietermaritzburg and the Sisters of Mercy to Mafeking. All this meant for South Africans—Protestants and Jews as well as Catholics, since the schools were open to and used by them all*—the introduction of a variety of tested teaching methods and traditions and of a healthy rivalry not only between individual staffs but between world-wide organizations properly anxious for their reputation as educators.

These conditions would no doubt of themselves have secured a large measure of efficiency, but there was, throughout the thirty years following the complaint of Rome, a deliberate effort to create a strong Catholic public opinion on the subject. Father Kelly and Father FitzHenry and Father Walmesley in the Eastern Vicariate, Dr. Kolbe and Dr. Welch at the Cape, Bishop Gaughren in Kimberley, Father Schoch in the Transvaal, Dr. Sormany in Natal, all with experience both of teaching and administration, urged on their fellow Catholics, by lecture and print, the duty of a better intellectual formation, and themselves provided some of the material for it.

* Save the Jesuit college at St Aidan's, Grahamstown, which, as has been noted, was for Catholics only.

Chapter VI

SOUTH WEST AFRICA

I. First Arrivals

THE development of Catholic life within the established vicariates is only half the story of the Catholic Church in South Africa in the last quarter of the nineteenth century. It saw the establishment of missions, scattered indeed but permanent, in that great strip of 500,000 square miles of barren, sometimes desert, land, comprising Namaqualand and Damaraland, which stretches from Port Nolloth to the borders of Portuguese Angola. During the same period the area comprising the valley of the Zambesi, from the Limpopo in the South to Latitude 10°S., comparable in size to Western Europe, was dotted with Catholic stations. Meanwhile churches were being built in the districts of Kimberley, the Transvaal and the Witwatersrand, as miners, European and African, flocked to the diamond and gold fields. At the same time the work amongst the Zulu tribes of Natal, abandoned by Bishop Allard for Basutoland, recommenced on a large scale with the coming of the Trappist monks.

In every one of these fields, schools and hospitals were established as well as churches. The missionary work was no longer measured by the occasional journeys of a priest. When Bishops Ricards, Leonard and Jolivet were appointed it is scarcely exaggeration to say that their labours were effectively limited to the coastal strip of the southern tip of Africa. Their successors found themselves part of an ecclesiastical organization which covered all the country up to the Portuguese colonies of the centre and which had made contact in Nyasaland with the Catholic missionary effort from the north.

Our historians write so often of the discipline and centralization of the Roman Church that it is tempting to describe this expansion as a sort of military campaign. But the parallel breaks down at many points. The opening of each new mission field was due to the initiative of one of the vicars apostolic: he sometimes asked the Congregation of Propaganda for approval or, if necessary, authorization, but the interest of the Congregation became serious only when some sort of reorganization had to be made. It is true, of course, that the missionaries understood the mind of Rome; to gather communities professing one faith, using one liturgy, living by the same sacraments. To that extent the work satisfied one test which St Thomas Aquinas and Napoleon independently recognized as essential to an army. But the missionaries had to deal as best they could with local difficulties, of topography and politics and resources, and their efforts seldom show much sign of a preconceived plan, and met little success for many years. Especially was this true of the work in South West Africa, and perhaps in that way it was not unlike many British military campaigns.

Namaqualand and Bushmanland, between the Olifants and Orange rivers, formed a semi-desert tract included in Cape Colony. Across the Orange the same sort of sandy country, liable to long periods of drought, continued for nearly a thousand miles up to and beyond the Kunene river, and was inhabited by Hottentots, Hereros, Damaras, Ovambos, and other nomadic peoples. To the east of this and separated by the Kalahari desert was an area held in the south by the Griquas or bastard people begotten by the union of men from the Cape with Hottentot or Bantu women but occupied for the greater part by Bechuana tribes. The whole area covered about 650,000 square miles, roughly the size of France and Germany together; but the comparison is misleading because of the great difficulty of movement for the traveller.

In all this great area there had been little spread of white settlers from Cape Town. A mining company—Namaqualand was rich in copper—employed a number of half-breeds and some natives. A few itinerant traders did business with them. Port Nolloth on the coast had been established to serve these interests. The different tribes, especially beyond the Orange river, were nomadic, and wars between them were frequent when they claimed or tried to use the same grazing areas. The Hottentots had killed off most of their Bushmen predecessors in Little Namaqualand (south of the Orange), and were themselves being attacked by the Hereros north of the river. Inter-tribal warfare was common on both banks of the Kunene river.

The presence of white settlers did not mitigate the general

disorder. Some of them made their profit by selling fire-arms to one or other of the native groups. The farmers who pushed across the Orange river regarded the purchase of land as giving them sovereign rights, and this conception was unknown to tribal custom, so that the nomads continued to graze lands which their chieftains had "sold". It seems that there was a measure of invincible or affected ignorance on both sides, and it was not difficult for the whites to set one tribe against another. Though the Protestant Rhenish missionaries often arbitrated and made peace, it was natural that they should support those who responded to their teaching, as in the war between the Hereros and Hottentots in 1881-2.

Three European governments, Portuguese, British and German, put forward claims to parts of this territory, sometimes to protect their traders and missionaries, sometimes to impose order and peace on the native peoples, occasionally and vaguely for strategic reasons. But until the 'eighties their several claims were subject to hesitation and vacillation, save for the area south of the Orange river, where the British government of Cape Colony was recognized.

As one result it was often difficult for missionaries to be sure what authorities they would have to negotiate with even though a formal agreement had been published in Europe before they set out. The whole of Damaraland, indeed all the territory from the Kunene to the Limpopo, was believed to be a British Protectorate in 1879, but when a mission of the Holy Ghost Fathers reached Ovamboland two years later, they found that the Portuguese claim had been conceded.

Even in the 'sixties the Rhenish missionaries reported that the Prussian government intended to annex the area north of the Orange river.[1] The Cape government, or rather the British Colonial Office, was then reluctant to accept any extension of territory, and Bishop Grimley, like most of his contemporaries, thought of Prussia as a Protestant power. In 1864 he suggested secretly to Napoleon III, whom he had already met and whom he regarded as a patron of Catholic missions, that he should anticipate the German move. The Emperor of the French, however, found himself unable then to provide the necessary naval and military mission, and, after ten years of hesitation and ineffective claims, both Portugal and Britain at the end of the 'eighties recognized the territory as a colony of the new German Reich. Meanwhile, on the other side of the Kalahari desert, the British had first protected and then annexed Griqualand after the rush of diamond seekers and then claimed a protectorate of Bechuanaland and recognized the practical rule of the Chartered Company of Cecil Rhodes between the Limpopo and the Zambesi.

The political uncertainties made missionary work difficult, because the Portuguese government usually insisted that religious superiors in their territories should be Portuguese subjects, while after 1870 French missionaries did not work very willingly with German officials. In addition, the Catholic efforts in this area suffered because they were regarded for many years as offshoots of greater tasks.

An Irish trader, Henry Edward Barry,[2] wrote to Bishop Grimley in 1864 a lengthy account of the Damaras, Hottentots, Bechuanas and Matabeles, and urged the opportunity for missionary work among them. Since these peoples dwelt north of the Orange river, and so beyond the bounds of his vicariate, the bishop forwarded the information to Cardinal Barnabò, Prefect of Propaganda, who wrote to the Congregation of the Holy Ghost in terms which gave them the impression that the whole vast territory was to be added to their vicariate of the Two Guineas.[3] This impression was probably confirmed when Bishop Grimley at the Vatican Council approached their superior with the suggestion that the Holy Ghost Fathers should take over the northern part of his vicariate, including, if they so wished, Little Namaqualand. Sir Philip Wodehouse, the governor of the Cape Colony, had urged that some of the " same sort of people " as the Oblates he had seen at work in Basutoland should go to Bushmanland.[4] It may have been with this in mind that Bishop Grimley approached the Holy Ghost Fathers, but his offer to them was concerned primarily with the more settled lands to the east.[5]

As no agreement was reached, Bishop Grimley seems to have approached another congregation, the *Missions Africaines de Lyon*, and their superior in Mauritius arrived in the Cape in January 1871, only to find the bishop on his death-bed. His successor, Bishop Leonard, found priests of the Lyons society already at the Cape when he arrived in September 1873, and promptly agreed to their taking over the Central Prefecture, including the towns of Mossel Bay, George, Oudtshoorn and Beaufort West, which had formed Catholic communities, and the area between the Olifants and Orange rivers in the west.

Little Namaqualand was still only an outlying district of the new prefecture. During the episcopacy of Bishop Grimley its scattered two hundred Catholics[6] had been visited once every two years either by the bishop or by one of his priests. The Society of African Missions in 1873 sent Father Gaudeul to Springbok, but the mine there was closed soon after his arrival and the population scattered. A Catholic farmer named Hayes at Pella, five miles from the Orange river, where the Lutheran schoolmaster had recently been killed by Bushmen, gave him lodging; the government granted him the use of the school, since there was no one to replace the Lutheran, and so Father Gaudeul settled there in 1875. There seems to be no record of his work, but his successor, Father Simon, who arrived in 1882, found that he spoke English and Hollands with ease, was in touch with two dozen Catholic families in Bushman-land, and was living in apostolic poverty with his little library of the Bible, Liguori, Aquinas, and English and Dutch catechisms.[7]

The Catholic effort north of the Orange river was even slower and on a smaller scale during the 'seventies. The very energetic Father Duparquet, of the Congregation of the Holy Ghost, sup-posing that the area would soon become a British protectorate, decided to approach the tribes from the south. In 1878 he went to Kimberley, but soon found that it was useless as a headquarters for his work; next he went from the Cape by boat to Walvis Bay —the British had proclaimed Damaraland a protectorate—and established a mission at Omaruru, a hundred miles or so inland, in the middle of the Rhenish and Finnish Protestant missions.[8]

His plans, however, brought him into conflict with the Society of African Missions. Their superior, Father Planque, claimed that all this area must be the field of work of the Central Prefecture, and therefore of his society; alternatively he offered to hand it over to the Congregation of the Holy Ghost in exchange for their vicariates on the Gold and Ivory Coasts.[9] There had been misunder-standings already between the society and Bishop Leonard, or rather his vicar-general, since the Central Prefecture was formed. A chief cause of complaint was that the civil government preferred to work with the vicar apostolic, and so the titles of grants of land were made out in his name. Perhaps Cardinal Barnabò's confidence to Bishop Grimley, that " from his long experience he would rather have secular priests for work in foreign missions ",[10] was caused by such complaints, though it must be said there was a case for the point of view of the religious congregations. However, Cardinal Barnabò settled the quarrel by handing back the Central Prefecture to Bishop Leonard, giving the Society of African Missions the vicariates of the Two Guineas, and establishing for the Congregation of the Holy Ghost the Prefecture of Cimbebasia, to include the land between the Kunene and the Orange rivers, and Bechuanaland. It was at this time, too, that Bishop Jolivet, the Vicar Apostolic of Natal, urged on Rome the advisability of entrusting those parts of his territory north of the Limpopo to missionary orders. Father Duparquet, named vice-prefect of the new territory, installed Father Hogan and Brother Onophrios at Omaruru to work in the Walvis Bay area, sent Father Gogarty to Mafeking to try to penetrate Bechuanaland from the south, and himself made a rapid tour of Damaraland and Ovamboland, where the British had ceded their claim to the Portuguese.

These missionaries met with a difficulty which occurred indeed elsewhere in Africa and in Asia, but which was acute in Cimbebasia. The wars of the French Revolution practically brought to an end the major part of the missionary work of the Church, which had been directed and recruited, in the eighteenth century, from France and Portugal. The Protestant missionary societies, English, Prussian, Finnish, and French, recovered quicker from those upheavals, perhaps because they had always been less respectful to their civil governments. In Basutoland the Paris Missionary Society, in Griqualand and Bechuanaland the London Missionary Society and the Wesleyans, in Damaraland and Ovamboland and the south of Angola the Rhenish and Finnish Societies were at work for almost a quarter of a century before the Catholic missionaries appeared. When they made converts of tribal kings and chiefs, and even when they had only established friendly relations, they asked for a monopoly of missionary work, and especially a promise to exclude Catholics. In Basutoland Moshesh had refused their request, but the Bechuana chiefs were firm in denying any permanent stay to the Holy Ghost Fathers. The Hereros and some of the Ovambos were equally firm, and used the presence of Catholic missionaries as an excuse to attack other tribes. When

the British civil authorities abandoned the Protectorate of Damaraland to concentrate on the port of Walvis Bay, the Hereros,
attacking the Hottentots, drove the Holy Ghost Fathers from
Omaruru, and two of them with their converts fled to the Portuguese area in the north of the Prefecture. The war of the tribes
soon spread to these parts, and two of the missionaries, Father
Delpuech and Brother Lucius, were murdered in 1885. The
anarchy was only brought to an end when the Portuguese government sent garrisons to the territory north of the Kunene, and the
German government, with the agreement of Great Britain, annexed
the area between the Kunene and the Orange rivers as South-West
Africa. The Congregation of the Holy Ghost asked to be relieved
of their task in Cimbebasia; in April 1888 Great Namaqualand up
to the tropic of Capricorn was handed over to the Oblates of St
Francis de Sales, and in the following year Bechuanaland, and two
years later Damaraland, were entrusted to the Oblates of Mary
Immaculate.

II. Bishop Simon

When Bishop Leonard had resumed the administration of the
Central Prefecture he had asked another missionary society, the
Oblates of St Francis de Sales, to help him, and they sent the small
group under Father Simon to work in Little Namaqualand. In
1909 Simon, now a bishop, wrote a memoir of the twenty-seven
years he had spent in South Africa. Probably he wrote from some
sort of diary, or else he had the admirable gift of seeing the past
unmodified by his more recent experience. It is difficult otherwise to account for the completely different outlook which he
attributes to himself, without comment or judgement, when he
was first sent to Pella as a priest in 1882 to take over, for his order,
the work which Father Gaudeul of the African Missions had been
doing for nine years. His account suggests a man naturally
unsuited for the conditions. When he disembarked at Port
Nolloth, after the three days' voyage from Cape Town, he found
he had to disembark by ladder, a feat easy enough, he remarks, for
athletes, but difficult for those " gênés d'un certain baggage mi-
aphérique, présent de la nature ". His mind was coloured by
French provincialism; it seemed funny to him that the priests
Colgan and McCarthy, whom he met at the Cape and whom he

admired, should speak French so badly, and that the waiters at Port Nolloth should not understand that *merci* was a refusal. He was in no way conscious of his own linguistic deficiency, and records without comment that he had no common tongue with the priest at Southampton, though the latter tried him in English, Spanish, German, Italian and Portuguese. They fell back on writing because their pronunciation of Latin was so different. The first sign the memoir gives of the desire for a gift of tongues is when Father Simon found Father Gaudeul able to catechize in English and in Dutch and apparently word-perfect in both languages. When he was taken to visit the dozen Irish families around Pella he began to wonder why he had not learned the two languages they used before leaving France.

Many other qualities made up for these incapacities. His first companions, a secular priest and his brother a deacon, a lay brother and a priest of his own society, all left him very soon, the first three apparently as soon as they saw the physical conditions and the last because his health broke after a few months. But the paunchy Father Simon went on working in that climate for nearly half a century. Knowing neither language, he set himself to learn them by teaching the schoolchildren Father Gaudeul had assembled, though he remarked on his good fortune that the school was not inspected that first year. After six months of loneliness his superior-general sent two priests and three sisters to help him, and they found his French almost unrecognizable. Clearly he had no gift for languages, but he persevered, finding Dutch more difficult than English, and was proud to report after a dozen years that he was able to preach in the former tongue when his church at Pella was consecrated. But he insisted that all missionaries sent to him from Europe should have some grounding in these languages before they arrived.

It was not an easy country for travel. After landing at Port Nolloth he was to make the first part of his journey by railway, but the train was a caravan of thirty wagons drawn by sixty mules and went over ravines and narrow passes which Father Simon found nerve-racking. From Springbok he was taken to Pella, close to the Orange river in Bushmanland, by wagon, and had to walk much of the way through sandy desert because the wagon

broke down on several occasions. These settlements in the
northern part of the territory had grown around the copper-mines
which had been opened there, and even when they were abandoned,
as at Springbok, a small community remained, keeping herds or
trading with the Hottentot tribes. But the seasons forced them to
be semi-nomadic, and after six months in Pella Father Simon
found himself left behind with a stray European who had joined
him as half-servant, half-postulant. Having little taste, so he wrote,
for the contemplative life, they made their way on foot back to
Springbok where, being without funds, they had to rely on the
charity of the good widow Malone who kept a food shop there. An
Irish " itinerant merchant " gave him a necessary pair of trousers.

Back at Pella in 1884, he was visited by Bishop Leonard who,
despite feeble health, taught him apparently the practice of touring
the country in search of those who were or ought to be papists.
After that lesson the area between the Olifants river and the Orange
was made into a prefecture for Father Simon. Making his own
first visitation of the farming district of Calvinia two hundred miles
to the south, he discovered what the climate could do in the way
of frost, fog, and frightful cold during July. In the three years
following 1894 he saw the effects of drought. Many cattle died,
and the able-bodied took the remainder away to search for water.
Only children and the aged were left at Pella, and they suffered
famine until help could be sent from the Cape. On one of his
missionary journeys during these years Father Simon and another
priest almost died of thirst in the desert. Their sight was blurred,
they lost the power of speech, got separated and were afraid for
their reason; in this state they were luckily found by some natives
who restored them to health, knowledgeably giving them a little
water at a time.

As could be expected, the material circumstances of the population
were wretched in the extreme. Even at Port Nolloth, a galva-
nized-iron town and a centre of trade and communication with the
Cape, Father Simon noted that the standards of the magistrates,
ministers and mine company officials, the aristocrats as he called
them, were only just tolerable. At the other end of the village the
out-of-works lived in misery; their children unclad, of morals none.
He came to the mining village of O'okiep; its population was two
thousand and there were two or three deaths a week, sometimes the

result of the sulphur fumes but more often of enteric or typhoid. When there was a fall-in of the mine, panic spread among the workers but hunger drove them back to their only possible employment.

Even so, after twenty-seven years of observation, Bishop Simon (as he had become) recognized that the mining company was " behaving well ". Despite heavy taxes and low profits and the exhaustion of the copper, they did what they could for their workers, planting trees, installing improvements in the townships and making the refinement process of the metal less dangerous by substituting motors for coal power. From the beginning they had helped to provide education for the children and made grants for any missionaries who were willing to settle near their mines. They had given Bishop Grimley a site at Springbok and a grant of money; they provided free passage for persons and a 50 per cent reduction on goods for all missionaries. The government itself was not less co-operative; in, for example, giving Father Gaudeul his school at Pella. The regulations only allowed direct payment for teachers in European schools, but in 1885 Bishop Leonard obtained from the Cape authorities a money grant for the boarding-school that Father Simon had founded at Springbok, though it admitted coloured as well as white children. On several occasions in his memoir Father Simon, like Bishop Allard, exclaimed in admiration of the real " liberalism " of the English government, comparing it favourably with that of his own country. He formed the same opinion of the English whom he met. They were very " unprejudiced " as a rule, though they did not appear to practise their own religion very noticeably. Their ministers were respectful, friendly and helpful, and some of them believed all Catholic doctrines save that concerning the papacy. This was true also of many laymen, and Father Simon believed the English to be on the path back to the Faith. The Catholics whom he met among them were chiefly Irish, and the widow Malone, who kept the little food store at Springbok, was a stalwart of the Faith. She had provided hospitality for the visiting missionaries in the days of Bishop Grimley, and though she lost most of her money in the 'sixties she was still the benefactor of the very poor and, as Father Simon noted, showed no desire to enrich herself.

Though Lebanese, Italians, Jews and Germans were all to be met with among the itinerant traders, they were comparatively few;

JOSEPH GERARD, O.M.I.

Apostle of Basutoland
(died 1914)

Right

MARIE JEAN FRANÇOIS
ALLARD, O.M.I., D.D.

First Vicar Apostolic of
Natal (1850–73)

Left

JACOBUS HOENDERWANGERS, O.PRAEM.

Pioneer Catholic priest of the Orange Free State

Below

Father Hoenderwangers with his congregation at Bloemfontein, c. 1852

besides the English the Boers formed the only sizeable element of the population. For these farmers in his mission area Father Simon had little use. A little of this was due to his disdain for their speech, which he called a jargon and despised for its lack of verb-inflections. But he charged them further with being often unable to read and write, more ignorant than any peasant in Europe, inferior indeed to the indigenous population, and for that reason often called " white Kaffirs "—which sounds like an echo of the education inspector who confided to him that no progress would be made till their children were compulsorily educated. It is more surprising to read his observation that they were not only rude and " bossy " in manner, but refused help to strangers and lied readily, and that their houses were dirty and miserable. Like most missionaries he complained of their treatment of the " blacks"; a century before they had been slave owners, and bad ones at that; they still treated their black servants in the same way, cheating them of their legal wages, talking of them as brutes without souls, worse than cattle.

Though he claimed that in his mission territory there were few exceptions to this description he added that he had heard that the Boers of the Transvaal and Orange Free State were not very much better. He attributed their lack of generous sentiments, however, to their brand of Calvinism.

It consists of reading some verses of the bible which they don't understand, and singing canticles in an appalling tone. Once a year at their Cena the minister tells them they are saints and must keep apart from other races and religions to avoid damnation. Especially they hate Catholicism, which they regard as the religion of anti-Christ.

Bearing in mind Father Simon's kindly observations on the English Protestants, and his willingness to believe well of the Calvinist Boers elsewhere, it is not easy to dismiss his testimony as mere prejudice.

He made converts among the Damaras, the Hottentots and the half-castes of the country, and they rarely apostatized. But they were culturally very different peoples. The Damaras lived in a fertile land and therefore had no liking for work. As they prac-tised circumcision and worshipped God by the name of Elo, he suspected they were of Jewish origin. The Hottentots showed much more energy, could fast long, but could eat hugely when opportunity came. Without aptitude for manual work or agriculture, they were experienced nomads with marvellous memories for country and skill in tracking animals, and generally in desert travel. For this reason they were especially troublesome to the German settlers north of the Orange river. He seems to have made little contact with Bushmen, who had, by his account, almost disappeared. But on the evidence of their pottery and paintings he supposed that they were more intelligent and cultured than the Hottentots, and, quoting Storr's account, that they only became savage when cruelly treated by the first colonists. His highest praise was kept for the coloureds, or half-breeds; physically and in every other way, as workers and as founders of families, they were the best type in the country; a lone testimony but not one to be cursorily rejected, for Father Simon was observant.

Teaching the faith to his converts and their children, teaching secular subjects in his schools, visiting the whole country committed to his care and the little groups of scattered Catholics were the normal occupations of Father Simon's life before and after his consecration in 1895 as bishop and vicar apostolic for what is now the diocese of Keimoes. In addition he had to turn his hand to other work. For two years he spent his spare time building a house for the sisters he brought to Pella, learning from an encyclopaedia and his mistakes. Another seven years went in building a church, quarrying and making the bricks, but for this he had the help of many amateurs. After making some experiments in water catchment and irrigation he discovered that he could grow vines at Pella, and was able to form a little settled community of about five hundred Catholics.

There were plenty of disappointments. A house of six rooms and some land were offered for sale at Springbok, but its owner, a Protestant minister, would not sell to Catholics. Through a third party, and a commission of over a thousand francs, Father Simon obtained the property, installed two sisters, a priest and a lay-brother and opened his school. But it succeeded so well that the government sent a Protestant teacher to the place and the Protestant children transferred to his school, leaving the Catholic classrooms nearly empty. One of the sisters opened another school at Matjeskloof, but as soon as it was flourishing she went back to Europe, and that venture had to close down till she could be replaced a year later.

Again and again in his memoir Father Simon has to record the departure of priest or brother or sister for reasons of health. Only about one in three, apparently, could stand the climate, and in each case the superiors at home had to be persuaded to risk the health of another young man or woman. Despite it all, by 1888, when the Holy Ghost Fathers abandoned the Prefecture of Cimbebasia, Father Simon was prepared to take over the area from the Orange river to the Tropic of Capricorn which had been offered to his Oblates of St Francis de Sales.

Here he ran into new difficulties, which were to some extent at least of his own making. In his memoir he reports as his opinion in the 'eighties that the English diplomats were blind to allow the Germans to make a settlement on this side of Africa because they would soon have the Transvaal and Orange republics in their economic grip. The people at the Cape, he says, sent agents to the disputed territory to bid for the support of the tribes, but it was too late, for the treaty between the two governments had already been made. One of the agents of the Cape was a merchant named Herridge who had traded for long in the territory, selling firearms as well as other goods to those who would buy; he was friendly with the Catholic missionaries, and became a convert, along with his family, in 1895. The situation was saved, in Father Simon's opinion, by Cecil Rhodes and his chartered company who kept an armed force in the corridor between the new German possessions and the northern republics.

These views, written in the memoirs, may not have been expressed publicly, but it would seem that they were known or guessed at. As soon as Great Namaqualand was entrusted to him by the Sacred Congregation, Father Simon visited the native chiefs to find out their attitude to religion. He found their " captain " Willem Christian at Warmbad and was met with a blank refusal of missionary work, on the ground that it would divide the tribe. The Oblates were French and from English territory, whereas Willem's people were Protestant and under German protection. Indeed, it was added, to permit them to found a mission would be against the tribes' treaty with the Germans.

Two years later Father Simon heard of a farm for sale in this area and re-opened his negotiations. This time Willem Christian brought in some Lutheran ministers as assessors, and they produced a report in *Salesian Annals*★ (by Father Simon) in which a Lutheran minister was ridiculed; such insults, they insisted, would not make for peace. Though poor Father Simon tried to explain that it was a joke and offered to apologize, Willem Christian put the tribal ban against Catholicism.

Roughly every two years Father Simon repeated his attempt, unsuccessfully, till in 1896 he was offered an immense property (stretching twenty-five miles from north to south) for 150,000 francs. The owner, Mr Wheeler, had obtained it from " Captain " Willem Christian, who granted him sovereign legislative rights over it, though the Germans would only acknowledge him as proprietor. The sale was finally arranged in 1898 for 125,000 francs and the tribal people immediately became respectful, especially when the missionaries sunk wells and made a reservoir. But the Lutheran missionaries still considered the German government as officially Protestant (and indeed Father Simon seems to have shared this belief) and appealed to them with confidence to eject the papists. They found, however, that the German military governor was himself a Catholic, and Bishop Simon (as he now was) was left in peace and could reckon on three established mission stations, Pella, Matjeskloof and Hierachabis (the new estate). But with that capacity for correcting his own habits and prejudices which is so marked in all his career, Bishop Simon urged on Rome that the area under German political rule should be formed into a separate prefecture and entrusted to the German province of the Oblates of St Francis de Sales. By 1906 he had obtained their consent[11] though it was not put into effect for another three years.

When the Congregation of the Holy Ghost gave up their mission field in South West Africa the northern part of it was offered to the Oblates of Mary Immaculate, who were in process of forming a German province. Though they were desirous of some such work there was considerable delay at Rome, and the brief establishing the

★ " Salesian " here is the adjective for the Oblates of St Francis de Sales, of whom Father Simon was one, and has nothing to do with the Salesians of St John Bosco. The Oblates of St Francis de Sales have charge of the diocese of Keimoes to this day.

Prefecture of Lower Cimbebasia, from the Tropic of Capricorn to the Kunene, from the Atlantic to Bechuanaland and the Transvaal, and entrusting this area to the Oblates of Mary Immaculate, was not published till 1892. Even after that step another four years elapsed before Father Schoch, the Prefect Apostolic of the Transvaal, was sent as the first Oblate to visit the new territory and plan the missionary work. At the end of six months he had completed his task, made friends with the German officials and sent the missionaries, two priests and a lay brother, who were to stay in the country. One of the difficulties which Bishop Simon had met was eliminated by sending German priests, but the delay of eight years had accentuated another. The Protestant Rhenish Missionaries, and later the Finnish, had already been working amongst the Hereros and Ovambos even in the time of Father Duparquet, and had persuaded the chiefs, as we have seen, to refuse facilities to Catholics. As an administrative measure the German colonial government decided to continue this arrangement and gave the Oblates permission to minister only to German Catholic settlers, of whom there were about five hundred, and indigenous groups where Protestant missions were not yet founded.

This restriction remained until after the Herreros rebelled against the Germans in 1904, and till then the strictly missionary work of the Oblates was limited to some coloured (half-breed) people at Windhoek and a group of Bechuanas who had left their own country in search of cultivatable land. As very few priests were yet available from the Oblate German province, and as money was scarcer even than personnel and travel very expensive, it may have been an advantage that the Catholic work was confined at first to these two localized but definite tasks. Certainly they were successful; the trade school established for the coloureds at Windhoek earned the respect and appreciation of the civil officials, and they were able to convert almost an entire village of Bechuanas at Aminuis. Meanwhile more priests were found for the mission, and in 1904 five German Franciscan nuns trained as nurses came to the country. At first they worked in the military hospital, but after the Herrero war they opened a Mission hospital at Windhoek. When general permission was given to preach the Catholic Faith there was a personnel ready with considerable experience of the country and some knowledge of the different tribes.

Chapter VII

THE NATAL VICARIATE: 1851–1903

I. Invitation to the Oblates

LACK of provision for the future could not be charged against Bishop Devereux's plan for forming a vicariate in Natal. He had persuaded Rome to entrust it to a religious order, and the necessary replacements of men and money should have followed as a matter of course. Bishop de Mazenod, the superior-general of the Oblates of Mary Immaculate, who accepted the task, sent Bishop Allard, two priests, a deacon who was to be priested after arrival, and a lay brother. The new vicar apostolic was not the first choice of his father-general, and was reluctant to undertake the work, and the consequent delay put off his arrival in the province till 15 March, 1852. In the interval, however, Father Murphy had spent seven months at Pietermaritzburg and Durban, had discovered several hundred Catholics and left the list of their names for the new bishop, had obtained a grant of land for him at Pietermaritzburg and the promise of another at Durban, and had persuaded the Catholics to collect a fund towards the building of a church.[1] In 1853 Bishop Devereux arranged a collection in all his churches for the new vicariate and gathered £163.[2] Father Hoenderwangers had been working for more than a year in Bloemfontein, and been given a site for a church by the British Government there, and Bishop Devereux promised to lend him to the Natal vicariate until he could be replaced.[3] The Colonial Secretary in London had given Bishop Allard introductions to the Governor of Cape Colony and the Lieutenant-Governor of Natal,[4] and the latter, after Father Murphy's negotiations, received the new bishop well and offered him protection.[5] Major Donovan and John Ford at Bloemfontein, Captain McDonnell and John Bird, all personal friends of Bishop Devereux, were willing to help, and the Catholics both at Durban and Pietermaritzburg gave him a warm welcome.[6] He said Mass after landing in the house of Mr

Edward Snell, a relatively wealthy citizen, who was three times mayor of Durban (in 1856, 1867 and 1868), whose wife was a Catholic, and who became treasurer for the fund to build a church in Durban.[7]

Before leaving France Bishop Allard had read in Father Murphy's report that drunkenness, debauchery and indifference were to be found among the nominal Catholics, and that in some cases of concubinage the parties were not free to marry. Perhaps for this reason, he wrote from Cape Town to Bishop Devereux asking him what the canonical position was and what was the practice.[8] Where the decree of the Council of Trent about clandestine marriages had not been published the Church recognized the validity of ceremonies which satisfied the civil requirements and did not positively exclude the Catholic concept of marriage. With regard to " mixed " marriages the bishop was obliged in conscience to insist on the Catholic upbringing of all children, but no single and universal method of doing so had yet been formulated. Bishop Allard could of course have discovered in Europe that the decree about clandestinity had not been published in South Africa, but it may have been wise for him to verify the fact, and in any case to learn the practice of the neighbouring vicariates. Devereux's reply was quite clear. The Tridentine decree had not been published, he explained, but the clergy were told to do what they could to secure that the marriages of Catholics should be civilly recognized. This was now the case if they were celebrated before a priest and two witnesses, if they were registered, and if a copy was sent to the civil authority. Mr Bird in Pietermaritzburg would get the bishop a copy of the law. The Congregation of Propaganda had never given a rule on mixed marriages for South Africa.

Some bishops get a promise from the husband of liberty for the wife to practise her religion and to bring up the children as Catholics. If I tried to insist on it here I shouldn't obtain it, and even if I obtained the promise (as has sometimes happened), I have always found that this written promise acted as a temptation to the husband to do the contrary, especially in this Colony where such a promise is not legal. So I prefer to ground my decision on the character and disposition of the Catholic party. If I have not a good opinion of the faith of the Catholic party I refuse to marry them. In the contrary case, if I judge in her a firm faith, I do not hesitate to marry them, not even where it is the woman who is Catholic, and experience proves that we gain by this practice in this vicariate. For in general the zealous wife succeeds in bringing her husband to the true fold. In the other case I try to dissuade the Catholic party, but in a colony like this one can scarcely act rigorously, as the parties can renounce the faith and marry in the Protestant Church.[9]

Bishop Devereux clearly knew the canon law and the discretion it allowed him to exercise, and employed it with a prudent care of the circumstances and consequences. In that letter he had not referred to the Protestant ceremony which was customary and even perhaps obligatory in the case of a mixed marriage. He sent this supplementary information a month or two later: " When I approve a mixed marriage I allow the Catholic to appear before the Protestant minister, but make it clear to the Catholic that it is only a legal form and not religious ".[10]   But Bishop Allard was not satisfied, and put the objection to Bishop Devereux: " If the Protestant minister makes it a service, isn't this allowing idolatry?"[11] In reply he received a lengthy and patient historical explanation of the position:

The Irish penal law made it a felony for a Catholic priest to marry a Catholic and a Protestant until they were first married by a Protestant minister. In England until very recently it was invalid unless celebrated by a Protestant minister. Hence by necessity arose the custom of going to the Protestant church, and the bishops did not scruple to give a dispensation. Others held (as Protestants did) that it was a mere civil ceremony and there was no necessity for a dispensation. That was the case when I left Ireland. Since that time the Government has introduced civil marriage (as in Ireland), and that alters things. When I came to the Colony the civil tribunal was in existence, and this did away with the difficulty. Since then the law has changed and difficulties increased. According to the practice of England and Ireland the parties could go to the minister, but I never considered it a safe rule on this point, and I don't think it was the intention of the Congregation. I ought to have explained that I tolerate it as *minus malum;* the greater evil would be apostasy. I don't use a censure against them. I did not mean I advise, but on the contrary I try to make them content with the Catholic marriage which is legal and valid here.[12]

To the specific objection of Bishop Allard he replies very shortly: "We must make a wide distinction between Protestants here. Some hold marriage to be a civil ceremony, some religious. I would regard it as they do and apply the principle."[13]

Bishop Devereux then added one point of some interest. The Congregation of Propaganda, repeating the decisions of the Holy Office, had insisted, against the suggestions of missionaries in many parts of the world, that Protestant marriages and pagan marriages were valid in themselves, and the intention of single and perpetual union must be presumed since it is natural to the human race—even though the social custom may allow divorce or polygamy. The exception they made was when conditions against the essential character of marriage were positively introduced into the ceremony, and in two rescripts they had given as examples a Calvinist practice of reading the text Matthew 5. 32 or 19. 9, or Hebrews 13. 4, on which they based their practice of dissolving marriages when adultery was proved.[14] Bishop Devereux clearly had this in mind when he added to his letter:

> Marriages where there is no clause *contra essentiam matrimonii* I take to be valid. But where there is, as in the Dutch Reformed Church, where the intention is 'as long as faithful and then divorce', it is invalid.[15]

To make the whole position absolutely clear he then enumerated his practice point by point in every case, even to requiring both parties who are married in a Dutch Reformed church to affirm publicly that they regard the marriage as binding for life in all circumstances.[16]

II. *The New Vicariate*

Bishop Allard's desire to be clear on the questions about matrimony was reasonable, since the matter was important. But it is not so easy to understand his attitude to the limits of his vicariate. The indications in the brief of appointment were vague because Rome had not very clear information about the political situation or even the geography, and he appears to have been told that he must in time supply this. Bishop Devereux explained that he had merely indicated the " Keya on the West, the Portuguese possessions on the East, the Tropics in the North" and quoted a letter of the Congregation of Propaganda to show that this was the intention of the brief.[17] He had told them too that "later you would probably ask for a new division".

Even before his arrival in Natal Bishop Allard began to worry about the Portuguese at Delagoa Bay, because he had formed the opinion they were in schism, and on his reading of the brief they appeared to come under his jurisdiction.[18] Bishop Devereux replied that he did not think the few priests in Portuguese territory were in schism, but that he knew very little about them; he made it clear that they were excluded from the Natal vicariate he had suggested. This opinion was confirmed by a letter from the Congregation dated 1 November, 1851, but received by Bishop Allard shortly after his arrival in Natal in the following spring. It stated that Bishop Griffith had been consulted and thought that the new vicariate should not include Portuguese possessions. However, Bishop Allard was to consult the other vicars apostolic before making definite suggestions. But Bishop Allard was not satisfied. Despite the work for the Catholics of Pietermaritzburg, Durban and Bloemfontein which was keeping his priests busy, despite the clamant need of a mission to the Zulus which Bishop Devereux had urged on his attention, he told Father Sabon at Durban to make enquiries about the state of religion at Delagoa Bay.

That was early in 1854, and during that and the following year Father Sabon collected information and rumours. There were fairly frequent three-day passages by boat to Delagoa Bay, which was three hundred miles distant, and the number of Catholics was said to be five hundred.[19] On this the bishop sent a letter to a priest he had heard of in the Portuguese colony, asking again about the spiritual jurisdiction of Delagoa Bay.[20] No reply appears to have been received, but the rumours reached the Congregation in Rome, perhaps indirectly from Bishop Allard himself. In 1862 Cardinal Barnabò, who had succeeded Franzoni as Prefect of Propaganda, sent Bishop Allard faculties for the four hundred Catholics said to be at Delagoa Bay, "although they were outside the limits of the Natal vicariate".

It is not easy to understand why the bishop had not by this time obtained the true facts of the Delagoa situation, or why he could

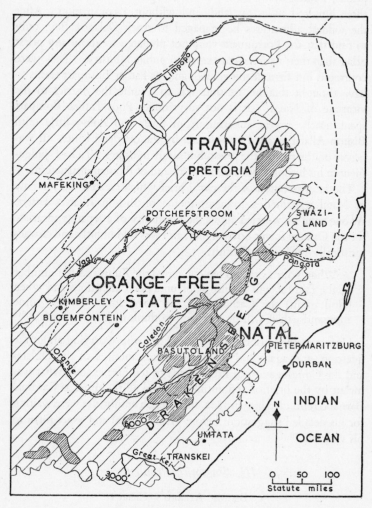

3. THE ORIGINAL VICARIATE OF NATAL

not have waited until one of the occasional boat passages was available. In fact, after waiting almost a year, he sent one of his priests, Father Bompart, on foot through the almost unexplored three hundred miles by land, and without a companion. After the wildest adventures he managed to reach Delagoa Bay, only to find that the Portuguese were not prepared to allow any priest other than their nationals to exercise a public ministry. They were courteous but firm in this refusal, and, as Father Bompart seems to have thought that his mission was to " unite the district to the vicariate of Natal ", it is not surprising. Poor Father Bompart spent nearly a year suffering from fever and doing little until Bishop Allard recalled him—again by the overland route. It was heroic on the part of the priest, but surely indicates a lack of judgement in his bishop—both of his work and of Roman instructions.

The interpretation of the papal brief which created the vicariate of Natal remained a frequent theme of Bishop Allard's letters. At one time he worried about the possibility of a separate vicariate for the Orange River Sovereignty, and was told bluntly and characteristically by Bishop Griffith:

> When your Lordship has converted the Zulus and the number of the faithful will require your undivided attentions and when (God grant) the Catholics of the Sovereignty number some thousands, then will be the time to think of a new vicariate.[21]

Unfortunately Bishop Allard could not stop worrying about the question, and again and again asked the canonists of the Oblates and the Congregation of Propaganda to tell him exactly what was meant by the brief of appointment. And all the time, as Cardinal Barnabò reminded him in 1862, the Roman authorities were waiting for his detailed suggestions before giving a final and exact form to his vicariate.[22]

III. Pastoral Problems

1. Bishop Allard's Clergy

The only English-speaking priest of his party, among those who accompanied Bishop Allard to Natal, Father Dunne, wanted to leave the Oblate congregation as soon as he saw Natal, and so had to be sent back to Europe. Though about a third of the Catholics in Durban were French-speaking when the bishop arrived, the proportion elsewhere was much smaller, and until the priests became fluent in English their work was naturally much restricted. The bishop thought it easy enough to learn, and assured the father-general of the Oblates that he had done so in four months, but as he was still accusing himself of the reception of letters some years later his standards cannot have been very high. It may be that this accounts for the lack of cordiality in his relations with the official and military groups, despite his excellent introductions and the presence of Mr Bird at Pietermaritzburg. All negotiations seem to have been conducted by correspondence, and he was much less successful than his colleagues at Cape Town and Grahamstown in obtaining salaries for priests who acted as chaplains. Though he forced himself and his priests to drink tea instead of wine because it was "the English way", they wouldn't eat or drink in the houses of the Catholics they visited.[23]   And it looks as though they did not visit other houses at all, so that the opportunities for English conversation must have been few.

The plan of Bishop Allard for his work seems to have been different from that of the other vicars apostolic. At first he kept his priests with him in Pietermaritzburg and prepared to build a house large enough also for those who would join him later. Only the insistence of the Catholics at Durban persuaded him to allow Father Sabon to live there (despite Father Sabon's difficulty in learning English the bishop would only allow Father Logegaray to go and help him very occasionally); and he left that zealous priest to struggle as best he could with a somewhat quarrelsome congregation[24] and, after 1860, with the fifty Catholics among the Indian labourers whom the Government had brought to the sugar-cane farms.

There was at first a shortage of priests, but not more so than when the other vicariates had been started. Indeed, Bishop Allard refused to accept the services of the Belgian Father van Caulewaert, who wanted to be transferred to Natal.[25] Though this may have been wise, for Bishop Devereux had already found him difficult to work with, Bishop Allard reported to the superior-general of his congregation: " I did not want to introduce other than Oblates ".[26]

This may be the explanation of his somewhat strange treatment of Father Hoenderwangers. The latter was doing remarkable work in the Orange River territory. At Bloemfontein, Faure-smith, Smithfield and Harrismith he collected Catholic congrega-tions and obtained the grant or promise of sites for churches;[27] he visited as far as the villages across the Vaal river;[28] at times he taught the Catholic children, both white and black, where he was trying to establish a mission;[29] and above all he established friendly relations both with the English garrison, when it was maintained, and with the Dutch government which replaced it. Of course, the work cost money and the collections of his tiny congregations were insufficient; though he begged for and obtained help from the priests he knew in the Eastern Province and at the Cape (to the reasonable annoyance of Bishop Griffith), he had to ask the Vicar Apostolic of Natal to pay the debts incurred on each new venture. " He ask money " or " he ask more money " was Bishop Allard's frequent summary of the letters of Father Hoenderwangers. But the latter had been keeping himself on gifts made either by his family or by his monastery, and naturally enough they called a halt; so that at the end of 1855 he told Bishop Allard that he would have to go home if not given a subsistence allowance of £50 a year[30]

Bishop Allard made the grant at once, but the curious thing is that he had not troubled, during the past three years of correspon-dence, to ask Father Hoenderwangers how he was keeping himself alive. It is even stranger that for the first ten years of his vicariate the bishop did not make a complete visitation of these scattered missions, and only did so in 1862, and met Father Hoenderwangers for the first time, after Bishop de Mazenod had written firmly about his episcopal duty.

2. MISSION TO THE ZULUS

It was more than three years after his first arrival in Natal before Bishop Allard opened his first mission to the Zulus.[31] It is difficult to see any good reason for this long delay. There was of course the need to learn the Zulu language, but only in 1854 did he send two of his priests, Father Barret and Father Gerard, to pick it up as best they could by living in a native kraal. Besides the gentle reminders of Bishop Devereux about the purpose of the Natal vicariate, and Governor Pine's expressed wish for a Catholic mission to the natives,[32] there was the desire of Bishop de Mazenod, the superior-general of the Oblates, of which Bishop Allard was well aware,[33] to hear that such work had commenced. It may be that Father Murphy's kindly work of preparation for the coming of the Oblates, his forming of a nucleus congregation of Europeans in Pietermaritzburg and Durban, was too well done. Certainly the new vicar apostolic set himself and his priests to building up these congregations as though the situation in Natal was the same as it had been in the Cape Province. Six months after his arrival he could write to a friend in France, " We have to minister to Catholics first ".[34] He was far from optimistic about native missions in his first report to Bishop de Mazenod,[35] and this because of their lack of civilization and, in particular, their nudity, " about which ", he said, " the government does nothing ".[36] But in his second report, a year later, he thought differently: " I often think my chief work should be for the Kaffirs. The Protestants say their missions are sterile. . . . The Kaffirs have no religion." The patience of the superior-general may have been somewhat strained; at the least it must be said that Bishop Allard was very slow in summing up a situation, and it is not surprising that there are traces of holy impatience in some of the superior-general's later letters.

The general told him plainly in 1857 that he was not doing the work he had been given, and this severe judgement is not contradicted by the evidence of his own correspondence. It suggests, too, some reasons for the failure. On several occasions his preoccupation was with the exact sense of his instructions when he might more profitably have used his discretion; Bishop de Mazenod had given him all possible powers within his religious obedience, while Bishop Devereux had reminded him more than once that Rome left a lot to the prudence of vicars apostolic. He often seems to have expected opposition from the English officials, and was always fearful that the Dutch in the Orange River State hated all Catholics; so that he could not adopt the attitude of Bishop Griffith and Bishop Devereux to the one group, or accept the assurances of Father Hoenderwangers about the other. And he was reluctant, seemingly, to make all the use he might of the work of that vigorous priest because he found it difficult to work with those not of his own congregation. All of these were temperamental qualities, of course, rather than defects of character, but not helpful to the pioneer work he had been assigned.

Here, as always in historical estimates, there is the danger that our documentation is incomplete. Because of his austere spirituality he won and kept the devotion of Father Gerard, who was a very great missionary;[37] his advice was sought and used by Bishop Ricards, an intelligent and thrusting ecclesiastical ruler, before inaugurating his own work for the conversion of the pagans. The quality they recognized in Bishop Allard, whatever it was, may explain why he was able apparently to change the whole approach to his problems when in 1862 he penetrated with Father Gerard into the country of the Basutos.

The work of Bishop Allard in Basutoland during the last fifteen years of his twenty-two years as vicar apostolic is the subject of a later section of this book. The striking contrast between the first ten years of his vicariate, in the 'fifties, and the second, in the 'sixties, is a contrast between his work in Basutoland and that elsewhere. The hesitant, scrupulous and almost timorous Bishop Allard became a different man when he crossed the Drakensberg mountains. Nor did he change his old attitude to his European problem. The discovery of diamonds at Kimberley in 1867 brought a rush of miners, many of them Catholics, to that part of his vicariate. He sent priests to visit them, and in 1871 arranged for one to stay in the camps. But it was apparently not till two years later that he went to see for himself the work which was being done or could be done. And meanwhile he was still asking the Congregation of Propaganda about the interpretation of the limits of his vicariate. Perhaps it was this appearance of scruple, perhaps it was consideration for his age (for he was by then nearing seventy), which made them suggest that he should resign.[38] Bishop Jolivet, who succeeded him in 1874, was instructed from Rome not to shut himself up in Basutoland as his predecessor had done. But for all that the present Catholic culture of the Basutos, including a third of the whole nation, owes a great deal to Bishop Allard.

IV. Bishop Jolivet

Charles Constant Jolivet, successor to Bishop Allard, landed at Port Natal on 4 March 1875, and was Vicar Apostolic of Natal till his death on 15 September 1903. A Breton, short and spare, he had been regarded as lazy and light-minded when he first entered the novitiate of the Oblates of Mary Immaculate, and all his days he was fond of puns and jokes. But his ability had been recognized early; after ten years as rector of the Oblate parish in Liverpool, he had been employed as visitor of the Canadian province and as one of the assistants to the father-general of the society. In that post Father Jolivet knew at first hand both the reports of Bishop Allard on his work and the complaints of many of the Catholics of Natal that they had been neglected.

After a fortnight in Durban the new bishop went on to Pieter-maritzburg, the capital of the province. A couple of months there gave him time to meet the governor, the magistrates and some dignitaries of the Anglican Church, to found a convent of nuns of the Holy Family, fourteen of whom had travelled with him from France, to celebrate the Easter liturgy and to ordain a deacon who had been one of six Oblate companions on his voyage. On 28 May he set out by horse-wagon for Bloemfontein and Kimberley. Without great exaggeration it could be said that Charles Jolivet was travelling around his vicariate for the next twenty-five years, either on horseback, in post-carts or in wagons, and even increasing age—he was in his fiftieth year when he began this work—did not bring much diminution of his activity.

These journeys, however, were not like the "visitations" of Bishop Griffith, a method of bringing the sacraments to isolated Catholic groups. In most cases Bishop Jolivet was enquiring where he could suitably build a church, or more often a school, and fairly often he had purchased a plot of land, or, later, engaged teachers and arranged for a visiting or resident priest before he had left the neighbourhood. His predecessor had bequeathed him the missions of Durban, Pietermaritzburg and Bloemfontein and two stations in Basutoland. Within a few years Bishop Jolivet had doubled the number of priests, established nuns in four convents, opened some half-dozen elementary schools and started a college for boys and three high schools for girls. The schools founded in Natal during his vicariate alone form the record of his travels: Pietermaritzburg, Durban, Newcastle, Ladysmith, Estcourt, Oakford, Mount Edgecombe, Kokstad, Cala, Umtata, Mariannhill, Centocow, Lourdes, Mariazell, Reichenau, Mariathal, Oetting, Maria Trost, St Michael, Maria Ratschitz, Emoyeni.[39] In addition to these there were the foundations he had made in the vicariate of Kimber-ley and the prefectures of the Transvaal and Basutoland before arranging for the separation of these ecclesiastical areas from the old Natal vicariate, at Bloemfontein, Pretoria, Kimberley and other places. In 1899 the *Natal Mercury*, summarizing his labours, said that Bishop Jolivet had built ninety churches and chapels, eighty-two schools and fourteen convents, orphanages and hospitals; had raised the number of his clergy from six to one hundred and fourteen, and had brought two hundred and eighty-four lay brothers and nine hundred nuns to South Africa.[40] It is Charles Jolivet, and not Bishop Allard, who should be regarded as the effective founder of the Catholic communities north of the Orange river, with the exception, perhaps, of Basutoland, where the influence of Bishop Allard, already acknowledged, played a great part.

None of these schools or mission stations would have survived without hard work by the priests and nuns whom Bishop Jolivet sent to them. And in some cases the labour was really heroic; Father Mathieu spent years in the Oakford district with hardly any pecuniary resources, living on mealies for the most part, travelling from kraal to kraal, or round the sugar farms, sometimes on horse-back, often on foot, learning the Zulu language by living with Zulus. The lives of such men were far harder than that of the bishop, but his constant travels showed him what he could ask of them, enabled him to spend what funds he had to the best advantage, and made sure that the expenditure of men and money was not wasted.

V. The Division of the Vicariate

The remarkable quality in a man of Bishop Jolivet's active and masterly temperament is that he was ready to hand over any part of his charge as soon as the opportunity came for it to be done more effectively by another. In Rome at the end of 1874, before leaving for Africa, he had asked for a clarification of the bull about the limits of Natal, and had suggested the Zambesi as its northern boundary. Within eighteen months of arriving in Africa he had grasped the impossibility of the task he had given himself and recommended that the area from the Limpopo northwards to the Zambesi should be made a separate prefecture or vicariate,[41] and that the territory west of the Vaal should be similarly with-drawn from his jurisdiction. His first plan was that his own congregation should supply the missionaries to work north of the Limpopo, and he wrote in this sense to his superior-general.[42] The latter was not able to supply priests at the time, and Bishop Jolivet readily agreed to Cardinal Simeoni's suggestion that the area should be given to the English Jesuits. At the same time he agreed to the Holy Ghost Fathers taking over the territory west of the Transvaal and the Harts river.[43] Bishop Ricards and Bishop Leonard had separately recommended these divisions before the boundaries of the Natal vicariate had been decided; canonically it was now a matter for Bishop Jolivet and the Cardinal Prefect. But when Father Weld, the English Jesuit Provincial, wanted to take over the Transvaal, Bishop Jolivet, though reluctant, discussed the pros and cons with him; after it had been made a prefecture for the Oblates he insisted that matters should be left as they were.[44]

One of the reasons put forward by Bishop Jolivet for the division of his vicariate had been economy. The long journeys necessary for its supervision were a heavy expense, and much of it would be saved if the units were smaller. On one occasion, however, writing about the Transvaal, he put this argument another way. Cardinal Simeoni had supposed that his difficulty was to obtain Oblate priests for the work; it was not men who were unobtainable, he replied, for the superior-general had never refused his requests for them; it was money that was lacking.[45] He supposed apparently that the congregation would find funds for new vicariates without restricting their grant to Natal. And the same might be true of the great Society for the Propagation of the Faith, whose headquarters at Lyons had been the largest benefactor of all to the missionary work in South Africa since its beginning. Bishop Jolivet, having been a parish priest in Liverpool, knew the value of a second collection.

The curia of the Oblate father-general, however, took a different view. In their minutes they observed that Bishop Jolivet's new foundations meant so many debts which the Kimberley vicariate and the Transvaal prefecture must meet in the future. Though the Oblate Congregation were not legally responsible, they would be so morally, and would be held so by the Roman authorities. Indeed, as the vicariates were accepted by them first, and on their presentation given to one of their fathers, they had the right to be consulted before large debts were incurred, and with regard to the division of resources. All this was made clear by a visitor of the congregation when he met Bishop Jolivet and his council in 1888.[46] In consequence the Transvaal was allotted the lion's share in the division of the resources (the " Viaticum "), despite the bishop's protest, which he wrote into the *procès verbale*.

VI. A Period of Expansion

At this time the debt of the Natal vicariate was £7,500, and the bishop had to promise not to start new works without leave of his council. Unlike Bishops Grimley and Ricards, however, he does not appear to have worried unduly about this situation; though the council cut down his estimates and plans occasionally in future years, it looks as though he had foreseen the likelihood of this and was able, with a little delay, to carry through the work he intended. In 1895 the debt was £10,000, on which the interest only amounted to £500 a year, a considerably lower rate than that paid by Bishop Ricards; and the visitor of that year expressed himself as satisfied by the bishop's promise of reducing it.[47] And in all probability this was reasonable; Charles Jolivet's constant activity gave him a detailed knowledge of the conditions of every part of his vicariate, and when he made a foundation it was likely to be successful, to repay the debt he incurred and to become a centre of Catholic life and a source of income for more pious works. Of all the schools and hospitals and orphanages established by him, under the care of nuns of the Holy Family, of Loreto, of the Holy Cross Sisters, of Augustinian Canonesses, only one school failed so badly as to be a financial burden to his successor.*

The father visitor of the Oblates told Bishop Jolivet in 1895 that zeal for the African missions was dying out among the scholastics preparing for priesthood because the missionaries were being used to look after a few Europeans.[48] It was of course an exaggeration. Three new centres had been founded in Basutoland before it passed to the Orange vicariate. There were Oblates working among the Zulus and the Indians in Natal, and when a whole community of Bantu from Portuguese East Africa settled on the Bluff south of Durban, Bishop Jolivet sent them first Father Zimmermann, a secular priest, and later Father Bryant, a former

* See Chapter XIII.

Trappist, only because he had no Oblates available.[49] He had founded missions, too, at Kokstad and Umtata, and schools for native children in several places. But it was true that a disproportionate number of the bishop's foundations, schools and hospitals, were for the whites, and he intended asking the Congregation of Propaganda to create separate prefectures of Kaffraria and Zululand.[50]

He could, however, reasonably have answered the criticism by pointing to the missionary work of the Trappists. When they were a broken and quarrelsome community he had welcomed them in his vicariate and after one rapid glance had recognized their possibilities for missionary work. After a short experience he had seen the virtues of the difficult Prior Franz and confirmed him as abbot, leaving him free to follow his own methods and allowing him to bring out for work among Bantu women some young ladies who later became a community of religious. Complaints about the Trappists and quarrels amongst them did not cease. Partly these were due to Prior Franz's habit of regarding canon law, as Bishop Delalle was to say later, as written *in scrinio pectoris*. To protect the Trappists in the work they did well and at the same time save them from their blunders, the vicar apostolic needed prudence of no mean order and ability to distinguish what was of importance.

It is a pity that Bishop Jolivet did not use the idiomatic vigour of his drafts for letters in his pastorals. Their rather flat language may be because they were first thought in French; though thoroughly at home in English conversation, he may not have trusted his pen when it came to a lengthy public exposition of doctrine. And the same explanation may account for the failure of his efforts to establish a Catholic journal; in the 'eighties he started a *Monthly Record*, and again in 1902 the *Catholic South Africa*, but neither lasted more than two or three years. His priests were mainly French, and none of them had the flair for journalism of Dr Kolbe and those who helped him at the Cape.

But it would be unjust to suggest that Bishop Jolivet's success was limited to matters of immediate government. In any case the Roman authorities drew his attention on several occasions to the long-term effects of his policy. Particularly they did so in regard to two matters—mixed marriages between Catholics and Protestants, and the acceptance of a colour-bar in Catholic institutions;

the one might easily lead to indifferentism and the other to a loss of Catholicism itself.

In regard to mixed marriages Bishop Jolivet urged his case, that the rules of avoiding them should not be made more severe, by an analysis of those of ten years of his episcopate. There had been eighty-eight in the ordinary sense, a marriage before a priest, and twenty-one before a civil official or a Protestant minister (which was valid but illicit in the canon law of the time). Of the eighty-eight the promises about the religion of the children had not been kept in eleven cases only. Five of the Catholic parties had apostatized, but the number of converts in the other cases was larger. Even out of the twenty-one who had married "outside the Church", some five or six had brought up their children as Catholics. In some cases, the bishop concluded, the result of these "mixed" marriages in towns (with a local Catholic community) was good, and their families were most religious. It was a defence difficult to fault, but possible only to a bishop who was well acquainted with the lives of his scattered flock.

He adopted a similar method in answering the complaint about schools, which was a double one, that non-Catholic children were admitted to the high schools and that a racial division was adopted. The bishop opened his reply with a list of his fifty schools, the number of their pupils, Catholic and non-Catholic, the races to which they belonged, and the teachers, almost always religious, employed. He admitted that 768 out of the 3,076 children were non-Catholics, and that these were taken to their own churches by one of their number or by their parents. Religious disputes among the children were forbidden, and the parents of non-Catholics usually forbade their attendance at religious instruction; at Umtata and Kokstad, however, under the Holy Cross Sisters, it was given to all pupils. He claimed that the results were good, and led to the break down of prejudice against the Catholic faith.[51]

With regard to the racial question the bishop pointed out that though a small fee was charged in parish schools and the government gave a subsidy, the schools for Indians and Bantu were supported mostly by the alms of Europeans, whose wishes had to be respected. Consequently there was, generally speaking, a racial separation in the schools, and this was necessary at least for teaching language, but he had secured that the coloured were usually admitted to the white schools. He claimed to be gradually and prudently eliminating the colour-bar feeling. All churches were of course open to Indian and Bantu as well as coloured and whites, but the former still needed in places their own churches where sermons and devotions could be in their own language.[52]

No corrective instructions seem to have been sent from Rome in either case. Whether Bishop Jolivet could have done more to remove the evils which he tolerated is of course arguable, but he made a solid defence of his policy and the large development of Catholicism in Natal during his vicariate is an added justification.

Chapter VIII

THE BOER REPUBLICS

I. The Orange Free State

ONE of the two great areas of Catholic expansion in South Africa in the last quarter of the nineteenth century was that which included the Boer republics between the Orange and Limpopo rivers. In this case the missionary priests and nuns followed on the heels of the immigrant miners, although the way had been prepared by the Premonstratensian Father Hoenderwangers. For ten years Father Hoenderwangers had visited Catholics in Bloemfontein, Bethulie, Fauresmith, Plattberg, Harrismith, Glendover, Thaba Nchu, Vlakfontein, Rouxville and Potchefstroom; he bought a house at Bloemfontein which he used as chapel and school and a site at Smithfield.[1] Then in 1869, when the rush of diggers began to the Vaal River Territory, where diamonds had been found, this energetic priest had both his legs broken in a wagon accident and returned to his native Belgium. Bishop Allard, who had left to him practically all the mission work of the Vicariate of Natal outside Basutoland, Durban and Pietermaritzburg, now sent first Father Le Bihan and then Father Bompart to Bloemfontein. The former soon went across the Vaal to the Boer Republic of Potchefstroom and the latter to the diggers first at Klip Drift, where Barkly West now stands, and then to the " New Rush " fields, where the new town was named Kimberley in 1875. There were already some five thousand and soon ten thousand Europeans at work, as well as three times that number of Bantu, and Bishop Allard accepted Father Bompart's enterprise, naming him the missionary for the area. Father Hidien had succeeded Father Bompart at Bloemfontein but found that most of his Catholics had packed up and gone to the diggings; without delay the priest followed them and established himself in what is today the town of Beaconsfield.

The missionaries set up temporary churches of canvas and soon found about a thousand Catholics, largely Irish, in the area. When fever, probably typhus, began to make ravages, in the winter of 1871, Father Hidien made himself nurse, and even physician, and put up a tent hospital at Du Toits Pan; he fell a victim of the fever in November. His place was now taken by Father Le Bihan, who built a couple of wood and iron churches and started some rudimentary schools for the children.

In these early years there was little planning because no one believed that the diamonds or the population would continue for long. Bishop Allard resigned, and Bishop Jolivet, in a rapid six months tour of his vicariate, partly on horseback and partly by wagon, reorganized it completely. Much of the activity of his early years in South Africa was devoted to the Orange Free State and the diamond fields to the west. By the good grace of the government of the Orange Republic he obtained a site for a convent at Bloemfontein, had it built, and sent four sisters of the Holy Family to open a school there in January 1877; it did much to break down the prejudice against Catholics, and President Brand sent one of his nieces to be educated there. In the diamond fields the bishop saw that the time for makeshift work was over; Fathers Le Bihan and Bompart were sent back to Basutoland, and Fathers Walsh and Lenoir, who had worked with the new bishop in England, were left to organize and build.

Their task was not too difficult, because the Catholics were generous. In 1871 the churches in the Eastern Vicariate had given a collection to enable Father Hidien to do his work in the diamond fields, but in 1878 Father Walsh was able to build a stone convent for the Sisters of the Holy Family in Kimberley and, despite storms and accidents, Father Lenoir had his church in Kimberley ready by the end of 1880. By that year Bishop Jolivet was able to report to the Congregation of Propaganda that this Orange River and diamond fields area, the Republic and Griqualand West which was annexed to Cape Colony, had more Catholics and more Catholic oeuvres than Natal and the Transvaal combined.[2]

Gold was found in Lydenburg and Potgietersrust in 1874, and prospectors began to move across the Vaal, though it was not till 1884, with the finds, first at Barberton and later on the Witwatersrand, that the real rush began. Money was reasonably plentiful at the " diggings ", and the Catholic population were mainly of Irish origin, the people among whom the bishop had worked successfully in Liverpool; it was a field where his activities and talents would have found the material specially suited to them. Yet those were two of the reasons, the *oeuvres* and the Irish, which he urged again and again as demanding the erection in this area of a new vicariate which should be placed under an Irish vicar apostolic.[3]

Bishop Allard had been excessively scrupulous about the interpretation of the brief erecting his vicariate. In its original form the limits given were indeed unintelligible, perhaps because of some error by the drafting *minutante* in Rome, but the bishop considered that his mission probably ended twenty leagues beyond Potchefstroom and accordingly forbade Father Hoenderwangers any further penetration.[4] The same instruction was probably given to Father Le Bihan in 1870. This priest, however, having found more than a hundred Catholics around Potchefstroom, succeeded, with the help of some Portuguese officials on a mission to the Republic, in gaining legal freedom for Catholic worship from the *Volksraad* and a plot of ground for a church from the President. Charles Jolivet adopted a wider interpretation of the limits of his vicariate,[5] and at once sent Father Walsh to Pilgrim's Rest and Lydenburg to found missions. When the English annexed the Transvaal, in 1877, the bishop went to the capital, Pretoria, and obtained grants of land from Shepstone, the acting governor. He then left Father Walsh to build a convent and school and in the following year installed there the five Loreto nuns whom he had persuaded to leave Ireland for South Africa. The energy of Bishop Jolivet made communities of the scattered Catholic immigrants of this part of his vicariate.

The Orange River Republic was firmly established, and, though the English government had with some legal chicanery claimed the diamond fields as a crown colony, its communications linked it with Bloemfontein, and this was also true of Basutoland. These political and economic considerations were put forward by Bishop Jolivet to support his proposal for a separate vicariate in these areas.[6] Even after 1880, when Kimberley and its district were formally annexed to the Cape Province, he continued to urge this regrouping. The Catholics there were, as he pointed out, mainly Irish and it would be well for them to have a vicar apostolic of their own nationality.[7] At the back of his mind there may have been the awareness, to which he refers in other letters,[8] that he himself was very grateful for the liberty and assistance given him by the English officials, an attitude not shared at the time by Irishmen in South Africa.

II. The Transvaal

When Bishop Jolivet first came to Natal the country north of Parys and the Vaal—the Transvaal—was also a Boer republic, and the bishop suggested that this also should be separated from his vicariate, as a prefecture. But after its annexation by Theophilus Shepstone in 1879 and the friendliness of the English governor he asked that the missions there should be left in his charge for the time being.

This was not due to his loyalty to British rule, or to dislike of the Calvinist politics of the Boers, but to a doubt about the viability of the Transvaal as an independent republic. In 1880 he sent a letter to Bishop Ricards urging him to write to the papers in favour of British rule:

If the Boers had stood for their independence when Shepstone annexed them I would have admired their pluck, and Shepstone would never have used violence. They had neither the wish nor the means to do so, but welcomed annexation to save them from the Kaffirs. Now the British have done that they want their independence back. The British rule is really tolerant in the colonies, but the O.F.S. have just re-enacted a law excluding Catholics from all government. If the English retired now it would be a breach of faith for those who trusted her.[9]

It came as a surprise to him when the revolt of the Transvaalers was successful,[10] and they captured him with his friend the English Major Marshall Clarke at Potchefstroom at the end of 1880. He could recognize their good qualities—excellent as cavalry, his comment in one letter, shows sound judgment in one accustomed to the formal tactics of French and all European mounted troops of the time—and he liked the appreciation one Boer gave him of his sermon to their Catholic prisoners: " you preached the Christian faith ". But he still urged the Roman authorities not to erect the Transvaal into a prefecture, partly because of the fluctuation of its Catholic residents with the vicissitudes of gold-mining, partly because he believed the British would have to annex the area again in time. The Congregation of Propaganda did not agree.

with his reasoning, but many would say that Bishop Jolivet's prognosis was correct, and that the Anglo-Boer war of the end of the century, and its outcome, were inevitable from the end of the 'seventies.

After the Boer rising of 1879–80, he pointed out that two-thirds of the Catholics had left the Transvaal with the British government.[11] However, the discoveries of gold at Barberton and De Kaap in 1884 brought a new flood of immigrants from Kimberley, and later from overseas, and there was every likelihood that they would be able to support Catholic schools and churches. On this advice the Congregation of Propaganda took action, and a papal bull of 4 June 1886 created both the vicariate of the Orange Free State, to include that republic and Basutoland and the Kimberley district, and the prefecture of the Transvaal, to include the lands of the South African Republic. The vicariate was entrusted to Bishop Anthony Gaughren, an Irishman whose name Bishop Leonard of the Cape had also put forward (along with two others) as a co-adjutor for himself.[12] Father Monginoux, also an Oblate of Mary Immaculate, was appointed prefect of the Transvaal.

Money was soon available in the diamond and gold fields. In 1889 Bishop Gaughren was able to open an orphanage in Kimberley, conducted by the Nazareth House sisters whom he brought from Cardinal Wiseman's institute in London; the De Beer's company contributed £2,000 for the building, the town council gave generously, and the citizens were constant in their support. The following year the bishop bought a farm at Clocolan in the Free State for £1,800 and built on it a college for boys to be directed, like St Charles's in Pietermaritzburg, by his own Oblate priests. Seven years later he was able to persuade the Irish Christian Brothers to open their boys' school in Kimberley itself. More expensive, though less striking and successful, was the effort to found a mission in Southern Bechuanaland, which was added to the Kimberley vicariate in 1890. The people there were thoroughly loyal to the Congregationalist London Mission which had worked amongst them for half a century or so, and Father Porte journeyed from chieftain to chieftain seeking in vain for leave to found a permanent mission. Only in 1895 was he able to start work at Taungs, on the banks of the Harts, just inside the borders of that country.

Along with these developments went the establishment of little churches, each with a school and a priest's house, up and down the country. As a result, by 1895 the estimated 5,600 Catholics of the vicariate were served by seventeen priests, twelve brothers and sixty-four sisters; there were ten churches and seven chapels, with eight schools for four hundred and twenty boys and thirteen for six hundred and seventy girls, in addition to Nazareth House, which cared for eighty orphans.[13] In 1897 the generosity of the citizens of Kimberley enabled the Christian Brothers to open their college and to start with a hundred pupils in their first year. Soon afterwards the Sisters of Mercy (also from Ireland) came to found a school for girls there and to prepare another at Mafeking. But before the latter was ready the Anglo-Boer war had begun, and the first employment of the nuns was to be nurses for the wounded.

An equally rapid formation of a Catholic community took place on the Witwatersrand during the 'nineties. When the Transvaal Boers successfully asserted their independence of England, in 1882, two-thirds of the Catholics, as Bishop Jolivet observed, left the country.[14] But the later discovery of richer gold mines at Barberton and on the Reef brought them back in large numbers among the prospectors. Soon temporary schools and churches were being built in the new town of Johannesburg—temporary because at first men thought of it as little more than a mining camp. In the next decades the Catholics could afford to build, and did build, substantial and lasting churches. Along with them they founded schools, and the Marist Brothers opened a college for boys in the town. Most striking of all these *oeuvres*, perhaps, was the staffing of the hospital by the nursing sisters of the Holy Family on the invitation of the town authorities.

Opposition was not lacking, and it did not come only from the extreme Calvinists who ruled the Transvaal politically. A controversy about the work of the nursing nuns filled the columns of the Johannesburg newspapers in 1895. Two of the doctors complained that the staff was " out of date ", but the board of management found after enquiry that the charge was unproved. It was agreed, however, that more nurses were needed, and the resident surgeon who was sent to recruit forty of them in Europe was told to bring lay nurses if he could not get nuns. The complaints died down after six more trained nuns arrived and the Johannesburg Medical Society recommended that the Holy Family sisters should remain in charge. Two of the hospital board, however, resigned, and one of them made it a religious issue.[15]

Not all the Catholics of the Cape took the trouble to understand the difficulties of a mining camp. Alexander Wilmot, experienced in affairs and usually level-headed, praised the hospital as a credit to the Transvaal government and the citizens of Johannesburg. They had made a capital bargain, he said, when they got the nuns for its staff.[16] But otherwise he wrote disparagingly of the Catholic works both of Kimberley and the Transvaal; "religion", he concluded, "is at a low ebb". Dr Kolbe, after a visit, said this was a mistaken view, at any rate as far as Johannesburg was concerned; Nazareth House was a model of its kind, the Marists were conducting the best school of the town, and so on, though he admitted that the scramble for gold made for the neglect of the arts and sciences.[17]

Father Schoch, who became prefect apostolic in 1892, also wrote in defence of the Catholics of the gold and diamond fields, pointing out that they had a nucleus of Catholic families as honourable as any in South Africa; in ten years the Catholic population of Johannesburg had risen to four thousand, the majority of whom were English speaking, and many of them, of all races, were a credit to their faith.[18] More valuable, perhaps because more detached, was the similar judgment expressed by Father Kenelm Vaughan when he visited South Africa trying to collect funds for his brother's missionary society,[19] the Mill Hill Fathers.

III. The Catholics and the Dutch

1. RACIAL CONTRASTS

At this point of the story politics must enter.* The quarrel

* For those who like a framework of dates the following may serve:

1852　Sand River Convention by which the British government recognized the independence of the Transvaal farmers.

1854　Bloemfontein Convention recognized the independence of Orange River State.

1877　Annexation of Transvaal republic by Shepstone.

1881　Pretoria Convention recognized complete self-government of Transvaal State, " subject to the suzerainty of Her Majesty ".

1895　Jameson's raid into Transvaal.

1899　Outbreak of Anglo-Boer war.

1902　Peace of Vereeniging.

1910　Union of South Africa proclaimed.

between the British government at Cape Town and the republics of the Orange River and Transvaal, the Anglo-Boer war of the turn of the century and its aftermath, and the establishment of the Union of South Africa, brought about changes in the Catholic outlook. It is a subtle matter, and even today the political facts are disputed, so that any expression of views must be largely a personal judgment. Nevertheless, it must be attempted.

The history of South Africa in the nineteenth century is sometimes presented with the tacit assumption that the English-speaking section of the people was represented by and supported the government at Cape Town which strove persistently to anglicize those of the Dutch tradition. Such a view calls for many qualifications. The journals of the time, and especially those of the Eastern Province, were filled with bitter criticisms of the policy of Cape Town, and still more often of the remote rule of Whitehall. Again, there were many English officials whose sympathies were with the Boers, of whom only a small proportion had crossed the Orange river to set up independent states. Sir William Butler, who held military posts under the Cape Town government on three occasions, and was himself the head of it for a few years at the end of the period, put it on record that:

> There were new names in the offices and over shop fronts in the towns, but out in the big country the old names were still in the farms. Men who had made money in trade or commerce had largely gone back to England to spend their days there. The children or grandchildren of the Dutch were still on the old sites. This dominating difference between the two races first convinced me that it was necessary to accept the fact of the permanency of Dutch life in South Africa and the consequent greater necessity of cultivating friendly relations with this permanent population.[20]

He claimed that the old soldiers who were sent as governors in the first half of the nineteenth century always came round to this view,[21] and he quoted Sir George Grey as saying that the Boers were " a quiet, orderly, industrious and hard-working people, hurting no one if let alone, but resentful of injuries, and especially of calumnies against their character ".[22]

The groupings and antipathies of the nineteenth century cannot, it is clear, be determined on racial lines. Especially is this true of the Catholic community in relation to the Boers, who were for the most part Calvinists in religion. There were of course Catholics of English race and tradition, like Colonel Bird, and his son John, who tells how, during his boyhood at Cape Town, language and social habits kept the Dutch for the most part aloof from the large military and naval force. The English regiments often remained for ten or twelve years, and the officers at least had their families with them, so that the English society in which his father lived was almost permanent. But when he returned forty years later conditions had changed; the military were a mere handful, and, though there were some English immigrants, the Dutch generally were fluent in English and there was no race distinction.[23]

The Catholics, however, were of many races. Many of those in Natal were of French descent and came in the middle years of the century from Mauritius. After the Crimean war a number of German soldiers, of whom several hundred were Catholics, were settled around King William's Town. There were also, as Father Devereux remarked in 1841, a number of farmers with Flemish and Brabant names whose parents had been Catholic,[24] and the Dutch governors, before the British occupation, had been aware that many of their soldiers and some of their settlers were of that faith.

But the majority of Catholics were undoubtedly Irish; some were deserters, some discharged from the British army, and they were reinforced by those who came as settlers from Ireland in 1820 and later in the rush to the diamond fields and gold mines. Further, the early vicars apostolic of both Western and Eastern provinces, and most of the priests, were Irishmen who formed the attitude of Catholics both *ex officio* and by the vigour of their personalities. Irishmen abroad, and especially the clergy, usually got on well with the English officials, especially when, as often in South Africa, they acted as chaplains to the soldiers. The newspapers and books of the time often refer to the popularity of Bishops Devereux and Ricards and Monsignor Murphy; the diaries of Bishops Griffith and Grimley contain many acknowledgements of help received from the civil authorities. But this attitude did not cause them to adopt the policy of the British government as their own. When preparations were being made for the celebration of Queen Victoria's golden jubilee, Bishop Ricards told his clergy not to take an active part because so many of the Catholic people were, he said, rightly displeased with the recent treatment of Ireland.

2. VIEWS OF THE AFRICANS

With regard to the settlers of Dutch origin the Catholic opinion varied considerably. Father O'Haire in his recollections says that South African history amply attests that they had robbed the Bantu of vast flocks. The natives " are treated more like beasts than human beings, even to this day, by very many masters and employers. . . . I have seen them kicked about like dogs and whipped like mules on farms in the Nieuw Veldt and elsewhere." [25] In generalizing he was, as he said himself, relying on the reports of Dr Livingstone and other Protestant missionaries, and in some cases on books and reports of the eighteenth century. His other general charge against them was that of bad husbandry: " the rain that falls would be sufficient, if damned up, to serve the farmers' purpose; but the Dutch farmers generally have been too supine for the task ".[26]

Though Bishop Simon made the same charges against the Boers of Namaqualand, he expressly said that his information did not go beyond that area, and that he had been told better things of them elsewhere. In no writing by other Catholics have I found these charges—the typical Exeter Hall accusations—repeated without qualification, though there are references to what Dr Welch once called the notorious negrophobe propensities of the Boers.[27] Even on his first tour Bishop Griffith commented on the hospitality usually shown him by the Boers, and gave more than one instance of marriages with Bantu women, uncommon indeed but not openly disapproved, at any rate by the layman of Dutch descent. As Dr Kolbe wrote in 1891, " the Bishop found it hard, and we find it impossible, to arrive at the truth about their treatment of the Kaffirs ".[28] There was of course, as John Bird wrote in the 'eighties, a tradition which was a remnant of the old slave laws and which should be expunged. The English government and many high-minded men in Natal agreed, he claimed (citing Sir Henry Bulwer), with his view that severity should not be used towards natives. But he and Bishop Moran, both men of wide experience, seem to have been alone among Catholics in foreseeing the exacerbation of the problem which would follow responsible self-govern-

ment by the white population;* the latter, as Bird said, could not
represent the vastly more numerous uncivilized majority to whose
interests they were naturally opposed, and so had no right to representative government.[29]   This was not, however, a charge against
the Boers more than against the English settlers, and Bird, indeed,
was writing of the latter only.   His judgment was followed by
Sir William Butler, who claimed to follow the opinion of the
soldier-administrators, but who also brought to the situation a fine
and experienced Catholic culture.   The worst treatment of the
natives, he alleged, was given neither by Boers nor by old-time
British but by Uitlanders, first at Kimberley and then on the
Rand.[30]   In so far as he attacked the farmers, it was those in Natal,
and for much the same reason as Father O'Haire had attacked the
Dutch; everyone in Natal wanted a life of leisure, their farms were
but territories for kraals, and the native was taxed till he was in
the hands of the moneylenders.[31]

Sir William Butler, indeed, is a witness that the attitude of the
early vicars apostolic to the Bantu was not extraordinary.   The
apartheid—and worse—practised in the republics of Potshefstroom
and Pretoria and in Natal was a new development.   " Cape Colony
stands alone ", he wrote, " in its wise and far-seeing policy to the
native race."[32]   Bishop Griffith had noticed in his first tour that,
though the marriage of white and coloured was rare, it did occur
sometimes, and was regarded as not outrageous by those of Dutch
descent, and even, by laymen at least, as better than concubinage.[33]
The Cape Synod of the Dutch Reformed Church did not exclude
the coloured from their congregations, and this was, in fact, one
of the grounds for the repudiation of their authority by the Calvinist
congregations formed in the north by the trekkers.[34]   So when
Bishop Grimley had " the blacks, at least eleven of them, walking
in his [May] procession ",[35] and when the Marist Brothers admitted
the sons of Cape Malays to their college (as the South African
College had done before them) there was no protest, or even
opposition.   It was not difficult then for Catholics there to preserve
Christian charity of outlook.   Only north of the Orange river
did they begin to adopt the racial heresy, and Father Hoenderwangers had to write to Bishop Allard in 1856 (in the bishop's
words): " Some Catholics think it bad to marry white with black;

* The Anglican Bishop Colenso also foresaw it.

he asks for a letter to shut them up ". The episcopal reply was unequivocal: " As to colour the Catholic Church does not pay attention to it. Jesus Christ died for all without distinction ". And this was effective, for the would-be moralists came and asked pardon.[36]

3. VIEWS OF EACH OTHER

While the Catholic missionaries did not generally associate themselves with the exaggerated denunciations of the Dutch tradition which were made annually in London at Exeter Hall by some English Protestants, they were regarded as enemies by the Dutch population who in fact, in course of time, came to think of them as their principal opponents.

As the Dutch were almost all convinced Calvinists, there was naturally religious opposition. Anyone who claims that he teaches the revelation of Christ must of necessity deny the authenticity of another interpretation. When he further claims, as the Catholic does, that the constitution of the Church and its sacraments are part of that revelation, he denies the Christian origin of other religious bodies. On these grounds, however, the Catholic was as strenuously opposed to the Anglican and to the Wesleyan as to the Dutch Reformed Church.

It is also true that each of these bodies preserved a tradition of bitter and savage persecution by the Catholic Church. There was perhaps more ground for this belief in the case of the French Huguenots and the Calvinists of the Low Countries, from whom the Dutch of South Africa were descended. Historical research had only just begun to put the wars of the sixteenth century in their political setting, and so the myth was hardly questioned.

Further, it was the habit of the nineteenth century to identify religion with nations, so that the English thought of papists as chiefly Irish. There was less excuse for the Dutch to do this, as Catholics had been a large numerical minority in Holland since the sixteenth century, but since the penal laws excluded them from political life it was easy to believe that their Faith was alien to the national tradition.

It is part of the tradition of the Catholic Church to persuade men by argument of the authenticity of her claim, and therefore to overcome by controversy the attitude of mind which at any time makes men unwilling to listen. The spirit of the ghetto, of being content to live their own life among themselves, is never dominant for long; it is alien to the genius of Catholicism. In the nineteenth century, aware of the Church's history as a maker of European nations, European Catholics like Görres and Montalembert and Lingard were soon arguing that the real national traditions had taken birth in the Faith and could all find a place in the Catholic fold. And as detailed historical research increased it was becoming clearer that secular politics played a very large part in the tragedies of the sixteenth century, and that they could not in reason be laid to the charge of the Church.

In South Africa it was naturally the priests who took the lead in this approach to the outside world, for, as a rule, they alone were acquainted with the literature of recent studies. It could be directed to those of the Dutch Reformed Church equally with those of other religious bodies. So Father Devereux in 1841 tried to get hold of Dutch Catholic books to circulate among them.[37] Later Dr Ricards adapted and published Dr Döllinger's study of the Lutheran movement, which had more relevance for the Dutch than for Anglicans. After the *Catholic Magazine* was founded the contributions of Dr Welch sought to correct what was mythical in the Huguenot tradition.

There were, however, some special stumbling-blocks to contact between Catholics and Dutch in South Africa. The first of these was the continual appearance of stories of debauchery and sadism in contemporary Catholic institutions. These of course had been a commonplace among all kinds of Protestants, and one of the reasons for the foundation of the Catholic *Colonist* had been their rebuttal. For practical purposes the early numbers of that newspaper had silenced the slanders current among Anglican and Wesleyans.[38] Only rarely did they obtain public recognition in those bodies afterwards. But they unfortunately persisted among those of the Dutch Reformed Church. Down to the end of the century Catholics tried to maintain the view that the unreasoning and incredible slanders were circulated only by what Dr Kolbe called the Protestant underworld,[39] and on occasion the Dutch Reformed Church gave them grounds for making this distinction. After one of the outbursts against Catholics in 1891 the Dutch

Reformed Synod warned its members to be careful whom they admitted to their pulpits, and Dr Kolbe could reasonably infer that the agitation had been the work of a narrow and noisy clique. But it was the latter who appeared to gain ground, and in the following year Kolbe commented:

With the higher aspect of the Dutch Church as shown by the Rev A. Murray, Rev Professor Hofmeyer, Rev Dr Kotze and some others I have no quarrel; but I take it as evident fact, painfully evident to us, that the average rank and file of that Church are animated by a narrow-minded, scandal-mongering, persecuting spirit.[40]

By 1898 the situation seemed worse: " There is going on in this country an active propaganda of personal libel against us Catholics which ought to be incredible."

Kolbe quoted a Transvaal paper which called priests and nuns " emissaries of Satan ", " liars, murderers and doers of everything that is abominable ". But the worst was that similar books and pamphlets were being " scattered throughout South Africa under the encouragement and even instigation of high officials in the Dutch Church ". Even so, Dr Kolbe insisted, " all the better class of Protestants are quietly dropping it "; but, he added, " the purpose of it is the practical boycotting of Catholic schools and often of Catholic individuals in favour of Protestant schools and Protestant individuals ", and " this purpose is favoured by the silence of those better-minded Protestants who nevertheless share in the spoils ". And he concluded with an appeal that Protestant public opinion should openly denounce the mass of calumny which lay to its charge.[41]

4. THE BARRIER OF LANGUAGE

Besides that campaign of slander there was another difficulty in the way of contact between the Dutch and the Catholic Church. It was the matter of language, and the difficulty was really the fault of Catholics. It is certainly surprising that the missionary priests did not set themselves to learn Hollands, since first Father Devereux and then Bishop Allard recognized that no headway could be made without it. But Father O'Haire is the only priest of whom it is known that he set himself to the task while doing his mission work; in 1864 he " learned the local patois (a mutilated

Dutch) from a Catholic lad named Keating ".[42]   It may account
for his evident popularity, despite his no less evident bellicose
temperament.

During the years when Catholic work was developing in the
Cape Colony the population of Dutch descent were learning to use
English (a practice encouraged by the government schools), and
many of the Irish priests may have thought this would become
general.   But the successful insistence on the recognition of Dutch
in the law courts and in education should have warned them.
The vicars apostolic were not altogether negligent.   They tried to
secure the services of Dutch or Flemish priests.   When Bishop
Griffith visited the Crystal Palace exhibition in 1851 he found there
a fellow Dominican in his habit, as we have already seen, and,
discovering that this Peter van Ewyk was a Dutchman, brought
him to Cape Town and set him to preach in the new cathedral.
Bishop Devereux persuaded three Flemish priests to come to the
Eastern Vicariate; of them, Father Hoenderwangers was, as we
have likewise seen, very successful in establishing friendship with
the Dutch farmers of the Orange Free State, and Father de Sany
made many friends among those at Uitenhage.   A similar attempt
by Bishop Grimley in the Western Vicariate was not so successful;
the story of the Belgian, Father Kums, has already been told.
Nor was Bishop Grimley much more successful with another plan.
Through his vicar-general, Monsignor McMahon, he sent two
Irish students, O'Connell and Sheridan, to Utrecht to train for his
vicariate there and to learn Dutch at the same time.[43]   The prior
of St Dominic's reported in effect that they were huskies but
ignorant.[44]   Even after four years' residence he could only report
that they talked Dutch fairly well,[45] and though they came to Cape
Town in 1869 after ordination, they do not seem to have done any
work worthy of record.   The best effort to bring Dutch-speaking
priests to South Africa seems to have been made by Bishop Ricards,
who, at the time when the Society of Jesus took over St Aidan's
College at Grahamstown, asked their father-general to send him
two Dutch fathers who were to be placed in charge of the mission
at Graaf Reinet.

The growing use of English had undoubtedly been helped by the
earlier policy of the government, who had refused to allow
the use of Dutch in the elementary schools.   The attitude of

the educationists was expressed by Dr Kolbe who, writing of the university on whose board he served, denied that Dutch was on the same level as English for educational purposes. " Nearly all the children in this country ", he added, " who speak both Dutch and English, speak both inaccurately, and I would far rather know one language properly than blunder in half a dozen."[46]   He was a just man and could recognize that it was natural for Hollanders to want to preserve their mother tongue,[47] but he regarded their attempt to force it into the elementary curriculum as " wanting to put brakes on their decline ", remarking also that " a lot of them think they talk Dutch but do not ".

Opposition on the language question was undoubtedly exacerbated by the use which Dutch Reformed *predikants* make of their influence to exclude Catholic teachers from the public schools.   In 1892 they dismissed a Miss Crosby from her appointment at Riebeck College for this reason, although they had always known she was a Catholic.   Dr Kolbe's comment was:

It was done, and rudely, by a Rev Mr Pienaar.   In ordinary affairs he is a kindly, genial, straightforward gentleman. But at the *word* Roman Catholic he loses his balance.   Of the thing he knows nothing.   What sort of religion is it which has this effect on natural character?[48]

Instances of the sort appear several times in the *Catholic Magazine* during these years.

For practical purposes the public taxation was made to provide schools which, though called undenominational, were in fact Calvinist, to which Catholics could not in conscience send their children, while Catholic schools received a grant which did not cover half the salaries of the teachers.

In the 'nineties the movement to adopt the patois of the farmer as a language in its own right was growing.   For those formed in the classics or in European languages, like Father Simon in Namaqualand or the writers of the *Catholic Magazine*, as also for many of the Dutch Reformed *predikants*, the grammatical simplifications seemed barbarous.   Despite these causes or excuses for criticism, the leaders of the Catholic community did not identify themselves with a radical, racial or linguistic opposition.   When a Father O'Brien attacked the Bond (formed by Mr Hofmeyer to develop

Afrikaans) as " apes and fools ", his remarks were promptly disowned by Dr Kolbe in the *Catholic Magazine*.[49]   Dr McCarthy,
it is true, wrote:

> The Bond-man wants the reins of government drawn tight
> for the townsman and loose on his own neck, dreams that he can
> maintain an oligarchy of more or less Dutch descent amid an
> increasing population of more recent accession from Europe.
> It is an idle dream, and its temporary triumph is a sad thing even
> for those who believe in it.[50]

But in the same year Dr Kolbe published a tribute to the Dutch
farmer; he " is a genuine man as a rule, and knows a man when he
meets him ".[51]

IV. The Anglo-Boer War

Alexander Wilmot, best known of Catholic lay publicists, gave
several lectures at Paarl in 1893 on the rise of the Afrikaner nation,
and the substance of these was published without criticism as
articles in the *Catholic Magazine*.   He denounced the policy of the
British government down to the Great Trek; " extreme toryism,
extraordinary illiberality and gross want of judgement characterized
the way of Downing Street for a quarter of a century ".   Their
treatment of the Dutch language, the Dutch courts and the currency
were given as examples, and Wilmot claimed that the new British
settlers became " champions of free speech, critics of the government and leaders of the Dutch ".   The tales of the Protestant
missionaries were exaggerated and gave a false picture, and the
methods used in the emancipation of slaves and the award of compensation caused injustice to the farmers and were often contrary
to the advice of the governors of the Colony.   This was not mere
partisanship, for Wilmot had already made some serious and
documented studies of South African history.   With equal sympathy he described the founding of Natal and the Orange Free
State and the Transvaal republics: " these men were Afrikaners
and so were all the other leaders who have been pioneers of civilization in South Africa to drive back savagery and open fair fields and
new empires to the world ".   But he insisted that the title Afrikaner included " people of all extractions who make South Africa
their adopted country and home ", and that " it is desirable that we

should all consider ourselves as one Afrikaner nation from the
Zambesi to Agulhas ", and again that " the time is not far off when
the Afrikander [sic] nation will not only rule the Cape Colony and
the Orange Free State—as it does at present—but also the South
African republic ".[52]

The last quotation reads strangely to-day, but in 1893 it was the
South African Republic of the Transvaal which seemed to many
besides Alexander Wilmot as the difficulty in the way of Afrikaner
nationalism.   It was not because of the Uitlanders of the mining
camps, but because Paul Kruger and his large following among
the burghers wanted to emphasize and maintain their connection
with Holland.   Wilmot praised the culture of the government
officials in Pretoria, especially of the real Hollanders whom President Kruger had imported.   But he maintained that they were
alien to the Boer, and " the Afrikaner from the Cape who speaks
the taal fits better ",[53] and this was the policy of Joubert.   It serves
to remind us that the quarrel which was developing cannot be
stated in terms of Whitehall and Pretoria alone.   In addition there
was the viewpoint of the Cape Colony, which was shared for a time
by the Orange Free State; it differed from Chamberlain and it
differed from Kruger, for it assumed that the people from the Cape
to the Zambesi should be an independent nation.

Wilmot's Afrikaner thesis did not provoke any criticism in the
Catholic Magazine.   Five years later it seems to have been urged in
a speech by Sir William Butler, then both commander-in-chief and
administrator of the Cape.   Dr Kolbe commented with approval:
" Let Afrikaner nationality have free play . . . let Englishmen
drop their swaggering attitude of perpetual superiority ".[54]

It would be easy but mistaken to interpret these statements in
terms of more recent movements.   Dr Kolbe made it clear that he
was not attacking the Uitlander: " surely a man of the British
Isles is at home anywhere in the Empire ".[55]   And Wilmot
expressly claimed that his Afrikaner thesis was not republican,[56]
since the Queen had given a liberal constitution to South Africa.

The attitude of the writers in the Catholic Magazine to the Transvaal question followed naturally enough.   Though their emphasis
differed, they regarded President Kruger's treatment of the Uitlanders as a denial of justice.   For them the immigrants were a

mining community, of whom some were Catholic and most were British or Irish, and should, therefore, be given political and above all educational rights equally with the Boer farmers.   But while insistent on the injustice of the Transvaal government, all these writers agreed in condemning the attempt at armed revolt against it, and especially the interference of Jameson's forces from Rhodesia. Even Dr McCarthy, least sympathetic among them to the Boers, commented in 1896:

> Transvaal government, whatever its shortcomings, was deeply sinned against—and so the Transvaal and the Orange Free State have drawn closer together. . . . It ill becomes any of us to lecture Kruger on how to govern.[57]

These views were those of the Catholics of Cape Colony, but there was a different tradition in Natal and the Transvaal. Though Father Hoenderwangers had made friends with President Boshoff of the Orange River State, and though Bishop Grimley had found President Brand "a very liberal man and not bigoted against Catholics ",*[58] Bishop Allard had deliberately avoided meeting the Boer leaders.   His successor, Bishop Jolivet, was more friendly, but, as we have seen, he also kept in close association with the representatives of English rule.   Since both bishops, like Father Simon in Namaqualand, often referred with appreciation and apparent surprise to the large measure of real liberty accorded to the Church by the British Government, and assumed as natural and even desirable the efforts of the British to re-establish their rule in the Transvaal,[59] it seems likely that they regarded the Boers with a French dislike of all frondeur movements.   It must be added, however, that the anti-Catholic attitude of the governments of the republics was more obvious to them than it could be to the priests at the Cape.   The Orange Free State law of 1880, requiring all teachers to be Protestant, and the denial of grants to Catholic schools in the Transvaal (modified slightly just before the outbreak of the Anglo-Boer war), were grievances which almost forced them to throw in their lot with the Uitlanders.

From 1897, when Sir Alfred Milner took over the direction of

* President Brand had studied at Cambridge and was a member of the English bar.

affairs at the Cape, these issues were publicized. General Butler believed, from what officials told him, that it was deliberate and exaggerated propaganda, a policy to provoke President Kruger to make war or to give an excuse for war.[60] But the Catholics of the Transvaal and Kimberley, and even of the Cape, did not possess that information. Even so Dr Kolbe sounded a note of warning when the crisis came in 1899. He deplored what had been done by President Kruger, but urged that force was not the solution. He would not support the war party or the revealed designs of the English government, for " Mr Chamberlain aims directly at war ". " Everything is being calculated to force Kruger into war." He denounced it as an unrighteous war even if England was unanimous for it, and he praised General Butler for striving for peace.[61] When protests came in from other Catholics Dr Kolbe reminded them that he spoke for himself and that he had made this clear. He recognized that Catholics were treated as helots in the Transvaal, but urged that this was matter for protests, not invasion.[62] Though Father de Lacy, O.M.I., one of the leading priests in Johannesburg, attacked Kolbe's attitude, the latter thought he had the majority of the clergy and even of the Catholic laity on his side.[63] A month or two later, however, he admitted that the South African Catholics were so divided that there was no prevailing opinion about the justice of the war. By March 1900 Dr Kolbe concluded that " some of the bishops have taken an open stand for what is to me the cause of injustice ", and so, fulfilling an old pledge, he resigned at once.[64]

During the course of the war the sympathies of the Catholics were mainly but mildly with the English forces, and this sentiment was stronger probably in the areas within the British lines or besieged towns, in Estcourt, Ladysmith and Kimberley, than in the Cape Provinces. Some priests acted as chaplains to the Imperial troops and hospitals; a few Catholics fought in the Boer commandos. Fortunately the government had not learned how to make propaganda efficiently, except for home consumption, and the soldiers were able to respect their opponents' good qualities and ability. Many of them openly questioned the wisdom and humanity of the police methods by which Kitchener overcame the resistance, and it seems a pity that no protest was made publicly by Catholics against his harshness. There was at least an excuse for those of Dutch tradition to think of the Catholic Church a supporting their foes.

V. From the War to the Union

During the first ten years of the new century, a number of influential men of both traditions strove honourably to undo some of the stupidities and worse which had caused the war. The greatest honour belongs to the great Boer leaders, Botha and Smuts, Hertzog and Steyn, who, accepting the fact of defeat, did their best to restore the unity of the country within the Empire which, in their judgement, had treated it unjustly. Many English officials, even Lord Milner to some extent, appreciated their attitude and tried not to insist on their military victory. So lightly were the feelings of the Catholic bishops engaged on the British side that, before the war was over, they asked Dr Kolbe to resume the editorship of their official magazine. He did so in January 1901, but insisted that politics should be avoided " except where they touch directly the interest of the Church ".[65] In the following years some efforts were made to approach those of the Boer tradition. Kolbe editorially took an unnamed Irish priest to task for a tirade against the Dutch language, protesting that Catholics generally found its users a God-fearing people; " they dislike us, it is true ", but this is " because they are smarting under unfair treatment ".[66] At the Cape a Catholic Reading Guild was formed to supply parcels of books to outlying villages and towns, and they tried through Father W. Leeson to include Dutch Catholic literature.[67] Under Dr Welch's direction the Catholic Association of Cape Town arranged in 1906 a discussion with the debating society of the Adderley Street Dutch Reformed Church on the " creation of separate states for the use of all South African aboriginals ".[68] Meanwhile, Bishop Miller, who had become the first vicar apostolic of the Transvaal in 1904, had arranged that a Father van Laer should translate some of the available Catholic literature into Dutch.

The rapprochement extended to the leaders of the people. Father Hecht, O.M.I., a chaplain to the British forces during the war who had won the C.M.G. for helping the wounded at Bloemfontein, made friends with the Boer Generals, Hertzog, Steyn and de Wet, and Dr Kolbe met them in Pretoria.[69] On this same visit he also had interviews with Botha and Smuts. The latter reminded his visitor of the time when Kolbe had examined him for his degree at Cape Town University; Botha talked with enthusiasm of Robert Emmet and the Irish Home Rule movement.[70]

Unfortunately the presence and perhaps the behaviour of the Uitlanders in the Transvaal was still a difficulty. Sir William Butler, writing as a visitor and old friend of the country but no longer a British official, published, first as newspaper articles and then as a book, *Naboth's Vineyard*, an out-and-out denunciation of them as parasitic speculators belonging neither to the British, Boer nor Black groups of the population, worthy only of the name of Bounders.

This attitude of dislike had spread by this time to the Cape, and Dr Kolbe was known apparently to share it. His friend Dr Welch, who descended from a family already prominent in Cape Town when Bishop Griffith arrived, argued cogently against the general xenophobic view. "Civilization", he maintained, "should welcome the civilized stranger"; "the Uitlander who goes home to revive ideas and bring them back confers a benefit on us"; "a spreadeagle patriotism is not indigenous to our land . . . and we may be allowed to hope that no foreign influence will ever change this quality of our people".[71] And with a gentle malice he pointed out that van Riebeck himself was an Uitlander.

The editor replied that he had Dr Welch's assurance that the article was not political—and so an answer could not be so either. He admitted that he himself supported the *Cape Times*, which urged that the Uitlander should go home and stay there; and that it was based on the belief that the Uitlander only came for his own good.

The disputants, by choice probably, did not get to grips. Dr Welch kept to principles which it is unlikely that Dr Kolbe would have challenged. The latter kept his attention on the financiers in the Transvaal, and they were for the most part a sorry lot. Unfortunately the Catholics there had little chance to show that they had come to settle and were not to be included among the market speculators. They were largely immigrants, and their community had obtained a large measure of liberty under the English rule, marked among other things by a public procession of the Blessed Sacrament at Braamfontein.[72] They built a Johannesburg Catholic Club at a cost of £11,500, and the first Mayor under the new régime was St John Carr, a Catholic and a great friend of Father de Lacy.[73]

But the structure of government was determined neither by Boer farmers nor Uitlander business men but by the able if theoretical young men whom Milner had collected. These were politicians of the new sort, who took it for granted that the state was a secularist institution. So their education commission ruled that all denominational schools were outside their terms of reference, and they put into that category all in which religion (as Catholics understand it) was taught at all.[74] It went for nothing that the Marists had hitherto given most of the boys' secondary schooling in the province and that they had received a subsidy for the last two and a half years of the Dutch rule.[75] It went for nothing that St John Carr suggested the formula " where no religious test is imposed or compulsory religion ",[76] and that the Catholics were willing to have subsidies dependent on examination results.[77] The Dutch-speaking community, who had their own legitimate grievances against this educational commission, still regarded the Catholics as their enemies, and unfortunately the friendly contacts with the Afrikaner leaders had not begun early enough or developed far enough to enable a joint defence against the English civil servants. So for the first time in South Africa the theory (as distinct from practice) that public education should be of a kind unacceptable to Catholics was embodied in the laws of a province.

The establishment of the Union of South Africa in 1909 did not bring better conditions for the relation of Catholics and those of the Dutch tradition. There were two able Catholics, members of the Convention which met in Durban and worked out the plan for the new state, and one of these, Charles Coghlan (the future Prime Minister of Southern Rhodesia), was fervent and practising. But the educational system of each province was left untouched. Dr Welch, who had succeeded Dr Kolbe as editor of the *Catholic Magazine*, was uncertain about the effects of the new constitution. He considered that the colour question was the greatest source of anxiety, and regretted that the fateful phrase " European descent " had now been consecrated by the law.[78] Wilmot remarked that the fierce race jealousies (of Dutch and English) had been unknown at the Cape when he came there in 1853. In one important respect an immediate result of the Union seems to have been that the spirit of the Transvaal overcame the Cape. A bill was gazetted in the following year of the union of the Dutch Reformed Synods in the different provinces, and it virtually excluded the coloured peoples from equal rights in that Church.[79] It was the end of the more liberal traditional practice of the Cape Calvinists, but it was also an additional if accidental cause for disdain and dislike between Catholics and Dutch; the one regarded as a vice what the other reckoned a Christian duty.

Chapter IX

THE CHURCH AND THE AFRICANS

I. The Cape

1. A MATTER OF EMPHASIS

IN 1911 Dr du Plessis published an account of missionary work in
South Africa which was given, and deserved, a good review in
the *Catholic Magazine*. It contained one friendly grumble against
papists: they would list as missionaries all priests and religious
under the rule of the Congregation of Propaganda, whether
engaged in converting Protestants or preaching to pagans. The
practice made it impossible to arrange the figures of missionary
endeavour in a neat table.

The quarrel of the statistician with his material seems to be part
of his science, but in this case there was some ground for complaint.
When Bishop Griffith came to the Cape he occupied himself first
of all with " those who ought to be papists ". Much later Bishop
Ricards was to write, in *The Catholic Church and the Kaffir*, that the
papal instructions to him and his predecessors had been: " Attend
first to the wants of the children of the household of the faith.
When the wants of this portion of your flock have been provided
for, turn your attention to the native population." Dr du Plessis,
had he known of that directive, might well have argued that it was
parallel to the attitude of the Protestant missions, though he might
have been surprised at the absence of reference to heretics. The
two tasks, the provision of religious teaching and worship for
European Catholics and the advancement of the Faith among the
natives, seemed to be clearly separated.

The phrase of Bishop Ricards has often been quoted by Catholic
writers as though it was intended to have that effect. But no
explicit brief of the Sacred Congregation has been quoted to show
that it was a plan of organization. Almost certainly it was a remark
of Pius IX, given maybe in answer to a question, at the private
audience of the vicar apostolic. As such it was to guide him in

making up his mind about the priority of duties to which he should give attention; a matter of emphasis in what was a single task.

Certainly it had been understood in that way by the earlier vicars apostolic. Even in his first tour when he was looking for those who should be papists, Bishop Griffith had stayed on at Fort Beaufort for a few days to instruct and baptize an elderly black woman who had been living in concubinage with an Irishman. He obtained their public promise—before the Commissioner—that they would live apart in future. In the same town he was seriously considering whether to baptize the native wife of a Protestant who promised that their children should be brought up in the Catholic religion. Some time later he wrote[1] that in the previous two and a half years he had converted twenty infidels (i.e. native pagans) and had received thirty-eight abjurations of heresy (i.e. of Protestant whites). And pleading for more priests to help him he mentioned two areas of work; one was at Beaufort, where there were four hundred Catholics, and secondly, on observation which we have already quoted, "the Kaffirs of the Black River seem to promise to the missionary a precious acquisition".

From the time of his arrival, then, Bishop Griffith did turn his attention occasionally to the native population. Either he had not been given the instruction of which James Ricards wrote, or he understood it differently, and his successor followed the same policy. When Bishop Grimley sent Father O'Haire to found a mission at Malmesbury he urged him again and again to evangelize the natives; he spoke of it as the first attempt to convert South Africa, and rejoiced when O'Haire reported the baptism of twenty-two Hottentots who afterwards walked eighteen miles every Sunday to and from Mass.[2] Nor was this a special task assigned to one priest. The bishop himself, on his first tour of the vicariate, baptized " two blacks, one Afrikander, and one Scotsman ",[3] and on a similar tour towards the end of his life he " received five adults, two of whom were Zulu Kaffirs ".[4] At church ceremonies in the cathedral at Cape Town, he boasted, " I have the blacks, at least eleven of them, walking in procession ";[5] and there too in 1864 he opened a school for native children, though it had to start with only three pupils.[5]

The practice of the vicars apostolic and the different " instruction " of Bishop Ricards are most easily explained by the history of the Church in Europe. The French Revolution and the rule of Napoleon had completed what the Bourbons and Habsburgs had begun in the eighteenth century: the Church was stripped of its property, and out of this was given a bare stipend to continue as a privileged private corporation under the control of the civil government which claimed absolute sovereignty over the people. It is not surprising that the Catholic missionary endeavour came to an end during those years. With the restoration in Europe of the monarchies which claimed the loyalties of the Christian tradition the popes of the nineteenth century set themselves two tasks; one was to persuade the civil governments to accept Christian law as binding their behaviour, and the other was to regain the affection of the peoples for the Church, whatever their rulers might do. The events which led up to the Syllabus of Errors, and later to the seizure of Rome, were stages in the failure of the first task, but the second was so far successful that out of it there grew missionary work on a larger scale probably than that of the sixteenth century.

Looking back on the past it is easy enough to suppose that the new direction of Catholic activity was planned by Rome—curiously, historians were always ready to attribute great worldly wisdom to the popes—as a suitable way of using the wealth and energy of the Church. The Catholic missionary record, however, shows clearly that the work had to be manned and financed by contributions, often the small collections of poor congregations, made all over the world. The support of governments on a large scale was no longer available as it had been in the days of Philip II of Spain or Louis XIV of France. Before any plan could be seriously made it was necessary for the Church to rebuild the Catholic life and charity of the faithful. As Chevalier pointed out in a long-forgotten monograph on Church and State, the visit of Pius VI to Vienna, in the days of Josephism before the Revolution, can be taken as the starting-point of the new direct appeal to the people; their enthusiasm showed the eighteenth-century system to be unnecessary, for the enthusiasm of the crowd was addressed to the Holy Father. When the popes, after the Revolution, set themselves to restore that attitude in the faithful

they could be confident that it would in time re-kindle the flame
of all the old traditions. It is in that sense, I think, that we must
understand the "instruction" of which Bishop Ricards wrote.
Gregory XVI and Pius IX, like their predecessors, knew that the
beginning of all Catholic enterprise must lie in the vigorous
sacramental life of the faithful of a country, and they directed their
vicars apostolic to that as their first task. In the measure of its
restoration the old Catholic traditions of missionary work would
come into play, and only in such a sense was it planned in the early
stages.

For Bishop Griffith and for Bishop Grimley, then, the instruction was a matter of emphasis. They would try to convert the
pagan races whenever time and men could be spared from the
task of rebuilding the Catholic life of those who should be papists.
Though the "Kaffirs of the Black River" were a promising field
for Bishop Griffith in 1841, the work had to wait for many years;
though Father O'Haire made a good start at Malmesbury with his
twenty-two Hottentot converts, the bishop was forced to send
him to Oudtshoorn because of the hundred and fifty Catholics
there without a priest, and for six years the Malmesbury mission
was closed.

2. Catholic and Calvinist Approaches

These attempts to convert the pagans, sporadic though they were,
aroused the antagonism of the Protestant clergy; especially, it
seems, of the Calvinists. It was not seemingly the old fierce hatred
of the Roman priest; that was spoken of as something of the past,
though the recent past. Those of Dutch tradition, like the Anglicans, appear to have accepted Catholics as a backward group of
families, adhering to old unreformed ways, and therefore needing
a chaplain of their own denomination. But they thought of their
country as Protestant, and therefore denied the right of anyone
to use its civilization, culture and influence to enlarge the Catholic
Church; the heathen inhabitants were material, to their mind, for
the Calvinist Church if they were Dutch or Scotch, the Anglican
if they were English; all others were interlopers.

Subsequent history and the Afrikaner myth might lead us to
look for the motive of segregation to account for this jealousy.
The evidence is certainly not clear. Du Plessis' insistence on the

distinction between those who ministered to Europeans and those who preached to the natives is one of statistics; his own factual account gives many instances of a Protestant missionary who also had a European congregation. Indeed, the Cape Synod of the Dutch Reformed Church insisted after 1838, against the protests of the groups among the Voortrekkers, in treating the converted Bantu as members. The London Missionary Society and some of the German ministers did form separate congregations of natives, but this followed from their social policy of trying to organize their converts into villages independent of the Boer farmers. On the other hand Du Plessis gives several examples of the spirit of segregation, and it may have been the motive of that " Presbyterian Calvinist parson" of whom Bishop Griffith heard at Beaufort West, who despite " the strong desire here among the free black or liberated slaves to be baptized and married and become Christian . . . will not do it for them till they have gone to school for years ".

Perhaps we should understand the various attitudes better by remembering that national culture was an integral part of each Protestant religion as it had developed historically. Calvinism was either Scottish or Dutch, Lutheranism German or Swedish, just as Anglicanism was English, and, unconsciously, they thought of Christianity as necessarily national. Some would conclude that the natives must always remain dependent Christians, since they could never become fully English or Scottish or Dutch; others, with a more imperial outlook, would think it possible to incorporate the subject people in their own national culture. All would regard an intellectual training, in the language and especially in the sacred poetry of the missionaries, as essential.

The attitude of Catholics is a little more complex. In a country like South Africa they would not be tempted to regard the " white " culture as a necessary part of their religion, but they did not criticize this national approach as the chief fault of their rivals. Their principal comment was that these efforts had ended in failure. In his *Catholic Church and the Kaffir* Ricards noted that the farmers regarded raw natives as preferable to those who had had contact with the missionary school, but he was not satisfied that the opinion was justifiable. Better evidence, as O'Haire had pointed out, was the testimony of the missionaries and their supporters; the *Christian*

Remembrancer, d'Urban, Napier, Calderwood and Livingstone could all be quoted to the same effect. This was a sad result after almost a half-century of very generous efforts on the part of the Europeans interested. Calvinist missionaries had been sent liberally by the Dutch, then came the German Rhenish and Moravian, and then the English; according to *The Times*, Bishop Ricards wrote in 1866, their missionary societies had spent not less than two million pounds on the work.

Nor did the Catholics impugn the quality of the Protestant missionaries; certainly some of them, wrote Ricards, are men of integrity and every good quality. But from observations which extended over more than a quarter of a century Catholics blamed the system of training of the Protestant converts, because it put all emphasis on the habit of Bible reading. Of one of their missionaries Bishop Griffith wrote in 1839: " He wants men and women of sixty years old to go to school and learn psalm singing (the only religion they appear to me to be taught) and reading and has some younger ones at it these ten years to no effect." Thirty years later Bishop Grimley's impression was only slightly more favourable: " The natives have benefited a little intellectually, I grant; morally, I deny."

Bishop Griffith, Father O'Haire, and Bishop Ricards all left comments on the coloured races in Cape Colony. From these I think it would be fair to say, first, that they started with the expectation of finding the native degraded in morals. Griffith asked himself what new thing he had learned in his first tour of visitation and answered that the difference in colour causes not such variety in morality as we are led to expect; O'Haire found the Bantu brave and intelligent, the Korannas wicked, the Bushmen savage, the Hottentots degraded; " but ", he added, " I believe them all capable of civilization, knowledge and religion ". Yet these quotations show also that, though free from the myth of the noble savage, the Catholic writers were equally certain of the capability of any human being to learn and practise the moral law. For this they believed the Catholic discipline and the Catholic sacraments to be normally necessary, and so they were ready to baptize natives, and especially native children, wherever there was reasonable likelihood of their continuing in the practice of Catholic worship and sacramental life. Bishop Ricards recognized more clearly

than his predecessors the difficulties which would be caused by
native traditions and native institutions, but he also was confident
that the living force of Catholicism would be able to overcome
them in time.

In some ways their attitude was not unlike that of the majority
of the clergy in the Spanish and Portuguese dominions of earlier
centuries. They took it as a matter of course that the " Kaffirs "
would accept the ways of the whites along with their language,
even though the assimilation might take some time or be imperfect
at best. Meanwhile there would be no segregation in religion,
and it would not be absolute in social matters. Nor was this,
indeed, very different from the general attitude of the inhabitants
of Cape Town and the older districts of the colony in the first half
of the nineteenth century. It had brought the coloured population
of mixed parentage into being. One of the earliest lieutenant
governors of the Eastern Province had been the child of such a
marriage, and even his political opponents do not appear to have
objected to him on the score of his birth. His brothers were
fair but his sisters took after their mother; yet one of them was
married to the Dutch civil commissioner at Beaufort who entertained Bishop Griffith on his first visitation. And the latter was
told, in another town, that the laymen, farmers for the most part,
and Dutch, compelled their unwilling parson on some occasions
to marry them to their black concubines. This society had
accepted slavery as an institution but had also accepted the practice
of emancipating those who became Christians, and were accustomed
to shopkeepers and artisans who were legally slaves but economically independent; they had not shown much opposition to the
British decree of freedom and, though many protested that they
were cheated of the compensation promised, very few of them took
part in the treks out of the Colony which were organized in the
Eastern Province where there had been far fewer slaves.

It must be recognized that conditions were different on the
borders, and the Eastern Province was largely border country.
There was, as on many frontiers, a thoroughly bad tradition of
violence. Father O'Haire was able to quote from a *landdrost* of
Graaf Reinet in 1792 and from Moodie's Records of 1777 to show
that the Boer farmers had killed off the Bushmen and seized their
land.[7] He could have cited equally the complaints of the old

Dutch governors at the Cape that the Hottentots were " descendants of those whose vast flocks were torn from them by the early
European civilizers ".[8] But this long past history had left its
trail of revenge and counter-punishment, so that it was all but
impossible to restore a peaceful justice. There were undoubtedly
some farmers in the Nieuw Veldt who, as Father O'Haire said,
kicked the natives like dogs and whipped them like mules. But
there were also occasions where the Bantu tribes working down the
Eastern coast robbed the farms and attacked the inhabitants.

There is of course nothing contradictory in the two testimonies.
On the frontiers the two systems of society were in contact and the
Bantu there had not accepted or even known the law of the white
man. Clashes were bound to come about from opposed conceptions of property and of contract, and the tradition of past injustices
was an excuse for barbarous outrages on the part of some Bantu
and for savage cruelties on the part of some colonists. The
experience of the Catholic Church of similar problems had accustomed its rulers to distinguish between the rights of natural law,
which should be respected and defended by all civil governments,
and the social systems which, even if they started with cruel wrongs,
could be ameliorated and made tolerable. So, though the popes of
the renaissance had fulminated against the slavery introduced by the
early Portuguese and Spanish Colonists, their successors had been
more insistent on the strictly natural rights of the slaves, to life and
sustenance and a secure family life; provided the commerce in
slaves was forbidden and those natural rights were safeguarded,
the Catholic Church had not joined in the outcry against the
practice of economic slavery. It is indeed doubtful whether the
speed with which the British governments brought the system to
an end did not bring about, for a generation, even worse conditions
for those who had been enslaved; it relieved their former owners
of legal responsibility before the slaves were in a position to fend
for themselves.

Nor was it likely that Catholics would support the pressure
which Protestant missionaries organized at Exeter Hall to compel
the government to a general condemnation of the colonists irrespective of detailed enquiry and as a matter of public policy. They
looked to the civil government to impose on all a respect for known
law, rather than for new plans or policies. Accordingly they

expected the Cape government to impose its authority both on the farmers and on the Bantu of the border, and their complaint, often repeated, was that it did not keep consistently to that course.

3. "The Catholic Church and the Kaffir"

Before the publication of Bishop Ricards' *Catholic Church and the Kaffir* there does not seem to have been any statement by a responsible Catholic layman or priest on the general problem of the treatment of Bantu society. It is clear from the book, however, that its author had learned a great deal from others; and the respect with which he was always received, as well as the pride with which Catholics referred to the book, shows that his views were either commonly held or won general agreement.

He deals only with the Bantu living in what was then called Kaffraria, and points out that these, Xhosas and Thembus, must be distinguished from the Zulus further north. They had arrived in the area after the middle of the eighteenth century and had exterminated the Bushmen and Hottentots. The Dutch from Cape Town had reached the Great Fish river in 1783 and there met the Bantu tribes coming from the north-east. After an unsuccessful effort to establish a no-man's-land by agreement, the British Government had established settlers in Albany District, and after many raids and a few massacres the British claimed the area between the Great Fish and Kei rivers and installed their own magistrates to superintend the rule of the chiefs. The wars of 1846, 1850, 1877, all caused, according to the bishop, by blunders of the home government, had shown that the system was unsound.

He then gave a good factual description of the Xhosa society; the position of the chief and his authority, his wives and his heirs, the principles of their criminal law, their marriage law, their religion and theory of medicine, healing and witchcraft. He was careful to see their institutions, as far as he could, from their point of view; so he reminded his readers that the cattle given for the bride were considered in their law to be held in trust for her by her male relatives, for her benefit and her children's should she be widowed. At the same time he was realistic and recognized the almost universal practice of abortion in this tribe.

The sobriety of the account gives greater weight to his conclusion that the Bantu would benefit by the abolition of the powers of the chief and the consequent destruction of the native social institutions and law. The insecurity of the people under the authority of their chiefs was, he said, the principal cause of their indolence and of their failure to develop a settled civilization. Their own tradition had failed them, and hope of their improvement could come only by the substitution, gradually if need be, of British law administered by resident magistrates.

Nor was this mere prejudice in favour of European notions and standards. He gave one example of the response which the Thembus had made to such European-directed efforts. A Mr Levey had organized some of that tribe outside their tribal system into a " native agricultural society ", and in four years they had constructed seventy square houses where they had formerly had but eight, had made two hundred water courses in an area which had been served by only thirty, and produced ten bags of wheat a year where four only had been raised before. He urged, therefore, that these people would respond equally as those in Algeria had done to the establishment of Trappist monasteries which would farm on a large scale, and so bring material improvement along with the preaching of Christian doctrines.

For a variety of reasons, of which Bishop Ricards' unskilful planning was one, his project failed in that territory. It may be doubted whether he had a clear picture of what he wanted, but it certainly included (as his book shows) the acceptance of English law by the peoples in the borderland. The Catholic priests of the Cape Province had taken it for granted that their converts, whether Hottentot or Bantu or coloured, would become part of the colonial society. Many of them were critical of its Protestant outlook and customs, but the Catholic community had established their way of life within it, and they were satisfied that their converts would do the like. Bishop Ricards wanted above all the conversion of the border peoples to the Catholic faith; but, aware of the social problems involved, he considered it should be accompanied by the acceptance on their part of English law and administration as the best security for their economic advance.

The practice of Catholics in the vicariates of the Cape Province remained true to this habit of mind. It was not very different from that of most Spaniards and Portuguese in Central and Southern America. They, it is true, were thinking in terms of a European society which in theory rested on Catholic values and could be recalled to them at times. But their converts were assimilated to existing Catholic congregations, and as the Church developed in the Cape Province this also became the pattern. The parishes included both European and coloured, worshipping together, receiving the sacraments from the same priest, often being taught together in the same school. It was a work which obviously could not fit in to the statistical tables of Du Plessis, and some of the Mariannhill writers refused to regard it as proper missionary work. It started very slowly but gained momentum as the Catholic organization was more firmly established among the " whites " after the turn of the century. Today the proportion of Catholics in the coloured population of the Cape is roughly the same as in the white population, so that the fruits of this method were by no means negligible.

II. Bishop Allard and the Zulus

In some respects the conversion of Bantu and coloured peoples in the Cape Province had followed the method of the Spanish and Portuguese Colonies in South and Central America, where Europeans had established their rule and some of their culture. Their outlook in turn was derived from the tradition, more or less historical, of the incorporation of the barbarians in Europe during the eighth, ninth and tenth centuries. The memory of all that work was sufficiently alive to make it natural to think of missionary work as an extension of Christian civilization.

But other methods had been employed both in America and in Asia, and the first vicars apostolic were aware of them. Bishop Griffith and Bishop Devereux urged the Roman authorities to take into consideration the organized tribes who were known to live north of the Orange river and who had been establishing themselves for a considerable time in Natal. It seemed unlikely in the 'forties that the country would be colonized effectively by Europeans—the numbers who had trekked there were relatively few, and the English government, in so far as they had a settled policy, were disposed to treat them as subjects of the native chiefs with whom they had bargained for lands. The missionary approach must be made directly to the Bantu rulers, especially as most of the trekkers held to the Calvinist tradition of intolerance of the Catholic name. When Bishop Devereux was in Rome in 1848 he urged the importance of such a work, showed the Congregation of Propaganda on their maps the territory he had in mind, and recommended strongly that it should be given to a religious order so that the vicar apostolic would not himself be responsible for the provision of men and money. The Oblates of Mary Immaculate accordingly accepted the commission from Propaganda, and Bishop Allard arrived at Port Natal.

Two years later, at the beginning of 1854, Father Barret and Father Gerard came to Pietermaritzburg; the bishop set them to learn first English and then Zulu (the latter, as we have noted, by living in native kraals), and in September of the following year he sent them, apparently without material resources or any backing from the government, to preach the faith to some Zulus south of the Umkomaas river. They dedicated their mission to St Michael. In the following May a local chief, Dumisa, chased away the people among whom the missionaries had settled and replaced them with members of his own tribe, although offering to let the missionaries stay and continue their work. The bishop decided to withdraw them, however, and in July 1856 ordered them to return to Pietermaritzburg.[9] Early in the following year he applied to the Lieutenant-Governor for a grant of land on the usual conditions, and after some correspondence[10] was assigned five hundred acres in the area of the abandoned mission. Work started again at St Michael's in 1858, and two years later a second mission was opened for those who had fled from Dumisa. This time the mission, dedicated to Our Lady of the Seven Sorrows, had a recognized and legal position; it had become clear even to Bishop Allard that the prestige of the civil government could be helpful. He asked that native boys might be indentured as apprentices to him until they were eighteen years old, to be brought up as Christians and to work for their expenses; though the authorities agreed it was probably fortunate that the scheme fell through, as this indenture system was certainly unpopular with the Zulus.

Bishop de Mazenod had written to Bishop Allard saying that the conversion of the Zulus was his first duty, and asking whether it were not possible for him to take part in the work himself. He set himself at once to learn Zulu (without any success) and helped Father Gerard both at St Michael's and at Our Lady of the Seven Sorrows. It would seem from a phrase in one of the bishop's letters that the latter mission had some promise of success, but before it was really established the bishop had made contact with the Basutos and decided to abandon both missions to the Zulus[11]—that of the Seven Sorrows in July 1861 and St Michael's two years later.

The trouble was partly that the Zulus saw at once that Christianity meant the end of polygamy and consequently the changing of their social structure, and partly that they raised astute philosophical difficulties on which neither the bishop nor Father Gerard satisfied them[11a]. Father Gerard explained the failure—and the bishop endorsed his remarks—by accusing the Zulus of a lack of simplicity. The examples sound odd. Though living in relative luxury themselves, the Zulus did not admire the strict poverty and austerity which the vicar apostolic both practised and insisted on. Nor did they show the slightest readiness to give aid to Europeans in building their simple church and dwelling unless it was well paid for. When the mission opened they seemed attracted by the ceremonial, and joined in singing the *Veni Creator*, but later they were inclined to make jests during the lengthy instructions, as though the idea of religion was of no interest. Yet when the priests taught the immateriality of the soul they objected at once by citing the Catholic doctrine of hell fire; as Allard complained, they were *rusés*.

The basis of this attitude seems to be surprise that the Zulus would not recognize the superiority of the virtues and thought and way of life of the European. As the vicar apostolic remarked soon after he landed, " though they have mixed with Europeans for nine or ten years, they have made no single step in civilization but are still as nude as ever ".[12] Now the Europeans had to learn that the Zulu simply did not admire what they valued, and yet was no fool. Of course Father Gerard laboured untiringly to explain the Catholic Faith—but apparently he thought at this time that its European setting would be sufficient to attract respect for it and the desire to obtain it.

Akin to this attitude was Bishop Allard's treatment of the Zulu social order, or rather his neglect of it. True, that society had been largely broken by the wars of Shaka, Dingane and Mpande, but the people still maintained some coherence under their lesser chiefs. The founding of St Michael's mission ignored this situation; it assumed quite simply the right of European priests to expound truth to any who cared to listen. After that first failure, the mission was re-established on a farm granted by the Lieutenant-Governor. Bishop Allard did not indeed claim to represent the English rulers, but these first efforts bore the imprint of a religion of the superior race.

That outlook seems to have been very common in missionary work of the nineteenth century—the only one when European civilization was undoubtedly superior in a material sense, and thought itself to be as clearly so intellectually. But there were older and stronger traditions in the Catholic Church: Columba, if Adamnan reports truly, did not so regard the Druids, any more than St Paul the Athenians, or Ramón da Lull the Tunisians or Father Ricci the Chinese, or Father Nobili the Brahmans. Even in the sixteenth century in America the Spanish Franciscans tried to fashion an Indian Catholic state in California, and the Portuguese Jesuits did so successfully in Paraguay.

The " reductions " of Paraguay, especially after their suppression by the anti-clerical secular rulers, was one of the great epics of Christian missionary work even in Protestant countries. Bishop Allard must have known of them in any case, and he may well have pondered the casual suggestion of Father Murphy (in his report to Propaganda)[13] that Natal could be the field for a like effort. Certainly when he went to Basutoland in 1862 he adopted a method of approach quite different from his earlier one, though neither he nor Father Gerard seems to have thought the change worth mentioning.

III. Basutoland

1. BISHOP ALLARD AND MOSHESH

Basutoland, then a country of some 15,000 square miles, was formed by the mountainous highlands where the head-waters of the Orange river gather, a triangle shut off from Natal by the Drakensberg, cut off from Cape Province, which it touched in the southern pointed extremity, by the Witteberg, and falling to the Caledon River and the Orange Free State to the north-west. For a hundred years from the middle seventeenth century some half dozen Sotho tribes had penetrated the country in flight from the stronger and better organized Nguni kings and had themselves exterminated or expelled the pygmoid Bushmen. In the twenties of the nineteenth century Shaka, the Zulu ruler, sent several expeditions to subjugate the country, but a local chief, Moshesh, partly by tactical skill but more by diplomacy, managed to unite the different tribes and to repulse the attacks. The wars of the Europeans against Dingane finally freed him from the Zulu danger, but at the cost of disputes with the Boers which soon developed into armed raids. The different legal conceptions gave sufficient excuse for both parties to claim breaches of agreement, and in 1852 this brought an invasion by a regular Cape Town force under General Cathcart. Moshesh was successful in the first battle, but astutely asked Cathcart for terms which would include the friendship of the British and so give him some protection against the Boers in future.

But the Basuto contact with European culture was not merely that of war and diplomacy. From the early 'thirties missionaries of the *Missions Evangéliques de Paris* had been established in the country and had made many converts but lamented many apostasies (including one of the sons of Moshesh).* As bible-reading was almost essential to a Calvinist they laboured always to teach the use of writing, and by 1860 their chief foundations were some fifty schools under native instructors. The king—now more than seventy—and many of his chiefs encouraged the movement in so far as it brought the European accomplishments to the people. As yet there was no sign of their abandoning polygamy or accepting Christian law, but it would be inaccurate to say that their attitude was a cynical one of seizing temporal benefits; when Father Gerard got to know Moshesh he found him an admirer of the Old Testament patriarchs and puzzled by, but not disdainful of, the teaching and example of Christ.

The biographer of Father Gerard gives two sources for Bishop Allard's interest in Moshesh; one was an Irish trader in Pietermaritzburg and the other was the houseboy whose father had been the king's envoy to Shaka and Dingane.[14] Both are likely enough

---

* According to their own historian they were accused of engaging too much in politics and commerce, and Moshesh had tired of their ways (Ellenberger, *Un siècle de missions au Lessouto*).

(the Irish trader reappears in later letters), but Father Hoenderwanger[5] may well have been a third. In 1853 he had written to the bishop about two Catholics " *ex famosa tribu Mosha* " who were in prison at Bloemfontein, and it was after meeting the Flemish missionary for the first time in 1861 that the vicar apostolic and Father Gerard made their way to the chief Molapo, the son of Moshesh.

At the audience which was granted them the missionaries had to explain how the religion they wished to expound differed from the Protestant one, and why they claimed it to be that of the gospels which Molapo already knew of. The bishop spoke through Father Gerard, whose Zulu was interpreted. At the suggestion of Molapo they went on to the hill fortress of Moshesh and repeated their request and explanations.[15] By this time they must have realized that even if the Basutos were, as Allard said, straightforward (in contrast to the " double-faced " Zulus)[16] they were certainly not the " poorer simpler Kaffirs " they had set out to find.[17] Necessity alone would have compelled them to ask the permission of the chiefs before opening a mission, but they did more than ask permission. Molapo asked if he might attend their service, and when he came Bishop Allard " used the mitre before and after Mass ".[18] When Moshesh promised them an answer in a few days' time they carefully performed their devotions in as public and ceremonial a manner as possible, knowing that they were under careful observation. The bishop showed no impatience nor any curiosity about the country, rightly guessing that the Basutos wanted to observe their behaviour. So they occupied themselves with their devotions, and only answered such questions as were put to them. When asked about their religion Father Gerard read passages from the gospel in Zulu, which was translated to the audience by one of the Basutos. When some Protestant converts asked questions on matters of dogma the missionaries based their replies on texts from the Bible, which they had already discovered was a convincing method to their hosts.[19]

At a second formal interview with Moshesh Bishop Allard had grasped the necessary diplomacy and after asking through an interpreter for leave to preach the Catholic faith, he promised, if the people would respond, to teach them reading and writing and skilled crafts. When Moshesh mentioned that he wanted his people to learn how to make European clothes, Bishop Allard promised to bring out those who could teach weaving.[20]

As a result of these negotiations the bishop was given a site for a year, and the villagers were instructed to assist them, and indeed to be responsible for their welfare, and apparently to see that they had a congregation.[21] Leaving Father Gerard to start the work, the bishop went back to Pietermaritzburg to collect a lay brother and tools and equipment. Returning with these in October 1862, he was ready for a "solemn" opening of his mission on 1 November. When Moshesh expressed a wish to be present the bishop received him in state, gave him a seat in the choir and granted his request to address the people after the sermon. He treated the Basuto chieftain, in fact, exactly as he would have done a King of France, and without any scruples about his practice of polygamy or other vices. The reward of his excellent and surprising common sense was that Moshesh added to his exhortations to obedience and loyalty a recommendation to the people to examine this new religion, to find out if it were the authentic religion of Jesus Christ.[22] He further told his chiefs to see that the chapel was always full and that no harm was done to the priests.

The Basutos did not imitate the curiosity and friendliness of their ruler. They soon tired of the Catholic liturgy as a show. Father Gerard's work began seriously at that point. He had to build up a dictionary and then to construct a scheme of dogmatic teaching; first an explanation of doctrine and then its crystallization in question and answer.

It would be interesting to know what process had led the vicar apostolic to change his approach. It may be that his superior-general had convinced him that there was something faulty about the earlier methods of Father Gerard. It seems from later letters that he was attracted by the mind and character of Moshesh himself. But since he treated his new line of conduct as not requiring explanation I am inclined to think he was simply following the French tradition of great and even ecclesiastical respect for the central government. In Natal the British held that position, and Bishop Allard was generous in praising, though surprised at, the liberty and help they gave him; but in Basutoland he was free from any obligation to them, and found instead a ruler whose political behaviour answered in many ways to his traditional concept of a personal monarch.

The Oblate priests emphasized their respect for the authority of the Basuto rulers whenever there was occasion for doing so. During the years 1865-8 the Boers of the Orange river made repeated attacks on the country, and Moshesh was beleaguered in his hill fortress and all but starved out. The missionaries did what they could to feed the scattered Basutos, and Father Gerard managed to penetrate the siege lines in order to encourage Moshesh and to bring him provisions.[23] They appear to have helped the negotiations which led to the British declaration of a protectorate over the country, by which Moshesh made himself safe from further attacks by the Boers. Certainly the British officials held the work of the Oblates in high esteem, and it was explicitly for this reason that the Governor of the Cape asked Bishop Grimley in 1869 if he could arrange for these missionaries to undertake work in Namaqualand.[24]

It would be interesting, though still more in the realm of guesswork, to speculate on the reasoning of Moshesh. Naturally the Calvinist missionaries tried to persuade him against welcoming the Catholics. The latter believed from the beginning that the domineering character of the wives of the pastors was one reason for native reluctance to accept their religion; certainly an African would regard it as unseemly. Celibacy, however, was not any more welcome to them, and was indeed scarcely credible; but it was reported very early that when the Calvinists urged Moshesh to refuse admittance to celibate missionaries he asked them what had been the practice of the Lord Christ on earth. Another remark, made much later by a chief who was defending the Catholics, sounds as though it may have started in the court of Moshesh; he had been told that the Catholics paid exaggerated honour to the Blessed Virgin Mary, and asked whether the mother of the king was not the queen in Basuto society and the most honoured of women. Ellenberger, the historian of the Calvinists' mission, commented that his people had become greatly involved in politics at this time. Probably this refers to the internal affairs of the different Basuto chiefs, and there may have been good reasons for their action. But Moshesh, who was clearly an astute ruler, may well have thought it useful for his own authority for two opposed groups of missionaries to bring to his people the European accomplishments that he desired.

Bishop Allard kept his promise to Moshesh, and in April 1865 brought six Sisters of the Holy Family to the country to teach sewing and weaving as well as Christian doctrine. By this time, however, the Basutos had grasped the fact that conversion meant the end of polygamy, and would not allow their women-folk to attend the nuns' school. Moshesh was friendly and even wished his people to learn about the Catholic religion but, as in all historical cases, the royal power stopped short of destroying the pagan prejudices of a people.

At this time the Boers made a determined attack, destroying herds and crops and obtaining the submission of many lesser chiefs. During this war and the consequent famine the missionaries and the nuns did what they could for the Basuto children and the wounded. Bishop Allard dedicated the nation to the protection of Mary Immaculate[25] and did so in the name of Moshesh. A tradition, which the bishop did not contradict, says that he had the king's authority to do so and his promise to put an end to the circumcision rites and to protect those who separated from all subordinate "wives". Though there is no documentary record of such an agreement, the king certainly showed no disapproval of the bishop's action, and when Setlopo, one of his chief officials, made from his death-bed a public and dramatic announcement of his conversion, it was done in the presence of Moshesh himself. It is also clear that Bishop Allard now identified his work with the independence of the Basuto people, and even when the English, at the request of Moshesh, declared the country a protectorate he continued to treat with the chiefs as the civil authority. Though this exposed the Catholics to considerable Protestant and pagan mockery, and to an amount of unofficial physical persecution, it saved the converts from the charge of becoming Europeanized. Father Gerard was able to make a beginning with a Basuto Catholic culture, with its own daily greetings and its own publicly worn emblems. Very slowly the number of baptized increased; the fewness of number was in part due to Father Gerard's insistence on a long testing catechumenate. In his lifetime, and after, some missionaries held that the policy of caution was exaggerated and, strange to say, this was the opinion of Bishop Allard himself.[26]

When Jolivet succeeded Allard as vicar apostolic, in 1874, he at once adopted the same policy of close and friendly contact with the chiefs. Moshesh had died at a great age five years earlier, but the bishop, sending Father Gerard to the northern part of the country, obtained for him, through an English military officer, a recommendation to Molapo, the local pagan ruler, whose luxury shocked the missionary. In 1881 Bishop Jolivet was sending another missionary, Father Le Bihan, from Kimberley into Basutoland, and again he instructed him to pay his respects first to Lerotholi, the eldest son of the paramount chief, although neither of these chiefs showed any disposition towards Catholicism.[27] Good fortune attended the move, though Father Le Bihan was as reluctant as St Boniface had been when sent to Charles Martel. The English had somewhat stupidly demanded the surrender of the muskets treasured by the Basutos, and a party of the latter had made armed resistance, complicated by a civil war between the "loyalists" and the "rebels". Father Le Bihan was able to persuade Lerotholi to sue for peace, his cousin Masupha, another chief, to pay his taxes, and the British administration to suspend the law about the muskets. In return Lerotholi promised him permission to found missions wherever he wished.[28] Though Father Le Bihan complained that lesser officials were allowed to put difficulties in his way, he continued, reluctantly at times, the contact with the sons of Moshesh, and in 1898 Masupha was publicly received into the Church just before he died. A dozen years later Griffith [sic], the second son of Lerotholi, became a Catholic after a long catechumenate, and on the death of his elder brother was accepted by the British and the Basutos as paramount chief.

2. METHODS AND MOTIVES

In their first approach to the Zulus both Bishop Allard and Father Gerard had been impatient for conversions; after less than a year's teaching they had abandoned the effort as unpromising. They remembered this lesson in Basutoland. The first adult baptisms, seven in number, took place in 1865; in the following year there were nine in January and twenty-nine in December. Though the increase was steady after that slow start, it never became really spectacular. There were 230 adult baptisms in 1871. When Bishop Jolivet, the second vicar apostolic of Natal, made his first visitation of Basutoland, in 1875, there were five hundred

Catholics; by the end of the century the number was ten times as great, by 1904 it was 8,000, and by 1912 it had risen to 15,000. Roughly speaking the figures indicate an increase from 0·5 per cent to 5 per cent of the population.

The influence of the reigning house on the movement is as hard to evaluate in this case as in others. The explanation that when a ruler became Christian or friendly to Christians his people followed suit does not stand investigation, though it has been often stated for the European barbarians. In their case of course, notably for Clovis the Frank, the ruler was more usually afraid to change lest he be murdered by his nobles. In Basutoland something of that psychology appeared. The "rebel" chiefs in the war of the muskets attacked the sons of Moshesh as negligent of the ancestral religion. Others of them later drove Masupha from power, and confined him to a village where finally he became a Catholic. It seems likely that the death-bed conversions of one or two of the lesser chiefs had been postponed from fear of the political consequence of their action.

Certainly, the friendliness, and still more the conversion, of a chief made it easier for the missionaries to obtain sites for churches and schools. But they had also to fear the possibility and the consequences of a later apostasy. One of the earliest converts was a niece of Moshesh but, returning to paganism, she became a bitter, knowledgeable enemy of the Christians. When Griffith Lerotholi first asked for instruction from Father Foulonneau, the latter dreaded a like sequence and was very reluctant at first to accept the chief even as a catechumen.[29]

It is perhaps natural that European writers should assume missionary work to be facilitated by its association with their material culture. In support of the view Moshesh's expressed desire, in his early interviews with Bishop Allard, for teachers of European arts might be quoted. Surprisingly, at least to the uninformed mockers of missionaries, he wanted the women of his people to learn how to make European clothes, an attitude very common and very reasonable in intelligent African rulers, who have little use for the sentimental attachment of journalists and trippers to native dress. It was partly because of this request that Bishop Allard brought the sisters of the Congregation of the Holy Family to Basutoland in 1865. But the menfolk, and especially the lesser chiefs, soon found, as we have seen, that the nuns gave their pupils ideas of monogamy and even virginity which ran counter to Basuto custom. Moshesh was powerless (in this as in other cases) to impose his will, and the first attempt at a " trade " school was a failure. Some of the prejudice against the nuns was overcome during the wars of 1865–8 and the subsequent famine, when they looked after a number of children, and they were able to teach the rudiments of nursing to a small number of convert widows. At this time, however, such work was on a minute scale and the improvements of a material sort, like the beginnings of secular education, came after the conversions and were not a cause of them.

Nor was this due merely to the reluctance of the pagans to be bribed into the Christian faith. Partly it came from the fewness of missionaries, priests, lay brothers and nuns, so that these had little or no time to spare for direct cultural instruction. Bishop Allard seems always to have tried to do his work with the smallest number of helpers. It is true that he sometimes told the superior-general of the Oblates of the opportunities, but his requests were never framed in a way to gain generous help from those at headquarters who had several fields open to their available personnel. When Bishop Jolivet became Vicar Apostolic of Natal, in 1874, he asked for and obtained many more helpers—on one occasion he wrote that the superior-general had never refused a reasonable request for men—but he opened up so many new missions in his vicariate that there were never enough priests in Basutoland to instruct all those who wished to become catechumens. The same condition obtained when Basutoland, having been cut off from Natal to form part of the new Kimberley vicariate under Bishop Gaughren, was consecrated by him to the Sacred Heart of Jesus in 1888. Many would-be converts who presented themselves after the event had to be taught largely by catechists from those Basuto who were already Catholic. Only after 1894, when the country was made a prefecture apostolic, first under Monsignor Monginoux and later under Monsignor Cenez, and its needs were therefore presented directly and separately to the superior-general of the Oblates and the Congregation of Propaganda, did the number of priests reach double figures.

The absence of the motive of material culture in the early presentation of the Catholic religion to the Basutos was due not only to the paucity of missionaries but to the remarkable character of Father Gerard. As the only linguist in the early days he was responsible both for instruction and for training newly arrived priests. The appeal of material culture depends at least in part on the display of comfort and wealth and calls for some care in administration. Father Gerard despised, almost hated, both one and the other. Only an official " visitor " of the Oblates in 1871 and the order of Bishop Jolivet in 1875 brought reasonable and necessary repairs to the mission buildings.[30] The attitude of Father Gerard was adopted deliberately. He seems at first to have favoured Bishop Allard's plan of using the Holy Family sisters to teach the Basuto women to sow seed crops and to weave cloth. But after the failure of that first attempt Father Gerard concentrated almost entirely on appeal to individuals and their instruction. Quite early he abandoned the original centre, where he had tried to attract by the music and the liturgy, in order to visit even distant villages. At the same time he insisted on a longer and more rigorous preparation of would-be converts, even against the wishes of Bishop Allard, whom he regarded almost as a saint.[31] What is remarkable about him is the perseverance with which he followed his chosen method—he called it fishing with line rather than net[32]— and his ability to impose it on his fellow workers until arthritis limited his physical activities in 1897. The devotion he displayed was regarded by his fellows as heroic, and the Basutos were so impressed that they regarded him as a miracle worker.

3. Pagan Beliefs and Christian Faith

Such a method presupposed some point of contact with the beliefs of the pagans. This was not difficult. Like many peoples who have passed the animistic stage, and especially those whose culture is an amalgam of the sky-gods and animist levels,* the Basutos retained the notion of a high god or creator, *Molimo*, but believed he took no active part in their affairs; they found it " worked better " to placate some at any rate of their chief ancestors. The God preached by Father Gerard was easily identified by them with the old god, but they had to be persuaded of his

* Accepting the theory of culture-developments of Schmidt in the *Ursprung der Gottesidee*.

interest in them. They had also legends of a virgin-born divinity who refused kingship but delivered men from the threat of the mountains, and they addressed themselves at times to a saviour whose hands were pierced and bleeding.[33] It does not seem to be established whether these images were the result of contact with Christians at some remote period of their history. They are unlikely to have started with the Calvinist missionaries, since these had only been in contact with them for a generation, and the pagans believed the legends to be their own. Father Gerard apparently made use of them when preaching on the Passion of Jesus Christ. Father Le Bihan reported to Bishop Jolivet the use he made of them. " At bottom ", he told them, " you are very religious. Though God is unknown to you now, your fables contain in germ the truths which Christianity reveals. If you listen to my explanations you will see that you are not so far from Christianity as you suppose ". Then he outlined the Catholic religion as belief in a good God, the fall of man, the redemption by Jesus Christ, and fitted the Basuto legends into the plan.[34]

Though some modern missionaries lay great stress on this approach to pagans, and imagine they are improving on the methods of their predecessors by adopting it, unfortunately without as much success in conversions, they sometimes overlook the real difficulty. The Basutos had long been convinced that the high god and those connected with him lived in realms which did not demand their co-operation. They could consider and in a sense believe in divine redemption, but treated it as outside practical affairs. Of course, the men of western civilization are not so very different; almost every heresy from the strict Catholic doctrines of the incarnation and grace had led in the end to doubt of human merit, and even of man's responsibility. When Father Gerard began his instructions to the Basutos he soon found that the practice of their religion was mainly to placate the enemy-gods or to defeat them (and to cheat *Molimo*, who was a strict upholder of the moral law) by the tricks of magic. Social custom, which had almost replaced morality based on religious doctrine, recognized drunkenness as a legitimate form of thanksgiving for prosperity— and so habitual for the wealthy—though still associated with a vague sense of guilt. More important, social life as well as economic had been rationalized on the basis of polygamy. Men and women had learned to think that marital intercourse was wrong and even perverse during pregnancy and until the child had been weaned, and this moral rule was made the justification for the taking of additional wives.

These facts were recognized by Bishop Jolivet (on the testimony of his missionary priests) and reported by him to the Congregation of Propaganda. Though dealing specifically with Zulu society, a great deal of his account applies also to the Basutos. They do, he said, regard marriage as a fixed and permanent contract for the procreation of children, but, believing it " against nature " to have marital relations until the child is weaned, they must either be celibates for one or two years when a child is born or take another wife. For converts to the Catholic Faith there will be difficulties, since they will still " feel " they are disobeying the natural law. The heretics, he notes, have had sad experience of the sexual morality of their converts, for adultery and other vices have taken the place of polygamy, and only divine grace can save our converts from a like result.[35]

It has often been supposed that the Christian missionaries attacked the general Bantu practice of paying a *lobola* of cattle to the father of a bride. Some of the Calvinists in Basutoland certainly did so, and there are one or two allusions in Bishop Allard's early letters which suggest he shared their views that it was a traffic in wives. But the Catholic missionaries very soon learned to distinguish between the essence of the practice and some of its deleterious results. In the report already quoted Bishop Jolivet expressly likened it to the European customs of the bride's dowry. It was a settlement between two families, one of which had lost an economic worker while the other had gained an economic worker. It served sometimes as her guarantee of honourable behaviour: should she desert her husband, her family must restore the *lobola*. And it was also the guarantee of the approval of the marriage by the family of her husband. But in a society where polygamy was accepted it could unfortunately help to maintain that system. Though it did not mean, in Basutoland or amongst the Zulus, that women were given in marriage against their will, or at least not more so than elsewhere, the wealthy, who are usually the older, could afford several wives, and this naturally led to a high *lobola* and greater difficulties in the way of the young unmarried men. It is not surprising then, that, in the interests of their converts, the Catholic missionaries always strove for the reduction of the head of cattle needed for a legal marriage.[36]

There were other difficulties for convert women. A widow " belonged " to the family of her late husband so long as her father retained the original *lobola*. The system, therefore, put pressure on her as a rule to become an additional wife for one of her late husband's relatives. Again, the idea of consecrated virginity, which occurs, though of course rarely, among Catholic girls, would demand an economic sacrifice on the part of her family, and naturally increased their opposition to the Faith.

Several times over the centuries missionaries in Africa had suggested to the Congregation of Propaganda that the marriages of pagans were all invalid because they had no intention of fidelity to one wife. Rome, or more strictly the Holy Office, had again and again rejected the argument on the ground that the first marriage was made according to natural law and a permanent natural bond was, therefore, created during the lives of the two partners. In a letter to the Congregation of 9 May, 1887,[37] Bishop Jolivet acknowledged that these first marriages must be valid, but urged that the Church could dissolve the natural bond for a convert even though his first or " great " wife did not refuse to be a Catholic, and so give ground for the Pauline privilege. The bishop's argument has been accepted by canonists, but then and since then the Holy Office has shown itself very reluctant to give a dispensation from the natural bond.

To make effective conversions, therefore, the Catholic missionaries had to do more than convince the Basuto of the truth of Christian doctrine. The convert had also to learn the new habit of directing his life by what he believed. It is not surprising to read of Father Gerard[38] that his course of instruction usually included what would be called a " retreat " in Europe. And in many cases it would be necessary to require the convert, if a man, to send away but still support all his wives save the first married, who though honoured was not the most favoured; if a woman, to persuade her still pagan husband to monogamy, or to let her live as a widow though not returning to her father's house. It is surprising indeed that there were so many conversions and, in the circumstances, so few apostasies and not more violent opposition

The austerity of the missionary appeal was not merely personal to Father Gerard. When Griffith Lerotholi asked what he must do to become a " Roman " he addressed himself to Father Foulon- neau, a young missionary who was trying to negotiate with the chief the grant of a site of a new mission in his territory. The chief gave as the reason of his desire that Moshesh and other ancestors had appeared to him in his dreams and urged on him that it was the only way of salvation. The missionary thereupon explained that, though the mercy of God works in many ways, men must not base their religion on dreams. Protestations of sincerity finally brought the real objections: the priest knew that the chief was an habitual drunkard and had many wives (actually thirty).

An essential preliminary to baptism would be sobriety and the sending away of all but the first, the queen-wife. Griffith promised the first reform quite easily; when his fellow chiefs tried on one occasion to keep him in the ancestral paths with brandy, he guessed the plan and went on official business till they had time to finish the brandy themselves. Apparently there was only one known outbreak (about Christmas time, too) during the many months of his catechumenate.

The marriage problem was not so easy. To twenty-eight of the wives Griffith readily bade farewell, but besides the queen there was a well-beloved younger wife. The queen herself had no wish to be sole wife, but the priests were adamant, and at long last Griffith promised to ask the queen to consent. Astonishingly to our notions, she promised to pray God to remove her from the scene. Shortly afterwards, being given chloroform for an opera- tion, she died under the anaesthetic and Griffith was able to enter the Church along with the wife of his desire.[39]

From quite early in this missionary effort the priests had recog- nized that there were three great obstacles to conversions—the social habits of drunkenness, polygamy, and magical practices and their ramifications. In the preparation of converts they certainly took all reasonable steps to eliminate the first two. It would seem that they supposed the addiction to magic would fall away before a sincere belief in the Christian faith.   Certainly they recognized the dangers of the initiation, training and rites which extended over several weeks and were obligatory for girls as well as boys.   In these secret preparations for tribal adulthood the power of magical practices to give courage (for young men) or charm (for young women) played a part, but the missionaries seem to have been more worried by the kind of sexual instruction and experiments which accompanied them.   They knew well enough that those habits, strengthened by the physiological urges of adolescence, would be appallingly difficult to unteach.   They may have supposed that magical practices, being fundamentally unreasonable, would not gain so strong a hold.

The effects, however, have not worked out so simply.   Though sins of the flesh have of course been harder for Basuto Christians to overcome after an indoctrination (a condition not peculiar to the Bantu peoples), the relapses to ritual murders to obtain courage or good fortune of one kind or another have reappeared distressingly even after years of freedom, and even though they have never become a general practice.

In his report on the Bantu missions Bishop Jolivet stressed the physiological and sociological difficulties of the converts.   He was by all accounts, and as his letters show, a very intelligent observer of facts, and he saw no remedy save in the work of divine grace, hoping that would operate through the children who were trained in the Faith from infancy.   His prognosis could be defended, because the really large accession of converts came after 1920, when the Marist Brothers and other religious orders established Christian schools and hospitals and other institutions.

But, looking more closely, it must be observed that there was already a strong and faithful Christian community among the Basutos before these foundations.   Their success was a result as much as a cause of very many sincere and effective conversions. If the historian asks, as he should, what prepared the way, I think attention must be given to some seemingly trifling and even unsuccessful efforts of Father Gerard and those who worked with him.   Though the missionaries in the country asserted that conversions increased considerably after the consecrations of Basutoland to the Sacred Heart by Bishop Gaughren and Monsignor Cenez,[39a] the causal connection, if there, is almost inscrutable.   But the same is not true of Father Gerard's repeated efforts to create a novitiate for Basuto nuns, and to give the idea of a religious or priestly vocation to the young men. These efforts lasted only for a time, and in 1896 other experienced missionaries reported that celibacy as a possible life for men would take a century or more to establish. More long-lived was Father Gerard's custom of insisting on public penances for those of his catechumens and adult converts who had been known to break the Christian law. He himself did penance with a rope round his neck on one occasion, and the practice of penitential dress and the sinner's place of scorn were common in his time; his preparation for baptism could be likened by the Basutos to some of their own initiation ceremonies.

These practices were much modified or abolished by his successors, though the memory of them seems to have survived. But another has continued down to the present. In 1867 Father Gerard taught all his converts to greet one another with the Christian wish, *Ho rorisoe Jesu Kriste*, " Jay Jesus Christ be praised," and to reply to it, *Le Maria ea se nang sekoli*, " and Mary Immaculate too". Even earlier than this he had taught all the baptized to wear a cross or other Christian emblem prominently.

Small though they were in themselves, these habits meant that every loyal Catholic Basuto gave concrete form, by word or thing, to his faith; they were related to and expressive of the doctrine he believed; they formed, better, probably, than any economic organization because simpler, and more general, the beginnings of a culture which would be both Catholic and proper to Basutos. Even the frustrated efforts to introduce the (technical) religious life would show the Basutos that the Church was not in any way reserved to Europeans.

There must always be a temptation to describe missionary work in terms proper to political methods. The latter have already been studied over and over again in the usual subjects of historical writing and we forget that they are appropriate only to political organization. Not only theory but the facts of the first half century of Catholic work in Basutoland should warn us not to force religious history into such a frame. But it is not easy to say what the pattern should be. The attitude of the missionaries, the attitude of the pagans, the motives of the converts are all difficult to evaluate.

The long traditions of the Catholic Church make available two or three general methods of missionary labour; in Basutoland perhaps the nearest parallel would be that of Augustine of Canterbury and his companions in England of the seventh century, and the chiefs behaved at times like the pagan rulers of that time. If there was such a repetition of method it was quite unconscious but, given the continuity of Catholic traditions, it may have been historically inevitable. Certainly the dominant and successful feature was the preaching of Catholic dogma and morality as supremely valuable; Father Gerard made sure of that. And the result by 1920 was a community of 40,000 Catholic Basutos. The time had come for cultural works calling for greater organization, more capital expenditure and personnel. It was fortunate that the Oblates of Mary Immaculate were able to entrust the task to their Canadian province, which was well equipped to supply these needs.

IV. In Natal

While the European Catholic community was in process of formation the work of the Church in purely Bantu areas such as Basutoland, and elsewhere, was, in organization as in geography, largely independent. But missionary efforts for the coloured and Indian peoples, as well as for the Bantu in the areas of European settlement, had never been entirely neglected, and the success obtained in the early twentieth century deserves notice.

Before the end of the nineteenth century the Congregation of Propaganda was reminding the vicars apostolic that they were responsible also for these peoples. In June 1884 Bishop Jolivet had to give an explanation of the absence of Catholic missions in the Transvaal, where Protestant work was plentiful.[40] His excuse was mainly lack of funds, and the divisions of his vicariate soon afterwards absolved him from further responsibility there. But he realized that it was not possible to do his duty through the Trappists of Mariannhill alone. In October 1887 he purchased for £1,580 the property of Oakford, twenty miles north of Durban, in Zulu country where a priest was already at work, and in the following year could report native missions there, at Durban and Pietermaritzburg, at the Bluff south of Durban, and at Umtata and

Kokstad in Griqualand East.[41]   Optimistic though Bishop Jolivet was, he could not find the money for these new ventures, or even the men, and at the same time maintain his " works " for the white population. The visitor of the Oblates' Congregation and his own Council were worried by the debts he had already incurred.[42] His suggestions were to sell Oakford to the Trappists, or, failing them, to the Dominican sisters, and to ask Rome to create separate prefectures of Kaffraria and Zululand.[43] But he was firmly reminded by the father visitor, again making an inspection, and by his own priests, that zeal for Africa was dying out at the scholasticates of the Congregation because of his policy: " they had no wish to come to his vicariate to look after a few Europeans ".[44] Accordingly the bishop had to persevere with these missions, and he did so by persuading nuns of various congregations to open schools in them.

Small though they were in all cases, ranging in numbers from twelve to seventy, Bishop Jolivet was able to report in 1897 that there were orphanages for Indian girls and native boys in Durban, run by Augustinians; schools for Indians and natives at Pietermaritzburg run by Sisters of the Holy Family; for coloureds and natives at Oakford under the Dominicans; schools for coloureds at Kokstad, Cala and Umtata in the care of Holy Cross Sisters.[45]

The first mission in Zululand proper had been opened in November 1895, following the death of John Dunn in the previous August. John Dunn was a European hunter who had become a Zulu chief. On his death-bed he expressed a wish that his numerous coloured children should be brought up as Catholics. Sir Marshall Clarke was at the time the government agent in Zululand. Since making the acquaintance of Bishop Jolivet as a fellow prisoner of war in Potchefstroom, he had renewed the friendship while commissioner in Basutoland. He lost no time in asking the bishop to supply a missionary, and Father Anselme Rousset set out from Oakford with some Dominican sisters and an Oblate brother. This was the beginning of Holy Cross Mission at Emoyeni, near Gingindlovu. Soon the Dominican sisters were replaced by Franciscan Missionaries of Mary, and in the course of time other Oblate fathers and brothers came and went, among them Brother Leo Gumede, the first Zulu Oblate of Mary Immaculate. Although the first care was to provide for Dunn's offspring, work for the Bantu began at once and the government granted a nearby site in the Zulu reserve at Ebuhleni. It was here that Father Bryant worked at his carefully compiled dictionary during the following years.* On the whole, however, Father Rousset was to labour almost single-handed throughout Zululand for the twenty-eight years he spent there. When he handed over to the Benedictines, in March 1924, he had established only one other central mission, that of St Jules, at Mbongolwane. Yet it could almost be said that there was scarce a footpath that he had not trudged over at some time during the course of his many and prodigious journeyings.[46]

There were other Oblate priests in Natal whose whole life was given up to work among the Bantu. Father Louis Mathieu was newly ordained when he was sent in 1880 to re-open the abandoned mission of St Michael, eighty-three miles south-west of Durban.[47] Two years later he went to found a mission twenty miles north of Durban, and in 1925 he was still in that area and could boast that there were now eight missions in action on the circumference of a circle of thirty miles diameter, originating from Oakford and served by five priests. He had planned it, by his account, so that each priest could get into touch occasionally with his neighbour.[48]

When this basic idea, as he calls it, first came to him is not documented; certainly he was, in his own words, a lonely sentinel at the start and remained so for many years. There was no great institution like Mariannhill to support him, and its methods were therefore out of the question. He found " a few Portuguese black Christians "—Bantu from Portuguese East Africa—but " they were not very edifying ". He had managed to learn enough Zulu to explain himself; in fact he gave the Mariannhill fathers, including David Bryant,† their first lessons in the language; but his Zulu would not have passed the later standards of his own pupil or of Father Wanger.

But he soon grasped an essential fact about the people among whom he was to work. Their military power had been broken by the British Zulu war of 1879, just before he came to South

---

* See page 251, *infra*.

† Later author of the Zulu-English dictionary and lecturer in the University of London.

Africa. English accounts often supposed that the defeated dynasty of Shaka had ruled over a homogeneous and loyal people, and the legend has persisted. Father Mathieu learned and stated the historical fact that the inhabitants of Natal were really the remains of ninety-four tribes who had been harried and smashed by Shaka some fifty years earlier, and that the Zulus were merely the dominant minority among them.[49] The people to whom the Catholic missionaries came had lost their own traditions, were often remnants of several different tribes, and had been in hiding from the ruling minority, or serving as their " dogs " in servitude, for years before the British made war on them. Like all such people they had lost many of the natural virtues their ancestors may have possessed and were likely to be extremely unreliable. Father Mathieu did not enjoy the advantages of the missionaries in Basutoland any more than the organization of Mariannhill.

The few letters of his which have survived give the credit to native catechists, or more often to young Zulu women, and indirectly to the Dominican nuns. At their Oakford Convent the nuns opened their boarding school for Bantu girls as well as for Europeans. Several of the former became fervent Catholics, and three of them, according to Father Mathieu, were practically foundresses of the missions of St Peter (Montebello), Itafamasi, and Kruisfontein. In some cases the missionary and his catechists had been able to visit the district once a month, but their instructions would soon have been forgotten had it not been for the work of Oakford pupils. Lucy Luthuli of Isinembe did more. She collected a small group in her kraal and so trained them that they were ready for baptism and absolution as soon as priest could come;[50] it was the beginning of the Kruisfontein mission.

The Europeans who knew Father Mathieu during these years still remember his own labours and devotion. Perhaps he gives a hint of it in describing the country of his " parish ", which covered an area of more than twelve hundred square miles. Some of the journeys could be done on horseback, but in places there were almost vertical paths of ascent (Montebello was more than 3,000 feet above sea level). Other places could be reached only by clambering over rocks, and where there was a ford one day there would be a swollen river the next.[51]

Nor were his difficulties only physical. In 1915 Julius Mthembu, a convert from Mariannhill, had collected and instructed some catechumens in his kraal at Umhlali. He sent for the priest several times, and when Father Mathieu was at last able to make a visit he found a well-kept thatch chapel, a school of thirty-five children, and a handful of catechumens. But before he could do anything the colonists (i.e. the whites) drove these Bantu away from the site and this promising little Christianity was dispersed. The trouble was that native tenure was insecurely at the mercy of the proprietor of the land. Father Mathieu had to be a prospector as well as a teacher. After the disappointment at Umhlali he found an abandoned farm on the upper Tongaat and persuaded Bishop Delalle to buy it; so he obtained a place near a native location, but one which could not be taken over and cleared of Bantu by Europeans.[52] Afterwards he built a school and, here as elsewhere, persuaded the Dominicans to teach the children.[53] Without the help of these nuns, as he said on several occasions, the missionary work would not have been possible.

If more priests had been available—after forty-five years he had only four to help him in the area—or more lay brothers, more might have been done. But it was slow work in any case. It took seventy years, as Father Mathieu pointed out, to collect fifty thousand converts in the whole of Basutoland, and the mixed hordes who were called Zulu were more difficult to deal with; it was line fishing always, as he said.[54] He was content apparently with a year's catechumenate (or in some cases six months),[55] though he knew that in the north of Africa Cardinal Lavigerie had insisted on a much longer one.[56] But at the end of forty years, when there were five to six thousand Bantu Catholics in his area, he could write: " The results are small but good; practically all keep their Easters, a good number receive Holy Communion daily; a few begin the religious life."[57] Some of them certainly showed an almost native grasp of theological truth, like the adult catechumen who, when asked what he knew of Satan, replied that he was the policeman of the good God[58]—which is not far from the concepts of the prologue to the Book of Job. Towards the end of his ministry Father Mathieu organized a savings club for his converts— a difficult lesson, as he said, for blacks ; and a discussion circle where " some preach better sermons than I do ", but which served especially to correct the " bolshevism " picked up by the Bantu in cities.[59]

Elsewhere in the country similar developments were occurring. Priests aided, and how greatly, by the nuns, to whom a later chapter of this book is devoted, and financed if rather meagrely by the established white Catholic community, were attending more and more to the conversion and education of the other races. In the Cape Provinces and in the Transvaal it was work among the Coloureds, and the great increase of Catholics among them seems to date from this quarter-century. In Natal at long last the Indian population received more attention. Already when they came to work on the sugar farms as indentured labourers in the 'sixties there were some Catholics among them and a priest went occasionally to administer the sacraments. It was assumed then that most would return to India on completion of their agreed years of service, but the farmers, and even more the railway contractors, persuaded them to stay for further terms. By the end of the century a new generation, born and brought up in South Africa, were engaged in gardening, business and other occupations as well as on the sugar farms. As early as 1884 Bishop Jolivet had discussed with his council the opening of a school for the children, and two years later Father Baudry had found an Indian schoolmaster for it. In November 1887 a small brick and zinc hut twenty feet by thirty was built which served both as school and chapel, and Father Gourlay took charge of it. A small orphanage was opened by the Augustinian sisters for Indian girls until the local whites objected to their presence in the Berea residential area.[60] Similar beginnings were made at Pietermaritzburg and Newcastle. Only by 1909 was the work properly developed. By that time Father Maingot was in charge of an Indian parish at St Anthony's in Durban, with Father Tanguy to help him; he had built a church as well as a school and orphanage with the Holy Family Sisters as teachers. Pietermaritzburg also had its church and school for Indians, and the Dominican sisters had opened a school for them in Newcastle.

It could not be said that the local missionary efforts had yet captured the imagination of the Catholic laity in South Africa. They were proud indeed of the work in Basutoland and Mariannhill, but they thought of it as separate from their own community. Local " native missions " were still the business of priests and nuns. But the beginnings were established, and with the greater unity which followed the appointment of an apostolic delegate in 1922, all Catholics were being prepared to recognize the Church as independent of the racial origins of its members.

Chapter X

MARIANNHILL

I. The Trappist Plan

1. PRIOR PFANNER'S FOUNDATION

A DIFFERENT method of missionary work to that which we have been describing was undertaken among the Zulus of Natal by the Trappist monks.

In his doctoral thesis on the history of Mariannhill[1] Father Dahm claims its legitimate succession in the line of the great monastic missionary institutions of Europe. Evidence for that view is clear to the eye. The churches, the workshops and farms, the hospital and training college, the schools and guest houses of the mother-town correspond to the descriptions of our medieval historians; and in the outlying country of Natal there are the many villages, each with its own church and farmlands, its school and the rest—a sort of colony or grange settled from the monastery.

It could easily be shown that such a development was in the mind of Bishop Ricards when he brought the Trappist monks to Dunbrody.* Quotations from *The Catholic Church and the Kaffir*, or from his letters and speeches, would suffice. His reading of Montalembert and his short visit to the Trappist foundation in Algeria would be enough to fire his ready imagination. But to change a romantic picture of the European past into a vigorous, lively institution of Africa in the nineteenth century, with all its laws and customs having a present purpose and utility—that was the real difficulty; and though many people and many quarrels contributed to the solution of its problems, Bishop Ricards had no part therein. Indeed, it would seem that he did not understand in 1882 the basic necessities of his own plan, for he wanted the Trappists to begin evangelization before they had established their material abbey, and he wanted them to be a monastery without either sufficient men or capital for that purpose.

* See pp. 104, sqq.

The Dunbrody monks came to Natal in two parties, one on 27
November and the other early in December, 1882, with their
wagons and equipment, and were directed by the Oblate fathers
to the Bluff, a ridge to the south of the bay. Their sub-prior,
Father Joseph, had seen Bishop Jolivet on 27 November and had
been offered by him the mission land at St Michael's which the
Government had granted to the vicariate in the time of Bishop
Allard. They were preparing to trek there when, in mid-
December, Prior Pfanner arrived back from Europe with money
and more monks. The next few days were busy ones for him.
As he wrote in a pamphlet four years later:[2]

> I came to Natal and found my brothers in desolation; their
> clothes worn out, lacking food and houses. I arrived on Sunday,
> made arrangements with Bishop Jolivet on Monday, on Tuesday
> inspected a terrain of 2,000 arpents, bought it on Wednesday and
> registered the purchase on Thursday. The following Monday
> we all turned up just as we left the place of thorns.* We slept
> on our boxes under wagon-covers the first night, but after that
> under canvas tents. I then hurried back to Europe for more
> novices, and to publish our new foundation at Mariannhill and
> to resign the priory of Bosnia.

He had persuaded Bishop Jolivet that St Michael's was unsuitable
for his work, and had purchased from the Land Colonisation
Company " Zeekoegat farm "—the land on which Mariannhill
now stands. A tradition of the Trappists said that he learned of it
from a Lutheran missionary who was unaware that this German
stranger was a Catholic priest.

The pamphlet was written for the friends of Mariannhill in
Germany at a time when there was much criticism of Abbot
Pfanner, and he naturally dealt mainly with his own part in making
the foundation. He made no allusion to the fact that his friendly
reception by Bishop Jolivet, and his permission to settle in Natal,
had depended on the good offices of Bishop Ricards, with whom he
had quarrelled. On 27 November, the day when the sub-prior
visited Bishop Jolivet, the latter made a careful note of what he
granted, and it began: *Reverendissimo Domino Episcopo Ricards
assentiente ac volente.* Even if the little red-haired prior remembered
that Bishop Ricards had given his consent, he probably thought it

* The prior's pet name for Dunbrody.

unimportant; his mind was set on the work of the future, and as a result of his collections in Europe he was now able to accept Bishop Jolivet's other condition—that the Trappists should be wholly responsible for the cost, " *suis tamen impensis* ".

The fifty monks were put to work making the necessary roads and bridges, erecting buildings, breaking the land, setting up their printing machines and tannery and so on. By August 1884 they had made 188 acres of waste arable, had three and a half miles of road completed, and as much half ready, and 1300 square yards of buildings.[3]

As yet no single baptism had taken place at Mariannhill, as the prior called the new foundation.* But employment was given readily to Bantu willing to work with the monks, and from the beginning, or at least very soon afterwards, the prior adopted and defended this as his method of missionary work. His own pamphlet of 1887 describes it:

> Our first buildings were temporary, for sleeping rooms and work rooms. Then we separated them by streets and so formed a village with its square, dormitories, refectory, church, chapter-house, workshops, kitchens, cellar, workshops for the marschal, the smith, the saddler, the cobbler, the tailor, the printer and photographer. . . . We built large schoolrooms for 82 boys who are maintained completely by the convent. All this building was in any case necessary against the rains, but our work-shops were put up only as need arose for them. We made a mistake by building too small a convent, not realizing that we should number 130 in four years' time; and we didn't know about the local stone available.

After more detail about the road-making, bridge building, installation of pumps and a turbine, about the draining of the land and the crops and the first attempts at forestry, he continued:

> All this astonished the blacks, who are very susceptible to externals. They think that our dams work like the rod of Moses, and think more of the earth because it produces new crops for us. Soon they ask to work for us. That is our ordinary way of

---

* According to Dahm, quoting the prior, the name was a conflation of Maria and Ann: the former because all Trappist foundations are called after the Mother of God, the latter because Prior Pfanner wished to record his gratitude to his own grandmother.

bringing them to the mission. We all, abbot* and monks, work and do what to them are wonders. When they want to join in, we tell them it is impossible unless they go to school. So they send their children and hear about God from them.[4]

This decision of the prior's was not made to justify, to his helpers in Europe, the course of events at Mariannhill. Four years earlier he had written:

> Manual work is an essential part of real civilization, and no missionary will convert the Kaffir if he does not bring him to accept it. We have to teach agriculture and crafts to this undisciplined people. If we want to arrive at that goal, we must work on the soil and with our hands and must found industries. It would be absurd to want to teach the Kaffir bricklaying or ploughing if we could do neither ourselves nor even show him how.[5]

2. MISSIONS AND AUXILIARIES

The aim, then, of Prior Franz Pfanner was to build a Christian community of Bantu on the estates of his monastery   Even before this took shape a chief whose kraal was 135 miles from Mariannhill asked the monks to establish a school for his people. The prior bought a large farm nearby and set to work to create a Mariannhill on a smaller scale. This mission of Reichenau was commenced in 1886 and was followed by others, for the same method was used both by the prior and his successors. A large farm was necessary so that a native Christian community could be formed, with its workshops and schools, and later other institutions, grouped round and dependent on the church and the monks who served it. By the year 1909 there were twenty-eight[6] dependent settlements of the abbey, groups of Christian families who, in that year, brought 2,155 infants to baptism.[7]

It was by permission of a General Chapter of the Trappist order that the priory of Dunbrody had been founded in 1880. The difficulties of the situation there were put before the meeting in 1882 by Father Pfanner; the transfer to Mariannhill was made on his own initiative, but he obtained the approval of the General Chapter of 1883 for the move and two years later the elevation of

---

* Prior Franz Pfanner was consecrated Abbot of Mariannhill in 1885.

the priory to an abbey with himself as abbot. Not only was the foundation an act of the Trappist order but the Trappist rule and training were necessary for the work. The monks who formed the cadre of Mariannhill came from Father Franz's priory of Maria Stern in Bosnia, and the discipline and spirit of the Trappists, their combination of manual work and contemplation, provided the example by which he hoped to build up a Christian civilization among the Bantu, and guaranteed a continuity of effort.

Within a few months of buying the land in Natal Prior Pfanner decided that the normal growth of a European monastery must be speeded up. In the spring of 1883 he left his community again to make a further recruiting tour in Austria and Germany. By the end of that year he had assembled at Mariannhill a community of eighty-five persons.[8] As the enterprises he planned took concrete shape he had need of more and more Trappists, and therefore repeated his quest for postulants in Europe. Two years after becoming an abbey Mariannhill was probably the largest, numerically, in the world.[9] By the end of the century there were 285 monks, novices and postulants, of whom 137 were in the mother-house and the rest at the different mission stations.

To keep touch with his friends in Europe Abbot Pfanner had begun from the Dunbrody days to print a little magazine, *Fliegende Blätter*. Under other titles, *Der Trappist unter den Kaffern* and *Vergissmeinnicht*, it was continued at Mariannhill. From 1886 onwards circles of supporters for the missionary abbey were established in several cities of Austria and Germany, and at the same time the abbot began to send a "collecting brother" to Europe with a letter soliciting help for the missions.

None of these developments was in principle novel for a Trappist monastery, whatever might be said of their publicity. But it would be difficult to find precedent for two other institutions founded by Abbot Pfanner. The first was his establishment of a dependent congregation of nuns. In 1884 he explained to Bishop Jolivet that it would be necessary to bring some from Europe to work amongst the Bantu girls and women. The vicar apostolic agreed, but insisted they must be a French congregation as were all the other religious of the vicariate. While not disputing this rule, the abbot appealed in the pages of his *Vergissmeinnicht* for

Austrian and German laywomen to help with his missionary tasks. When the first five of these mission-helpers arrived, in 1885, he gave them a uniform, appointed a superior, and presented them to Bishop Jolivet. As the latter made no protest, the abbot gave them a rule and admitted them under their private vows to a congregation of which he would be superior. Their uniform became a religious habit, a novitiate for further candidates was set up, and at the end of 1888 they took public vows. These Sisters of the Precious Blood had by that time obtained a favourable mention by the Congregation of Propaganda, and in 1901, when their numbers had risen to three hundred, Bishop Jolivet gave them his official approval: his original ruling had not been contested, but it had been circumvented.

The second novelty introduced by Abbot Pfanner was to form a men's congregation, under religious rule, for those who were willing to help in the work of the mission but were either unwilling or unsuitable for the Trappist rule. They would be half-Trappist, he wrote, when he announced their establishment in 1888 under the patronage of St Francis of Assisi.[10] This society does not seem to have grown as did the other enterprises of the abbot, but it survived his resignation and its troubles often appeared on the agenda of the Abbey Council of Mariannhill.

3. DIFFICULTIES

It was but natural that development on the scale and with the speed which Abbot Pfanner employed would leave many disgruntled. Some of the recruits he won in Europe found the reality of Mariann-hill different from what they expected; some again were unsuited to Trappist life but did not learn the fact till after they were in the novitiate; even if they had made a year's postulancy in Europe to test their vocation they had come to a monastery of a very special sort. If they could not fit into the life they had no choice but to find some secular occupation in South Africa or to return home at their own expense. Within Mariannhill itself there were those who thought that the Trappist rule was being unduly subordinated to the missionary plans of the abbot, and who quarrelled on this account with the day to day decisions of the superiors and disliked the work required of them. Questions were raised by them, or independently, about the money collected in Europe—

was it for mission work only, and was it right to spend it on the abbey buildings? For the abbot and those who thought with him the enterprise was one undivided thing, but others did not see this so clearly or trust entirely to his discretion.

On 16 April 1890, the Cardinal Prefect of Propaganda wrote from Rome to Bishop Jolivet saying that a report had reached him from a Father Adolph, one of the Mariannhill Trappists, complaining that Abbot Franz had collected vast sums from the faithful for purposes almost foreign to mission work, that the Trappists lived like hermits rather than missionaries, and that some of their postulants were sent away to live miserably in Durban. This letter would have reached Bishop Jolivet about the middle of May. The draft of his reply is dated 3 June, and his character guarantees, I think, that it was a factual, balanced estimate of the situation in Natal.

I have recently visited all Trappist establishments in my vicariate. . . . Father Adolph is an *exalté* whose word is not worth much, but the abbot has treated him too brusquely (according to his bad custom. . .). I wouldn't say all the abbot's expenditure was judicious (it is a matter of opinion), but all will bear fruit sooner or later, and in any case Adolph is not a serious judge. . . . I visited eight missions. In five missions the work was more or less developed, in three they were only at the material stage of building. Of these two are only " halts " between missions and not expensive: probably Adolph referred to these as hermitages. . . . Mariannhill is the envy of Protestants, and I am proud of it.

The bishop also reports well of the missions at Reichenau, at Oetting and, especially, at Lourdes, and continues:

Pater Franz has brought more than four hundred recruits from Europe. I have often urged him to be more careful in choosing them. And he does put the unworthy out without provision. More often they leave of their own wish, and come to Durban and complain to the Oblates. We have tried to fix them up. Some behaved badly, but I don't know that any of them is destitute. Adolph exaggerates. The scandal which I deplore is rather of drunken priests who go to La Trappe to reform, like Martin and Torpey. They wouldn't stay, though everything was done to make their life easier than the Trappists'.

The denunciations of Adolph do more harm than the postulants who leave, though these naturally speak ill of Abbot Franz. ...

One should encourage the collections for the Trappists, who do a work no one else could do. They give the best lesson of all to the negroes, that of work. They are humble, pious, mortified, and full of affection for their abbot (of course there are some who grumble). A man like the abbot will always have admirers and enemies. I cannot but admire his fine qualities, though I don't deny certain defects. He knows what I have written.[11]

With Bishop Jolivet as Vicar Apostolic of Natal the virtues and the failings of the Abbot of Mariannhill would have been reasonably balanced, and the local causes of complaints remedied in time without much trouble. But more serious was the doubt growing in the minds of the Trappist General and his Council about the fidelity of the work at Mariannhill to the rule of their order. Abbot Franz had had a stormy past. When he entered the novitiate he already had a dozen years of priestly experience of pastoral work behind him. Very soon he was appointed sub-prior and quarrelled with his superior, who was later removed from office. In 1867 Father Franz was sent to make a new foundation, and on this occasion came to loggerheads with the mother-house of his priory, Olenburg, whose abbot was also vicar-general of the order. The latter told him to return to the secular priesthood, but he went to Rome, secured the support of a German Cardinal in Curia, and argued his cause for a year with the Congregation of Religious. Again he was justified and he was given the task of founding the priory of Maria Stern, in Bosnia, which was to be independent of Olenburg. After successful work there he offered himself for Bishop Ricards' African project and obtained the approval of the General Chapter of his order.

Now, after ten years, the doubts were accumulating again. Abbot Franz's successor at Maria Stern complained that he had carried off the professed monks to Africa without regard to the interests of his old priory. The arbiter appointed by the Congregation of Propaganda had decided his quarrel with Bishop Ricards about the original loan of £2,000 in favour of the latter, and Abbot Franz, while appealing against the sentence, was claiming that either Maria Stern, who had benefited by the original £2,000, should repay it, or that it was an obligation of the whole order—as indeed the Congregation seemed to regard it.[12] Finally some of the professed monks[13] at Mariannhill complained that the abbot's government made it difficult to follow the Trappist life; that the novices were being trained for mission work rather than to observe the rule; that the organization of the distant stations (some of them more than a hundred miles from the mother-house), of the Society of St Francis of Assisi, and of the nuns, showed that the abbot was developing the missionary work at the expense of the monastery.

A General Chapter of the Trappists was held in Rome in April 1891. Abbot Pfanner was present and made a report on his monastery and its daughter-foundations. Though the Chapter congratulated him on its unexampled prosperity, they put on record that some of the religious there made a pretext of missionary work to neglect the monastic rule, and appointed Father Franz Strunk, the Abbot of Olenburg, to conduct a canonical visitation which would in effect make him its ruler till the next General Chapter, when his report would be considered.

A visitation is part of the normal government of monasteries of the Reformed Cistercians (as the Trappists are more formally known), and it was chiefly the great distance of South Africa which had delayed it in the case of Mariannhill. The Abbot of Olenburg proceeded in the ordinary way, checking the life of the monks by the rules and constitutions of the order, and restoring where he saw fit practices from which the monks had been dispensed in the past. So the conduct of the novitiate, the relations of the mission stations to the mother-house, the hours of worship and of manual work were altered. All this occupied Abbot Strunk's attention during his six months' stay at the beginning of 1892, and he gave instructions on leaving for the further carrying out of his "reforms".

During the visitation Abbot Franz Pfanner had stayed at the Einsiedeln mission station, but his influence had been consistently against most of the changes. When he resumed office, on Abbot Strunk's departure, he openly did his best, within the limits of his authority (or as the English would say, by all constitutional means), to defeat the spirit of the "reforms". This was known to the Trappist General Council of October 1892, to which the visitor made his report, and they suspended Abbot Franz Pfanner from his position for a year and appointed a Father Amandus as administrator.

Before the year was out Abbot Franz resigned and took up his residence at the mission station of Emmaus, where he worked on till his death in 1909.

It would be easy to describe these events as a clash of personalities. Though it was Abbot Strunk's predecessor at Olenburg who had told Prior Pfanner to leave the order but had his decision over-ruled by Rome, it seems likely that Abbot Strunk himself expected to find matter for reform at Mariannhill. It may be that the legal form of the record hides the personal feelings in this case, but the effective difference seems to have been one of two policies which were bound to clash.

It would be over-simplification to say that the visitor would allow no change from the Trappist discipline as it existed in Europe, while Abbot Pfanner had no loyalty to the order. The rule itself, as with all Catholic institutions, made room for dispensations to meet changing circumstances, and Abbot Strunk granted many, and provided for them to be habitually granted, so that the work of the mission stations might continue. But the starting-point in his mind was the Trappist monastery and the limit was the developments which were possible within the rule. Abbot Pfanner, however, had a single purpose, the building up of a Zulu Christian civilization, and he held that the Trappist monastery he had founded could be and should be adapted to that end. The reason he gave did not arise out of the rule, but from an instruction of Pope Pius IX that the Trappists should undertake missionary work in South Africa.[14] It seems likely, since there is no other record of such a decision, and since Pius IX died in 1878, that the abbot was reporting what Bishop Ricards had told him of one of his own audiences when he was urging the matter in Rome. It would not be the first time that a kindly comment by a pope had become a declaration of policy to its sanguine supporters.

The history of Mariannhill after Abbot Franz's resignation confirms my reading of his quarrel with the authorities of his order. The General Chapter accepted Father Amandus Schölzig as abbot, and, after his death in 1900, Father Gerhard Wolpert. Though they tried loyally to give effect to the visitor's regulations, the work of Mariannhill developed under them essentially on the lines of its original foundations, with the emphasis necessarily on the missionary work. Abbot Wolpert may have found it easy to plan outside the Trappist tradition, for he had been trained as a soldier and a Protestant and came to Mariannhill before ordination. Though he was critical of some of Abbot Pfanner's methods (he said so later in some correspondence with Bishop Delalle) his interests were in the mission stations, and he resigned the office of abbot in 1904 to return to that task.

Meanwhile the Trappist general and his curia did their best to bring the institution into the traditions and ways of the Reformed Cistercians without destroying its missionary purpose. Abbot Strunk was sent to make a further visitation in 1900, and after Father Wolpert's resignation Abbot Obrecht, of the American Abbey of Gethsemani, was sent as apostolic administrator, explicitly, as the abbot-general wrote, to expel any spirit of isolation and independence.

4. THE SOLUTION

To assist the pope in the government of the Catholic Church the Congregation of Propaganda directs all the missionary effort of the Church. But it makes use for this purpose of the religious orders, each of which works within its own constitution. Some of the Mariannhill fathers had brought their complaints to the congregation but had been told, as is customary, to be obedient to their own authorities. But, as is also customary, the congregation began deliberately to take into consideration the essential cause of the difficulties which arose. Consultations with the abbot-general of the Trappists followed, and the latter consented to a general synod of the Mariannhill monks to make recommendations on all their problems.

It met in May 1908 under the presidency of Bishop Miller, O.M.I., the vicar apostolic of the Transvaal (1904–1912). The weight of the testimony given insisted that the office in choir, the silence and the enclosure of the Trappist rule could not possibly be observed in the twenty or more mission stations of Mariannhill where considerably more than half the monks had to live. Only by the constant granting of dispensations could the apostolic work continue, and this would cause friction at every canonical visitation. Though the rule could be observed more strictly at the mother-house, to do so would mean a division of the community into two parties, monks and missionaries. After some discussion the conference decided to ask the Holy See that Mariannhill might become a congregation affiliated to the Reformed Cistercians, so that they would retain the solemn vows of the order and the canonical exemption which would make them self-contained within the vicariate where they laboured, but with a constitution of their own adapted to missionary work. If it should be impossible to make these changes within the Trappist framework, it was suggested that Mariannhill might become a separate congregation of the " unreformed " Cistercians.

Bishop Miller took the report and recommendation to Rome, where the questions were discussed between the abbot-general's curia and the Congregations of Propaganda and Religious. In February 1909, the decision of the Holy See was published. Mariannhill was separated entirely from the Cistercian Order; it became a collegiate church under a provost, with canonical exemption and the duty of governing its present mission stations and any others it might establish; the Religious Missionaries of Mariannhill, as they were to be called, would take simple vows, and only the priests residing at the collegiate church would be bound to choir office; the novitiate would be at Mariannhill, and there the studies for the priesthood would be made; a general synod of the religious would meet in three years' time and submit a definitive constitution for Rome's approval.[15]

The decision to separate Mariannhill from the Trappist order in which it had been born was made explicitly because of its own past history and of the missionary problem in South Africa. But it did not carry with it any criticism of the work of Abbot Pfanner; indeed, the papal decree expressly praised his achievement. Nor was there any hesitation at this point on the part of any one interested; the advice of the Congregation of Religious fell in with the desire of Propaganda; the tone of the letter of the abbot-general of the Trappists announcing the decree could not have been more friendly; almost certainly the decree followed the lines of the advice of Bishop Miller, who knew the local problems at first hand.

II. The Training of the Zulu

1. Farming

The struggle to adapt the Trappist rule lasted a quarter of a century. It was the background to an intensive missionary effort, of which it must at times have impeded the progress. But on balance the Trappist origin of Mariannhill brought many advantages. It gave Abbot Pfanner and his successors what no other religious order at the time could have given—a large number of lay brothers with the Trappist formation of contemplation and manual work. It gave too the tradition for training which could not have been improvised easily in the conditions of Africa. The external behaviour of the monks, the silence and the prayers and the habit, so combined to impress Europeans and Bantu that for a generation after they had ceased to be Trappists they were still so called in Natal. And though Abbot Pfanner with his lively and original intelligence seems to have understood what he wanted almost from the beginning, it is unlikely that his particular kind of missionary work would have been accepted habitually and intelligently by his monks, would have become an institution, without the insistent claim of the Trappist life fighting against the pressing needs of the missions.

Nineteenth-century historians in both Germany and France had written much of the work of early monasteries in teaching agriculture and the arts of Roman tradition to the peoples of Northern Europe; they had civilized as well as converted the pagans. This picture recurs often in Abbot Franz's writings, and he gave it to his monks as the purpose of their coming to Africa. It was not mere romanticism, for some of the conditions did correspond. The Zulus were poor agriculturists,[16] and though they reckoned wealth in cattle they had little skill as breeders or even herdsmen. The unity imposed by the ferocious rule of Shaka and Dingane had been broken, and their several small tribes under lesser chiefs were kept in comparative order and peace by the astute administration of Theophilus Shepstone. They had less political cohesion than the Basutos under Moshesh, and they were already attracted by and becoming dependent on the urban life established by the English.

It would, however, have been unrealistic to pretend that a

ABBOT FRANZ PFANNER
Founder of Mariannhill

Left

MGR. FREDERIC
KOLBE, D.D.

From the portrait by
E. Roworth

Right

EMMANUEL
'MABATHOANA,
O.M.I., D.D.

FIRST BISHOP OF
LERIBE

monastery in nineteenth-century Natal represented in any way the religion of the dominant class, or to expect the support which Frankish rulers of the eighth century were supposed to have given to St Boniface and his successors. The same sort of prestige could, however, be given in nineteenth-century Natal by the ownership of large estates. Though the Zeekoegat farm which became Mariannhill was bought as suitable for a large Trappist foundation, Abbot Pfanner soon realized how impressed the Bantu were by the appearances of material wealth. The same consideration entered into the later purchases by him and his successors of the mission stations; at the larger and more distant ones, a hundred or two hundred miles 'away, like Reichenau, Lourdes, Maria Ratschitz, the prestige of the mother-monastery was established among a new group of Bantu people; the smaller ones were at first only resting places, halts for the monks on the necessary journeys between the main stations.

On all of them the first care of the Trappists was to provide for their own sustenance. They introduced new crops, and they looked after their cattle with care. Under the direction of their Brother Nivard, a talented engineer-architect who was later often employed by the civil authorities, they put up the buildings they needed, made the roads and bridges, and for this purpose organized their own workshops and trades. Abbot Pfanner, writing of his enterprise, modestly supposed that it was the fact of better crops, better cattle, impressive buildings which won the respect of the Bantu and their desire to have some part of this life. Bishop Jolivet and other observers remarked rather on the lesson of the monks, the priests as well as the brothers, all doing as a matter of course the manual work necessary for the creation of this wealth. Hitherto the European had been known to the Bantu as a planter or rancher; these were husbandmen and herdsmen and workers and did not shirk the labour of it. And its rhythm was maintained by a routine of prayer both in the fields and in the church.

With their farms the Trappists took over the tenants. Before long the Bantu were asking help and were given it, provided they worked as the monks directed. Their huts must be built human-wise—i.e. with door and roof and window—the standard being fixed by the landlord. So also with their agriculture and herds; they must learn the economy of the monastic farmers if they were to share in their success. There was no pretence made of encouraging the customary way of the Bantu; the condition of their remaining tenants was that they took no more wives than they already had, and new tenants must promise to remain monogamous.

Naturally there were attacks in the local papers on these methods, and Mariannhill was accused of making Christians by bribery. In the ordinary meaning of words the charge is absurd. The rules made by the monks imposed practically the condition of work, relatively hard for the Bantu, for those who wished to benefit by their enterprise, and the offer was open to pagans. Indeed, on most of the farms no one was baptized until two years had gone by. At first occasional free distributions were made, of seed sometimes but chiefly of European clothing because it was much sought after by the Bantu as more convenient or more picturesque than their own. But Abbot Pfanner soon saw the danger of the practice and he and his successors set their faces sternly against the " bread-Christian " mentality, even though they did not attempt to preach to the recipients of their alms. Abbot Amandus pushed the principle to the extent of forbidding baptism to anyone who would not promise to engage in manual work.[17]

2. MARIANNHILL'S SCHOOLS

Those who charge missionaries with bribery, however, sometimes assume from ignorance of language that the Christian Faith should be described as a system of dogma unrelated to life. The principle of Mariannhill was indeed a challenge to such a view. It sought to show the Bantu one way at least in which the Catholic religion worked out, with its advantages as well as its burdens. The choice for or against could then be fairly made.

In no respect was this more clearly shown than in the development of education. Almost at once after the foundation of the monastery some of the local chiefs wanted their boys to be taught reading and writing, since this was the avenue to profitable trade and employment in the European towns. As yet the monks were not ready to give instruction; they were too busy on their own buildings and they had not yet learnt either Zulu or English. At the same time a Basuto Christian, trained by the Oblates at Roma in Basutoland, offered himself as a catechist, and he was set to work to teach boys, and continued to do so, for a year—

perhaps with more enthusiasm than technical skill. When the monks were ready to start the education of boys—the work was organized by a young English novice, Alfred Bryant, not yet twenty years old, of whom we shall say more shortly—it remained distinctly confessional; Catholic teaching was part of the curriculum even though the boys did not intend to be baptized. The same was true of the schools for girls which commenced under Maria Lassak, the daughter of a Polish tenant of the monastery, and were continued by the German helpers who later became the sisters of the Congregation of the Precious Blood.[18] The monastery provided a Catholic civilization which included instruction for children and it was open freely to any whose parents were willing for them to attend. On the farms owned by Mariannhill this was the only education available, and the confessional character of their schools was maintained in after years.

Characteristic of Mariannhill education throughout was the insistence on manual training. From the beginning only a part of the day was spent in the classroom; for the rest the children were sent to one or other of the workshops or (in the case of girls) to the kitchens. "We do not want the Kaffirs to be inspectors on the railways or station-masters", wrote the abbot in 1889, " . . . but we want them to become good artisans and trustworthy agricultural labourers. A scientific explanation of the rules of English grammar, as well as an infinite number of standards, is totally unnecessary."[19]

It must be remarked, however, that Abbot Franz recognized a distinction between the first school generation and later ones. As better standards of living became general among the Bantu it would be reasonable to train suitable children for teachers and administrative posts. At the end of that same year, 1889, he instituted a year of " high school " for selected boys and girls. The following year a teachers' training college was opened at Reichenau, and by 1901 there were sufficient Bantu teachers to staff the primary schools of the stations; in 1909 there were 48 Europeans and 30 Bantu teaching 2,622 children in the 78 Mariannhill schools. But the curriculum remained on the same general lines: 4.15 a.m., rise; 4.30 a.m., Mass, wash and bedmaking: 5.30 a.m., first school; 8 a.m., breakfast; 8.45 a.m., manual work; 11.45 a.m., break; 12 noon, dinner and free time; 1.30 p.m., manual work; 4.30 p.m., school; 5.30 p.m., free time and supper; 7 p.m., school; 7.40 p.m., night prayers and bed.[20]

The decision to found boarding rather than day schools was made originally so that the pupils should not lose in their homes the standards and practices of Christian civilization they learned during the day. It was regarded as a need for the first school generation which might cease when Christian families had been formed.[21] Experience, however, brought its continuance, and in addition hostels were soon established. Young women could stay in them earning money for their dowries while they were also part learners; in others young men, as journeymen in the workshops, could accumulate something towards the *lobola* they required for marriage. In 1909 there were four trades open for girls and thirteen for boys in which they could earn wages while staying at Mariannhill.[22]

The education provided by the Trappists, then, was openly religious, and, indeed, Catholic; was directed to learning a trade, and was largely residential. As the years went by more and more Bantu asked for and completed the catechumenate, a two years' instruction for children and three for adults, and were baptized. But the methods of education were not varied, because, as Abbot Franz wrote, " we must aim to form not merely instructed Christians but Christian families ".[23] It resulted in the village community which Abbot Wolpert built up on the farm at Centocow, and the social programme which Father Huss was to advocate, and to implement in part, after 1923.

This determined effort by a Catholic monastery to bring the Bantu into a Christian civilization, complete in all details of life, was surprising to the nineteenth century, which was already coming to regard education and the general arrangement of life as the affair of politicians only. There were not wanting letters to the Natal newspapers to complain that Mariannhill methods would keep the Bantu from seeking work in the towns, as house-maids or as labourers. There were others to complain that the monastery allowed none but Catholic schools on their farms.

3. RELATIONS WITH THE CIVIL POWER

The position of the monastery as owner of its farms enabled the abbot to push on with his schemes with the prestige which wealth and successful work gave. In fact, however, he considered that his methods were rational and would be recognized as such when they were explained. So the Mariannhill printing press—one of the first workshops to be established—produced pamphlets in defence, and the abbot wrote vigorous replies in the local papers. If Bantu, he urged, were given culture without religion, or were taught religion without the love of work, they would be perverted rather than converted. The girls should be prepared to become good wives and mothers, not servants. The boys should be trained to be able to farm for themselves, and to make their clothes and implements and houses for themselves, so that a Bantu community could become self-supporting.[24]

This frankness in stating his case served Abbot Franz well. He soon won a good press, not only in the pages of the *Catholic Magazine* and the *Natal Record*, but almost equally in the secular newspapers. And that friendliness to Mariannhill remained; even in the days of the 1914–18 war, when internment of those of enemy origin was applied (for the first time in history) in the belligerent countries, the South African government of General Botha allowed the monks (with one or two exceptions) to remain at their missions; it was the influence of Brother Nivard, as well as the recommendation of Bishop Delalle, and Botha's common sense, which won this privilege, but the friendship of the press spared the monks from any public outcry.

In time the Mariannhill approach to the Bantu, openly different though it was to the official view, gained recognition and some assistance from the civil power. The education law of Natal from 1856 had not imposed compulsory schooling on the Bantu but had left its development to the Christian missionaries, subject to an annual inspection. If the officials were satisfied with the educational practice, any school of more than twenty pupils could be given a grant in assistance of its work. In 1889, when there were more than three hundred children in the Mariannhill schools, the abbot applied for a grant, and two inspectors of that year were asked to make recommendations. Mr Russell urged that the grant should be made as a simple act of justice, since the Trappists were doing more than all other missionary bodies together, their proficiency in Zulu was far beyond the standards hitherto accepted, and the progress of their Bantu pupils in English could almost be described as wonderful; for the first time, he added, the Trappists have proved that the Zulus can be both intelligent and applied. The other inspector, Mr Plant, opposed the grant because it would mean an advance in Roman Catholic propaganda, and because the Zulus might some time choose the Trappists as their political representatives.[25] After considerable discussion the Lieutenant-Governor of Natal and his Council conceded the grant to the Mariannhill schools, and it was continued.

The success of the Trappists as an instrument of civilization, and perhaps the skill with which Abbot Pfanner defended his methods publicly, made it easy for him to win over the English administration. In any case, the latter, as usual, had no very definite plan or even principles of their own, and, at times, had favoured on paper a religious basis of education, of an indefinite sort, and certainly had recommended trades schools; Mariannhill could almost be regarded as officially approved.

4. The Problem of Polygamy

Relations with the English administrators and colonists were not the major difficulty for the Trappists. Although they presented the Catholic religion to the Bantu as part of a concrete civilization they soon learned, as other missionaries had done, how great an obstacle the Zulu practice of polygamy could be. The sincere and intelligent Anglican Bishop Colenso had recently decided to allow converts of the first generation to retain the practice and had been violently attacked by his co-religionists; for his critics even the Zulu practice of *lobola*, the payment in cattle by a bridegroom to his father-in-law, was merely the buying of a woman.

The marriage customs of the Zulu were the subject of a report by Bishop Jolivet to the Congregation of Propaganda on 28 May 1888. The Zulus, he insisted, regard marriage as a fixed and permanent contract, entered on by a public ceremony. In their own tribal law no divorce is admitted, but they rid themselves of a wife sometimes by alleging sorcery, which is a capital offence. Normally, therefore, each wife is for life and has a separate establishment. With a commoner the eldest son of the first wife is the heir of his father's property, but a chief usually chooses which wife is the mother of his successor. The bishop pointed out, too that a traditional sexual morality had grown coherent with this polygamy; the

Zulu, as we have already noted, regarded marital intercourse with a pregnant woman, or with one who had not weaned her child, to be unnatural vice; but for polygamy they would have to be celibate again and again for periods of one or two years. This attitude of mind made it relatively easy for a Bantu to accept the law of Islam; but convert Christians would feel they were disobeying the natural law if they could not be heroically celibate. As yet there was no evidence of the effect of Catholic teaching on the younger generation, but the " heretic " missionaries had sad experience with regard to the sexual morality of their converts; too often polygamy had been replaced by adultery and other vices.

The bishop further recognized that *lobola* was not in itself the purchase of a woman. It corresponded in a way to the European practice of a " dot " or a settlement; the bride's father, having received the cattle, was bound to look after her marital interests, and to insist that she perform her duties to her husband. It was a treaty of alliance between two families. At the same time it integrated the tribal marriage customs with the Zulu ceremony. Daughters were a potential source of wealth, reckoned usually among the Zulu in cattle, for their father and their brothers. Additional wives were an investment, both as potential mothers and because tillage was the women's business.

From those facts the bishop reasonably concluded that polygamy was the basis of the social life of the Zulu. Those then who sought, like the Trappists, to build a Christian Bantu civilization, had double reason to oppose it; it was not only contrary to the Christian law of marriage, it was also the corner-stone of the system they wanted to replace. And in consequence they took less account than Bishop Jolivet did of the theory of tribal law and more of the practical abuses it led to. It was already possible in Natal for Bantu to qualify by an educational test to be ruled by the English law of marriage, and after 1887, when the privilege was extended without the educational test to anyone who applied for it, the children of such marriages were no longer free to marry in any other way. But the Bantu men soon realized that their daughters or sisters might prefer the loss of family wealth. Accordingly they tried to prevent the Bantu girls from being educated, and above all from becoming Christians. More than had been customary, they compelled their womenfolk to accept tribal marriage custom, and insisted on their being part of the estate of their husband. These practices—abuses, they could be called, of polygamy, but abuses for which tribal law offered no remedy—were denounced by Abbot Pfanner as " *Die Sklaverei* in Natal ", in an essay published in 1889;[2] and he urged that they should be fought as fiercely as had been the slave trade of East Africa. His practical suggestion was to reduce the *lobola* payment for a legally mono-gamous marriage; one third should be given by the government, one third by the monastery as landlord, leaving the bridegroom to find the remainder only. Even though this was not adopted, he did give considerable help to many of his tenants. For the future he arranged that those brought up in the Mariannhill boarding schools could continue in the hostels earning, as employees of the monastery workshops, the *lobola* or an equivalent dowry until they were of marriageable age. Along with the rule that new tenants on the estate could have but one wife, provision was made by the Trappists for the livelihood and housing of those wives who were discarded on this ground.

These measures succeeded in breaking the institution of poly-gamy, and did so as quickly as that has ever been done. Some of the later studies by Mariannhill missionaries suggest that useful tribal customs were destroyed in the process.[27] They see the struggles in terms of a western individualistic outlook imposed on a native collectivism which bound two families into a greater unity by the *lobola*. Even if this is the true analysis of the institu-tion, by the nineteenth century it was integrated with and dominated by polygamy; and that practice, in a society where males and females are found in equal proportions, enforces and perpetuates the rule of the wealthy and elderly. Nor does monogamy neces-sarily result in an individualistic type of society; it merely makes it difficult for collectivism to become a tyranny. For those who hold that a human being comes to normal full development in founding his own family, and that the essential of law is to protect the personal dignity of man and woman, the only reasonable conclusion is that Zulu culture was impeded and fossilized by polygamy, and its removal was a necessary preliminary to further progress.

III. *Zulu Prayers and Catechism*

1. THE PROBLEM OF LANGUAGES

Another difficulty which the Trappists met arises from the very nature of missionary work. To teach the Christian religion it is necessary to describe it in the language of those to be converted. Abbot Pfanner and his monks came to Mariannhill without any knowledge of Bantu tongues. As they were also ignorant of English they could not at first make use of the smattering of that language which some Zulus had, nor of those colonists who had learned the native language. Fortunately the Oblate missionary working north of Durban, Father Mathieu, a Frenchman, was able to ride over from his station once a week to give the German monks their first lessons in Zulu. Fortunately, too, the prior on his recruiting journey in 1883 visited London and won the interest and admiration of the young Englishman, Alfred Bryant, who promptly came to Mariannhill and offered himself for the novitiate; the prior welcomed him, gave him the name of David in religion, and set him to teach the others English while he learned Zulu himself. His flair for languages enabled the Trappists to make use of the sound scientific grammar and dictionary compiled by the Anglican Bishop Colenso.* This somewhat makeshift preparation for missionary tasks was greatly assisted by the printing press at Mariannhill. A catechism in the language of the Basuto was printed in 1883, a prayer book and extracts from the gospel in Zulu four years later. Soon the need for larger prayer books, hymnaries and so on increased and was met; in 1909 the Mariannhill printing press had published in Zulu six short histories of the Church, six catechisms, two gospel books and ten books of hymns and prayers. With them in hand the monk or the Bantu catechist was no longer entirely dependent on his knowledge of the language, or even on his knowledge of theology; he had a sound form of words by which to teach the Christian revelation.

Or thought he had. This distinction is necessary because some of the practical missionaries, including sometimes those who compiled these books, did not grasp the fact that Zulu is a highly developed and subtle language. Their direct renderings into it

---

* Father David Bryant made this acknowledgement in the preface to the more advanced dictionary which he published in 1905.

appeared to be understood and they were content; it scarcely occurred to them that the concepts of Christian revelation were not more likely to find ready-made expression in Zulu any more than they had found it in the Greek of the early centuries of the Christian era.

Father David Bryant soon embarked on a study of Bantu speech, using such philology as he could gain from books, and educating himself on scientific lines. He soon recognized several historical layers in the speech used in Natal. Many distinct but related tribal languages had been lost when Shaka, the Zulu "tyrant", had destroyed the other tribes early in the nineteenth century, but words from them had often survived in the scattered groups under British rule, especially among the women. The latter indeed would use phrases among themselves which must not be said in the presence of men, and again would impose on themselves a *tabu* on all words with the same root as the name of their husband.[28] Such historical developments naturally made the study of the language a difficult affair, and Father Bryant took the opportunity of missionary work in Zululand proper at Ebuhleni in order to concentrate on the speech used by the Zulu royal house. In 1905 he produced a dictionary of more than 20,000 words.

This specialist work naturally directed the interest of Father Bryant to Zulu institutions and Zulu history.* Most of his publications were on these subjects, and although he took no direct part in the Mariannhill controversies about the language of prayers and catechisms, his labours had the indirect importance of teaching the exact meaning and the overtones of words used in catechisms and prayers. Two missionaries at least—Gerhard Wolpert, who after being abbot of the monastery became first superior of the Congregation of Mariannhill, and Willebald Wanger, the author of a grammar of Zulu—were convinced that the more exact knowledge of the language must be employed for teaching the Faith, and became the two great protagonists of change.

2. PROBLEMS OF TRANSLATION

Father Wanger set to work on a new catechism in 1910, consulting for the meaning of words and their usage with several Zulus,

* In 1920 he was appointed lecturer in Bantu studies at Witwatersrand University, and later at London University.

among them two catechists, Mathias Maphalala and Vitus Khathi, and a member of the royal family, Maria Zulu. When the manuscript was completed Abbot Wolpert and another member of his community, Father Reiner, went through it carefully, and the book was printed in 1912, [29] but owing to criticism was submitted to the Holy See. Rome suggested modifications[30] on theological grounds but did not make any judgement on linguistic issues, and a prayer book containing Father Wanger's prayers was published together with a small catechism. The two books were issued with the approbation of Bishop Delalle, the Vicar Apostolic of Natal, as the official texts for the vicariate, in September 1914.

A storm of protest burst at once from many missionaries, and some refused to employ the new prayers at all, asserting that the Zulus in their districts regarded the new expressions as blasphemous. At first Bishop Delalle defended the publications and issued a printed circular to this effect,[31] but he nevertheless asked Abbot Wolpert to call a series of conferences among his priests to hear their complaints.[32] Then he sent out a questionnaire among all his missionaries, both Mariannhill and Oblate fathers.[33] The volume of complaints impressed the bishop, who was not competent himself in the Zulu tongue, and convinced him that some words accepted in one locality were offensive to Christian ears elsewhere. Accordingly he set up a committee of priests, some Oblates, some of the Mariannhill Congregation, as an advisory board to make an acceptable translation which he hoped would " put an end to all controversies, which unfortunately have divided the missionaries, to the great detriment of the missions ".[34]

All the members of this advisory board had considerable experience as missionaries; Father Mathieu, who had taught Zulu to the first Trappists, was among them. But for that very reason they were likely to favour the phrases and words with which they had instructed their converts and made practising Catholics of them. Two examples will illustrate the main arguments. The missionaries had hitherto used Latin in a sort of Bantu form to express some of the technical words of the Catholic religion. Father Bryant had protested as long ago as 1905 against bringing in " these bastards of English or Latin derivation ".[35] " Grace " was one such word. Father Wanger had replaced it by a Zulu word for a royal gift, but the advisory board rejected the change. They were alleged, rather frivolously, to have acted on the consideration that the Zulu word was extremely difficult for European tongues, and their opponents pointed out that the Zulus had the same difficulty about the Latinism which it was proposed to retain.

In this case it does not appear to have occurred to either party that they could have cited precedents from the history of theology. The early fathers, both Greek and Latin speaking, made use of current words of near-meaning in their own language, while the Christian teachers of the Celtic and Germanic peoples often enriched those tongues with Latinisms. In neither case could the explanations of the missionary be avoided, for the Faith introduces concepts, and exact defined concepts, of things not previously known and for which there is naturally no single adequate word. But pedagogically it would seem easier for a convert to start from a word already known and to give it a technical Christian meaning.

The second class of words constituted a more serious difficulty. An example is that Father Wanger proposed using the word *wamithwa* for *conceptus est* in the creed. The advisory board accepted the view that this translation although very close for practical purposes was nevertheless not entirely correct and anyway was generally avoided in ordinary respectful conversation;[36] those who supported Father Wanger, including three of the four Zulu priests, denied this and indignantly accused the other side of suggesting that the word was indecent[37] (although all they had really meant was that it was "indelicate", even if the word "indecent" had been used). Abbot Wolpert, who with Father Wanger was not a member of the advisory board, had nevertheless put their case before the bishop in a very able—though clearly partisan—report of a conference he had called from 27 February to 2 March 1915,[38] before the appointment of the board. The same contentions were later to be more vigorously repeated in a petition to Rome signed by three Africans.[39] In his memorandum the abbot pointed out first that the question among the Bantu Christians was whether a special word, rather than the ordinary *mitha*, ought to be used for the conception of Our Lord; and opinion apparently was divided according to locality. Secondly, his enquiries among Christian Bantu women showed that they did not object to the word itself, but did not use it before men out of reverence for human fruitfulness. *Tabu*, as he pointed out with examples, is not directed against indecent words among the Bantu but more usually indicates a mark of respect; just as a wife covers her breasts before her husband but not before other men. Of course, *mitha* to the Zulu, though an honour for the married, would be a disgrace to the unmarried. Even so, they would not use the word in the latter case but would rather say " has met with an accident " or " has caused a quarrel ". Abbot Wolpert's third and strongest point— although the board accepted the arguments to the contrary which the vicar apostolic later called " very convincing and very logical "[40] —was that the word *thabatha* used as an alternative meant that the incarnate God dwelt in Mary's womb as in a temple but did not say that He was formed of her flesh.* And on enquiry, the abbot said, he had found that four priests, whom he named, objected to *mitha* just because it did mean conceived.[41]

It is not altogether surprising that in the heat of controversy Father Wanger accused some of his opponents of ignorance both of Zulu and of theology.[42] Abbot Wolpert regretted that there was some truth in this; under Abbot Franz there was little training in philosophy or theology and the curriculum was mainly of obedience, devotion and manual work; he himself with some others had had to put in hard study privately after ordination.

Those who were pressing so hard for a more careful theological discrimination in the choice of Zulu words for Catholic prayers were a small minority at Mariannhill. It was Abbot Wolpert's authority which secured a hearing for their case. But the decision rested with Bishop Delalle, Bishop Jolivet's successor as Vicar Apostolic of Natal (1904–46), and he treated it as a matter of discipline. There was a schism among the missionaries of Mariann-hill on the Zulu forms of prayers, published in 1914. After the outburst against the Wanger translations the bishop had appointed a committee of priests to draw up more acceptable ones which he had imposed on all missionaries; the great majority had accepted the new translations but a few, jealous and ambitious, claimed to find heresies and blasphemies in them, and made a complaint to the Congregation of Propaganda. Such was the vicar apostolic's

---

* Since the board ruled out the use of *mitha* on grounds of propriety, and as there is no Zulu word which gives the exact meaning of *conceptus*, they used the phrase " was taken from the Holy Ghost " for " was conceived of the Holy Ghost ".

report,[43] and he concluded: " If their complaint is accepted in any way my authority is done with and I must either abandon mission work or resign ".

It is only just to recall that a scholarly approach to the dispute was not favoured by circumstances. While considering Abbot Wolpert's arguments Bishop Delalle was preparing a plea to the Union Government that the Trappists, as they were still called, should be left at liberty despite the German origin of most, and pledged himself, a Lorrainer and a naturalized British subject, as warrant for their good behaviour.[44] It was a distraction to have quarrels among them involving the Bantu Christians.

Nor was the record of Father Wanger a peaceful one. He had been sent away from the community by Bishop Miller as apostolic visitor, and expelled by a vote of the Council of the Congregation in 1912. Abbot Wolpert's predecessor had taken him back at Mariannhill, and Abbot Wolpert agreed with that step because the original charges were clearly calumnious.[45] Bishop Delalle had given his permission and had entrusted him at first with the task of drawing up a new Zulu prayer book and catechism. Yet the result had been a storm of protest, and now Father Wanger was fighting hard for his own views against those of the majority of missionaries, both of the Oblates and of Mariannhill.

Moreover it was not calculated to make a favourable impression on Bishop Delalle when Father Julius, a Zulu secular priest working at a Mariannhill station, wrote to defend the use of *mitha*, saying it was only from white missionaries that the natives learned to think it indecent :[46] nor when, after the new prayers of the arbitration board had been imposed, another Zulu priest, Father Alois, protested against them, insisting that Europeans cannot correct Zulus in the use of their own language.[47] Before their ordination Bishop Delalle had had misgivings about two of the Zulu priests and now one had written to Rome in support of Father Wanger and another had translated into good Italian a plea signed by Mathias Maphalala, Vitus Khathi and Maria Zulu, who, as we have said, had been associated with Father Wanger in the preparation of his catechism.[48]

Bishop Delalle saw these protests and the refusal to use the prayers he authorized at the beginning of 1916 as resistance to his legitimate authority. Accordingly he imposed suspension *ipso facto* on all priests who did not employ the official form of prayers,[49] and excluded the signatories of the petition from communion for three months.[50] He ordered Father Wanger to leave Mariannhill for a named and distant mission station until the war was over when as a secular priest (he had not been readmitted to the Mariannhill Congregation, though residing at the monastery) he was to return to Mozambique, the diocese to which he then belonged.[51] This order was later supported by two apostolic visitors after investigation,[52] and on their report Rome rejected the appeal made by Father Wanger to remain. In the opinion of prudent and unbiased men (which is the only way to judge of discipline) the method of the vicar apostolic was necessary to restore peace in this mission field. But it seems a pity that he did not pay more attention to Abbot Wolpert's reasoned criticism at first, or, as the apostolic visitors suggested in 1920, ask the opinion of Father Bryant on the question of language.[53]

Inadequacies which may have resulted from acceptance of the conservative attitude in the controversy were remedied in time by the normal life of the Catholic Church. Because faith is a matter of doctrine and not of formula the missionaries were bound to explain what they meant by the Latinism *igrasiya*, for *gratia*, and did so, of course, in Zulu words or by the analogy of Zulu customs, of royal gifts or adoption. Since Mary is the Mother of God they were forced in the last resort to explain the meaning of the phrase in the official prayer by the *mitha* which at least expressed the fact of being with child.* The general improvement of studies made the old misunderstandings impossible, and in time the native catechists received a better formation. With the development of the Teachers' Training College at Mariannhill after 1920 Catholic Zulus became interested in the scientific study of their own language —Benedict Vilakazi became a lecturer in Zulu at Witwatersrand University and joint compiler of the first scientific Zulu dictionary since Bryant had published his valuable work more than forty years before—and standards of the missionaries were correspondingly improved; there is indeed something to be said for the view that in 1914 the learning of Father Wanger might have imposed

---

* The Doke-Vilakazi *Zulu-English Dictionary*, published by the Witwatersrand University in 1948, considers that the word *mitha* " should be entirely avoided in theological terminology ".

inadequately studied expressions on the Catholics. Nor could
Bishop Delalle's misgivings about the first Bantu priests stand
against the tradition of Rome. The quarrels and suspicions were
healed in time, and in 1925 a seminary was founded for training
Bantu priests, either diocesan or religious, under the direction of
the Mariannhill Congregation. With that and the organization
of the African Sisters of St Francis a normal Bantu Catholicism
was in process of formation.

3. The Catechism Controversy

The large catechism of Father Wanger which had been submitted
to Rome after being printed in 1912 contained the explicit condemnation by Catholic doctrine of many Bantu practices. It
was amended and given an *imprimatur* by the vicar apostolic in
1915, but was reserved exclusively for the use of priests. For the
faithful a translation of the catechism of St Pius X was made
containing indeed references to Bantu customs, but only such as
were considered strictly necessary, and Bishop Delalle imposed its
use on all missionaries in his vicariate.

While the advisory board was still at work, on 15 October
1915, Abbot Wolpert had stated his views at length:

> These same opinions I had . . . before 1900, and it is really
> Father Wanger who got them from me . . . only . . . he
> went further. . . . There can be no question of myself com-
> plaining about the writing of a new catechism . . . what
> troubled me . . . was . . . that in such a book . . . nothing
> about native heathenism would be found. . . . Through
> speaking so little about heathenism . . . many of our Christians
> have been left *in bona fide* on important points. . . . Confession
> is no remedy for this.[54]

The petition sent to the Holy See on 26 September 1916 went
further:—

> Father Wanger's book is attacked as explaining too much.
> But surely this is what it should do to remove our ignorance.
> Especially it is clear on what pagan practices must be abandoned
> by Catholics; again, surely it is well that this should be put
> clearly. . . . It is said to use bad language. But we have
> read it from end to end and there is nothing in it to scandalize a
> native; on the contrary it would be of the greatest use because

it goes to the root of the paganism and Protestantism which are widespread among the natives. How can it be said that this [Father Wanger's] catechism teaches the faithful the evil customs of paganism they have never heard of? We say there is no native who is ignorant of these customs.[55]

The criticism of Father Wanger's large catechism answered here was not the principal one brought against it. His critics objected mainly to the fact that it was too difficult for children.[56] And in fact Father Wanger wrote his small catechism of 1914 in response to this criticism. But the same objection was raised: there were too many highly technical theological expressions. After due allowance has been made for this criticism, the fact remains that two policies for the training of Bantu Catholics were in opposition. In regard to the facts there was no dispute. Tribal custom included initiation exercises both for boys and girls. Ceremonies and material with alleged magical properties were employed to give courage in one case and attractiveness in the other. Sexual practices forbidden by Christian law were taught, and the eating of human fat was at least a pretended gesture. In adult life the use and supply of charms was part of the practice of the Bantu herbalists and medicine men. But as a general rule the cause of all illness or misfortune was attributed to the malpractices of others, and the witch-doctors (a separate trade) would discover these " enemies " for their clients, often inducing mass hysteria to ensure that their accusations were readily believed. In extreme cases, especially where the client was a chief, they would demand the murder and mutilation of a victim to provide the ritual magic, and would obtain the assistance and non-interference of others necessary for their prescription.

Father Wanger and his supporters held that these practices should be described in detail and in accurate Zulu terminology, and the reasons for their condemnation by Christian law clearly stated. Catholics would then consciously reject them and know why they were doing so, and they would in consequence be less likely to revert to them or to tolerate them.

The missionaries who took the opposite view held that many Zulu Catholic children would grow up ignorant of these customs and that detailed catechetical instruction on them would have the ill-effect of awakening their curiosity. Even with regard to adults it would be sufficient for a confessor to forbid them to penitents who accused themselves of the sins involved, and the practices would thus die a natural death as the number of converts increased.

The decision of the vicar apostolic to make the catechism of St Pius X obligatory for missionary work among the Zulus was welcome to those who held this second view. But even when the converts were grouped into Christian communities they did not cease to have contact with their pagan neighbours and relatives, and the spread of the Faith could only be by individuals and families penetrating the pagan areas. For years to come the practice of magic and witchcraft, and the ideas on which they rested, would occasionally present themselves to the minds of the Christian Zulus, and in some circumstances would solicit their assent and patronage. Again and again missionaries have found it necessary to denounce and forbid these evils—but they have had to frame the Christian judgement in their own words with the sole help of the 1915 revision of the large Wanger catechism. They did not possess any other authorized form of words, accurate theologically and linguistically, which they could employ or on which they could build. And greater difficulty confronted the native catechists, who had not the use of even that book.

To some extent the dangers were lessened by the introduction of European medical methods and notions. Almost from their beginning the missions of Mariannhill provided rough and amateurish dental and medical care for those in need of it. At a conference in 1915 Abbot Wolpert invited a full discussion: the need for professional clinics, dispensaries and hospitals was urged, though there were those who insisted that the Zulu magic aimed rather at the security of their social order than at cures.[57] The Abbot and his council went ahead with the work as far as war conditions allowed, and by 1918 a provisional hospital had been built. It was in time for the epidemic Spanish influenza of that year, and the efforts of the religious, men and women, and of the students at the teachers' training college who volunteered to help, won many from employing the medicine men and witch-doctors who had failed badly to fulfil their promises. With the appointment of a mission doctor, the training of nuns as nursing sisters, and later the training of Bantu nurses, the belief in magic was further eliminated. But there remained much confidence, and not always unjustified, in the native herbalists, some of whom were licensed by the government. Their honest trade was often linked with charms and potions, and scoundrelly European traders could be found to make money out of the Bantu weakness. In circumstances which tribal custom regarded as desperate—especially where the life or strength of a chief or the foundation of a new kraal were concerned— witchcraft and ritual murder or mutilation would be attempted. And these evils were given new social vigour by the formation among the Bantu and by the Bantu of sects which incorporated them with imitations of Christian words and ceremonies and doctrines.[58]

The survival of the animistic and magical outlook among the Bantu suggests that Abbot Wolpert and Father Wanger were prudent in urging an explicit attack on those notions in catechetical teaching. Certainly the problem did not disappear, as their opponents hoped, with the passage of years; the Christians had too many contacts with the pagans to allow them to forget the beliefs of their ancestors. Perhaps a wise line of attack was adopted by Father Bernard Huss when he became director of the training college for teachers (Catholic and non-Catholic) in 1915. He set himself to " teach the Bantu to think white according to the psychological laws of the western mind."[59]

Such an approach, working through the lay teachers in all subjects of instruction, might well have co-operated with religious doctrine in forming a strong resistance to atavistic notions, and have led eventually to their elimination. Unfortunately at this time the Bantu were being employed more and more in the factories of the urban areas and were leaving their own families to settle in shack towns outside the European cities. The white mentality they met was materialistic, and many learned Communistic doctrines and believed Communistic promises. It was indeed an easy transition for those whose tribal memories told them of the days of Shaka when they were a conquering people with an organization that emphasized the community rather than the individual. The enthusiasm of the movement was in revolt against the settled family life, basically agricultural but with auxiliary trades, which Abbot Franz and his monks had tried to create for the Bantu. Its aim was to capture and control by revolution the industrialism of the whites. Though the latter were alarmed, their own use of migrant labour and their reluctance to allow the Bantu secure freehold of land brought about the conditions favourable to the spread of the new secular doctrines. It was not difficult for the missionaries of Communism to direct first suspicion and then hatred against the Christian faith, and particularly against the Mariannhill institution which had provided a working alternative to their proposals. The answer to it, a campaign which Father Huss originally organized, by co-operative unions, by lectures, by journalism, belongs to a later period and still continues.

4. The Later Years

When Bishop Ricards invited the Trappist monks to South Africa his historical imagination pictured the work which Benedictines accomplished in the European Middle Ages. Abbot Franz, with a better grasp of the real problem, set himself at Mariannhill to impart a technical and social culture to the Bantu along with instruction in the Christian Faith. And in that effort he built in a few years the numerically largest monastery of the world.

In 1921—after less than half a century—when the Trappists were transformed into the Missionaries of Mariannhill, their new constitution, which made their institution very different from the traditional monastery, was finally approved, and a large area of southern Natal and the Transkei entrusted to them as a vicariate apostolic. But the work for which Ricards and Franz had hoped, the creation of great Christian communities growing under the guidance of the monastery and reflecting its religious outlook, was no longer possible.

Partly this was due to the change in civil government. The British colonial system under which the Mariannhill estate was bought and organized had not then entirely abandoned its tradition of accepting and encouraging communities which had their own customs, provided these were free of slavery and paid their taxes; it was prepared to spend these taxes, in part at least, according to the wishes and customs of each community, and to enforce those customs by way of administration. Though a central bureaucracy was gaining control, it would still accept the pattern of Abbot Franz's schools, and might in time have accepted his suggestions for the reform of the native marriage laws, even though they ran counter to the scheme which the officials had first planned. In such circumstances it was possible to re-create a monastic settlement on the estates which the Trappists bought. But with the formation of the Union of South Africa in 1910 the political representatives of the white population, democratically elected (insofar as those qualified to vote were concerned), became the effective government, and any enclave of separate customs, such as Mariannhill, was assumed without question to be an anomaly. The pattern of social life for the African population would be fitted, not violently but gradually, to the requirements of the ruling section of the country. The extension of freehold ownership in land was made difficult and the legality of that already existent was called in question; the direction of schools and trades was subject to the regulations of government officials; the migration of African labour was made easier. No direct attack was made on the work of the Mariannhill missionaries, but they were treated, even in the areas they had cultivated and civilized, as a voluntary religious body, and their customary prestige as directors of social life ceased to develop.

Apart from the matter of politics, there was an inherent difficulty in Abbot Franz's plan. The size of the African population to be given a Christian culture was far greater than had been the case in medieval Europe. The circumstances led him to enlarge his monastery and to form twenty or more outlying stations. Even so the strain of maintaining anything that could reasonably be called the Cistercian rule was too great, and despite many efforts its abandonment was at last generally agreed. Looking back now it seems surprising that no attempt was made to form separate monasteries with only one or two out-stations apiece. In that way the rule might have been preserved, for the visitors generally found that the real difficulties lay in the organization of the missions rather than at Mariannhill itself. But in such documents as I have seen that solution does not appear to have been seriously discussed.

The very concept of a basically agricultural community dependent on a monastery could be attacked as a piece of historical revivalism, bound to fail since the conditions of the original work were not present. Certainly the development of roads and methods of travel at the turn of the century made Abbot Franz's concept more difficult of realization. The communications between the Christian communities and the pagan Zulus became more frequent, and the lure of employment in the " European " towns more general; as a result the creation of separate Christian communities was less complete and durable.

Along with this criticism of Mariannhill as a transplanted institution, it is sometimes claimed (even by its own historians) that Abbot Franz would have been better advised to accept and build on the tribal customs of the Bantu rather than to re-make them. But this suggestion itself suffers from the very fault of historical revivalism. Most of the vigour of the real tribal traditions had been destroyed by Shaka less than a hundred years earlier. The customs that were left no longer served the functions for which they had been created—maintenance of the independence and liberty of semi-nomadic groups by war—and were either fossilized or exploited by the chiefs. A factual account of human cultures must recognize the occasions when institutions derived from the past are no longer relevant because their usefulness or their power of development has ceased. Europeans with their "noble savage" sentiments seem blind to the fact, though many of the Africans recognize it—to take a trifling example, they prefer the white man's shirt and trousers, as being much more convenient to their work than the " native " dress.

Abbot Franz may have judged wisely when he held it to be impossible to build a civilization on the tribal customs of the Bantu. It might well have been the better course to take those customs that could be adapted and incorporate them into the way of life which had been fashioned in Christian Europe, with the monogamous family for foundation. But in that case the monastery, the school-master first and then the patron and support of the system, giving it the benefit of accumulated capital used communally, would have had to become fairly soon a Bantu institution. And the genius of the Catholic religion, independent as it is of race, seems to demand that development for far graver reasons. If the Trappists were to accomplish in Africa the work of the Benedictines in Europe they would have had to take the admitted risks of forming African monks.

By 1921 the opportunity of putting this idea into action had passed. But from the efforts which had been made because of that ideal there were valuable results. A new missionary order with its own methods had been formed, and it continued to work successfully both in Natal and Rhodesia; its converts were numerous enough for its territories to be later subdivided into several dioceses; it trained some Africans for the priesthood, and formed them into religious congregations both of men and women; and it continued to teach the African laity both book-learning and trades.

Chapter XI

FREDERIC KOLBE

I. New Standards in Education

IN 1885 Bishop Ricards wrote to a young priest, Frederic Kolbe, of the Western Vicariate, to congratulate him on an address entitled " The Art of Thinking ".[1] His father was a German from Westphalia who had come to South Africa at the age of twenty-three as a member of the Rhenish Missionary Society. His mother was the daughter of a member of the London Missionary Society, to which his father transferred. Besides being a practical botanist, his father had already published a dictionary of the Otyi-Herero tongue, and, ten years after Ricards' letter, was to publish a *Comparative Analysis of the Bantu Verb*. Frederic Kolbe insisted strongly on this parentage when an Irish monthly described him as " a Dutchman, or at least the son of a Dutch Reformed Minister ".

> One of my great-great-grandfathers was a Smuts, so I suppose I have a fractional claim to the title of Dutchman. I do not usually claim it, nevertheless, as I have a much bigger fraction of English and German. My father, moreover, is not of the Dutch Reformed Church but of the London Missionary Society, which is Congregational.[2]

The household spoke English—" English is my mother tongue " —and young Kolbe went to the University of Cape Town, where he won the Jameson scholarship which sent him to Europe to complete his studies. After taking a course in law and obtaining a first in jurisprudence,[3] he was received into the Catholic Church, and, desiring to become a priest, was sent by Cardinal Manning to the English College at Rome. The *Cape Argus* of 14 March 1878 called it " the perversion of Kolbe ", but agreed with the decision of the university, arrived at after debate, that " he could retain his scholarship, as religious opinions did not affect his status of prize-holder of the university ". The *Cape Times* of the following day protested against the use of the word " perversion " as illiberal, and was surprised that any debate had been thought necessary.[4]

After completing his studies at the Gregorian University in Rome and obtaining his doctorate in theology, Father Kolbe returned to South Africa in September 1882, and was soon busy with teaching and lecturing as well as in the ordinary pastoral duties. But in addition he found time to make himself one of the leaders of a group of botanists in the Colony, and organized the training of teachers for the Catholic schools. He was made a member of the board of Cape Town University (Bishop Ricards had not been able to accept the same invitation some years earlier).

In 1890 the bishops and prefects apostolic and the Jesuit superior of the Zambesi Mission, probably at the suggestion of Alexander Wilmot,[5] asked Father Kolbe to edit a *South African Catholic Magazine*. Its first number appeared at the beginning of the following year, and from then till 1925 this monthly of sixty pages or so was the principal literary instrument for commending the Catholic religion to all the people of the country.

Kolbe was a born lecturer. Indeed, he once remarked, after owning to pen-laziness, that he still found no difficulty in talking his ideas, and his work on the *Catholic Magazine* was only a transferring to print of the spoken comments he had made for some years in public lectures and in lessons to his pupils. Amongst his friends he was first a botanist and then later (as General Smuts once remarked) an ardent and argumentative student of Shakespeare. He became an intimate of Smuts, whose reputation as a scholar was earlier and perhaps more sound than as a soldier and statesman. Even late in the general's career his secretary tells a story of the old man studying *Hamlet* in one of his political tours, "because he must be ready for Kolbe's interpretation". But Kolbe's abiding interest seems to have been in the psychology of education. At Rome he had met and been captured by the revival of the doctrine and methods of Aquinas, which he regarded as the purest Aristotelianism, and he set himself deliberately not only to make all Catholics good Thomists but to recommend the system to South Africa generally. In his hands, however, it was not the repetition of a text-book thesis. He complained once, " Why does St Thomas stimulate original thought while some Thomists repress it?" Seldom if ever did he quote tags from Aquinas. Whether in the "Children's Corner" or in criticizing Newman's *Grammar of Assent* he started with the problem and argued it on logical ground, though he was not above pointing out that his treatment and conclusion were wholly in line with traditional scholasticism. The "originality", he urged, did not lie in strange or peculiar opinions but in starting from first principles and treating every question as new.

Meanwhile, with all the gifts needed for scholarship, Kolbe gave a lot of his time to teaching boys and girls in the Catholic schools of Cape Town, and if the traditions which remain are accurate he not only did it well but enjoyed doing it. At the same time he set himself to training the Catholic teachers. His position as a member of the governing board of the University, and as one of its examiners, gave him the opportunity to work with insight and prudence, for the University of the Cape of Good Hope had been founded in 1873 (on the model of London University) as an examining body and was largely occupied in forming and testing teachers for the schools. To obtain the proper official standing he entered for and passed the first-class teacher's certificate examination of the Education Department of the Province and so was registered as competent to train teachers. In 1894, with the assistance and goodwill of Dr Muir, the Secretary for Education, he made St Brigid's School at Cape Town a centre for Catholic teachers, taking charge of the instruction himself.

At this time Kolbe was administrator of the cathedral, with considerable pastoral duties, and editor (and chief contributor) of *the Catholic Magazine*. He was lecturing for the Education Department to their teachers in training, and to the general public on Shakespeare; he was writing and publishing—the solemn *Cambridge History of the British Empire* recognizes him among the few South African authors worthy of its mention, and his Shakespearean studies appeared in some of the English learned reviews—and he was also teaching small children in the Catholic schools, while doing much other pastoral work. A general breakdown of health in 1898 was followed by a gradual and increasing loss of hearing, and then of sight. Still more he was an over-worked man. It is natural now to blame Bishop Leonard for allowing the most gifted of his priests to dissipate his energies in this way. But it may be doubted whether the bishop knew enough about the way such work is done to have given a wise direction. Despite all this, however, he did not allow the formation of Catholic teachers to be limited to the examination requirements of the Education Department. The convents, he urged in 1904, should draw up their own curriculum and their own standard of graduation irrespective of the university.[6] It should be, and Kolbe argued could be, higher than that required by the State. He made out a good case for teaching logic to the highest standards of Catholic schools,[7] discussed the new methods of teaching geometry, and showed how to use Euclid intelligently.[8]

The evening classes at Cape Town were planned by him and Dr Welch as university extension lectures especially for the benefit of Catholic teachers. While Dr Welch gave them the results of his wide historical reading and research (which they certainly would not find in their text-books) Dr Kolbe showed them how to study English literature for themselves. Some fragments of his discussions found their way into print. Along with the psychological studies of Shakespeare, which were then novel, he defended for them, and with evidence, original and interesting views on grammar. Perhaps he was most proud of a longish dissertation on the mystery of the use of " shall " and " will " in English, on which he believed like so many others that he could demonstrate some certain conclusions.[9] A dozen years later he defended a principle which would certainly obtain general support today. The *Educational Gazette* had published an article laying down rules of grammatical analysis, and Kolbe expressed a fear lest teachers should follow this even against their own judgement. Though he agreed with much that was said, and praised it, he opposed the rules on some points and gave his reasons and urged Catholic teachers to join him. He pleaded for the principle that analysis is the examination of what are accepted as good sentences, and cannot be a set of rules by which we should always write. " In grammar of all subjects, and in English of all languages, let us beware of dogmatism ", was his conclusion.

Throughout these years Kolbe was formulating his own ideas on education, especially in relation to psychology. He used the occasion to discuss the merits of Aristotelian, and therefore Thomistic, theories in comparison with what he regarded as the defective modern systems. He lectured and wrote on the nature of memory, the priority of intuition to reasoning in the life of the child, and similar subjects. And from them he went on to the practical business of teaching a child religion or grammar. " Psychology and Education " was the subject of an article in 1894, of an address to the Teachers' Association of Cape Town in 1902, and in 1904 of a course of lectures sponsored by the Education Department to all teachers in training.[10]

In Dr Kolbe's judgement it would have been possible and was certainly desirable to establish a Catholic college. " My view ", he wrote in 1891, " is that we should try to improve what we have. We should take the best college we have and improve it gradually into a teaching university."[11] He was pressing the same point in 1904, but our [Catholic] educators take little or no notice of what I say ". It may be that the bishops considered not only the financial difficulty but the reluctance of Catholic boys to take up teaching as a profession.[12] But with full knowledge of the circumstances Dr Kolbe still urged his view in an attack on Catholic inertia.

> I am myself chronically alarmed at the small preparation we are making for a steadily approaching crisis. . . . Rightly no one shall be allowed to teach, even in private schools, without being on the teachers' registers. . . . For high schools this means to have matriculated and to hold the second-class certificate as a minimum; at the present moment the minimum is to most of our teachers an unattained maximum. . . . It was my ambition to found a Training Institute in or near Cape Town . . . but the money was otherwise expended. . . . My aims have not been even understood and the Catholic schools of the Cape Peninsula are now at a lower ebb than they were twenty years ago. . . . The bishops are speaking about the crying need of a Central Training Institute for South Africa . . . and it is one thing necessary to save us from educational ruin.

He dreamt, he added, of a convent for all religious in training, with a hostel for lay students, a chapel, class-rooms and laboratory; and a similar institute for men. With such it should be possible to carry Catholic teachers on to the university degree and the first-class teachers' certificate. It would be costly, but " bold finance is the truest economy ".[13]

Though the bishops would not take the steps he urged—neither he nor another priest suggested by him was allowed to accept the principalship of a training college planned by the Trappists in Griqualand East[14]—Kolbe was allowed in 1908 to resign all his other tasks and tour the Catholic schools of the Union to advise and stimulate them. This he did for several years, and his influence may have brought about the acceptance of the system of entering for teachers' certificates. Certainly the disqualification of Catholic schools on this count, which he had feared, did not take place. But far more valuable, at least in the memory of the teachers, was the understanding he gave them of what Catholic education could be. His own work and the work of his associates in the *Catholic Magazine*, of Alexander Wilmot on the history of South Africa and Rhodesia, of Dr Welch on Portuguese colonization as well as his own studies on Shakespeare, were made vivid to them by his lectures and conversation. They learned to think of their job as going far beyond the humdrum limits of the text-book and the information required by the public examinations.

II. The " Catholic Magazine "

Meanwhile, with the appearance of the *Catholic Magazine* in 1891 a change had occurred in the method of Catholic apologetic. Bishop Ricards was then already a very sick man. His coadjutor and successor Bishop Strobino, like the vicars apostolic of Natal, Bishops Jolivet (1874–1903) and Delalle (1904–1946), spoke and wrote idiomatic but often " translated " English, with its consequent flatness. Bishops Leonard and Rooney of the Cape and the two Bishops Gaughren who succeeded one another at Kimberley like Bishop MacSherry at Port Elizabeth, were not given to exposition.

Partly by accident, then, the apologetic work in South Africa ceased to be pontifical. But this brought it into line with a widespread movement. In England, and to a large extent in other European countries, it became the fashion at the end of the nineteenth century to believe that administration was an art beyond the work hitherto done by clerks, and the rulers of teaching institutions like the secular universities were chosen for their supposed proficiency in it rather than for their intellectual distinction. A similar criterion seems to have been used in the choice of the rulers of Catholic dioceses, or at least those who were appointed were usually content to leave the literary commendation of the Faith to their priests and layfolk.

The change of approach had some advantages. Though the exposition no longer had the authority of a Bishop Grimley or a Bishop Ricards, the writers of the *Catholic Magazine* were, perhaps for that reason, more concerned with the attractiveness of their arguments to the minds of their readers. They paid less attention to the controversial conclusion than a bishop would perhaps have felt bound to do, and could more easily discuss facts and philosophical theories with which they happened to be acquainted. The magazine did not claim to express an official opinion; indeed, the writers often insisted that their opinions were not binding on Catholics. It did not limit its subject-matter to topics which affected Catholic belief or practice, but (as Kolbe was to say in 1901) like an Olympian court viewed all things under heaven. But it set forth the considered and critical opinion of informed Catholics, and was known as such a forum by the secular and religious papers of South Africa. It was not the first journalistic venture of the Catholic community; the Grahamstown *Colonist*, as we have seen, had appeared regularly for ten years in the 'forties and 'fifties, and Bishop Jolivet had published a *Monthly Record* for his vicariate of Natal for a year or two in the 'eighties. But the *Catholic Magazine* circulated over the whole country, dealt with topics of wider interest and with better scholarship, and won the respect and hearing of many who were not Catholics.

Members of the Catholic Club which Dr Sidney Welch founded in Cape Town,[15] or the various Catholic Reading Guilds of the time, could find in the *Catholic Magazine* information and reasoned arguments on a multitude of subjects relevant to apologetics. They would find articles by men like H. Donoghue who, with his father, had known the old President Pretorious sufficiently to persuade him in 1870 to repeal the enactments of the *Grondwet* making the saying of Mass illegal in the Transvaal.[16] Colonel Schermbrucker wrote for his fellow Catholics with the mind of a man of public affairs. Chief of this group was Alexander Wilmot, who settled in Grahamstown, where he became a provincial councillor and adviser to many business companies. His writings on South Africa won such repute that he became the collaborator and continuator of the archivist Theal, then (and still) the classic historian of the country.   He provided the readers of the *Catholic Magazine* with a balanced and documented if for that reason rather dull account of the history of their country.   And it was due to him that selections from the Catholic records, from the diary of Bishop Griffith and the *Chronicon* of the Eastern Vicariate, were published from time to time.

The magazine served, too, to make the South African Catholics aware of what the Church was doing in other parts of their land. The civilizing work of the Jesuits in Rhodesia and the Trappists among the Zulus were factually recorded by those who saw it in operation.   And Wilmot, along with several priests, extended the survey to America and Australasia and India as well as to Europe. The generation which read this monthly could not but be aware of the Catholic Church as binding men of all nations into a common and visible society.

More directly apologetic, perhaps, were the discussions of past events.   Because of their own ancestry, the non-Catholics of South Africa, of Dutch Calvinist or Huguenot or English descent, were acutely aware of the Catholic Church as an historical body.   They knew it and spoke of it as essentially the same as it had been when their own religion was first formed by revolt from it, and their dislike of it was much more concerned with what they believed its past history had been than with its doctrine or contemporary practice.

It is not surprising, then, that articles on events of European history appeared fairly frequently in the pages of the *Catholic Magazine*.   They were written chiefly by two priests, Dr McCarthy and (later) Dr Welch.   The older man wrote with the verve and interest of his own generation, his reputation was that of an orator, but he seldom made any attempt at thoroughness.   Dr Welch, however, who returned from his studies in Rome in 1894, adopted from the first the attitude which Ranke had taught as proper to the historian. He strove to be strictly objective and to relate "events as they happened".   In this method the writer assumes that there is a neutral viewpoint, independent of the passions which moved the actors in the scene;   this is "history", and the historian has something of the position of a judge in a lawsuit.   More recent criticism claims that this technique prescinds from much that is relevant and even vital to the story of mankind and assumes without proof the relative importance of those facts which happen to be well documented. But at the beginning of the century it was generally held to be the only method of securing objectivity. Certainly it had won a hearing for Lingard, who made use of it in his *History of England* before the time of Ranke; and it refuted the charge of bias which opponents were very ready to make against Catholic writers.

Dr Welch,[17] accustomed to this method in his historical studies, and employing it with success in his writings on Portuguese colonial history, which began with an article in the *Catholic Magazine* in 1904, used it also when he wrote on the interpretation of the Bible, on prayers for the dead, or on the Anglican attitude to authority in religion, on contemporary politics, and other controversial subjects. On all these matters he wrote with the apparent detachment of an essayist. It could reasonably be called a judicial viewpoint, but for that very reason lacked sympathy and understanding and sometimes even grasp of the feelings of his opponent. This dignified approach—as of a summing-up from the bench—was common to much Catholic controversial writing in English during the first quarter of this century, and Dr Welch's articles are well constructed examples of it; maybe such writing was effective in the long run because of its accuracy, but it contributed at the time to the exasperation of Protestants, and may even have hindered their intellectual contact with the Catholic Faith.

For the first eighteen years the greater part of the *Catholic Magazine*, in space and still more in quality, was written by Frederic Kolbe. The issues of the magazine for its first decade—down to the Anglo-Boer war—are probably the best material for a study of his personality. His two or three books on religion, though partly autobiographical, are impersonal. But in the pages of the *Catholic Magazine* he wrote under pressure and without time to practise the detachment of an essay. By some standards he was not a good editor; several times he had to apologize for delayed issues, and one month, in 1903, for the magazine failing to appear altogether. It was hardly a recommendation to complain in print of the multitude of his tasks, as he did in 1898; or to tell his subscribers, " By prodding me you can't make me more willing and may make

ST MARY'S CATHEDRAL, CAPE TOWN
The Mother Church of South Africa

THE FIRST CATHOLIC CHURCH IN SOUTH AFRICA
Erected in Cape Town in 1822

The first Church erected in Johannesburg (1887)

SANCTUARY OF THE CHURCH OF BLESSED MARTIN DE PORRES
In African style, Orlando West, Johannesburg

me disgusted ".[18] Or perhaps it was; for this natural personal note, without any attempt at Olympian detachment, the engagement of the author with his readers in discussion, is the mark of all Kolbe's writings and makes them attractive.

Kolbe admitted in 1907, when complaining of a nervous inability to write, and of deafness, that he could not stop teaching and lecturing.[19] The same characteristic, *diffusivum sui*, certainly enriched the quality of the *Catholic Magazine*, for the editor was able to write from a variety of standpoints and to put himself wholeheartedly into each. His " Children's Corner " had all the grave seriousness which is the only way to talk to children, and yet was neither condescending nor impersonal; his " Professor's Armchair " discussed the questions that a Catholic layman might ask or be asked, without the apparatus of the schools but never pretending to slick or ready-made answers; his short stories were written in dialogues which could have been easily dramatized. And in all these he showed to different groups of readers the approach which an informed Catholic could make to their particular way of life.

While Kolbe was editor, from 1891 till 1909, with two short intervals, he was a hard-hitting controversialist against the writers in the Dutch Reformed Church *Kerkbode* and the Anglican *Southern Cross*, and gave an answer to every public attack on the Church which he noticed. Or perhaps it would be more accurate to say he commented in order to make fun of it. When the Anglican Bishop of Pretoria spoke of the " impudence " of Catholics in assuming territorial titles for their sees he asked what this bishop was doing in the Dutch republic of the Transvaal. After the *Volksbode*, which claimed to speak for the Dutch Reformed Church, had made a silly misstatement about Catholic doctrines, Kolbe " authoritatively " denied that the editor of the *Volksbode* was a Jesuit in disguise, " although he does his best to make Protestantism ridiculous ". On one occasion at least he expressly disowned the remarks of a priest who had been rude to members of the Afrikaner Bond; but he told the editor of *Ons Land*, who called it Roman Catholic rudeness, that he was being rude to Roman Catholics in assuming that the priest spoke for them all.

Kolbe made a similar distinction in answering the recurring and gross slanders on the Church of which the model was the Maria Monk story. Though its author had been judicially proved a liar and punished by the civil courts in Canada, her fables had a long start, and the disproof has never caught up with them. Similar stories about the Catholic Church had been put about in South Africa by Hammond and Muller in book form, and were sometimes sponsored in part by those who should have known better. Whenever he noticed their appearance in print Kolbe denounced them for the lies they were and took to task those who accepted them. In 1898 he wrote, " There is going on in this country an active propaganda of personal libel against us Catholics which ought to be incredible "; and he urged that Protestant public opinion should openly denounce the mass of calumny which lay to its charge. Still, he was ready to admit that " all the better class of Protestants are quickly dropping it ".*[20]

Similarly he frequently commented with laughter on the claim of so many of the Anglican clergy to be Catholic. " Outside themselves ", he wrote, " their belief in their continuity is not accepted by anyone "; and he attributed this opinion to the fact that " Englishmen do not think it possible for the English to be heretics ".[21] At the same time, however, he expressly welcomed their " manifest strengthening as a Church and as an establishment in England itself in the last thirty years and its expansion throughout the Empire; because their triumph is over our common foe: indifferentism . . . and we do not grudge it ".

Of the same sort but more penetrating was Kolbe's description of the religion of his own father, a member of the London Missionary Society:

> There was no book of controversy in his library, and he had no habit of it. . . . All the truths he believed were Catholic truths, and he found so much to obey in them that he never felt the need for more.[22]

But Kolbe does not appear to have followed up the line of thought which those comments suggest, or to have been interested directly in the dogmas of other religious bodies. Indeed, he seldom used the *Catholic Magazine* to expound the dogmas of the faith, though he published several books on that subject.[23] In the magazine he restricted himself to comments (and it is one of his journalistic virtues that most of his writings here was not in form or

* See also p. 183, *supra*.

content a slice of some larger work) on the relation of contemporary
thought to Catholic belief. And here he offered his readers many
an acute and pithy observation which did not profess to solve a
problem but suggested an attitude to it which Catholics might
easily overlook. When Mivart was accusing the ecclesiastical
authorities of ignoring science he wrote: " There is some truth in
saying that the Church looks upon physical science as a danger.
But dangers are meant to be overcome, and to be overcome they
must be entered into."[24] And in another connection he pointed
out that the Church had taken from the Greek philosophy and
the Roman law and grafted the cuttings into her theology, and " the
present age appears to have a mission for science, and probably (if
the world lasts) when this civilization is swept away and the
Catholic Church has emerged from the flood, she will be found to
have added the science to the philosophy and the law for the future
generations of society ".[25]

Besides these occasional comments Kolbe expounded what he
believed to be the best apologetic in the contemporary situation.
The last quarter of the nineteenth century saw the triumph of the
natural sciences and their method of enquiry. Newtonian physics
and evolutionary biology had won acceptance among the learned,
and were unquestioned by the well-read public as a sufficient
explanation of the material and living universe. Their conclusions and even their hypotheses did not alarm the Catholic
world as they had the Protestant theologians, and several writers
in the *Catholic Magazine* pointed out that the most controverted
one—that of evolution—could be understood in a way consistent
with sound Biblical exegesis, and indeed that a form of it had
been held by St Augustine. But, confident from their own success,
many scientists were claiming that the method of induction which
they used was the only valid way of arriving at knowledge. The
logical processes whose instrument was the syllogism, employed
in Aristotelian philosophy and in the Catholic tradition, were
explained as symbols to describe convictions really reached by other
paths than that of reasoning. Catholics, therefore, especially in
the English-speaking world, were met by opponents who rejected
the very method of their arguments.

Contemporary with this movement of thought was the revival

of scholasticism in the Catholic Church. The Vatican Council of 1870 declared doctrinally that the conclusions of human reason and the data of revelation are not in opposition, and that seeming discordances can be resolved by patient intellectual labour; in particular, that human reasoning can prove the existence of a Creator to whom also as an End the universe is directed, and that there are valid reasons for accepting the credibility of the Christian Faith. To make this teaching concrete and operative Pope Leo XIII set the Catholic universities to use the principles and methods of St Thomas Aquinas in their teaching. Their pupils studied, therefore, a close-knit system of metaphysics leading up to arguments to demonstrate the existence of God, while in theology the dogmas were articulated to a coherent scheme of the relations of man to God, and the reasonable grounds for each of them, of analogy or suitability, were developed. The instrument of enquiry was Aristotelian logic, and the structural completeness and intellectual beauty of Thomism gave its students confidence in that instrument as great as that of the scientists in their own methods.

Frederic Kolbe was sent by Cardinal Manning to Rome in the first years of renewed scholasticism, and he entered fully into the enthusiasm of the revival. But he had had an earlier formation at Cape Town and London universities in the natural sciences, and understood the confidence of their teachers in ignoring the arguments of Catholic tradition. In the *Catholic Magazine* he gave himself the task of showing that they were mistaken.

Kolbe opened his campaign with a criticism of Newman's *Grammar of Assent*. The great cardinal, profoundly interested in the psychology of religious conviction, had analysed the processes of the human mind, and, while admitting the force of the inductive argument, appeared to accept the current criticism of syllogistic reasoning, and explained assent by an illative sense which was a moral rather than an intellectual quality. Newman's was the greatest name as a thinker to English-speaking Catholics, and if they accepted this implicit logic (as it was called) as adequate they would never rally to scholasticism. They would then be deprived, in Kolbe's judgement, of the best defence of the faith and the best means of gaining converts to it. This attitude to philosophy was part of the intellectual antipathy between Manning and

Newman, and Kolbe, a protégé and admirer of the former, may also have thought that contemporary opinion was less than just to Manning's greatness. When Purcell's *Life* appeared his comment was, " Our whole sympathy goes with Newman, our whole judgement with Manning. . . . Be it remembered too that Manning spoke the first word of reconciliation and refused to answer to the last word of impatience."[26]

But neither veneration for Manning nor enthusiasm for his own intellectual formation kept Kolbe from recognizing facts. St Thomas Aquinas indeed, he says, stimulates original thought, but some Thomists repress it, and the *Grammar of Assent* was a reaction against the stiffness of scholasticism; smart syllogisms will never be sufficient to carry conviction by themselves. But while admiring the vigour and ease of Newman's approach Kolbe insisted that the Church has always used the methods advocated by him but in another connection. In its ethical science there is a perfect employment of the method of induction because here, as in the natural sciences, we have the proper material, a process to be examined, for that instrument. So also it was a commonplace of the schools that a good moral life was the best climate for intellectual work, and this could be called implicit thought. Indeed, education consists of passing through such climates, and they are necessary in the process of conversion. The scholastics, following ecclesiastical tradition, valued highly the judgement of the *ecclesiasticon phronemon*, and this was appealed to by the Council of Trent as the *universus ecclesiae sensus*. But just as the gift of music is not sufficient without training, so this moral sense requires the discipline of logical deduction before it can be used, and that is precisely what scholasticism gives. A factual analysis then shows that a man who reasons both syllogizes and uses induction implicitly. But by itself implicit thought is subjective and so provides no common measure for argument or conviction, and for that reason St Thomas recognized that there were two sorts of wisdom, one of spiritual judgement, the other of scientific theology. It is a pity that Newman did not realize that implicit thought is only useful as giving life to a system but is not a substitute for it. Nor is Newman's illative sense a way out of this conclusion. In itself it is personal, but the judgement of a purged and trained mind, of a *phronemon*, creates a probability, and the agreement of other such minds increases that probability, and not merely by addition. Finally, the consensus of a great number gives us moral certainty, and it is precisely as such—that is as a defence of authority—that the scholastic theologians employ it.

In the year when he published this article Kolbe was able to quote Judge Cole as having said that the *Catholic Magazine* was "the best magazine in the country ", and the *Cape Argus* that it " provided reading not obtainable elsewhere ".[27] But it is questionable whether the examples of strictly scholastic analysis which he published from time to time in later numbers were widely read or understood. In 1905 he justified himself with the remark that " those who say our magazine is over their heads thereby emphasize the need of it ".[28] But there may well have been need for a ladder of narrower rungs to make the ascent to Thomistic heights. To some extent it was provided by the discussions Kolbe provided in the "Professor's Armchair," and even in his "Children's Corner"— these would convince the Catholic reader of the reliability of scholastic training. So too Kolbe's philosophical articles would help priests, who would recognize in them the discipline in which their minds had been formed, to solve the intellectual problems they met with and to have confidence in the Thomistic method.

In the first quarter of the new century, then, Kolbe's work did much to being about in South Africa the state of mind among Catholics which he claimed as his purpose in criticizing Newman, that " for Catholics no other system [of religious philosophy] than the scholastic is to be thought of ". The same development occurred, indeed, throughout the English-speaking Catholic world. During these years, but quite independently as far as one can see, the value and importance of deductive logic was again recognized in the natural sciences by the work of men like Whitehead in physics and Collingwood in historical studies. It could fairly be said that the scholastic movement in the Church did, in this respect, lead the way in restoring the prestige of reasoning.

This common ground, however, was not discovered in the first quarter of the twentieth century, and there was then less contact of mind between Catholics and the rest of the world than there had been in the days of Wiseman and Newman. Catholic apologetic suffered because neither side seriously attempted to understand the position of the other. The argument for the credibility of the Catholic religion was cast more and more in a judicial form. Just before the outbreak of the world war in 1914 Bishop Cox of the Transvaal vicariate published several articles to demonstrate the necessity of authority in true religion, and the evidence of the authority of the Catholic Church. They had some of that stiffness which Kolbe had lamented in neo-Thomism, and which he almost always avoided. But their worst fault was one of omission; they forgot to show that true religion was desired or desirable.

Chapter XII

CHURCH, STATE AND SCHOOLS: II

I. The Change

BY the end of the century enthusiasm among Catholics for their own schools had become a matter of urgency because a change had taken place in the attitude both of the civil administration and of the citizens to educational questions. The Catholic leaders were perhaps slow to recognize it. They certainly had complaints to make and Dr Kolbe wrote in 1902:

> We have a claim to be more frankly and generously admitted into the national system than we are. It is for us (1) to assert our claim with moderation and firmness, (2) to show it is not inconsistent with liberty and justice, (3) to prove ourselves not unworthy of it.[1]

Dr Kolbe put the blame, as did others, on the administration. He assumed that the national system itself was capable of including the Catholic schools; in fact that it was the same system as he had praised twenty years earlier in a public lecture as more just than any other system in the world.[2]

Father James Kelly had stated the traditional Catholic view of education with entire clarity in 1892: the children belong to their parents and not to the state, and education is therefore a parental duty; the Church has rights given by God over the parents and therefore over their children; the state has the duty to correct and supply for the ignorance and weakness of parents, and therefore has rights in regard to the standard and competence of secular instruction but not to order and define the whole education.[3] Of these principles ten years later Kolbe welcomed the hustle which Dr Muir, the Secretary of Education at the Cape, exercised on the Catholic schools, but he urged that their existence was a real gain to the country:

> This question concerns a number of schools which it is for us a matter of conscience to maintain for our own youth and for

those whose parents entrust them to us . . . they are in the large towns only. . . . We think the variety is a distinct gain to secular education. But we cannot in principle cast them away. That this is so is a fact which the authority should legislate for just as they do for drought in the Karoo. . . . We are ready to enter the national system and submit to all their tests in secular learning. Surely it is profitable for the nation to use all energies, and so ours.[4]

The Catholics had learned already, as Kolbe put it in this article, that "the undenominational schools are Protestant . . . no Catholic need apply". In 1892 Miss Crosby's appointment at Riebeck College had been cancelled because of her religion. Many other instances occurred, and in 1900 an "undenominational" school, advertising for a teacher, stipulated: "who must not be a Catholic".[5] With some evidence the writers on education in the *Catholic Magazine* attributed such cases to the bigotry of individual Dutch *predikants* on the school boards who triumphed over Dr Muir's opposition. The official attitude was shown more correctly by the appointments of Dr Kolbe to the council of Cape Town University and of the Jesuit Father Walmesley to that of the new Rhodes University in 1904.[6] Even when the Bill to make schooling compulsory in the Cape Province was proposed in the following year and made mention of undenominational schools, Dr Welch, a realist in all political matters, opined that this was mere jargon and that the Bill would keep what was valuable at present but give impetus to the system ("including our own schools"). Though this meant, he said, secular education for South Africa, "it is practically the better though far from the ideal course".[7] When it became an Act of Parliament in 1905 he still insisted that it left Catholic schools as they were, but drew attention to the increasing endowments of "undenominational" schools which would force up the standards and so the expenses of Catholic schools while the grant-in-aid would not be in proportion.[8]

This seems to have been the first warning of danger in the structure of a national system. In the following year the recommendations of the Educational Commission in the Transvaal showed how serious it was. There the Marist College of Johannesburg held a unique position among the Transvaal schools for

popularity and competence.   For the last two and a half years of
Paul Kruger's government it had received a grant from the state,
and its principal had been on friendly terms with the old President.
They had done most for secondary education, and the rest had all
been given by other denominational schools.   The Mayor of
Johannesburg, nominated by the English victors after the war,
was St John Carr, a devout Catholic, and the commission represented the views of the English administration, not those of the
Dutch Reformed Church.   Though St John Carr proposed very
reasonably that all schools " where there was no religious test or
compulsory religion " should be reckoned undenominational and
qualify for grants, the commission defined as denominational any
in which religion was taught at all, and the government decided
not to give such schools a subsidy.[9]

This decision seems to have come as a shock to the Catholic
leaders, and its full import was not realized till 1911, when Father
FitzHenry wrote from a long experience:

> The educational conditions in South Africa and the relations
> of our schools to government and to public have changed
> altogether within the last five years. . . .   Before 1905 there
> was an aided voluntary system which obtained in all the provinces
> but which scarcely reached half the children. . . .   So there was
> full scope and welcome for Church schools, and right well we
> met the needs. . . .   Now the government has started a state
> system which aims at absorbing all others.[10]

Father FitzHenry saw rightly that the question was one of the
relation of Catholic schools to the government and the public, but
he was mistaken in dating it to the last few years.   The very concept of government had changed much earlier, and the educational
crisis was its late outcome.   In the days of colonial rule the administration had taken account of the grouping of the population.   For
some purposes the local units, for others the racial, for others again
the economic (farming and trade), for others a linguistic or religious
basis was considered.   Though it has become usual to talk of this
as an organic concept of the state, it is not very exact; a citizen did
not belong to one and the same cell in all connections, but was at
one time a member, say, of the farming class, at another a Catholic,
at a third the inhabitant of a district.   But the metaphor of a human
body is correct to this extent, that each community, religious or

local or linguistic, was in direct communication with the government concerning its own interests and spoke for all those who made it up. The business of the political rulers was to provide for the orderly prosperity of all by managing the groups of citizens as well as possible. Some governors might try to ignore a particular group, as Lord Charles Somerset was said to have neglected the Dutch element of the population, and Sir Harry Smith the Catholic; sometimes it was said that the English rule was one long series of blunders in this work; but the concept of such a system could always be appealed to with some success in discussions about patronage and finance.

II. *Representative Government and its Implications*

A parliament on the English model was established in the Cape Province in 1864, and, though some important matters were reserved, the government had to obtain its consent for taxation and for new laws. As in other countries where the system obtained it presupposed a class with leisure sufficient to devote themselves chiefly to politics, and the majority vote of elected representatives became the overriding condition of all administrative decisions. The influence of the groups based on economic or religious interests was thereby diminished, for the government when listening to them had to bear also in mind the views of parliament. If the latter had come into existence earlier this need not have made much difference. But, as [the late] G. M. Young has pointed out,[11] during the career of Sir Robert Peel in England the concept of parliament had changed from senatorial to representative, and it came to South Africa years after Peel's death in the latter form. The legislature was supposed to express the views of the electorate which had chosen them, and these had been obtained solely on the issues presented at the election. In practice the political class divided into two or three parties on some few controverted questions, and the electorate had perforce to vote on them. Only as a pressure group within those parties, sometimes only by relating their desires to what were being regarded as the sole political issues, could a religious or economic or racial community secure a hearing with the government of the day.

The course of history has made representative government an

accepted, indeed an unquestioned institution in South Africa, as in many other countries, and its advantages need no recapitulation. It is not so easy now to understand that it meant the loss of some social benefits possible under the older system. Yet there were those who pointed this out in the 'sixties. The Catholic laymen who were members of the assembly—Schermbrucker, Elder and Wilmot—were all in favour of the change. Dr Ricards had used the columns of *The Colonist* to urge it. He did so chiefly as part of his criticism of the treatment of the problems of the Eastern Province by the Cape government, and according to Wilmot he had but little interest in the theory of politics apart from education. Bishop Grimley did not discuss the matter in his autobiography, but his friendliness with Solomon and Schermbrucker showed where his sympathies lay.

On the other hand Bishop Moran was an ouspoken critic of responsible government. He urged that in practice the electorate would be overwhelmingly white and therefore only a small section of the inhabitants. Their interests would dominate all policy, whereas under Crown rule the interests of all sections of the community could be cared for. Until, therefore, the coloured and Bantu population were capable of taking part, responsible government was a misnomer and the pretence of it could only lead to trouble.

On this issue the bishop had few followers, though events have shown that there was substance in his warning. There were, however, other matters where the doctrine of responsible government also encouraged a trend of at least questionable social advantage. The education of children was one of these, in which it tended to prejudice the independence of minority schools. Bishop Moran expressed his views on this forcibly to Bishop Grimley in 1863; and six years later, in 1869, the two vicars apostolic differed on another matter of public policy. Mr Solomon, who had already helped Bishop Grimley in his negotiations about the schools, introduced into the assembly a measure called the Voluntary Bill. By its terms the grants made by the government to the ecclesiastical communities in the Cape would be abolished and the Churches as voluntary associations would have no claim on the administration for help of any kind. Among the supporters were several Catholic laymen, moved partly perhaps by the feeling that the Anglicans received an unduly large share, relative to their numbers, of governmental patronage. Bishop Moran regarded their action as wrong-headed, but worse was to follow. As he wrote to Bishop Grimley on 18 February 1869:

Schermbrucker not only opposed me but threw your opinion in favour of the Voluntary Bill in my face—the same was done in Port Elizabeth to Dr Murphy by Elder. In fact you have been quoted against us by Solomon's friends. I fancy they have maligned you, but if they have not I can only congratulate you on the happiness of possessing independently of government aid the means of supporting your staff of priests. We are not in that enviable position.[12]

Bishop Grimley's answer was: "I never told anyone I was for the Voluntary Bill, circumstanced as the colony is; but if the Catholics were able to support their priests, I would be a 'voluntary' heart and soul." Later, however, he began to remember some incautious remarks. When Schermbrucker wrote to him he regretted the need of letters on the subject and declared that he had never said he was " a voluntary " in the peculiar circumstances of the colony. He was only sorry that these circumstances " make it impossible for me to proclaim myself a voluntary ". And on 16 March 1869 he wrote to Mr Ford of Grahamstown asking him to recollect a conversation on the Bill. " I always expressed my opinion freely ", he said, and this opinion he summarized thus: " As we are it would be injurious, otherwise I would support ". So he asked Mr Ford to recollect if he (the Bishop) had ever said absolutely that he was " a voluntary ", or that he would vote for the Bill if he were a member of the Assembly.

It seems probable that Bishop Grimley's enthusiasm had led him to talk freely, but that later consideration of the " peculiar circumstances " had suggested that reticence would be more prudent. And it is clear that Bishop Moran was completely satisfied that his own clear-cut conservative decision was the only sensible one for a vicar apostolic, but that his colleague (whom he had known from their schooldays in Wexford) was likely to be muddled on the issues.

In fact Bishop Grimley was justified by the event. The Bill did pass, and the responsible government which was inaugurated a couple of years later began with purely secular interests save to the extent of the grants-in-aid of mission schools. Further, Bishop Grimley noted in his autobiography,[13] " whether the Bill pass or not the Church will expand ", and this also came true in the following years. And the Catholics of the next generation not only found the situation tolerable but would not have welcomed a return to the old system. This makes it the more difficult, and historically more necessary, to understand the strength of Bishop Moran's position and through it to see what was in fact accomplished in the relations of Church and State.

Any analysis of government, apart from that of a police state, must consider what is the moral authority by reason of which the subjects obey without being compelled, and, further, what is the limit or moral law which the rulers cannot transgress without justifying resistance. Under the colonial government, as in Europe generally, down to the middle of the nineteenth century, the answer was in both cases the traditional religions of the people. The only exception was the less than ten years period of the revolution in France; the Napoleonic régime restored in this matter the religious foundation of political obedience. In England the legitimation of Catholic life was in fact a recognition, denied hitherto in Protestant theory, that Catholicism taught loyalty to the state. And the guarantee that governments would not act intolerably was that they also accepted the principles of Christianity as taught by one at least of the received traditions. In such a system the secular rulers naturally supported, if need be financially, the traditional religious institutions which inculcated this morality and claimed a greater or less measure of influence in the appointment of the officials and conduct of their affairs. There were in consequence many disputes between Church and State both about the help the government should give from its revenues and about the extent of its interference in ecclesiastical affairs. But the system did do its work in teaching reasonable civil obedience and in providing some sort of check on the power of rulers.

There was no reason in strict logic why responsible government—i.e. the election of rulers by the subjects for a period of years—should not have taken place within that system. But it was simpler to press for responsible government with the plea that rulers should be bound in all things by the wishes of the majority of the electorate.   The corollary was that they were free from the traditional morality, and in fact the advocates of responsible government in Europe often sought as rulers the power to impoverish or otherwise destroy the influence either of the Church or of a class which embodied and preserved respect for that morality among the people; sometimes, even, they attempted to justify on this ground acts of aggression against neighbouring but weaker states.   Against this movement the papacy made protest after protest, culminating in the encyclical *Quanta Cura* and the Syllabus of Errors of Pius IX.   Bishop Moran had in fact considerable reason for suspecting the principle which underlay the Voluntary Bill.

But there were many, especially in the English-speaking world, who thought Christian morality to be so self-evidently right that the reasonable men who made up a nineteenth-century electorate would never call it in question.   A secular government responsible to the electorate would not, therefore, be guilty of a plainly unjust policy, even though it might be far from perfect.   They would certainly allow the traditional religious bodies to pursue freely their work of persuading the citizens, and there was no danger in their accepting voluntary status.   It would bring to an end the awkwardness of being partially dependent on a secular government, and at the same time there could be no discrimination of patronage in favour of a particular religion.   That seems to have been the view both of Bishop Grimley and of most Catholic laymen.   They did not think then that the Education Act of 1865 would in fact and naturally work out as the endowment of a Protestant system of schooling; even as late as 1883 Dr Kolbe could call it in a lecture a system more just than any other in the world.[14]

The assumption that secular governments would continue to be guided by Christian morality has not been verified in the twentieth century.   Indeed, it is now generally recognized that those principles cannot in practice continue to be held without the sanction of dogmatic beliefs or outside institutional religion.   In many countries, however, and South Africa among them, the fact was long unrecognized.   On the assumption of a common Christian morality it was supposed that the policy of the majority after election would be at least tolerable to their recent opponents, and, therefore, that responsible government would be workable; the divisions of political opinion could not be called religious in any sense. Perhaps it is true to say that the system broke down at the onset of the Anglo-Boer war and the subsequent world wars. But apart from these moments of crisis it was only the small minority of Catholics who regarded one matter of public policy, education, as a religious issue, and their scruples were largely overcome by allowing them a partial measure of help in paying for an exceptional position. Generally speaking, then, while the warnings of Pius IX and Bishop Moran have been justified by subsequent events in most of the world, the secularized responsible governments which, in fact if not in name, became common in the latter half of the nineteenth century have worked to their logical development only very slowly. Meanwhile, the Church as a voluntary association in law has been able to act more spontaneously and to proclaim its teaching more freely than when it was assisted and therefore influenced by its association with the secular power. Bishop Grimley might indeed claim that there were enough benefits to be derived from the voluntary system to justify his enthusiasm for it. But that its introduction was a fundamental change in human society, as far-reaching perhaps as the acceptance of the Catholic Church by the Emperor Constantine, will be recognized by historians when we are sufficiently distant from the event to see more of its effects. And it will be clear that the place of the Catholic Church in the new society depended on the preaching of an apologetic which stressed the independence of Catholic action—the importance, so far as South Africa is concerned, of the work which Bishop Grimley, Father O'Haire and Dr Ricards inaugurated.

Neither in England nor in Cape Colony was the change made deliberately. It is doubtful in fact whether many statesmen saw what the effect of representative parliamentary government would be. The process, therefore, by which the groupings of daily life, and among them that of religious faith, ceased to be part of social government or to have an admitted claim on the public revenue, was a gradual one. It is perhaps indicated (but unconsciously) by Wilmot in his life of Ricards when he says that the latter was unlike his predecessor, Dr Moran, who had been a great politician. The letters of Griffith, Devereux, Moran and Grimley show them negotiating with the governor and his officials, even with the

Colonial Secretary in Whitehall and the War Office, and obtaining from them building sites for churches and schools, grants of money as military or civil chaplains as well as for educational expenses, on the accepted ground that they were " chaplains of the Roman Catholic community ". But there is a marked lessening of that activity and co-operation* after 1870, when Grimley died and Moran went to New Zealand to be Bishop of Dunedin.

In some cases there was a special reason for the lack of episcopal interest in politics. Allard and Jolivet, the vicars apostolic of Natal, were both Frenchmen and were surprised and grateful to find themselves under a government which did not interfere with them. They consistently supported the British view in the troubles of the Orange Free State and Transvaal, which fell within the vicariate till 1886, in return for this liberty of private action. But in the case of Bishop Leonard, Bishop Ricards, and Bishop Gaughren it must be said that they accepted without question the new régime which excluded them from direct political bargaining or, to put it another way, which limited political activity theoretically to party issues. It was indeed a very common view of the Catholic hierarchy in England and Ireland and France; Manning was an exception among the English bishops, though very much of the English tradition, in speaking with authority on politics, and was the last Archbishop of Westminster to do so. When the Bill to make all religious bodies strictly voluntary associations was being debated in the Cape parliament of 1869 Bishop Grimley penned his remark to Colonel Schermbrucker about only circumstances making it impossible for him to proclaim himself a voluntary.[15] Among the circumstances was a very stern letter from Bishop Moran,[16] one of the old-fashioned conservatives who did not take the promises of liberation for real liberty.

It was the attitude of Bishop Grimley which prevailed. His successor and Bishop Moran's offered no opposition to the principle that the Church was purely a voluntary society in the new structure of the Cape Colony. Typical perhaps was Bishop Ricards' refusal of nomination by the Colonial Secretary to the council of the university in 1879.[17] He concerned himself only with the provision of schools and teachers for Catholics and refused a post

* Exception must be made for native territories which lay outside the rule of the Cape parliamentary government.

which would have given him voice and influence on the formation of South African youth in general.

III.   Religion and State Education

Taking 1870 then as a rough dividing line, it may be said that in the earlier period the Catholic Church was accepted in fact as a public body and part of the structure of society, whereas afterwards its status was that of a private corporation. The change was scarcely noticed by the hierarchy, because Catholic layfolk continued as before to accept voluntarily the law-making powers of the Church and the authority of its rulers to speak in their name, and such loyalty was the bishop's chief concern.

The effect of the introduction of responsible representative government on the Church was also hidden by the continuity of the civil service. After 1870 as before the bulk of negotiating about schooling (the chief point of contact between the vicars apostolic and the civil rulers) was the work of permanent officials. Langham Dale continued to be the Secretary for Education under the new constitution, and remained co-operative with the Catholics, as was also his successor Robert Muir. But, as Daudet pointed out many years ago, the important social change of the nineteenth century was the development of the administrative state, and this brought about, and was later preserved by, a civil service with new outlook and functions. The political rulers, elected as a party and for a time only, could form a policy and pass laws to implement it, but they seldom gave personal attention to detail. Nor did they leave it to the normal communities of citizens either to spend the revenue voted or to carry out the policy laid down. That was in future wholly the business of the permanent civil service, acting indeed scrupulously within the law and according to the given political directives, but giving them any needed interpretation.

The moderation and restraint of the civil servants concealed in the matter of education the social change which took place. They allowed former arrangements to continue, and even stretched the law, by gentlemen's agreements, to do so. The payment of half salaries to teachers in Catholic schools of the Cape Province, and the acceptance of what Scots law conveniently calls " use and wont " in regard to regulations, were not challenged, and the relations of the Catholic authorities with the Education Department remained as friendly as ever.   But the new attitude was not a dead letter.   The revenue expended on Catholic schools was no longer their proportion of the taxes paid but was definitely a special grant from state property, and continued because of the past history of these schools.   In general, education was to be a service rendered by the state out of its revenue because only the officials could be trusted to spend the money economically and wisely.   So the normal trend was to provide through the civil service a system of schools called free because the citizens anonymously and in general paid for them by taxation.   It was imposed on or given to (according to one's standpoint) European children at the Cape, in the Transvaal and in Natal.

But just as the finance for this came from or through the civil service, so the instruction provided must be that which the civil service approved.   Since the Catholics wanted to add or modify that instruction, they could not claim the state gift.   But, as a concession, the old system of financial aid to them was continued provided they satisfied the standards imposed by the department. When these rose, especially in the matter of buildings, the additional expense to the Catholic community was their own concern, as it was not included in the old arrangements which the civil service had taken over.   And when the educational structure was re-built from the foundations, as in the Transvaal in 1906, no place was made in it (and therefore no grant was made) for schools where a religious faith was taught.

To suggest that the main concern of the department officials was with expenditure would be unfair.   They wanted to give to the children of all citizens the culture they believed to be both possible and obviously desirable.   Consistently, then, they pressed on the politicians the extension of this benefit to all, and by general consent this was called, for men were not deceived into liking it, compulsory education.   It became the practice as well as the law for white children in all the provinces after the Union of 1910. Its nature and standard were determined by the curriculum imposed by the department, by their inspectors, and by their examinations. In South Africa as elsewhere (for the system was common to all " liberal " countries) the quality of this culture was limited by its examinable nature, so that the teachers were trained to give and encouraged to give only the sort of learning which the average child could absorb and could repeat in writing. It was seldom recognized in the first quarter of the twentieth century that the " school-board culture " takes up so much of the time and energy of children, and is assumed by them to be so complete, that it often prevents them from developing their natural gifts and takes away the zest for the arts and humane learning. Dr Kolbe did sometimes hint at this criticism (which was to become louder after his death), and with his friends provided some corrective. But generally the Catholic schools had to fall in line with those which were now called public. Where grants were given by the state they came under the same regimentation. Where the schools were wholly supported by fees and by the Catholic community the Department left them to their own devices, relying on the pressure of parents, and the need of passing public examinations, to secure to a great extent a similar result.

The matter of instruction in religion was admittedly difficult. The tradition of all sections of the community down to the turn of the century, and even later, was that it should be an integral part of education. Yet the civil service, as officials of a non-confessional state, could not adopt for teaching any one of the known and accepted beliefs. Probably the English and Dutch sense of humour saved them from the French stupidity of inventing an openly lay morality or religion. Instead they imposed a " Bible religion " on the public schools. In practice this meant at first the interpretation of the Scriptures given by the Dutch Reformed Church to which most of the citizens belonged. As the years went by and rationalism spread amongst teachers and inspectors the religious instruction was modified in the secularist direction (unevenly because according to the views of the teachers) and less place was given to the supernatural. But the legal permission to withdraw children from the religious instruction of the public schools for conscience' sake (used by Catholic parents and others) tacitly admitted there was no common religious foundation which could be given to all children, and that in fact the department had invented its own religion. And it was not long before intelligent people began to see that moral judgements were involved in the interpretation of history and literature, and that some of the fundamental issues—the field of reason and its relation to behaviour, the place of authority in social life and the right of revolution— naturally contain a religious element. With the growth of interest in the psychology of education this recognition increased, and it became more difficult to frame strictly secular subjects. As Father Kelly wrote in 1891, education is always in fact religious.

The department officials could not of course agree to that view. But their acceptance, reluctantly, of the practice of not appointing Catholic teachers in public schools shows them to be aware of what could be said in its favour. But for the Catholics also it implied a change of attitude. In earlier days they had upheld the view of the mediaeval scholastics that rational knowledge could be organized separately from revealed, and applied it to the teaching of children, and so explained and justified their reception of those who were entrusted to them by Protestant parents. After 1890 certainly the position was put differently. Dr Kolbe asked himself in the pages of the *Catholic Magazine* why Protestant children were accepted. His reply was: "To make the best of a bad job". " We must get government aid ", he argued, " and they won't give it without our taking all and any, and these want to come. So far from desiring the state of things in which it is necessary to have Protestants in our schools, we find them a drawback and an embarrassment, a check to our freedom and a clog upon our devotion."[18] If it were not Kolbe who wrote the passage one could take it as a plea for the formation of a ghetto for Catholics, but the author's whole life and activity, as well as his other writings before and after, show him an advocate of the frankest co-operation on the cultural level of all classes of the community. The words must be taken to apply only to the subject of the education of children. With many of his friends he had come to see that in school one could not make the distinction between a purely rational philosophy and revealed teaching. For the formation of moral character it was practically necessary as well as reasonable to incorporate religious truth with other instruction of the mind from the beginning. Consideration of how much could be proved by observation and argument and what was a corollary of revealed doctrine would come at a later stage.

Generally speaking this view was adopted by all Catholics, layfolk as well as bishops, and in theory they regarded the presence of pupils of other faiths in their schools as unfortunate. As the twentieth century advanced the proportion of Catholics in the schools of the religious orders increased. But no confessional bar was imposed even where, as in the Transvaal and in some Natal colleges, there was neither government assistance nor control. Occasionally the reason was economic, as Dr Kolbe had admitted, but with the increase of wealth and numbers of the Catholic community this was not always cogent. There was, however, the school tradition of accepting the children of former pupils, and there was the simple belief in the value of a Catholic education and pleasure that it was recognized by some who were not Catholics. And in 1921 Dr Welch (a realist who was not afraid of defending an unpopular view) praised the mixed schools (mixed, that is, as regards the religion of the pupils) as having worked well up to the present, as having the real control in Catholic hands, and as having been the nursery of many South African priests.

By the end of the first quarter of the century, then, the situation was this. Education was reckoned to be part of the business of civil government. All citizens, including Catholics, must pay for it through taxation, but the expenditure of the money allocated and the standards of instruction given were not subject to direct control of the parents who paid or whose children were taught. The officials of the education departments (it was largely a provincial matter) were deemed to know best what was good for the country. The type of instruction given in this system, even when non-religious, could not be called Christian in any sense understood by Catholics or accepted by them. But, almost as an historical accident, Catholics were legally entitled to provide their own schools, and for some of these schools in Cape Province and Natal the government bore part of the expenses in return for a control of the appointments and curriculum which was not irksome in practice. Security for this arrangement rested on no admitted principle either of parental right or Church grant, but on the natural tendency of a civil service to keep the system it has inherited. Should a political attack be made on it the Department could not be more than benevolently neutral.

It must be said that the Catholics had come to take the situation for granted. Though they grumbled occasionally at the small assistance given to their schools, when given at all, they did not seriously suppose that in the world of South Africa they could persuade their fellow countrymen to make a radical alteration. Education was something given free by the government, who had a right to the revenue collected, and as Catholics wanted to contract out of the system they must expect to pay for the privilege.

Dr Sidney Welch seems to have been almost alone in urging that another system was practicable, and was actually in action in a civilized and democratic country. In 1910 he reminded the readers of the *Catholic Magazine* of the law in Holland by which twenty heads of families in any given district had the legal right, should they demand it, to a denominational school for their children.[19] He returned to the same point in 1920 and 1923.[20] He might indeed have added in these years that the same parental right had been established in Scots law and was bringing about there a solution very similar to the Dutch.* Though Dr Welch professed to have hope that the Nationalist Party, which had just come to power, would give his suggestion favourable consideration,[21] it came to nothing, and in particular it did not inspire any political enthusiasm or efforts on the part of Catholics. The Church was able through the religious orders to produce men and women to devote themselves to teaching for motives which were free from the lawful desire of personal gain. The Catholic layfolk did not regret the great financial sacrifices of their forebears or refuse to continue the more moderate ones now asked of them. And they believed that the brothers and nuns who taught in their schools were able to give at least something of the Catholic culture which they admired in Dr Kolbe, and which was not to be had in the public schools. In these conditions the future of the Catholic schools was secure for one or two generations at least.

* But as it depended on the principle of use and wont in Scots Law the result may not have been obvious at so early a date.

Chapter XIII

THE NUNS AND BROTHERS

I. Orders and Congregations

AN informed Catholic of the 1920's would have chosen the work of the nuns as the best example of what the Church had been doing for " white " South Africa. Amongst these the Dominicans of King William's Town could claim the most striking successes. In 1876, as we have already seen, Bishop Ricards invited the Convent of St Ursula at Augsburg—a community with a long history but then affiliated to the order of St Dominic—to make a foundation in his vicariate, and six sisters and one postulant who arrived in the following year opened a school in King William's Town. Till 1908 they were, in canon law, a diocesan congregation, though daughter foundations—often entirely independent—had been established in Natal and Transvaal and Rhodesia. They were then affiliated to the Dominican third order, whose rule they had adopted, and in 1923 most of the houses were given a constitution as the African Congregation of St Catherine of Siena. During these years seventeen convents had been established, and some, like those of Oakford in Natal and Salisbury in Rhodesia, were already the parent-houses of others; in the case of Oakford, indeed, of the independent Dominican congregation of Newcastle. The development suggests a parallel with the growth of Cistercian priories and monasteries in the twelfth century, but differs from that by the comparative ease with which the daughter groups became juridically independent while remaining true to the rule of St Dominic. When the African Congregation of St Catherine of Siena was established the six nuns and one postulant of 1871 had expanded to twenty houses of four hundred and eighty-two sisters, scattered over five ecclesiastical vicariates, and the number of South African recruits was increasing constantly.

The original band of six nuns had come to South Africa to teach in schools, but when the need came for nursing sisters they were ready to turn to that work and did it well.   They supplied a staff to Dr Fitzgerald's Grey Hospital in its early years, and they made their own foundations at King William's Town, at East London and Queenstown.   At the request of the Jesuits in Matabeleland, Mother Mauritia, the prioress of the King William's Town convent, went with four other nuns to Mafeking in February 1890, to care for the sick of the Chartered Company's pioneer column.   From there she sent on five sisters under Mother Patrick of the daughter Convent of Potchefstroom to the camp at Macloustie.   Under the direction of the doctors, from whom they learned the art of nursing sick and wounded soldiers, they followed the movements of the troops during the campaign.   Their work was good enough for the Governor of Cape Colony to suggest their establishing hospitals at Salisbury and Bulawayo, and this was done in 1892 and 1894, with Mother Patrick as matron of one and Mother Jacoba of the other.[1]   Intended only as a temporary measure, they continued in these posts for nine years, winning great public praise from the colonists;   only in 1901 were the nuns able to hand the hospitals over to secular control so that they might concentrate on their educational work.

This remained their principal occupation, as it was also of the independent congregations of Oakford, in Natal, which was founded from King William's Town, and of Newcastle, which was founded from Oakford.   But in teaching also during their first half century they followed methods and a curriculum of their own.   From the beginning they offered courses in embroidery, painting, gardening and domestic science as well as in foreign languages which were not at that time taught in the government schools, and they won an early popularity even with Calvinist parents.   Both in the Eastern Province and in the Transvaal they opened schools for deaf and dumb children and, when opportunity occurred, schools for Bantu and coloured.   Within two years of their arrival they saw the need to train lay teachers as well as their own sisters, and between 1879 and 1914 King William's Town convent school had won more than five hundred teachers' training certificates in government examinations.   From 1906 they prepared a few senior pupils for the intermediate bachelor of arts examination of the University of the Cape of Good Hope, and in 1915 and 1916 two bachelor of arts degrees were obtained by the school.

The financing of these new enterprises was possible because the congregation could and did employ the profits from a successful institution to develop a new charity. But as soon as reasonable they claimed and were given grants-in-aid from the secular governments. The Cape Province and Natal were already making *per capita* payments for mission schools, and after 1906 a small grant (which helped some 50 per cent of the native schools) was also made in the Transvaal. Naturally there was bargaining with every development; the education departments wanted to secure control in return for the expenditure of public money, and the sisters wanted to preserve what Scots law calls " use and wont ". When the organization of training colleges was overhauled by the Cape Department in 1912 they recognized the King William's Town convent as a centre for training Catholic teachers, but two years later Dr Muir, the director, urged its amalgamation with the Girls' High Training College at Grahamstown as a non-confessional institution. The arguments in the matter of efficiency were in his favour, but on the same ground he appointed Miss Emery, of the convent training staff, as first principal of the new college, and agreed that the sisters in training should have free places, an arrangement which the department ratified after legal advice in 1922.

The Dominican congregations which started from King William's Town—Oakford in Natal and Salisbury in Rhodesia—attracted some novices from Germany, and retained at least a flavour of their German origin in method and discipline to enrich the Catholic tradition in South Africa. This contribution was of course more marked in the Sisters of the Precious Blood, the congregation which Abbot Franz Pfanner of Mariannhill organized for work among the Bantu women. They founded schools, orphanages, clinics and hospitals, and when the Trappists extended their work to Rhodesia the sisters also made foundations in the new territory. Like the Trappists, or the Religious Missionaries of Mariannhill as they were subsequently reconstituted, the Sisters of the Precious Blood remained for the most part German by nationality.

Mariannhill, however, was then an enclave of the Vicariate of Natal. The Oblate priests who served the latter belonged to an order founded in France and still largely recruited there. When

Bishop Allard had looked for nuns to work in Basutoland he had persuaded a French congregation, the Sisters of the Holy Family of Bordeaux, to undertake the task, and under his successor Bishop Jolivet they had opened schools in Durban and Pietermaritzburg. As the Catholic community in Natal included many families from Mauritius of French descent and speech—they formed a large element of the managers and owners of the sugar plantations— the educational advantages were obvious.

Bishop Jolivet also brought to his vicariate another French congregation—the Canonesses Regular Hospitallers of the Mercy of Jesus of the Order of St Augustine, or Augustinian Sisters, as South Africa more briefly called them. Tracing their own history to a convent at Dieppe in the twelfth century, they had been given a papal constitution in the seventeenth century, and in the nineteenth maintained some half-dozen hospitals in France. The bishop brought nine of them, all experienced nurses, to South Africa in 1891, gave them a site on some vicariate property at Estcourt, and persuaded them to open a school there while their hospital was being built. Their first nursing was of Bantu and then of Indians, for whom the Indian Immigration Board paid them two shillings and sixpence per day per patient. After a few years a separate hospital for " Europeans " was opened. During the Anglo-Boer war of 1899–1902 the English wounded and sick, and a few Boer prisoners, were nursed there. The same general pattern was followed at the neighbouring town of Ladysmith forty miles distant: a school first, in 1894, and later a hospital—or rather two, one for Europeans and one for Indians and Bantu, though served by the same staff of nuns. Both here and at Estcourt the schools continued largely as boarding schools, since the pupils often came from great distances.

The original suggestion for a hospital run by the nuns seems to have come from Durban citizens who promised Bishop Jolivet a suitable site. The Augustinians were settled in Estcourt while these negotiations continued, and in 1892 a nine-acre plot on the Bera—the ridge overlooking Durban—was ready, with a few small houses. Four sisters with French training and nursing experience were then sent to open the Durban sanatorium (the name given to their hospitals in South Africa by the Augustinians). Soon afterwards they began sending their novices to Johannesburg to obtain the South African training and certificates, and in 1910 the Durban sanatorium was itself recognized as such a school, with about ten or twelve, both nuns and laywomen, learning to nurse. In 1898 the Augustinians opened their fourth hospital in Natal, at Pietermaritzburg. By 1920 the community there numbered 28, at Durban 24. Most were still French, but half a dozen South Africans and as many Irish and Canadians and French from Mauritius had joined the congregation. At Pietermaritzburg they had accepted two postulants from the coloured Dunn family of Zululand, but these did not remain. In addition to their nursing at Durban they opened an Indian orphanage for twenty girls, but later, in agreement with the civil authorities, changed over to coloureds; and in 1921 another orphanage for coloured boys was founded by the nuns at Mayville, on the outskirts of the city.

The representation of Catholic life and work by religious orders, both of men and women, was nowhere more striking than in the vicariates of Kimberley and the Transvaal. Two conditions made their work especially valuable. Owing to the economic setting, the diamond and gold mines and the attendant gambling and economic fluctuations, stability of support was not characteristic of the Catholic laity and could be given only by those with the equivalent of capital reserves. The second condition was, as Bishop Jolivet had pointed out to Rome, the largely Irish character of the Catholic population in these districts; it was an advantage to have Catholic work directed by those of their nation. Shortly before the Anglo-Boer war the Irish Christian Brothers, on the invitation of the second Bishop Gaughren, founded a school at Kimberley on a plot of land given by the De Beers Company, and its numbers and fame grew steadily in the next quarter-century. In 1907 the Sisters of Notre Dame opened their first South African school for girls at Kroonstad—which was also in the Kimberley vicariate at that time—and this also was successful. The Marist Brothers were teaching in Johannesburg during President Kruger's last term, and, indeed, received a financial grant from him; though Milner's administration refused to continue this after the war, the work continued, and expanded considerably as more brothers became available as a result of the expulsion of religious from France.

These schools, like those of the Holy Family Sisters at End Street and Parktown in Johannesburg and the Convent of the Loreto nuns in Pretoria, were attended by "Europeans". The Sisters of Mercy, whom Bishop Gaughren brought from Ireland to Mafeking on the Transvaal border in 1897, opened a school there the following year, but had to learn, as their house chronicle puts it, that whites and natives must be kept separate. Though, like other Catholic congregations, they had to accept the uncivilized local prejudice in later foundations at Vryburg and Braamfontein, they opened a school for coloured children at Mafeking in 1915. Three years later the Holy Cross Sisters did the same at Pretoria, and followed up with Bantu schools at Alexandra Township and other "native locations".

Besides teaching, the nuns developed the other "good works" of the Catholic religion in this area with its fast-growing population. The Sisters of Nazareth opened orphanages, and the Good Shepherd Sisters a home for their specialized apostolate. At Mafeking during the siege the Irish Sisters took on the care of the sick and wounded and had their share of the fame which accrued to Baden-Powells defence, including an interview with the English Queen. For some years afterwards one or other of them worked in the Victoria hospital whenever there was need for assistance. That was amateur labour given because of emergency. The Holy Family Sisters however had always formed a section of their community as professional nurses, and it was they whom the Johannesburg citizens invited to staff a hospital in 1887 during one of the gold rushes. They continued the work until 1915, but by that time it was impossible for them to supply the number of trained nuns necessary even to manage the institution with lay nurses. By agreement they handed it back to the corporation of the city and devoted themselves to a small nursing home, the Kensington sanatorium, which they had already built.

These examples have been taken chiefly from Natal, Transvaal and Kimberley because the growth of population there created the need and the opportunity for new Catholic "works". At the Cape and in the Eastern Province the early twentieth century saw rather the development of already established institutions. But new ventures were also made. The Little Company of Mary, the Blue Nuns as they are popularly known, opened a hospital at Port Elizabeth in 1905[2] and their rule also allowed them to nurse in private houses. The Holy Family Sisters founded a hospital at Sea Point, near Cape Town, in 1915.[5]

II. Economic Foundations

All these institutions needed land, buildings and equipment as well as personnel, and the nuns and brothers had to be fed and clothed. Their successful establishment was, therefore, a matter of money as well as religious zeal, and the financial affairs of the Catholic Church in South Africa were no easier than they had been fifty years earlier.

Bishop Grimley and Bishop Ricards had worried themselves into illness because they were perpetually in debt. In their case the new churches they built brought in a return larger than the interest on their loans, and their successors were able to restore their vicariates to economic health. The old difficulties recurred in Natal and Kimberley, and they were accentuated in the Transvaal. The opening up of the gold mines brought a rapid increase of the Catholic population and the need for many more churches. Prices of land fluctuated rapidly because of the speculation which is the accompaniment and curse of all such " rushes ". Plots were bought and mortgaged by the ecclesiastical authorities, and in a period of general depression on the Rand in 1912 they allowed many of their creditors to foreclose rather than borrow more money. Within a year or two the value of the land had risen again and there seems to have been a lack of business acumen on the part of those responsible. But clearly the vicars apostolic had to manipulate their small resources almost to the point of gambling if they were to succeed in forming centres of Catholic life.

It was in such circumstances that the Catholic schools and hospitals were multiplied, and the financing of each venture was obviously a difficult and risky business. Three contributors were involved. An already established convent, in Europe or in South Africa, sent the personnel and paid the initial expenses of equipment and food. But it was the rule of every religious order that each house must in the long run support itself, and usually it was required to repay the costs which had been incurred. The second group consisted of the nuns of the new convent. In most religious orders every nun on profession brings a dowry which must be treated as capital, the use of which belongs to the convent she joins. When the Sisters of Mercy came from Strabane in Ireland to Mafeking they formally renounced this dowry, although they were leaving Strabane for good. A decision in canon law, however, in 1913, required the dowry to be returned to a nun if for any reason she left the convent of her profession, and the Congregation of Propaganda ruled, on the application of the Mafeking convent, that the earlier arrangement must be revised equitably. The dispute in this case was settled on a fifty-fifty basis. The dowries, then, did provide a small revenue (the capital was never large) for a new convent after it was established, but when the nuns were only lent from the mother-house, or were free to return, this source of income was not available. Thirdly, individual nuns sometimes received gifts from their relations for their work, or even made collections among friends in their home town, though it was never on the scale of Abbot Franz's organization of the helpers of Mariannhill throughout Germany.

Save in that exceptional case the religious orders could not bear the initial cost of land and buildings. The vicar apostolic who invited them had to provide these, and he could do so only by raising a loan and paying interest. It was understood that the new institution would gradually repay these, so that the vicariate could launch out on further establishments.

The Catholic schools and hospitals, then, for the most part charged fees like any private establishment. They made profits which provided the upkeep of the convent, which paid off the debts of foundation, which made possible the works they did freely for poor children or patients. Provided they were successful, there was no trouble; they were able to develop reasonably because their creditors, the vicariate and their mother-convent, wanted them to do their work well and were willing to wait for their money; after a few years they were free of the original debts and could undertake new tasks according to their own wishes, subject only to the conditions imposed by canon law.

In most cases new foundations had that measure of success, and it is the justification for the methods employed. Its weaknesses showed only when the enterprise did not make its expected profit. In 1897 Bishop Jolivet persuaded the *Filles de Jésus de Kermaria*, a congregation of nuns of the diocese of Vannes in Brittany, to send a group of their sisters to found a school or schools at Umzinto in his vicariate. He bought a property for them for £6,000, on which he had to pay interest of 7 per cent. In civil law the land belonged to the vicariate, but both the nuns and the bishop regarded it as belonging to the nuns, who were responsible for paying back to the vicariate the loan and interest as soon as they could. As was his frequent way, Bishop Jolivet did not bother to put the agreement in writing.[4]

Improvements and additions to the property were made from time to time, but the cost of these had to be borne in part by the vicariate, since the nuns could not afford them. In fact their first venture—the teaching of coloured children—did not succeed, and in 1900 they opened a school for European children. This made progress slowly; it started with fifteen pupils and had seventy-nine in 1911. But there was no surplus profit to enable the nuns to begin paying off the loan, and even the annual interest was beyond their means. Bishop Jolivet tried to persuade the congregation in Kermaria to take over the loan and the property formally, but they protested their inability.

When Bishop Delalle became vicar apostolic in 1904 one of his obvious tasks was to tidy up the somewhat haphazard finance left in the wake of his predecessor's energy. Like him he was prepared to be patient with the difficulties at Umzinto, and he wrote off some of the book debts for improvements. It was still possible, he thought, for the school to become a success, and he had confidence in the business ability of the superior, Sister Noemi, who managed by 1911 for the first time to pay the whole annual interest.

Meanwhile, however, the congregation at Kermaria were worrying. They sent their own visitor to Natal, who deposed Sister Noemi from office. She refused to hand over the finances to her successor, and was supported by Bishop Delalle, who appealed to the Sacred Congregation of Propaganda against this interference by the Bishop of Vannes. The latter ordered the nuns at Umzinto to return to France.

In the matter of discipline the judgement went against the vicar apostolic. The superior at Kermaria could recall her sisters from Natal within a year of the decree; meanwhile they must all accept the authority of the newly-appointed superior, and in particular

Sister Noemi must hand over the property to her; all of them must return to Europe, and, if they refused, they might not be accepted as nuns elsewhere.[5] There was, however, a further question. Kermaria claimed that the vicariate should pay them for the improvements they had made in the property, for its " movables ", for the expenses of sending the nuns originally and for their return, and suggested that they ought also to be paid a salary for the work they had done. Bishop Delalle on the other hand showed that the official valuation of the property now handed back to him was less than the original loan and interest which the vicariate had advanced. It was essentially a dispute as to the nature of the original contract. Did the nuns come to work as employees of the vicar apostolic, or was he merely the creditor who had advanced money for a work undertaken by the Kermaria sisters in Natal? There was no written contract, and some of the documents assumed the first relationship and others the second. After long consideration the Congregation of Religious, to whom the question had been referred, told the disputants to come to an amicable arrangement, " *placere de concordia* ".[6] Kermaria reduced its claim to 16,000 francs, being their outlay on the first sisters who had gone to Umzinto, and Bishop Delalle sent it them " as an appreciation of the work you sisters did ".[7]

Some of the trouble in this dispute came from the casual nature of the original agreement, but a measure of impatience and unhappiness was, humanly speaking, inevitable whenever a Catholic institution planted in South Africa failed to pay its way. The acceptance by all concerned of the authority of the Holy See and its Sacred Congregation and their slow judicial processes secured in the end that an equitable solution was reached, and it would be silly to describe the facts as a scandal in any real sense. The establishment of so many schools and hospitals in South Africa was worth the risk of these very rare failures.

III. Service to All

A very stupid Marxist might interpret the record of loans and interest, of titles to property and balance sheets, as showing a dominant economic motive, forgetting that there were many more profitable opportunities for investment in the country, and forgetting too the kind of life to which these religious consecrated themselves and which was required of them. While the welcome extended to them by Catholics is understandable, it is not so easy to explain the enthusiastic support accorded by the non-Catholics to their schools and hospitals.

Of the fact there can scarcely be doubt. At the beginning of the century roughly two-thirds of the boys and girls educated by the Christian Brothers, the Marist Brothers and the many congregations of nuns were not Catholic. By 1923 this proportion had fallen to about one half, but this did not mean fewer absolutely, for the size and number of the schools had grown. In the hospitals the numbers of the sick of different religions were always and naturally roughly proportionate to the population strength of the various confessions in the country. When these institutions were first founded they supplied of course a social need not publicly provided for: private schools and private hospitals were regarded as normal. But even when the new-type government developed and administered the public institutions out of the taxes of the community, and called these services free, the popularity of the nuns and brothers continued.

It was certainly well known, as the contemporary references in newspapers showed, that the individual religious worked without a salary; even if, by a government arrangement, they were paid, the money was ploughed back into the development of the school or hospital. It was not so generally known that the convents themselves usually carried out some work for nothing, accepting pupils or patients who could not afford fees, teaching or nursing native and coloured sick and children.

For the layman or laywoman, however, the convent school or the Catholic sanatorium was as expensive as any other private nursing home or educational establishment. In the early years, maybe, the teaching especially of girls was technically better and the subjects were more varied than elsewhere, but with the development of state examinations and inspections the Catholic schools more and more settled down to the common curriculum. Yet large numbers of Jewish and Protestant parents continued to send their boys and girls to be trained by brothers and nuns, despite occasional protests and warnings by their pastors. Certainly no attempt was made to influence the children against their parental religion. Indeed, the instructions of the Congregation of Propaganda and of all Catholic authorities strictly forbade any discussion of religion between children of different faiths—though it must be said that children have ways of evading the prudential regulations of their pedagogues. Generally speaking they seem to have gleaned considerable knowledge, more or less accurate, about the way of life of Catholic religious, and to have found it very interesting. Perhaps that was true also of their parents. Meeting the nuns or brothers was not like talking to a lay teacher; it could satisfy a natural curiosity about a strange culture which produced some attractive types. And it had become almost the only way of getting to know the Catholic religion; the tolerance of the nineteenth century had developed into the idea that religion was a private affair, almost a solitude; each faith had its own churches and lived apart, but in a Catholic hospital or Catholic school there was a chance to see these somewhat mysterious Catholics, and very authentic ones, at close quarters without any danger of having to argue about religion. And from the frequent journalistic praise of nuns and brothers it seems to follow that people willing to work for God under rule, without hope of personal gain, were still news.

For Catholics the permanent presence of convents had special importance. In one sense the life of the nun or of the brother is closer to the laity than is that of the parish priest. Teaching and nursing are occupations which do not demand ordination and can be more readily understood than the administration of the sacraments. And the washing and mending, cooking and housekeeping and needlework of a convent do not differ in kind from the work of the home. They make it easier for the housewife to talk to a nun than to a priest. Excuse for gossip maybe, but the occasion of that social intercourse which binds people into a community. And in this case the nuns—and the brothers—have surrounded the work with prayer and worship of a kind which the laity could also practise had they the time and the inclination. They tend to see the life of the religious, in the technical sense, as the thoroughgoing practice of what they themselves attempt at times and by half-measures. It is not of course an adequate view, but so far as it is accurate it explains why Catholicism cannot express itself concretely without convents.

The different habits in which religious dress have their importance. The lay Catholic not only remembers their details but realizes that each corresponds to a particular rule and way of life, some part of which at least is generally known. The vow of religion which follows so naturally from the common Faith is specified in several forms, and it seems that, as in an army with its regiments, the human sense of community demands these distinguishable examples of a principle accepted by all as a starting point.

And the lay Catholic grows up to be aware that every congregation of religious does work in some way for those regarded as under-privileged, or " afflicted by God " as the older phrase had it. The Dominican nuns at the Cape and in the Transvaal trained the deaf and dumb, the Sisters of Nazareth brought up orphans and cared for the aged and sick, the Salesian fathers taught trades to poor boys, the Sisters of Mercy and of the Holy Family and the Holy Cross and the Dominicans taught the coloured and the Bantu. The growth of these good works, as theology calls them, in the Cape and Natal took long years, for it had to wait on the build-up of the Catholic community. But the momentum gathered there helped to make their establishment in the Transvaal more rapid. By the end of the first world war, when men were vaguely aware of, and often alarmed by, the emergence of a new order much more dominated by politicians and governments, much more anonymous and impersonal, the Catholics of South Africa knew that throughout the country their nuns cared for the sick and poor and downtrodden as human beings, and did so for the love of God and not as administering a state service. The point was appreciated by many, probably by most, outside the Church. But the Catholic, even though he might be niggardly in the help he gave to the work, knew that it was part of the organic life of which he was also a member, an activity which issued from the Faith he professed, and kept thereby a sense of a community making its own proper independent contribution to the country.

The vigour and the success of the nuns in these years made the convent, in the eyes of South Africans, the typical Catholic institution. But the work was in fact fitted into the discipline of the life of the Church. Within the framework of canon law the vicars apostolic guided and controlled the developments. Their sanction was necessary for every large expenditure, even when the nuns themselves were ready to provide it. And they could and did act even more directly on occasion. Bishop Delalle decided in 1907 that the five sanatoria which he found in his vicariate were too many for the needs of Natal. The sisters, he decided, " have built foolishly and got into debt still more foolishly ", and in the economic depression of the time there was little likelihood of recovery. So he closed the Port Shepstone sanatorium and thought seriously of doing the same to the Durban sanatorium. Though he spared the latter he reformed its methods. The older sisters were not, as he put it, " up to modern surgery "; so he sent some of the older ones away and had others trained, and in this way " they seem to have regained the confidence of the doctors ".[8] His reforms bore fruit when the Durban sanatorium was later recognized as a school for training nurses.

In the records the vicars apostolic of this time appear most often as a check or correction on the enterprise of others. It is the penalty of becoming administrators. But it is also in part misleading. Their priests and nuns kept also a memory, and particularly in the case of Bishop Delalle, of kind encouragement and sympathy in difficulties—but this was given personally and could not be committed to paper. They also did much by delegation, and in no instance more profitably than when they allowed Dr Kolbe, as we have seen in an earlier chapter, to resign from the editorship of the *Catholic Magazine* in order to tour the Catholic schools and give them the benefit of his great wisdom and experience.

Chapter XIV

THE UNION OF SOUTH AFRICA

I. A Transitional Period

THE decade 1910–1920 was an important one for the structure of society in South Africa. Soon after the Anglo-Boer war the conquered republics of the Transvaal and Orange River were reconstituted as colonies, with large but limited powers of self-government, by Lord Milner and his team of administrators, while the Cape and Natal reverted to their provincial status. After negotiations between the colonies themselves, and with the approval of the British Parliament, a central government and, therefore, a Union of these colonies was created in 1909. The rejection of a federal form, the subordination, in essential political matters, of provinces to the central legislature and executive, was brought about mainly by Generals Botha and Smuts (perhaps chiefly by the advocacy of the latter) who had been among the leaders of the forces of the Transvaal in the recent war but who now accepted *ex animo* the imperial connection. The new state brought to an end the old predominance and prestige of the Cape Province: Pretoria was to share with Cape Town as the seat of the legislature and executive, the supreme judicial tribunal was to be at Bloemfontein. If a case could be made for describing the Anglo-Boer struggle as that of Cape interests against those of the Transvaal, then the act of Union would be the first step in the reversal of its decision. At the time Smuts certainly hoped to include Rhodesia as another province of this Union, and again secured the goodwill of the British government, but he was defeated by the white settlers who preferred a direct dependence on the British crown.

Four years later England entered the first world war against Germany and Austria. Botha and Smuts secured a majority in the South African Parliament to attack German South-West Africa at the request of the English government. One leading South African serving officer, General Maritz, rebelled openly and joined the German forces with as many soldiers as he could. Other men of distinction in politics certainly opposed the government and approved the step taken by Maritz. All this opposition was treated as treason and broken up by martial law. The successful generalship of Botha in South-West Africa, the strong position and prestige which Smuts attained in British political life during the war, and the victory of the side on which they had engaged combined to enable Smuts effectively to re-form the British Empire as a group of self-governing dominions of which South Africa was one. His success brought general acceptance of the doctrine, which he held as a theory in 1910 and acted on in 1914, that the majority decision of the South African Parliament, despite its recent institution, expressed the will of the country. Undoubtedly there had been a large minority who, on various grounds, disliked the conduct of the war and the settlement which was made after victory; they set themselves now, however, to reach power through the legislature, and the sovereignty of that body, as against the provinces or traditional custom, was accordingly accepted by all.

The traditions of Catholicism could easily have contributed much both to the principles of political society and to the just conditions of war and peace. When the establishment of the single unitary state of South Africa was being discussed everyone took it for granted that the governing or political class in the country was effectively the whites, or Europeans as they called themselves. But either of the two roads could have been followed. In the Cape Province it had always been the practice to grant suffrage to the coloureds—whether Malay or half-whites—on a cultural test, and they had been eligible for seats on the local government councils. Segregation had been a matter of social choice, and was not enforced by regulation. This attitude had been generally supported, and some of the leading families, from which members had been chosen for the legislative assemblies, were known to have colour in their ancestry. But the " Europeans " of the Orange River State and the Transvaal had always been bitterly opposed to what they called contamination. The exodus of the Voortrekkers which had founded those communities was caused even more by the desire to escape the Cape tradition in this matter than by grievances about the method of slave-emancipation. Among themselves they had made sure by legislation of restricting political authority for all time to " whites ", and had imposed white dominance as the pattern of social and economic life which Bantu or coloured must follow, and European juries effectively created different and unequal criminal justice for the two classes.

For the sake of securing an Afrikaner union between those of English and Dutch descent, of burying the memories of the Anglo-Boer war, Smuts and most of the other politicians were silent about or minimized the differences on the black and white racial question. But the two traditions were in operation, and the Catholics, though only a 5 per cent minority of the nation, might well have urged the principles they had inherited. For one thing the canon law of the Church could have taught them to consider slavery as a fact and not to think it was eliminated by using a euphemism. At the same time it would have taught them to distinguish between the condition which denies to men essential rights such as marriage and the mitigated form which compels them to labour away from home in return for mere subsistence. Again, the moral system of the Church had always discriminated between tolerating social situations, though not approving them, and barring by legislation all improvements in the future. And thirdly, in the long story of Portuguese and Spanish colonization the principles of the Catholic Faith had had to struggle hard against the greed and habits of merchants and settlers and, doing so openly, had in the short or long run incorporated people of different colour and culture into Christian civilization.

II. Dr Sidney Welch

1. RACE RELATIONS

Dr Sidney Welch did his best to direct the attention of Catholics to these issues. Already in 1907 he was writing in the *Catholic Magazine* (contrary to the views of its editor, Monsignor Kolbe) a defence of the Uitlander on the general ground that " civilization should welcome the civilized stranger ", and gave its application: " A spreadeagle patriotism is not indigenous to our land . . . we may be allowed to hope that no foreign influences will ever change this quality of our people."[1] When the Union was being discussed he pleaded for the recognition of the Lebanese population

of the Transvaal as " Europeans ",[2] and in this he was successful,
though possibly more through his friendship with and influence
on the *Cape Times* and *Die Burger* than through the *Catholic
Magazine*. He took over the editorship of the last in 1909, and
urged that the coloureds should be included among Europeans in
the new constitution, since their way of life had already been
assimilated to that civilization in the Cape Province;[3] he expressly
recognized, however, that the Bantu political problem was difficult,
and it seemed reasonable to allow " parental control " of them by
Europeans, since democracy could only be defended if it resulted in
good government. When the constitution was finally passed he
owned that its treatment of the racial question caused him the
greatest anxiety, for " European descent " was embedded in its
clauses and it was a fateful phrase.[4] He returned to this issue in a
presidential address to the Cape Town Catholic Association some
months later. Examining the prejudice which asserts that the black
man is by nature subordinate to the white, and that this relation is,
therefore, normal, Dr Welch pointed out that the situation was a
result of contingent historical conditions, had no scientific foundation, and in fact was not everywhere true. It would be more
prudent, he urged, to make concessions now in South Africa to the
non-Europeans. He asked his audience the question whether
white South Africa was doomed, and confessed he could not answer
it if survival meant predominance. But if they would grant full
democratic rights to coloured men of culture he could see no
reason why the whites should not remain an honoured section of
the population.[5]

It was clear from the address that Dr Welch expected opposition
to his views. He did not succeed in stirring Catholics to a sense
of urgency about the question. Dr Kolbe had already announced
that he was going to devote himself to educational matters.[6] Mr
Wilmot expressed his admiration for the system of native administration planned in Rhodesia, a system of " segregation, com-
munal land, regulations administered by themselves, prohibition
of intoxicants; a thorough system of self-government with a veto
by missionary or magistrate "[7]—a system scarcely applicable in the
Union, where Bantu and coloured and Indian were already often
city dwellers and employed in the trade and industry of the country.
The vicars apostolic may have thought that it would be an impru-

dent intervention in politics for them to speak on the matter. But in December 1910 an attempt was made in the Union Parliament to have marriages between European and coloured legally forbidden. On this occasion the younger Bishop Gaughren, second Vicar Apostolic of Kimberley, wrote to the *Transvaal Leader* urging that this was not merely a question of politics. Such marriages, he admitted, were generally undesirable, and the proposed law was well-intentioned enough. But while it would remove the physical evil it would do so by introducing the moral evil of creating conflict between the law and the conscience of good men. The Catholic clergy would continue to bless such marriages if called on to do so, and he thought other denominations would adopt the same view.[8]

Opposition to the proposal in Parliament was led by Mr Merriman, supported by most of the Cape members, and they were successful. It had been urged (by Mr Grobler) expressly as the Transvaal solution (Act 3 of 1897 and Act 39 of 1904) of the racial problem, the only way of "keeping the new nation pure ".[9] Though this first effort failed, there seems little doubt that the Transvaal view, regarding intermarriage as the greatest of social dangers and " purity of race " as the necessary and sufficient test of civilization, steadily gained adherents in the Cape and in Natal. It was already clear in the 1910 Act for the Union of the Dutch Reformed Church, which virtually excluded coloured members from equal rights in that Church[10] and so established the principle for which the Transvaal congregations had separated from the Cape Synod in 1853. Racial superiority, even in religion, was accepted as obvious by the great majority of the new Union of South Africa, and Catholics would grow up in that climate of opinion without any clear and repeated challenge of the principle.

2. THE FIRST WORLD WAR

When Britain declared war on Germany in 1914 Dr Welch was still editing the *Catholic Magazine*. Though regarding it as rash to say on whom blame for the war rested, he agreed that Great Britain had entered it with a good motive—the defence of Belgium's freedom, as Mr Asquith had stated—but hoped that this would remain their aim.[11] While refusing to believe the stories of German atrocities, he was bitterly opposed to the action of those

South Africans who had rebelled against the decision of their government.[12]

This attitude was fairly general in South Africa and in England at the time, and was reflected in many responsible journals. Even when in 1915 Dr Welch urged a consideration of peace terms and peace negotiations, regretted the expression of claims going far beyond those of the declaration of war, and especially deplored the note of hate which sounded in both British and enemy comments,[13] he could claim to be of the same mind as statesmen like Loreburn and Bryce.

In 1916 Pope Benedict XV began the series of notes in which he appealed to the belligerents to discuss and agree on a diplomatic peace which would distribute as equally as could be the losses caused by the war. As each note was published Dr Welch urged its acceptance in the pages of the *Catholic Magazine*.[14] He did so often with arguments appealing to all reasonable men; though the *Cape Argus*[15] controverted his views, it did so courteously, and the Afrikaner paper *Die Burger*, founded in 1915, welcomed the papal intervention.[16] Again and again Dr Welch insisted that his attitude did not imply any disloyalty to Britain: it was, he said, strictly in accord with the English tradition which followed the rule of *ne quid nimis* even in a just war;[17] he quoted Lord Milner, who had urged that the German descent of many South Africans should be borne in mind; he pleaded that a moderate peace would help to cement the Commonwealth.[18]

But while distinguishing between English militarists and sane Englishmen, Dr Welch was inclined to identify France with its rulers. His studies in Portuguese history had brought to his attention the piracies of the French even more than those of the English. His comments on the separation laws of France in the early years of the twentieth century had shown how bitterly anti-Catholic their present politicians were. The readers of the *Catholic Magazine* were reminded of the fact, and when the *Cape Times* identified the allied cause with that of Christian civilization Dr Welch asked with some point if it were truly represented by Viviani, Briand, Painlevé and Poincaré.

In this crusade for a Christian peace, as he was to call his campaign,[19] Dr Welch's aim throughout was to urge South African Catholics to follow the mind of the Pope and make it known both by conversation and in the public press.[20] Unfortunately the allusions to France brought in another issue. Already in October 1914, Bishop Delalle, Vicar Apostolic of Natal, had protested to him privately for saying that no provision was made for religion in the French army, whereas four chaplains had been provided to every division.[21] The Vicar Apostolic of Natal had followed Leo XIII's advice and "rallied to the Republic", even though it was against the tradition of his family. Like the other French Catholics who did so, he distinguished his country from the attitude of its government, even during the persecution of the Church in the twentieth century. The war was, in his eyes, an expression of national sentiment, the recovery of a Catholic outlook, with the just aim of restoring provinces which had been French. Though he was careful not to preach this view in his pastoral letters—he was always mindful that his people were not French—he was naturally pleased when English-speaking Catholics adopted it more and more as the war dragged on, and feelings became embittered. Dr Welch's writings might have persuaded South Africans that this view was—at least with regard to the conditions of peace—anti-papal. By 1917 Bishop Delalle found himself supported by the vicars apostolic of the Transvaal and Eastern Cape, and suggested that they should make it clear that the *Catholic Magazine* was speaking not for them but only for Dr Welch himself.[22]

No public expression, or at least no official expression, was given to this disagreement of Catholics with the editor of their magazine. He recognized it himself, however,[23] and though many assured him privately of their support the comment on war aims was always his own. After 1918 the proposals of settlement by the victorious allies, and then the terms of the Versailles Treaty, came under his criticism. There were two difficulties for a Catholic editor: the Pope did not publish any further detailed suggestions, though it was clear that the lines of his earlier notes were not being followed; and it was practically impossible not to take sides on concrete issues as far as they were known. The warnings of Dr Welch on the dangers for future peace created by the allied terms were probably not heeded by many of his readers, but there was a widespread weariness with discussion and little understanding of the European situation; the diplomacy of the Holy

See was directed to making the best of temporal conditions, and even of the injustices it could not alter. And it was unfortunate that Dr Welch's information led him to a favourable view of the Russian revolution in its early stages, and a very unfriendly one of the restored Poland. Less than a year after this comment Achille Ratti, the nuncio in Warsaw who was soon to become Pope Pius XI, showed that he had formed a contrary judgement. For all that, Dr Welch could fairly write in 1924 that his " crusade of peace " had been directed mainly to second every hint that the Pope gave, and he could quote the approval of the *Civiltà Cattolica* for many of his views: but though the *Catholic Magazine* still had subscribers enough to pay its way, its editor seems to have recognized his failure to win the support of Catholics in South Africa for his conception of their political duties, and the issue of March 1924 was the last one.

The questions of the political structure of the Union of South Africa and of the aims of the war of 1914–18 were undoubtedly important, and had a moral bearing; the case for a clear Catholic demand was argued well; but, to say the least, it rallied the support neither of the vicars apostolic nor of the general body of the faithful. With the twentieth century a change had become clear in the treatment of politics by Catholics. It was, indeed, already hinted at during the Anglo-Boer war. Dr Kolbe had resigned the editorship because some of the bishops, he wrote, had " taken an open stand for what is to me the cause of injustice " (March 1900), and when he resumed it, in December of that year, he insisted on the notice:

> The policy put out ten years ago will be modified as far as the secular part of the magazine is concerned; politics, except where they directly touch the interests of the Church, will be entirely avoided.

We " must abandon ", he wrote, " the Olympian court from which we viewed all things under heaven; . . . my position as editor, like my position in the pulpit and the university, will be a sacred neutrality ".[24]

Consistent with this new statement of principle Dr Kolbe seems to have directed all his activities of the following years to the questions of Catholic education. In doing so he was following what was becoming more and more the practice of the Catholic communities in France, England and Germany: save for the matter of education, they left public questions to the civil authorities. Perhaps it was the natural outcome, though seldom remarked, of the nineteenth-century development of political parties and what was called responsible government in all the European states. Opposition to the policy of the rulers of the moment was expressed by a party or parties in the legislature, and it was increasingly accepted that this was the only legitimate action which could be taken by the citizens. Even the verbal criticism of the press became much more restrained, and men began to think of the forthright action of their grandfathers as akin to subversion. That the Church should not interfere in politics was regarded as a self-evident truth, while the decisions of political governments frequently dealt, as they have always done, with matters of morality.

For the first quarter of the twentieth century and more the fundamental crux of this situation was obscured. The civil authorities claimed that their actions were within the framework of God's law, that their wars for instance were just, and Catholics in all countries, forgetful of the warnings of Pius IX in *Quanta Cura*, were content to accept these assertions with regard to fact which were set plausibly before them. They no longer contributed as a body to the settlement of public issues. In consequence the bishops seldom if ever took independent action on such matters, and this held good in South Africa as elsewhere. Dr Grimley had not thought it extraordinary to suggest to Napoleon III the annexation of unclaimed South-West Africa, Bishop Moran was known by all the politicans to oppose the move for responsible government on the ground that it would be used unjustly against the Bantu, Dr Ricards had publicly refused to encourage Catholic schoolchildren to celebrate Queen Victoria's Jubilee because of the ill-treatment of Ireland. Bishops Rooney and MacSherry and Delalle* were probably as forcible personalities as their predecessors, but action of that sort simply did not occur to them, and was probably not expected of them. They contented themselves with administering the works of Catholics, particularly in

---

* Respectively Bishop Leonard's successor at the Cape (1903–24); Bishop Strobino's in the Eastern Vicariate (1896–1940); and Bishop Jolivet's in Natal (1904–46): their very long rules were remarkable.

the educational field. Their negotiations were mainly with the civil service officials, a necessary and developed organization of the new type of political society—and they learned some of the outlook and methods of that body. Catholic activity seemed no longer to follow a lead given by each vicar apostolic; every institution, and indeed every vigorous personality, made an independent contribution, with the bishops approving and co-ordinating or occasionally checking the movement.

III. Summary of Achievement

What summary, then, can be given of the efforts to form Catholic communities among white South Africans which began when Bishop Griffith landed at Cape Town in 1838?

It must be remarked first that the setting had changed both in extent and social character. Soon after the end of the world war of 1914–18 the Union of South Africa was practically as well as legally established as an autonomous state, and it was so treated at the Versailles conference. There was still question, however, of its extent. If, as was possible, the British protectorates of Basutoland, Swaziland and Bechuanaland, the conquered and then mandated territory of German South-West Africa, and the Rhodesias, should be included in its bounds in the future its area, its resources and population would be enormously increased.

Nor was the ruling white population yet homogeneous. They had come from Dutch and English, Irish, French, and German stocks, and though intermarriage had taken place to some extent they still tended to think of themselves as either English or Afrikaner. The latter were predominant in the Orange province, the former in Natal, but they were living cheek by jowl in the Cape and the Transvaal. The constitution, however, ensured that the powers of the central government were bound to increase at the expense of provincial independence. Political parties in the legislature were not strictly on racial lines. Botha and Smuts, who were Afrikaans, had the support of most of those of English descent, and their opponents were also of Dutch or French Huguenot descent. The development was due in part to the greater interest in politics which was a tradition of the Boers, and to the opportunity, which their system of plantation farming gave, of devoting themselves to the business of administration. Political division was now being

accepted on cultural lines. One party claimed to have the monopoly of the Afrikanerdom which Wilmot and Kolbe among others
had urged as common to all before the Anglo-Boer war. And the
mark of it was taken to be devotion to the Afrikaans speech, developing now its own literature and status as a language from its origin
in a Flemish patois, although it could still be referred to, without
intentional insult, as Cape Dutch.

A second dividing line was discernible in the attitudes to Bantu
and coloured peoples, who had practically no share in the government of the country. The old liberal tradition of the Cape
Province, which had not regarded even intermarriage as unthink-
able, was dead; it had been abandoned at the Union in favour of
the Transvaal attitude, that the whites were a superior race because
of their colour. But while one section of the dominant minority
planned to make laws to perpetuate their dominance and to treat
Bantu and coloureds as forever *in statu pupillari*, with the corollary
of social residential and economic *apartheid*, the others were more or
less willing to permit a gradual integration, at least in industry,
and even to close their eyes to the passage of light coloureds into
the " European " community—which had, of course, occurred in
the previous century in many families now reckoned white.

The growth of the Catholic Church in South Africa during the
nineteenth century was not unaffected by these circumstances.
The scattered individuals, scarcely forming a congregation anywhere save in Cape Town, whom Bishop Griffith found in 1838,
had become by 1922 communities, each with their own church and
school, in every town of any size in all the provinces of the Union
of South Africa. The census showed them to be mainly urban,
and this was to be expected, both because it is normal for Christianity to start around a church in a town and because it was a population trend everywhere at the time. The families were mainly of
Irish, French or German origin, but with the passing generations
the South African born were more and more predominant. This
was less true of their priests, though many exceptions, like Monsignor Kolbe, Dr Welch and Father McAuliffe, were well-known
leaders. Despite the magnificent work of the Oblates of Mary
Immaculate, it was one of the drawbacks of entrusting several
vicariates to them that they could rely on recruiting from their own

congregation and were not under the necessity of fostering local vocations to a greater extent. And apparently Bishop MacSherry of the Eastern Cape Vicariate still insisted in the first quarter of the twentieth century that his priests must be born and bred in Ireland. Perhaps it is natural, as it seems to be usual, for the Catholics of a pioneering land to have few priestly vocations from their own families, but there seems to have been no adequate reason for refusing to encourage them.

As the linguistic division of South Africa began to take shape there was danger of Catholicism becoming a religion of the English-speaking only. Such a development would clearly be opposed by the genius of the Faith and had been resisted from the beginning. Bishop Devereux had brought in Flemish priests and Bishop Griffith a Hollander; Bishop Grimley and Bishop Leonard had sent some of their theological students to Holland, and as late as 1917 Bishop Cox of the Transvaal issued a Dutch translation of the Catholic catechism.[25] It was unfortunate that very few Catholics seem to have recognized the possibilities of Afrikaans as a literary language, but Dr Welch had welcomed the publication of *Die Burger* in 1915,[26] and the following year a Dutch priest in the Transvaal published a pamphlet in " Cape Dutch ": *Iets oor die Kerk van Kristus*.[27] The Calvinists who were so large a part of the citizens were certainly reluctant to learn about the Catholic Faith (save as it was presented in lying and scurrilous but widely circulated " revelations "), but it seems fair criticism to say that the Catholics might have done more to present the truth in a language which the others would read.

The partial acceptance of that linguistic obstacle may have had its effect on the part which Catholics played in public life. In the days of the provincial governments Fitzgerald and Dyer, Uppington and Gallwey in law, Schermbrucker and Wilmot and Coghlan in politics, had been important figures, but they had no successors of the same stature after the Union. Political life in particular became more and more the preserve of those of Afrikaner culture, and Catholics did not force an entry.

The absence of Catholic pressure groups during the years which led up to the world war of 1914–18 was noticeable in almost all the European countries which took part. The causes of it there, as in South Africa, were complex; and to presume to pass a moral judgement on a generation or a community would be to convict one's self of knowing little history and less morality. It is simply a fact that during the first quarter of the twentieth century the Catholics of South Africa did not possess adequate means of appealing to their fellow citizens in the Afrikaans language, or of making the Catholic principles of social and political intercourse audible in the legislature.

Corresponding, perhaps, to these failures is the fall in the rate of increase of Catholics in South Africa after the turn of the century. The census of 1891 had given the number of Catholics in the Eastern province as 7,891, while in 1904 they were 13,395, and this increase of about 70 per cent was true of the whole of Cape Colony. But in 1921 the figures showed that white Catholics in the Union had increased only by 14 per cent in the previous ten years, slightly less that is than the growth of the total population.[28] Allowance must be made for less accurate enumeration in the earlier years, for the general decline of the birth-rate and for the inclusion of the Transvaal and Orange River State in the post-Union figures, but the discrepancy is large enough to suggest a falling-off in immigration and conversions, a change in Catholic activities after the Anglo-Boer war.

In 1904 the first *Catholic Directory of South Africa* had been published. It gave the details of churches and schools throughout the country, and a statistical summary. Thereafter it appeared annually. A comparison of the issue for 1921, when the Holy See was about to appoint the first Apostolic Delegate to the country, with one of the early volumes should provide a rough picture of the history of the Church from the end of the Anglo-Boer war to the end of the Great War of 1914–18. In Basutoland a notable development had taken place—it was the beginning of a movement which brought a third of the nation into the Church in the next twenty years. But in the Union territory the overall growth seems to have been very slight—certainly not more than the natural increase of the Catholics would require.

The number of priests in the Transvaal province (the northern part had been entrusted to Benedictines in 1910) had increased by nine—but in the neighbouring Kimberley vicariate it had fallen by ten: an indication, probably, of the shift of population from the diamond fields to the Rand. There were many more Mass-centres or stations in the Western Cape and in Natal at the end of the period, but no corresponding increase of priests; the improvement of communications and the greater speed of travel, rather than more permanent churches, seem to account for the figures. By the end of the period there were about 5 per cent more schools than at the beginning, but there were 70 per cent more nuns in the country, and since these were usually engaged in teaching, the size of the Catholic schools, especially those for girls, must have grown considerably.

IV. A New Directive

It is a corollary of the doctrine of divine grace that anyone, however pagan or bad his background, can become a Catholic. For the same reason the vocation to become a priest can be given to a Catholic man of any race.   But it is true also that the particular discipline of mind and emotions necessary for that work, and the consequent stability, are more likely to be found in families which are Catholic by tradition.   Generally speaking, the first generation of converts is served by priests who are foreign by origin but who have identified themselves, if they are wise, with the people among whom they live.   Even so the tradition of the Church in its relation with the barbarians of Europe had been to accept, and even to call for, a few of the newly converted as candidates for the sacred office.   The same attitude was taken, with often admirable results, by the Spanish and Portuguese missionaries of the sixteenth century.   In later times, however, and until the pontificate of Pius XI, Catholics have been much more timid of scandals. Though Abbot Franz Pfanner, who was indeed free from that spirit of caution, had sent four young Zulus to Rome to be trained for the priesthood in the College of Propaganda, the practice was suspended by Bishop Delalle, who waited till near the end of his days before ordaining his first Zulu priests.

His reasons for delay had been the difficulties he had had with those few Zulus already ordained and his belief that their natural and traditional culture made them temporarily ill-fitted for priestly work.[29] Such considerations were obviously weighty, though one wonders why some effort was not made to find vocations among the coloured Catholics who had for long adopted European ways, or the Indians who came of an ancient civilization.

The cautious attitude of the vicars apostolic was finally queried by Rome. The hostilities of the 1914–18 war were barely over when an article in the journal of the Congregation of Propaganda urged the need of native clergy everywhere,[30] and later in the same year, 1919, Father Sykes, in Rhodesia, pointed out that the Holy See had imposed this task on the conscience of all vicars apostolic.[31] He thought that the preparation of such a clergy would be slow work in Rhodesia, where he was prefect, but pointed out that the Jesuit theologian Father Vermeersch, after his African travels, considered that Uganda was ready for such a development. Bishop Cenez, O.M.I., the last prefect and first vicar apostolic in Basutoland, thought it possible to begin training an indigenous clergy there.[32] On the other hand Bishop Simon in Namaqualand reported a deterioration of his African peoples. The whites had often displaced the natives and these were no longer united in tribes but intermarried. They were generally of low intelligence and morals and only the whites could keep them from fighting. Despite this gloomy report he insisted that they would become civilized if properly treated, and were indeed better material than many Europeans.[33]

The formation of a native clergy and the approach to the Afrikaans-speaking population were clearly two tasks for the Catholic Church in South Africa in the new age which opened, though men had not perhaps grasped the fact, with the end of the 1914–18 war. Both were tasks which called for the co-operation of the vicariates. In 1922 the strong minded and vigorous Pius XI was elected pope; a librarian and historian by training, and a very great one, he had already shown himself alert for new methods in the field of diplomacy and he wanted to win the title of Pope of the Missions. Amongst the early acts of his pontificate was the appointment of an apostolic delegate, who would be his personal representative and see to the carrying out of his policies, for the vicariates and prefectures of the Union of South Africa, South-West Africa, Southern Rhodesia and the native territories of Basutoland, Swaziland and Bechuanaland. With that appointment a new chapter opened in the history of the Catholic Church in South Africa.

EPILOGUE

I. Expansion since 1922

D<small>R BROWN'S</small> studies in the history of the Catholic Church in South Africa found their *terminus ad quem* in the decree of 7 December 1922 with which Pope Pius XI created the Apostolic Delegation to Southern Africa, with territory including the Union of South Africa, South-West Africa, Southern Rhodesia and the Native Territories of Basutoland, Swaziland and Bechuanaland. Southern Rhodesia, although it still comes under the same Apostolic Delegation, is now quite separate ecclesiastically as well as politically. Its hierarchy is an independent one, established four years later than that of South Africa, and politically it is now part of the Central African Federation. The history of the Church in Southern Rhodesia has therefore been excluded from the plan of this present volume. It might be argued that South-West Africa ought similarly to be excluded, where the two vicars apostolic, of Windhoek and Keetmanshoop, are not members of the hierarchy of South Africa; but politically South-West Africa is governed under mandate by the Union, and when in the fullness of time these vicariates become dioceses the reasonable expectation is that they will be attached to one of the metropolitan provinces of the Union. The dioceses of the Native Territories of Basutoland, Swaziland and Bechuanaland are likewise under bishop belonging to the hierarchy of South Africa, although they are governed politically, as Protectorates, from the United Kingdom.

The Apostolic Delegation was at first established at Bloemfontein, and was moved to Pretoria towards the end of 1946. Its first two occupants were both Dutch archbishops, the first of whom remained in South Africa for more than twenty years. The second was there for nearly seven years, and together they supplied, through a quarter of a century of great expansion for the Church, that personal link with the Dutch tradition which the rigorous exclusion of Catholic immigrants through the century and a half of Dutch ascendancy had made so conspicuously lacking among the Catholic bishops, clergy and people.

The first Apostolic Delegate, Archbishop Bernard Jordan Gijlswijk, O.P., was consecrated in Rome on the feast of the Immaculate Conception in 1922, the day after the publication of the decree establishing the Delegation. He arrived in South Africa in February 1923 and remained there until his death on 22 December 1944. He is buried at Bloemfontein. His successor, Archbishop Martin H. Lucas, of the Society of the Divine Word, a native of Haarlem, was appointed to be Apostolic Delegate to South Africa on 14 September 1945 and consecrated on 29 October. He arrived in South Africa early in 1946 and remained there until, in 1952, the year after his labours and those of his predecessor had been crowned by the erection of the hierarchy, he was transferred to India as Internuncio.* He was succeeded in South Africa by an American prelate of Italian origin, Archbishop Joseph Damiano.†

Through more than three-quarters of the period between the appointment of the first Apostolic Delegate and the establishment of the Hierarchy in 1951 the Church in South Africa benefited from the wise counsel and direction of Archbishop Gijlswijk. His death marked the end of a chapter that had opened with the end of the first world war and closed with the end of the second; an easier and happier chapter in the history of the Church both than that which preceded and than that which followed it. His tenure of the Apostolic Delegation covered the whole period of the pontificate of Pius XI, "the Pope of the Missions", which, in South Africa as elsewhere, was one of great and fruitful growth. In the early spring of 1926 the encyclical letter *Rerum Ecclesiae* laid down the principles of the missionary work of the Church in the changed conditions which followed the first world war and heralded a period of great expansion in which South Africa fully participated.

When the encylical *Rerum Ecclesiae* extolled the advantages of local-born bishops and clergy in the mission-fields, the first two South African-born bishops had just been consecrated: David O'Leary, O.M.I., as vicar apostolic in the Transvaal on 8 September 1925, and Cornelius Bernard O'Riley as vicar apostolic in Cape Town five months later, on 6 January 1926. Between 1921 and

* In 1959 Archbishop Lucas was appointed to be the first permanent Apostolic Visitor to the Scandinavian countries, residing in Stockholm.

† In February, 1960, Archbishop Damiano was appointed to the See of Camden, New Jersey.

1936 the number of priests within the territory of the Apostolic Delegation was more than doubled, rising from three hundred to seven hundred, and the number of brothers and nuns also doubled, from two thousand to four thousand. By the time the hierarchy was established, at the beginning of 1951, seven priests born in South Africa had been raised to the episcopate, nearly a hundred and fifty South African-born priests had been ordained, and nearly seven hundred South African-born women, including many non-Europeans, had become nuns.

The religious orders and congregations, and especially those of women, greatly increased their activities in South Africa in the years between the two world wars, many sending communities from Europe to open houses in South Africa for the first time. German Benedictine nuns arrived in 1922 and the Pallotini Sisters in the following year. The Brothers of Charity came to the Transvaal in 1928. In 1931 the Sisters of the Holy Names of Jesus and Mary arrived from Canada to work in Basutoland, and in 1932 Franciscan nuns from southern Germany came to Kimberley. The Sisters of Mary of the Catholic Apostolate arrived in 1933; and in 1934 the Servite nuns arrived in Swaziland and the Brothers of the Sacred Heart in Basutoland.

In March 1928 the Congregation of the Sacred Heart had opened a seminary at Indwe, in what is now the diocese of Aliwal, in the eastern part of Cape Province; it was moved to Aliwal North two years later. There for the first time it became possible for aspirants to the priesthood to complete in South Africa all the studies leading to ordination. Intended originally for the Aliwal vicariate only, the seminary was soon receiving students from other parts of the Union also, both native-born South Africans and immigrants. About a score of its students reached the priesthood altogether, the last being ordained in 1945. But this was, of course, far from sufficient to meet all needs; most South African students for the priesthood still had to go overseas; and when this became impossible, during the second world war, the long-cherished plan for a national seminary took shape. The knowledge that a national seminary was coming, and the difficulties created by the war, led meanwhile to the closure of the Aliwal seminary.

It was on 14 April 1948 that the National Seminary of St John Vianney was opened by the Apostolic Delegate. At first it had temporary quarters in Queenstown. The foundation stone of its permanent buildings was laid on Waterkloof Hill, Pretoria, on 26 February 1950, and in March 1951 these impressive new buildings were opened. They are capable of accommodating a hundred and fifty students, together with the professorial staff of Franciscan Friars Minor of the Irish province, to whom the seminary had been entrusted in 1950.

The Oblates of Mary Immaculate have had their own scholasticate near Pietermaritzburg since before the end of the war; and at Roma, Basutoland, they have conducted both a major and a minor seminary for Africans since 1924. At Ixopo the Mariannhill Fathers have a minor seminary for Africans founded by Bishop Fleischer in 1925, and at Pevensey, also in Natal, the African major seminary begun by Bishop Fleischer has become a regional one staffed by the Dominican Fathers of the English Province, who train their own students at Stellenbosch, near Cape Town. A minor seminary for Europeans has recently been opened in Johannesburg, and one for coloured students in Cape Town.

The Pius XII Catholic University College at Roma, Basutoland, is not a seminary, but exists to give a university training to Catholic Africans who will be not priests but an élite among the laity. Under the direction of the Oblates of Mary Immaculate, it was founded by the bishops of the South African Apostolic Delegation in 1945 in a centre which takes its name from the Eternal City and is the vigorous and exceedingly impressive intellectual focal point of Catholic life among the Bantu, the scene of many memorable expressions of the devotion sown by those who have devoted their lives to the mission among them since the days of Bishop Allard.

The best way of indicating the development of the Church in South Africa in the years since the establishment of the Apostolic Delegation is to glance at the diocesan history. But before doing that it may be recorded that in 1947, at a general meeting of the Ordinaries of South Africa held at Mariannhill, a permanent consultative body known as the Southern African Catholic Bishops' Conference was established for the purpose of co-ordinating and organizing, wherever possible, the various aspects of Catholic activity. The administration of the affairs of the conference is entrusted to an Administrative Board, consisting of the bishops who are chairmen of the various departments—African Affairs,

Catholic Action, Education, Social Welfare—assisted by a General Secretariat.

II. The Erection of the Hierarchy

The Bull *Suprema Nobis* of Pope Pius XII, dated 11 January 1951, which erected the Hierarchy of the Church in Southern Africa, created four ecclesiastical Provinces, with the four Metropolitan Archbishops at Cape Town, Durban, Pretoria and Bloemfontein.* The Province of Bloemfontein is vast and sprawling, extending from Basutoland to the Atlantic coastline of the northern part of the Cape. The other three Provinces are more or less compact— those of Cape Town; Durban, where all the dioceses have one border on the Indian Ocean; and, occupying the north-east corner of the Union, Pretoria. Since the erection of the Hierarchy there have been various changes, with the creation of a new diocese in Basutoland and another partly in Natal and partly in the Cape, and the re-naming of that which covers the Swaziland Protectorate. Today Cape Town has the suffragan dioceses of Aliwal, Oudt-shoorn, Port Elizabeth and Queenstown; Durban those of Eshowe, Kokstad, Mariannhill, Umtata and Umzimkulu; Pretoria those of Bremersdorp, Johannesburg and Lydenburg, with the Abbey *Nullius* of Pietersburg; and Bloemfontein those of Bethlehem, Keimoes, Kimberley, Kroonstad, Leribe and Maseru. In addition there are three new prefectures, of De Aar in the Cape Province; Volksrust, comprising parts of both Transvaal and Natal; and, most recently, Bechuanaland. Most of these circumscriptions which became dioceses in 1951 had been created for the first time, as vicariates or prefectures, during the previous thirty years—that is, since the end of the period of which Dr Brown tells the history in this book—and to summarize their history is to summarize the history of the rapid development of the Church in South Africa in the years following the appointment of the first Apostolic Delegate.

The original vicariate of the Cape of Good Hope had been divided, it will be recalled, in 1847, into the two vicariates of the Western and Eastern Districts; and these names remained in use

---

* By a decree of the Congregation of Propaganda dated 17 May 1951, a Military Ordinariate for the Union of South Africa was created, and the Bishop of Pretoria was appointed to be the first Military Ordinary.

for more than ninety years, until a decree of 13 June 1939* made
them respectively the vicariates of Cape Town and Port Elizabeth;
today they are, within borders constricted several times since
1847, the dioceses of Cape Town and Port Elizabeth. It will also
be recalled that on 24 May 1872 the prefecture of the Central
District was detached from the Western District. Two years
later, on 13 July 1874, the new prefecture was entrusted to the
French *Missionaires d'Afrique*, from Lyons, who were responsible
for it until 1882; then it was divided, part being entrusted to
the Oblates of St Francis de Sales and the remainder returning to the
Western vicariate until 1922, when it was again detached under the
name of the Central Prefecture and entrusted to the German Fathers
of the Society of the Catholic Apostolate (Pallottines). In 1939 its
name was changed to the Prefecture of Oudtshoorn; it became a
vicariate on 9 December 1948 and then a diocese in 1951. It has
a Pallottine bishop to this day; so also has the inland diocese of
Queenstown, to the north-east of Port Elizabeth, an area entrusted
to the German Pallottine Fathers when it was detached from the
Eastern vicariate on 20 February 1929. This became a prefecture
on 29 March 1938 and a vicariate on 9 April 1948, and was enlarged
after it had been made a diocese by the addition, on 7 February
1952, of seven districts transferred from the neighbouring diocese
of Umtata, in the Province of Durban to the east. The fourth
suffragan diocese of Cape Town is that of Aliwal, to the north of
the dioceses of Port Elizabeth and Queenstown. As the Gariep
prefecture, this was entrusted on 12 June 1923 to the German
priests of the Sacred Heart who are responsible for the diocese
today. It became the Aliwal vicariate on 27 January 1936; after
it had been a diocese for two years the western part was detached,
on 24 March 1953, to make the prefecture of De Aar, which was
entrusted to the American province of the same Congregation of
Priests of the Sacred Heart. Such in brief is the comparatively
simple story of the Metropolitan Province of Cape Town.

Virtually the whole of the rest of what is now the territory of the
Union of South Africa was included in the original vicariate of
Natal to which Bishop Allard was appointed on 15 November

---

* All dates, unless otherwise indicated, are those of decrees of the Roman
Congregation of Propaganda, under which South Africa still remains.

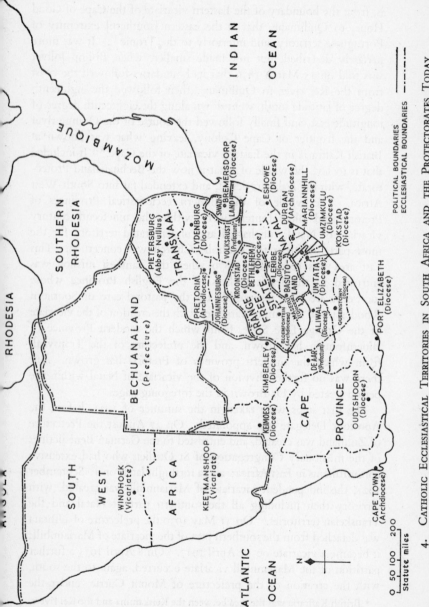

4. CATHOLIC ECCLESIASTICAL TERRITORIES IN SOUTH AFRICA AND THE PROTECTORATES TODAY

1850. It was then defined as extending "from the Kei river, that is, from the boundary of the Eastern vicariate of the Cape of Good Hope, to Quilimane, that is the eastern [southern] extremity of Portuguese territory, and interiorly to the Tropic". It was more precisely described, but not made smaller, when Bishop Jolivet was told on 15 March 1876 that its boundaries followed the coast from the Kei river to Quilimane, then followed the eighteenth degree of latitude south, went down along the eighteenth degree of longitude east, and finally followed the course of the Orange river and the frontier of Cape Colony, leaving what was known as British Kaffraria in the Eastern vicariate of the Cape.* It included that is to say, the whole of what is now the Bechuanaland Protectorate, with the Kalahari desert, and extended far into South-West Africa. The whole of the modern ecclesiastical Provinces of Pretoria and Bloemfontein were within the nineteenth-century vicariate of Natal; uncharted and unpenetrated territory for the most part, so far as the Catholic Church was concerned. This vast area was reduced in 1879 when the Zambesi mission was entrusted to the Jesuit Fathers of the English Province whose successors are now responsible for the pastoral care of Southern Rhodesia, and then nine years later with the creation of the vicariate of the Orange Free State, from which the modern Province of Bloemfontein has grown, and the prefecture of the Transvaal, from which the modern province of Pretoria has grown. But there was no further division of the vicariate of Natal within the period treated by Dr Brown in the foregoing pages.

The first steps were taken in the summer of 1921, before the Apostolic Delegate was appointed. On 27 August the Prefecture of Zululand was created, and entrusted to the German Benedictines of the missionary Congregation of St Ottilien who had extensive commitments in East Africa; and a fortnight later, on 10 September 1921, the independent vicariate of Mariannhill was created, with territory then including all the southern part of Natal and the Transkeian territories. On 31 May 1930 the prefecture of Umtata was detached from the southern part of the vicariate of Mariannhill; it became a vicariate on 13 April 1937. On 8 April 1935 a further partition of the Mariannhill vicariate occurred, again to the south, with the creation of the prefecture of Mount Currie, under the

* British Kaffraria was the area between the Keiskamma and the Kei rivers.

Irish Friars Minor; this became the vicariate of Kokstad on 11 July 1939. When the Hierarchy was established in 1951, therefore, the Metropolitan See of Durban had three suffragans to the south; those of Mariannhill, Kokstad and Umtata. To the north it had Eshowe, including almost the whole of Zululand proper; the original Zululand prefecture had become the vicariate of Eshowe on 11 December 1923. One further diocese was added to the Province of Durban after the establishment of the Hierarchy, with the creation on 21 February 1954 of the diocese of Umzimkulu, with territory detached from the southern parts of the archdiocese. Finally, the northern part of the archdiocese of Durban was detached in 1958 to form part of the prefecture of Volksrust under the English Franciscan Friars Minor.

The prefecture of the Transvaal, from which grew the Metropolitan Province of Pretoria, became a vicariate in 1904 and was first divided on 22 December 1910, when the northern part was entrusted as a separate prefecture to Cassinese Benedictines from Belgium. On 13 June 1939 their monastery of Pietersburg received the status of an Abbey *Nullius*, a status which it still retains in the Province of Pretoria.★ The next division came on 12 June 1923, when the Eastern Transvaal was entrusted to the Missionary Sons of the Sacred Heart as the Lydenburg Prefecture; it became a vicariate on 9 December 1948 and then a diocese in 1951. In 1958 the southern portion of the Lydenburg diocese was detached and included in the new prefecture of Volksrust. On 9 April 1948 the remaining part of the Transvaal vicariate had been renamed as the Vicariate of Pretoria. It was divided again when the Hierarchy was established with Pretoria as the Metropolitan See, the separate diocese of Johannesburg being then created to the south. Today the diocese of Johannesburg is easily the largest numerically in the Union of South Africa, with the greatest number of both faithful and clergy.† The other diocese in the Province of Pretoria is Bremersdorp, which is the old Swaziland Mission that was entrusted to the Servite Fathers in 1913; on 19 April 1923 it was

---

★ The abbot is a titular bishop and has jurisdiction over all clergy in his territory, whether members of his order or not. The word *Nullius* means that the territory forms part of no diocese.

† In 1959, according to the 1960 *Catholic Directory of Southern Africa*, its Catholic population was 165,928.

detached from the Natal Vicariate as a separate prefecture; on 15 March 1939 it became a vicariate, and when the Hierarchy was established it became the diocese of Bremersdorp; it has an Italian Servite bishop still.

Bloemfontein, the capital of the Orange Free State, became the seat of a bishop for the first time when the Hierarchy was established in 1951. The diocese of Kimberley was in area until recently the biggest in South Africa, including some territory in Cape Province, with, until the spring of 1959, the Bechuanaland Protectorate south of the Tropic of Capricorn. Pope John XXIII in April 1959 created the new prefecture of Bechuanaland from this part of the diocese of Kimberley, together with the parts of Bechuanaland which had previously lain in the Southern Rhodesian diocese of Bulawayo and the South-West African vicariate of Windhoek. The new prefecture of Bechuanaland was entrusted to the Passionist Fathers. To the south-west of the diocese of Kimberley and extending to the Atlantic is the diocese of Keimoes, of which the history begins with the original Namaqualand mission of the Oblates of St Francis de Sales in 1882, in what was then part of the Central Prefecture. A separate prefecture was created for them on 20 June 1885; this became the Orange River vicariate on 2 May 1898 (not to be confused with the 1886 vicariate of the Orange Free State) and the vicariate of Keimoes (where most of the faithful are coloureds) on 9 July 1940. To the north-east of Bloemfontein, by contrast, the diocese of Kroonstad is small and compact. It is the only diocese that gives its information in the Afrikaans language alone, and not in English, in the *Catholic Directory of Southern Africa*. It was the northern part of the Orange Free State when it was detached from the old Kimberley vicariate on 26 November 1923 to form a separate prefecture under the German Holy Ghost Fathers, and became the vicariate of Kroonstad on 8 April 1935. Then on 12 February 1948 it was divided, the western part, with the town of Kroonstad (which had attracted great attention two years before with the discovery of important new gold deposits) being given to the Dutch Dominicans, and the eastern part, with Bethlehem, being retained by the Holy Ghost Fathers. So it was that Kroonstad and Bethlehem became two dioceses in the Province of Bloemfontein in 1951.

We have left to the last in this catalogue two of the most remarkable dioceses of South Africa, both in the Province of Bloemfontein: those of Maseru and Leribe, which cover the territory of the Basutoland Protectorate. On 8 May 1894 Basutoland was detached from the vicariate of the Orange Free State to form an independent prefecture, and this, by a decree of St Pius X on 18 February 1909, was made into a vicariate. The Oblates of Mary Immaculate, who were in charge of it, confided it to their Canadian province in the 'thirties. It formed the single diocese of Maseru when the Hierarchy was established; a year later, on 11 December 1952, it was divided to make the smaller diocese of Leribe in the northern part of Basutoland, with a local-born African Oblate as its first bishop: Emmanuel 'Mabathoana, who was consecrated on 25 March 1953. Leribe remains a small diocese, with only a score of priests, but Maseru has well over a hundred priests—more than any other South African diocese except Johannesburg—with more brothers and nuns than any other South African diocese and over 200,000 Catholics. Nowhere was progress between the wars more marked than in Basutoland.

To round off this account of the ecclesiastical circumscriptions of South Africa which come within the scope of this book it remains to describe the two vicariates, of Keetmanshoop and Windhoek, the former to the south and the latter to the north, through which the Church is governed in the mandated territory of South-West Africa. The Vicariate of Keetmanshoop, under the Oblates of St Francis de Sales since the pioneer days of Bishop Simon, received its present name on 13 January 1949. On 7 July 1909 Great Namaqualand had been separated from the Orange River vicariate to form a prefecture which became a vicariate in August 1930. The other of these two vicariates originally formed part of the old prefecture of Cimbebasia, in Portuguese Angola; it was made into the Lower Cimbebasia prefecture on 1 August 1892, and the Oblates of Mary Immaculate began their work a few years later. On 10 January 1921 it became simply the Cimbebasia Prefecture, the Portuguese having relinquished that style; and on 11 May 1926 it became the Windhoek vicariate. It surrendered that part of its territory which extended into Bechuanaland when the new prefecture of Bechuanaland was created in the spring of 1959.

III. *Apartheid*

In the area with which this book is concerned, the Union of
South Africa, South-West Africa and the Protectorates, there are,
according to the most recent estimates, sixteen and a half million
people,* of whom a little over three million are of European origin.
Among the total population there are 1,200,000 Catholics† of
whom just over 12 per cent are of European origin and nearly
80 per cent are Bantu; Indian Catholics account for about 0·6 per
cent and the remainder are coloureds. In the population as a
whole, therefore, about 7 per cent are Catholic, and among those
of European origin about 5 per cent. To be more precise, the
Catholics of European origin number just over 147,000‡ in a total
population of European origin of just over 3,000,000.

In forming any picture of South Africa it is important to remember how small is the total white population in relation to the huge
area, and in considering the position of the Catholic Church it is
equally important to remember how small a minority among the
white people the Catholics are. The entire European population
of the immense area with which this book is concerned is substantially less than the population of many single cities—Paris or
Berlin, New York or Chicago, Moscow or Mexico City—but it is
dispersed through an area which (since we are including the vast
spaces of Bechuanaland and South-West Africa) is well over a
million square miles, or more than ten times the area of the
United Kingdom. Dramatic comparisons of this kind give a
distorted picture, it is true, and would only be valid if there was an
even distribution of population in both the areas compared. But
they serve to stress the point that all the white population of South
Africa is a small minority distributed through an immense area,
with its main centres separated by great distances. Herein lies a

* For the Union and South-West Africa the figures are from the *Monthly
Bulletin of the South African Bureau of Census and Statistics*, September 1959.
For the Protectorates the figures are taken from the 1956 census.

† 1959 figures from the 1960 *Catholic Directory of Southern Africa*. The
latest available government census figures of the Union (1951) give a Catholic
population appreciably greater than the *Catholic Directory* statistics for the same
year, 684,414 instead of 547,336, a difference of over 23 per cent. of the
Directory figure.

‡ *Catholic Directory* 1960. An estimate based on the 1951 Union Census
figure would be closer to 210,000.

large part, although not the whole, of the explanation of the apprehension for the future which in recent years has been so tragically translated into discriminatory racial legislation. And secondly, because the Catholics are but a small element in this widely scattered European population, the Church in South Africa, of recent origin by comparison with the Reformed Church and ministering to relatively recent arrivals among the Europeans, has been obliged to devote her primary missionary effort to the Europeans, and came relatively late into the field of missionary work among the Bantu, so that in the task of Bantu education, as one Catholic writer remarked not long ago, the Catholics began fifty or sixty years after the Protestants.

It was only after representations made during and following the visit to South Africa in February 1928 of Archbishop Hinsley, the future Cardinal Archbishop of Westminster, as Apostolic Visitor, that real impetus was given to the acquisition of government grants for Catholic mission schools, and a quarter of a century later came the Bantu Education Act to take them away.* The very scale of the blow then suffered is a measure of the progress made in that quarter of a century. It is true that the Catholic mission schools have a much longer history than that. The centenary of the Catholic contribution to Bantu education will fall in 1964; it was in 1864 that the Holy Family Sisters arrived in Basutoland, the Mariannhill foundation followed within twenty years, and the readers of the preceding chapters of this book will know with what devotion the foundations of a Catholic educational system among the Bantu were laid in the later years of the nineteenth century and the first quarter of the twentieth. But the second quarter of the twentieth century was the period of great expansion, just before the blow fell.

It was in the election campaign of 1948 that the word *apartheid* first made its appearance in the South African political vocabulary. The coalition of the Afrikaner and Nationalist parties led by Dr Malan gained only a narrow victory then, but it was enough to reverse the verdict of 1943 when Smuts and the United Party

---

* It is perhaps not necessary to point out that the Act did not touch the Protectorates, but we do so nevertheless, having just been stressing that the Protectorates are included in the area with which this book is concerned.

had polled more than twice as many votes as all other parties combined; and it led to Dr Malan's triumph in 1953. This is not the place to trace in detail the history of the measures by which *apartheid* was then put into effect.

One of the first major measures directly affecting the Church was the Bantu Education Act of 1953 which followed immediately upon Dr Malan's triumph. The application of this Act resulted in the progressive withdrawal of the government subsidies upon which the extensive system of mission schools had come to depend. Only about 15 per cent of the mission schools affected were Catholic, but it was among the Catholics that the measure had the most far-reaching effects because only the Catholics attached sufficient importance to the confessional character of their Bantu schools to declare the intention of shouldering the huge financial burden of keeping them open as far as possible without the subsidies. Great sacrifices were willingly made, by those who gave generously to the fund which the bishops established, and by the teachers who had to accept drastic reductions in their salaries so that the schools might remain open. Overseas benefactors also came to the aid of the stricken schools, particularly the pontifical mission aid societies and the German hierarchy. But the position remains critical, and the outcome of the grim battle to save the schools hangs very much in the balance.

By July 1959 about sixty schools had closed and the overall number of pupils had dropped by 17 per cent, from 112,000 to 93,000. Teacher training colleges and secondary schools had suffered most heavily. None of the six Catholic training colleges had been granted the recognition which the Act required, and the qualifications of the teachers trained in them were thus not recognized. Three had been closed. Ten Catholic secondary schools for Africans had disappeared, including four of the largest in the country, leaving only thirty-four training colleges and secondary schools altogether.* The extent of the loss is accentuated when it is remembered that before 1954 the number of pupils in the Catholic mission schools had been increasing by about 5 per cent annually and would have amounted now (in 1960) to about 150,000 but for the Bantu Education Act.

* Figures supplied by the Secretariat of the Southern African Catholic Bishops' Conference, Pretoria.

It is, however, not this Act alone that is causing such substantial losses. In fact it can be said that, apart from withdrawing subsidies, the government has not as yet made extensive use of the powers conferred on it by this Act in order to suppress Catholic schools. Perhaps it is relying on financial circumstances and the operation of other laws such as the Group Areas Act of 1950. It is this law that has been responsible for the major closures. Still more Catholic schools are likely to be affected by it in the future, because of their situation in so-called European areas. There is very little likelihood of making good the losses resulting from these closures by the opening of new Catholic schools in African areas, for, apart from the financial problem involved, it has been stated that there will be no permits for new Catholic schools in these areas. Secondary schools are confronted with a particular difficulty. Here graduate teachers are required, and the general shortage of African graduates has created keen competition in which missionaries cannot match the salaries obtaining in state schools. Indeed, but for the fact that a certain number of highly qualified religious teach in mission secondary schools, it would be quite impossible to maintain the required standard. As regards the teacher training colleges still in existence, applicants for admission must be impelled more by religious and apostolic ideals than by professional aspirations. A teacher's diploma not recognized by the state can promise little in the way of a professional career.

The Group Areas Act aims at achieving the maximum degree of separation between the races in regard to the ownership and occupation of land and premises. One of its consequences is the creation of insecurity on a disastrous scale among non-Europeans, who cannot tell what will happen to their homes and businesses as this legislation comes ponderously and clumsily into effect. As has been seen, it strikes at the Church in her institutions and moreover threatens to disrupt the common life of priests and religious of different races and to wreck their association in educational and charitable undertakings. The ecclesiastical authorities fear the day when white missionaries may be excluded from non-European areas and when grave obstacles may be raised to the training by Europeans of non-white aspirants to the priesthood and religious life.

This fear is aggravated by the importance, theoretical at least, which is now being attributed to the development of native reserves which, it is hoped, will evolve into satellite " statelets ", or " bantustans ", in which the Africans can develop " along their own lines " and achieve some degree of autonomy under the paternal supervision of the White South African state. The extent to which the *apartheid* policy is being pressed, regardless of religious or moral considerations, is illustrated by the Native Laws Amendment Act of 1957, which gave the Minister of Native Affairs power to order that no Bantu " shall attend any church in any urban area outside a native residential area ". Protesting, along with other religious leaders, against this enactment, the Catholic bishops denounced this "claim by the State to regulate worship and the religious practice of the individual person ", and affirmed that "we cannot admit such a claim ".

Rather than attempt here any further narrative account of these developments, we cannot do better than quote from the three principal collective utterances of the South African bishops since the problem of race relations moved into its acute phase. The first of these came in 1952, the year before Dr Malan's electoral triumph; the second in 1954; and the third in 1957. The third was a sequel to the first; these were statements published by the Bishops' Conference at Pretoria; and the second was a joint pastoral letter.

IV. *Principles of Race Relations*

The bishops' statement of June 1952 began by saying that, " as it is the duty of bishops to teach the truth committed to the Church by Our Saviour ", they had " judged it opportune to draw attention to the racial problem " in their country, " and to the Christian principles that must govern attempts to solve it ". A cautionary note was struck in this opening paragraph:

> This racial problem admits of no easy solution, and for that reason it can only be regretted that it is so frequently made the plaything of party politics, without regard for the real welfare of citizens. A problem so fraught with grave consequences should be kept on the highest level of earnest and prudent consideration; for no good purpose can be served, and only detriment can result, when the problem or any proposed solution is exploited for sectional interest or party gain.

The bishops went on to expound the Christian teaching of the dignity of all men, " and the great truth that all men, being bound together in one household of God, should love their Father in heaven above all things, and one another for His sake ". They added that "it is not easy for fallen men, even with the help of God's grace, to attain this ideal of the Christian life ". South Africa, they said, " has a particular difficulty in this regard; a difficulty that cannot be minimized when we consider the long and tragic history of inter-racial and international relations in the world at large ". " The South African people originate from various branches of the human family that differ greatly from one another in culture and institutions." The Europeans, representing about one-fifth of the population, hold, as a result of historical circumstances, " most of the land, wealth and, for all practical purposes, the entire political power ". The non-Europeans " have practically no share in the government of the country, and are debarred by law and custom from enjoying equal opportunity with Europeans in the field of gainful employ, and consequently in other spheres of social life ". As a consequence of " this political, economic and legal ' colour bar ' ", many Europeans " look upon non-Europeans as persons of inferior race who can never be entitled to full citizenship and complete equality ". " A stigma of social debasement is attached to the condition of non-Europeans. The natural consequence is the growth among non-Europeans of resentment, animosity and distrust." The bishops continued:

Were the attitude of the Europeans the sole reason for South Africa's racial problem, it would be simple enough to condemn it as unjust and un-Christian, and, by a determined process of education, endeavour to modify it. However, the problem is far more complex than that. Its complexity arises out of the fact that the great majority of non-Europeans, and particularly the Africans, have not reached a stage of development that would justify their integration into a homogeneous society with the Europeans. A sudden and violent attempt to force them into the mould of European manners and customs would be disastrous. There must be gradual development and prudent adaptation. Nor must they be required to conform in every respect to European ways, for their own distinctive qualities are capable of rich development.

The bishops recognized, however, that, " though the majority of non-Europeans are still undeveloped, there are many of them well qualified to participate fully in the social, political and economic life of the country; some because they have a long tradition of civilization behind them, derived from their ancestry in its entirety or along one line of forebears; others because they have risen beyond the cultural level of their people through education ". Yet " resentment and mistrust, almost innate in the illiterate ", is " aggravated in the literate through their experience and reading to such a degree that they can scarcely conceive that Europeans might want to help them to higher attainment ". " The majority " in " a group of non-European peoples in various stages of cultural development " is " still totally unprepared for full participation in social and political life patterned after what are commonly called western standards ", and in addition there are " divisions and animosity between various non-European groups ".

The bishops proceeded to apply to " this vexed problem of human relationships " the virtues of prudence, charity and justice.

Prudence is required to regulate the advance of less developed peoples, so as to impart to them gradually the benefits of higher civilization without bringing chaos and disruption into their social life. Prudence is essential when measures are taken for the welfare of various groups of citizens, in order that such measures may not aggravate suspicion or rancour, but promote peace and understanding. Prudence is the proper virtue of good government. However, not only those in authority are required to exercise it, but also the ordinary citizens, each of whom has a share of responsibility in the solution of a common problem.

Charity, " the supreme virtue ", " forbids the harbouring of dislike or contempt for any human person "; it " does not, of course, oblige us to disregard differences of condition and culture ", but no inequalities can " justify behaviour that is offensive and disparaging, for social inequalities in no way detract from the great truth that all men are the creatures and children of God." " Yet charity is not opposed to honest striving for the securing of one's true rights. For charity and justice must go hand in hand." " Justice demands that we give every man his due." The bishops distinguished between " fundamental and inviolable rights " and those which are "derivative or contingent", the first including "the right to life, dignity, sustenance, worship; to the integrity, use and normal development of faculties; to work and the fruit of work; to private ownership of property, to sojourn and movement, to marriage and the procreation and education of children, to association with one's fellow-men"; and the latter including "the right to vote in the election of legislative bodies, State aid in education, unemployment insurance, old age pensions and so on". No person or society may deprive the individual of the exercise of the fundamental rights:

> The State, though justified in controlling the exercise of rights to the degree required by the common good, cannot abolish them; for the person is superior to the State, which exists for his benefit. Contingent rights, too, cannot be arbitrarily denied or restricted. They are frequently the expression or adaptation to particular circumstances of fundamental rights; and it would be unjust to refuse them to persons capable of exercising them and of contributing their equitable share to the welfare of society. Further, it is the duty of the State by means of wise laws, efficient administration and the provision of public services, to create conditions that will foster the proper exercise of the rights of citizens. Should there be such neglect that this cannot be achieved, then obviously the State is not doing its duty. However, the State cannot be burdened with the sole responsibility of ensuring a decent livelihood for its citizens. All those who employ labour, and especially those who wield considerable influence over a country's economy, are bound in justice to do all in their power so to compensate their employees that these may live at least in frugal comfort.

After a passage stressing that all rights have duties as their counterparts, and that "those who demand the recognition of rights should remember this, and should base their claim on their ability and readiness to assume the duties involved", the bishops summed up their conclusions under four heads:

(1) Discrimination based exclusively on grounds of colour is an offence against the right of non-Europeans to their natural dignity as human persons.

(2) Though most of the basic rights of non-Europeans are in theory respected, conditions arising out of discriminatory

legislation (such as laws restricting employment), social conventions and inefficient administration seriously impair the exercise of these fundamental rights. The disruption of family life is a case in point.

(3) Justice demands that non-Europeans be permitted to evolve gradually towards full participation in the political, economic and cultural life of the country.

(4) This evolution cannot come about without earnest endeavours on the part of non-Europeans to prepare themselves for the duties connected with the rights they hope to enjoy.

V. The Call to Sacrifice

The Pastoral Letter of 30 November 1954, soon after the promulgation of the Bantu Education Act and the announcement that the government subsidies to the mission schools would be scaled down and would ultimately disappear, was signed on behalf of the Hierarchy by the Archbishops of Durban, Cape Town and Bloemfontein and the Bishops of Lydenburg and Kroonstad, the members of the Administrative Board of the Bishops' Conference. It admirably combined restraint with severity, temperateness with firmness. " In the midst of an atmosphere of bitter verbal strife," its second sentence ran, " of misunderstanding and misinterpretation, of allegation and counter-allegation, the Catholic Church, with calm serenity and untiring charity, has striven by every possible means to reach a conclusion which would be satisfactory to the Church, to the State and to the parents of our Bantu children." It was a high claim, and a justified one. The Pastoral Letter continued:

If the efforts of the Bishops have not as yet met with the desired results, this does not mean that Catholics will be less ready in the future than they have been in the past to strive, in a spirit of friendly co-operation, for good order in society and for the happy security of all the people. We may never allow ourselves to be less than Catholic in our thoughts and deeds. Even when our principles are misunderstood and we are deprived of what we consider due to us in the matter of education, such as the right to establish Catholic schools wherever they are required and the right to a fair share in the public revenues allotted to education, we may never descend to hatred or recrimination, or to any course of conduct which is not in accord with the spirit of Christ.

Only after this did the bishops go on to declare that " that very spirit which urges charity and forbearance upon us forbids us nevertheless to yield on principle ".

The bishops spoke " with deep regret " of " the reluctance of the State to give our Catholic mission schools any guarantee of continued financial support, though this could well be done in harmony with the provisions of the Bantu Education Act ". The withdrawal of the grants, whether wholly or in part, would inevitably lead to hardship " and a tremendous increase in calls for sacrifice on the part of parents and their children ". The bishops paid tribute also to the teachers who found themselves " now faced with the most painful choice ", predicting with a confidence which in the event proved well justified: " We know that, whatever decision they will have to take in relation to their future livelihood, at heart they will remain one with us in our struggle for the Catholic schools ". Within a very short time there were numerous reports of teachers in the mission schools agreeing to accept severe reductions in salaries that were in any case small, even in cases where alternative employment might not have been difficult to find. As the bishops went on to say in this pastoral letter, " In times of crisis and of special difficulty, it has always been the mark of true Catholics to unite their forces in a spirit of extraordinary mutual assistance and of generous self-sacrifice ":

United as we are in one Faith and sharing together in the same Life of Christ, we cannot say that our Catholic mission schools are not our concern because we are not parents or because we are not Africans. On the contrary, we realize now more than ever before that our Catholic mission schools belong intimately to the Catholic life of the whole of South Africa. We who have committed ourselves by our very profession of Faith to co-operate, under grace, in the consolidation and in the extension of Christ's Kingdom on earth can have no doubt about the importance and the necessity of our mission schools. As South Africans, too, we can make no greater contribution to the moral prosperity of our country than by a concerted and continuous determination to bring the genuine teaching and influence of Christ into the heart of African life through the length and breadth of our land.

The bishops therefore called " with unbounded confidence " on all South African Catholics first to pray for the threatened Bantu schools and then "to demonstrate their faith and loyalty by a generous and sustained response to the appeal that we launch for the support of our African schools". They announced the establishment of "The Catholic Mission Schools' Fund", and said also that "a special fund-raising effort" would be made, which would be known as "The Catholic Education Drive"*, the proceeds of which would be "allocated both to the mission schools and to the regional seminaries according to their requirements". They knew that the Catholics of South Africa were "generally not rich in this world's goods", but, they concluded:

> The present crisis of our African schools is a challenge to our loyalty and self-sacrifice. The struggle may be long and arduous, the immediate results discouraging, but we know that with God's help and the prayers of Mary, our heavenly Mother and Patroness, we will triumph in the end. We will come through the present difficulties stronger in the Faith of Christ, more fixed in hope and trust, more united than ever before in the life of grace and charity that flows to us from our crucified King and Saviour.

VI. "A Sin to Humiliate one's Fellow Men"

The statement of 1957, published at the end of the plenary session of the Bishops' Conference which met in Pretoria from 2 to 6 July, referred explicitly to *apartheid*, a word which had not occurred in the statement of 1952 to which it began by looking back. It opened with a severe and uncompromising condemnation:

> The basic principle of *apartheid* is the preservation of what is called white civilization. This is identified with white supremacy, which means the enjoyment by white men only of full political, social, economic and cultural rights. Persons of other races must be satisfied with what the white man judges can be conceded to them without endangering his privileged position. White supremacy is an absolute. It overrides justice. It transcends the teaching of Christ. It is a purpose dwarfing every other purpose, an end justifying any means.

* Later known as "The Catholic Bishops' Campaign for Mission Schools and Seminaries". It raised £750,000 in two years.

Apartheid is sometimes described as separate development, a term which suggests that under *apartheid* different races are given the opportunity of pursuing their respective and distinctive social and cultural evolutions. It is argued that only in this manner will these races be doing the will of God, lending themselves to the fulfilment of His providential designs. The contention sounds plausible as long as we overlook an important qualification, namely, that separate development is subordinate to white supremacy. The white man makes himself the agent of God's will and the interpreter of His providence in assigning the range and determining the bounds of non-white development. One trembles at the blasphemy of thus attributing to God the offences against charity and justice that are *apartheid's* necessary accompaniment.

It is a sin to humiliate one's fellow-men. There is in each human person by God's creation a dignity inseparably connected with his quality of rational and free being. This dignity has been immeasurably enhanced by the mystery of our redemption. In the words of St Peter, we are " a chosen race, a royal priesthood, a consecrated nation" (I Peter, ii, 9). Christ Himself has said " I have called you MY friends" (John, xv, 15). No man has the right to despise what God has honoured, to belittle one whom Christ has called friend, to brand a fellow-man with the stigma of inborn inferiority. It is an insult to human dignity, a slur upon God's noble work of creation and redemption. Christ has warned us against inflicting such injuries: " . . . any man who says, Raca, to his brother must answer for it before the Council; and any man who says to his brother, Thou fool, must answer for it in hell fire " (Matt., 5, 22).

From this fundamental evil of *apartheid* flow the innumerable offences against charity and justice that are its inevitable consequence, for men must be hurt and injustice must be done when the practice of discrimination is enthroned as the supreme principle of the welfare of the state, the ultimate law from which all other laws derive.

This having been said, the 1957 statement went on to counter fanaticism with moderation:

This condemnation of the principle of *apartheid* as something intrinsically evil does not imply that perfect equality can be established in South Africa by the stroke of a pen. There is nothing more obvious than the existence of profound differences between sections of our population which make immediate total integration impossible. People cannot share fully in the same political and economic institutions until culturally they have a great deal in common. All social change must be gradual if it is not to be disastrous. Nor is it unjust for a state to make provision in its laws and administration for the differences that do exist. A state must promote the well-being of all its citizens. If some require special protection it must be accorded. It would be unreasonable, therefore, to condemn indiscriminately all South Africa's differential legislation. It would be unfair to disparage the services provided for less advanced sections of the population and the noble and dedicated labours of many public officials on their behalf.

The bishops observed that " many who suffer under the sting of *apartheid* find it hard to accept counsels of moderation ".

Embittered by insult and frustration, they distrust any policy that involves a gradual change. Revolution, not evolution, is their slogan. They can see redress only in the sweeping away of every difference and the immediate extension of full civil rights to all. They do not stop to contemplate the confusion that will ensue, the collapse of all public order, the complete dissolution of society and perhaps their own rapid destruction in the holocaust. This is particularly true of those who find in atheistic Communism the inspiration of their present striving and their hope for the future.

A gradual change it must be: gradual, for no other kind of change is compatible with the maintenance of order, without which there is no society, no government, no justice, no common good. But a change must come, for otherwise our country faces a disastrous future. . . . The time is short. The need is urgent. Those penalized by *apartheid* must be given concrete evidence of the change before it is too late. This involves the elaboration of a sensible and just policy enabling any person, irrespective of race, to qualify for the enjoyment of full civil rights.

The bishops then addressed a candid word to the faithful:

The practice of segregation, though officially not recognized in our churches, characterizes nevertheless many of our church societies, our schools, seminaries, convents, hospitals and the social life of our people. In the light of Christ's teaching this cannot be tolerated for ever. The time has come to pursue more vigorously the change of heart and practice that the law of Christ demands. We are hypocrites if we condemn *apartheid* in South African society and condone it in our own institutions.

This does not mean that we can easily disregard all differences of mentality, condition, language and social custom. The Church does not enforce human associations that, because of these differences, can produce no good. She understands that the spiritual welfare of her children cannot be fostered in a social atmosphere wholly alien and uncongenial. But the Christian duty remains of seeking to unite rather than separate, to dissolve differences rather than perpetuate them. A different colour can be no reason for separation when culture, custom, social condition and above all a common faith and a common love of Christ impel towards unity.

In conclusion the bishops reiterated their plea to all white South Africans to " consider carefully what *apartheid* means : its evil and anti-Christian character, the injustices that flow from it, the resentment and bitterness it arouses, the harvest of disaster that it must produce in the country we all love so much ". They expressed admiration for " the splendid work done in many quarters to lessen prejudice, promote understanding and unity and help South Africa along that path of harmony and co-operation which is the only one dictated by wisdom and justice ". They expressed their deep regret " that it is still thought necessary to add to the volume of restrictive and oppressive legislation in order to reduce contacts between various groups to an inhuman and un-natural minimum ". And finally they made their own the prayer of Pope Pius XII with which this book may fittingly close: " that a task of constructive collaboration may be carried out in Africa: a collaboration free of prejudices and mutual sensitiveness, preserved from the seductions and strictures of false nationalism, and capable of extending to people rich in resources and future the true values of Christian civilization which have already borne so many fruits in other continents ".

Appendix

ECCLESIASTICAL JURISDICTIONS AND THEIR INCUMBENTS

Jurisdiction   *Incumbent*

1. PROVINCE OF CAPE TOWN

(1) CAPE TOWN

1805	Prefecture Apostolic of the Cape of Good Hope	Johannes Lansink	1805–06
1818	Vicariate Apostolic of Mauritius and the Cape of Good Hope	Bede Slater, O.S.B. William Placid Morris, O.S.B.	
1837	Vicariate Apostolic of the Cape of Good Hope	Patrick Raymund Griffith, O.P.	1837–62
		Thomas Grimley	1862–71
		John Leonard	1872–1908
		John Rooney	1908–24
		Bernard C. O'Riley	1925–32
1939	Vicariate Apostolic of Cape Town	Francis Hennemann, S.A.C.	1933–50
1951	Archdiocese of Cape Town	Owen McCann	1950–

(2) PORT ELIZABETH

1847	Vicariate Apostolic of the Eastern Districts of the Cape of Good Hope	Aidan Devereux	1847–54
		Patrick Moran	1856–69
		James David Ricards	1871–91
		Peter Strobino	1891–96
		Hugh MacSherry	1896–1938
1939	Vicariate Apostolic of Port Elizabeth	James Colbert	1939–48
1951	Diocese of Port Elizabeth	Hugh Boyle	1948–54
		Ernest Arthur Green	1955–

(3) OUDTSHOORN

1874	Central Prefecture	— Devernoille, S.M.A.	1874–88
		— Gaudeul, S.M.A.	1882
		Administered by the Vicars Apostolic of the Cape of Good Hope	1882–1922
		Francis Hennemann, S.A.C.	1922–33
1939	Prefecture Apostolic of Oudtshoorn	Theodore Koenig, S.A.C.	1934–48

	Jurisdiction			*Incumbent*	
1948	Vicariate	Apostolic	of	Bruno A. Hippel, S.A.C.	1948–
	Oudtshoorn				
1951	Diocese of Oudtshoorn				

(4) ALIWAL

1923	Prefecture	Apostolic	of	Francis W. Demont, S.C.J.	1923–44
	Gariep				
1936	Vicariate	Apostolic	of		
	Aliwal				
				Patrick L. Meyer, S.C.J. Adm.	1944–46
1951	Diocese of Aliwal			Johannes Lueck, S.C.J.	1947–

(5) QUEENSTOWN

1929	Independent	Mission	of	F. J. Vogel, S.A.C.	1929–36
	Queenstown			Johannes B. Rosenthal, S.A.C.	1937–
1940	Prefecture	Apostolic	of		
	Queenstown				
1948	Vicariate	Apostolic	of		
	Queenstown				
1951	Diocese of Queenstown				

(6) DE AAR

1953	Prefecture	Apostolic	of	Aloysius J. Dettmer, S.C.J.	1953–
	De Aar				

2. PROVINCE OF DURBAN

(1) DURBAN

1850	Vicariate Apostolic of Natal	Marie Jean Francois Allard, O.M.I.	1850–73
		Charles Constant Jolivet, O.M.I.	1874–1903
		Henri Delalle, O.M.I.	1903–46
1951	Archdiocese of Durban	Denis Eugene Hurley, O.M.I.	1946–

(2) MARIANNHILL

1921	Vicariate	Apostolic	of	Adalbero Fleischer, C.M.M.	1921–50
	Mariannhill			Alphonse Streit, C.M.M.	1950–
1951	Diocese of Mariannhill				

(3) ESHOWE

1921	Prefecture	Apostolic	of	Thomas Spreiter, O.S.B.	1921–43
	Zululand				
1923	Vicariate	Apostolic	of		
	Eshowe				
				Theodos Schall, O.S.B. Adm.	1943–47
				Aurelian Bilgeri, O.S.B.	1947–
1951	Diocese of Eshowe				

Jurisdiction	Incumbent

(4) UMTATA

1930	Prefecture Apostolic of Umtata	Emmanuel Hanisch, C.M.M.	1930–40
1937	Vicariate Apostolic of Umtata	Joseph Grueter, C.M.M.	1940–
1951	Diocese of Umtata		

(5) KOKSTAD

1935	Prefecture Apostolic of Mount Currie	Sigebald Blasius Kurz, O.F.M.	1935–46
1939	Vicariate Apostolic of Kokstad		
1951	Diocese of Kokstad	*Lucas Puerstinger, O.F.M. Adm.*	1946–49
		John Evangelist McBride, O.F.M.	1949–

(6) UMZIMKULU

1954	Diocese of Umzimkulu	Bonaventura Dlamini, F.F.J.	1954–

3. PROVINCE OF PRETORIA

(1) PRETORIA

1948	Vicariate Apostolic of Pretoria	John Colburn Garner	1948–
1951	Archdiocese of Pretoria		

(2) JOHANNESBURG

1886	Prefecture Apostolic of the Transvaal	Odilon Monginoux, O.M.I.	1886–91
		Aloysius Schoch, O.M.I.	1892–98
		John De Lacy, O.M.I. Adm.	1898–1902
		Matthew Gaughren, O.M.I. Adm.	1902–04
1904	Vicariate Apostolic of the Transvaal	William Miller, O.M.I.	1904–12
		Charles Cox, O.M.I. Adm.	1912–14
		Charles Cox, O.M.I.	1914–24
		David O'Leary, O.M.I.	1925–50
1948	Vicariate Apostolic of Johannesburg	William Patrick Whelan, O.M.I.	1950–54
1951	Diocese of Johannesburg	Hugh Boyle	1954–

(3) BREMERSDORP

1923	Prefecture Apostolic of Swaziland	P. M. Bellezze, O.S.M.	1923–33
		R. M. Migliorini, O.S.M.	1933–39
1939	Vicariate Apostolic of Swaziland	Atilio C. M. Barneschi, O.S.M.	1939–
1951	Diocese of Bremersdorp		

Jurisdiction	*Incumbent*

(4) PIETERSBURG

1910	Prefecture Apostolic of Pietersburg	Ildefons Lanslot, O.S.B.	1910–21
		Salvator Van Nuffel, O.S.B.	1921–39
1939	Abbey-Nullius of Pieters-Pietersburg	Frederic Osterrath, O.S.B.	1939–52
		Clemens Van Hoeck, O.S.B.	1954–

(5) LYDENBURG

1923	Prefecture Apostolic of Lydenburg	Daniel Kauzeor, M.F.S.C.	1923–26
		Aloysius Mohn, M.F.S.C.	1926–39
		Johann Riegler, M.F.S.C.	1939–55
1948	Vicariate Apostolic of Lydenburg		
1951	Diocese of Lydenburg	Anthony Reiterer, M.F.S.C.	1956–

(6) VOLKSRUST

1958	Prefecture Apostolic of Volksrust	Christopher Ulyatt, O.F.M.	1958–

4. PROVINCE OF BLOEMFONTEIN

(1) BLOEMFONTEIN

1951	Archdiocese of Bloemfontein	Herman Joseph Meysing, O.M.I.	1951–54
		William Patrick Whelan, O.M.I.	1954–

(2) KIMBERLEY

1886	Vicariate Apostolic of the Orange Free State	Anthony Gaughren, O.M.I.	1886–1901
1903	Vicariate Apostolic of Kimberley	Matthew Gaughren, O.M.I.	1902–14
		Charles Cox, O.M.I., Adm.	1914–24
1951	Diocese of Kimberley	Herman Joseph Meysing, O.M.I.	1924–51
		John Bokenfohr, O.M.I.	1953–

(3) KEIMOES

1882	Prefecture Apostolic of Namaqualand	John Maria Simon, O.S.F.S.	1884–1932
1898	Vicariate Apostolic of the Orange River		
		Odilon Fages, O.S.F.S.	1932–39
1940	Vicariate Apostolic of Keimoes	Henry J. Thunemann, O.S.F.S.	1940–
		Coadjutor Bishop:	
1951	Diocese of Keimoes	Francis Esser, O.S.F.S.	1956–

Jurisdiction	*Incumbent*

(4) MASERU

1894	Prefecture Apostolic of Basutoland		Odilon Monginoux, O.M.I.	1894–95
			Alexander Baudry, O.M.I.	1895–97
			Julius Cenez, O.M.I.	1897–1930
1909	Vicariate Apostolic of Basutoland		*Gerard Martin, O.M.I., Adm.*	1930–33
			Joseph Bonhomme, O.M.I.	1933–47
			Joseph Delphis Des Rosiers, O.M.I.	1948–
1951	Diocese of Maseru			

(5) KROONSTAD

1924	Prefecture Apostolic of Kroonstad		Leo Klerlein, C.S.Sp.	1924–48
1935	Vicariate Apostolic of Kroonstad			
1951	Diocese of Kroonstad		*Gerard N. van Velsen, O.P., Adm.*	1948–50
			Gerard N. van Velsen, O.P.	1950–

(6) BETHLEHEM

1948	Vicariate Apostolic of Bethlehem		Leo Klerlein, C.S.Sp.	1948
			Ph. Winterle, C.S.Sp., Adm.	1948–50
			Peter Kelleter, C.S.Sp.	1950–
1951	Diocese of Bethlehem			

(7) LERIBE

1952	Diocese of Leribe	Emmanuel G. 'Mabathoana, O.M.I. 1952–

(8) BECHUANALAND

1959	Prefecture Apostolic of Bechuanaland	Urban Murphy, C.P.	1959–

SOUTH-WEST AFRICA

KEETMANSHOOP

1909	Prefecture Apostolic of Great Namaqualand		Stanislaus von Krolikowski, O.S.F.S.	1909–23
			Matthias Eder, O.S.F.S.	1923–30
1930	Vicariate Apostolic of Great Namaqualand		Joseph Klemann, O.S.F.S.	1930–39
			James F. Eich, O.S.F.S.	1940–47
1949	Vicariate Apostolic of Keetsmanhoop		Francis Esser O.S.F.S.	1949–56
			Edward J Schlotterback O.S.F.S.	1956–

Jurisdiction	*Incumbent*	
	WINDHOEK, S.W.A.	
1892 Prefecture Apostolic of Lower Cimbebasia	Bernard P. Herrmann, O.M.I.	1896–1901
	Augustine Nachtwey, O.M.I.	1901–06
	Eugene Klaeyle, O.M.I.	1906–21
1921 Prefecture Apostolic of Cimbebasia	Joseph Gotthardt, O.M.I.	1921–
1926 Vicariate Apostolic of Windhoek		
	Co-adjutor Bishop:	
	Rudolph Koppmann, O.M.I.	1957–

SOURCES

I. MANUSCRIPT

A. IN THE DIOCESAN ARCHIVES AT CAPE TOWN

1. Diary of Bishop Griffith.
2. Book of Transactions and Memorials regarding the Building of the new Roman Catholic Church of Cape Town, by Bishop Griffith.
3. Unpublished autobiography of Bishop Grimley; two volumes.
4. Diary of Bishop Grimley on his journey to the Vatican Council from 19 August, 1869.
5. Letter Books No. I and No. VII of Bishop Leonard.

B. IN THE DIOCESAN ARCHIVES AT PORT ELIZABETH

1. *Chronicon* of the Eastern Vicariate, by Bishops Devereux, Moran, Ricards and Strobino.

C. IN THE DIOCESAN ARCHIVES AT DURBAN

1. *Registre comprenant la correspondance pour la mission de Natal:* a Letter Book of Bishop Allard.
2. *Actus administrationis in V.A. a Terra Natal nuncupata.*
3. *Actes du Conseil* (O.M.I.), Natal.
4. Draft Letters of Bishop Jolivet.
5. Draft Letters of Bishop Delalle.
6. *Les Trappistes dans l'Afrique du Sud.* MSS. by Abbot Pfanner.

D. IN THE DIOCESAN ARCHIVES AT KIMBERLEY

Kurze geschichtliche Übersicht über das apostolische Vikariat Kimberley (Zusammengestellt von P. Franz Hagel, O.M.I.).

E. IN THE DIOCESAN ARCHIVES AT KEIMOES

1. Memoir of Bishop Simon.

II. PRINTED

1. *The Catholic Directory of South Africa*, from 1904.
2. *The Catholic Magazine*, 1891–1924.

3. *The Colonist*, 1849–1858.

4. *Missions de la Congregation des Missionaires Oblats de Marie Immaculée* (Rome), from 1866.

5. *The Zambesi Mission Record*, from 1898.

6. *Aperçu historique et exercice* (Congregation du Saint-Esprit, Paris, 1932).

7. Bird, *Family Record*. Memoirs relating to the family history of the late Lieut.-Colonel Christopher Chapman Bird and John Bird, C.M.G. (Privately printed in Pietermaritzburg, 1922).

8. Rev. J. E. Brady, O.M.I., *Trekking for Souls* (Cedara, Natal, 1952).

9. Rev. A. T. Bryant, *Zulu-English Dictionary*, Preface (Mariannhill Mission Press, Natal, 1905).

10. Sir William Butler, *From Naboth's Vineyard* (George Bell, 1907).

11. Rev. Joseph Dahm, C.M.M., *Mariannhill* (Mariannhill Mission Press, *Abs. Manuskript gedruckt* 1949).

12. James Rose-Innes, *Autobiography* (Oxford University Press, 1949).

13. Rev. F. Laydevant, O.M.I. (and others), *Basutoland* (Editions Grands Lacs, Namur, Belgium, 1949).

14. Rev. F. Schimlek, C.M.M., *Mariannhill* (Mariannhill Missionary Press, 1953).

15. Rev. J. O'Haire, *Recollections of Twelve Years Residence* (Dublin: Cooke, Keating and Co., s.d.).

16. Alban O'Riley, *Notre Mère* (Maskew Miller, Cape Town, 1922).

17. Bishop Ricards, *The Catholic Church and the Kaffir* (Burns & Oates, s.d. [1879]).

18. Ricards, *Catholic Christianity and Modern Unbelief* (Benziger; R. & T. Washbourne (London); Gill & Son (Dublin); 1884).

19. Ricards, *Aletheia* (Benziger, 1885).

20. Aimé Roche, *Clartés Australes: Joseph Gerard, O.M.I.* (Editions du Chalet, Lyon, 1951).

21. A. Wilmot, *Life and Times of the Rt. Rev. James David Ricards* (Cape Town, 1908).

REFERENCES

Abbreviations

Allard	The Letter Book of Bishop Allard.
Autobiography	The Autobiography of Bishop Grimley.
Chronicon	The *Chronicon* of the Eastern Vicariate.
C.M.	*The Catholic Magazine.*
Diary	The Diary of Bishop Griffith.
Memoir	The Memoir of Bishop Simon.
Missions	*Missions de la Congregation des Missionaires Oblats de Marie Immaculée.*

CHAPTER I

1. *Irish Catholic Directory,* 1863.
2. *C.M.,* I, 471.
3. *Irish Catholic Directory,* 1863.
4. Diary, 85 v.
5. *Ibid.,* 39 v.
6. *Ibid.,* 53 v.
7. Bird, *Family Record.*
8. *Autobiography of Sir Andries Stockenstroom* (C.T. Juta, 1887), 78–9.
9. See Walker, *A History of South Africa,* Chapter VII.
10. Diary, 123.
11. *Ibid.,* 128.
12. *Ibid.,* s.d. 12 August.
13. *Ibid.,* 116.
14. *Ibid.,* 115 v.
15. *Ibid.,* 116 v, *ff.*
16. Archives of the Archdiocese of Cape Town.
17. Letter of John Bird to his son dated 3 February 1886, in Bird, *Family Record.*
18. Notebook of Bishop Devereux: apparently the edict was by Governor van Rheede.
19. *Annals of the Faith,* Vol. 4, p. 247. A Report by Bishop Griffith dated 18 April 1841, to the *Oeuvre de la propagation de la foi,* from whom he received a subsidy.
20. Diary, 85 v.

21. Allard, 344. The letters are numbered, and these references are to the numbers.
22. Book of Transactions and Memorials Regarding the Building of the new Roman Catholic Church at Cape Town.
23. See letter of John Bird (Christopher's son) to his son William dated 3 February 1886, in Bird, *Family Record*.
24. *C.M.*, X, 388.
25. Report on the State of Religion in the Central Districts: *Catholic Magazine*, VIII, 436, *ff.*
26. Diary, s.d. 22 August and 1 September 1838.
27. Letter to Dr O'Connell, P. P. Donnybrook.   14 March 1860. Bp. McC. Coll.
28. *C.M.*, XV, 74.
29. Transactions, s.d. January–July 1839.
30. *C.M.*, 1891, 473.
31. Printed *C.M.*, 1891, 595.
32. *Ibid.*, X 657.
33. Quoted *C.M.*, 1911, 28.
34. Book of Transactions and Memorials Regarding the Building of the new Roman Catholic Church at Cape Town.
35. Dom. Archives in Dublin, cited in *Irish Catholic Directory*, 1863, and *Annals of the Faith*, IV, 247.
36. *C.M.*, X, 388.
37. *C.M.*, VIII, 436.
38. Allard, 74.

CHAPTER II

1. *Chronicon*.
2. *Ibid.*, s.d. 1 January 1849.
3. Allard, 36.
4. *Ibid.*, 121.
5. The detail has been studied and set out by Professor A. F. Hattersley in his *British Settlement of Natal* (Cambridge University Press, 1950).
6. *Chronicon*, s.a. 1848, and Allard, 12.
7. Hattersley, *op. cit.*, 82 and 88.
8. Allard, 36.
9. *Chronicon*, February 1849.
10. Allard, 12.
11. *Ibid.*, 26.
12. *Chronicon*, s.a. 1847.
13. Allard 12.
14. O'Riley, *Notre Mère*, 50.
15. A full account of these negotiations and the foundation of the convent and school is given by A. O'Riley, *op. cit.*
16. Bishop Devereux's notes in the archives at Port Elizabeth.
17. *Ibid.*
18. O'Riley, *op. cit.*, 221.
19. Diary, *passim*.
20. Notes of Sister Mary Alacoque, O.P.
21. In O'Riley, *op. cit.*, and *Chronicon, passim*.
22. O'Riley, *op. cit., passim*.
23. Allard, 115.

24. *Ibid.*, 62.
25. *Ibid.*
26. Related by O'Riley, *op. cit.*
27. The description probably comes from Jeremiah O'Riley. It is given by his son in *Notre Mère*.
28. *Chronicon*, s.a., 1851.
29. Allard, 62.
30. *Ibid.*
31. *Ibid.*, 77.
32. *Ibid.*, 150.
33. *Ibid.*, 209.
34. *Ibid.*, 233.
35. *Ibid.*, 263 and 264.
36. *Ibid.*, 273.
37. *Ibid.*, 242.
38. *C.M.*, VIII, 436.
39. *Ibid.*, XIX.
40. Allard, 62.
41. O'Riley, *op. cit.*, 9.
42. Allard, 62.
43. Wilmot; *Life and Times of Ricards*, *passim*.
44. Allard, 62.
45. O'Riley, *op. cit.*, *passim*.
46. Notice in the *Chronicon*, s.a. 1856.

CHAPTER III

1. Autobiography, I, 6.
2. *Ibid.*, s.d. 11 January 1865.
3. *Ibid.*, I, s.a. 1865.
4. *Ibid.*, I, 119 (The pagination ceases after p. 121).
5. *Ibid.*, I, s.d. August 1865.
6. *Ibid.*, I, s.a. 1864.
7. *Ibid.*, s.a. 1865.
8. *Ibid.*, I, 7.
9. Quoted *C.M.*, XV, 130 *ff.*
10. O'Haire, *Recollections*, 41.
11. O'Riley, *Notre Mère*, 225.
12. Autobiography, II, s.a. 1874.
13. Letter of 26 March 1861.
14. Autobiography, I, 4.
15. *Ibid.*, s.a. 1864.
16. *Ibid.*, I, 4.
17. *Cape Argus*, 15 December 1863.
18. Autobiography, I, s.a. 1864.
19. *South African Advertiser and Mail*, 19 August 1869, quoted in *Recollections*.
20. O'Haire, *Recollections*, 364.
21. *Ibid.*, 258.
22. Letter of 24 August 1867, in *Recollections*, 350.
23. Autobiography, I, s.a. 1865.
24. O'Haire, *Recollections*, 270.
25. Autobiography, s.a. 1866.

26. O'Haire, *Recollections*, 364 *ff*.
27. *Ibid.*
28. *Ibid.*, 355.
29. Autobiography, II, 210.
30. *Ibid.*, s.a. 1868.
31. O'Haire, *Recollections*, 46.
32. *Ibid.*
33. Autobiography, s.a. 1864.
34. O'Haire, *Recollections*, 200.
35. Inserted in Autobiography, I, 50.
36. O'Haire, *Recollections*, 40.
37. Autobiography (continuation), II, 218.

CHAPTER IV

1. *In finem.*
2. Diary s.d. 11 December 1869.
3. *Ibid.*, s.d. 6 July.
4. The figures are analysed in *C.M.*, II, 465.
5. *C.M.*, VII, 235.
6. *Ibid.*, XII, 422.
7. *Ibid.*, VI, 165, reporting *The Standard and Digger News*.
8. Memoir by Wilmot in *C.M.*, XX.
9. *C.M.*, II, 327 *ff*.
10. Leonard, Letter Book I, s.d. 23 September 1881.
11. Autobiography (continuation), 218 v.
12. O'Haire, *Recollections*.
13. Autobiography, 218 v.
14. Leonard, Letter Book I, s.d. 22 May 1879.
15. Autobiography (continuation) s.a. 1874.
16. Leonard, Letter Book I, s.d. 21 June and 23 June 1880 and VII, s.d. 17 September 1885.
17. Autobiography (continuation) s.a. 1874.
18. Leonard, Letter Book VII, s.d. 25 August 1886.
19. *Ibid.*, VII, 675 *ff*.
20. See Bishop Simon's Diary, *passim*, and Leonard, Letter Book VII, 160 *ff*, 179, 221, 223, 231v, 245, 269v.
21. E.g., Leonard, Letter Book I, s.d. 19 October 1879 and 27 June 1880 and VII, 342v and 663.
22. *Ibid.*, VII, 407 *ff*.
23. *Ibid.*, I, s.d. 16 December 1879.
24. By Dr McCarthy on the history of the Church in South Africa and by Dr Kolbe on the history of education in South Africa; Notes by Bishop Leonard in the continuation of Grimley's Autobiography .
25. *C.M.*, XX, 27 *ff*.
26. Leonard, Letter Book VII, 809v.
27. *Ibid.*, I, s.d. 11 December 1879.
28. *Ibid.*, VII, 407.
29. *Ibid.*, 412 *ff*.
30. *Chronicon*, s.a. 1875.
31. Note by Mother Pius Galvin in Misc. Notes, Archives of King William's Town Dominican Convent.

32. *Chronicon*, s.a. 1877.
33. *Ibid.*, s.a. 1871.
34. *Ibid.*, s.d. 17 November 1879.
35. *Ibid.*
36. Quoted by P. J. Dahm, *Mariannhill*, p. 34.
37. Dahm, *op. cit.*
38. *Chronicon*, s.d. 18 June 1881.
39. *Ibid.*, s.d. 13 and 26 September 1882.
40. *Ibid.*, s.d. 30 June 1889, 28 and 30 April 1890.
41. *Ibid.*, s.d. 30 June 1888.
42. *Ibid.*, s.d. 14 July 1881.
43. *Ibid.*, s.a. 1886 and 1887.
44. Wilmot, *Life of Ricards.*
45. *Aletheia*, Preface.
46. *Ibid.*, 84.
47. *Ibid.*, 114.
48. *Ibid.*, 153.
49. *Chronicon*, s.a. 1890.
50. *Ibid.*, s.a. 1891.
51. *Ibid.*, s.a. 1893.
52. *Ibid.*, s.a. 1891.
53. *Ibid.*
54. *Ibid.*, s.a. 1894.
55. *Ibid.*

CHAPTER V

1. Autobiography, I, 45 *ff.*
2. Cape Superintendent's Report, 1882, quoted in Malherbe, *Education in South Africa* (Juta) 111.
3. Malherbe, *op. cit.*, 111.
4. *C.M.*, XVI, 329. Statement by Brother Callixte.
5. Bishop Strobino in the *Chronicon*, s.a. 1891.
6. *C.M.*, III, 716.
7. *Ibid.*, XVIII, 207.

CHAPTER VI

1. Autobiography, s.a. 1864.
2. *Ibid.*, I, 95 (s.a. 1864).
3. *Aperçu Historique*, 269.
4. Autobiography, II, s.a. 1869.
5. Diary of Journey to Vatican Council, s.d. 11 January 1870.
6. Autobiography, II, 210.
7. Memoir, 64.
8. *Aperçu Historique*, 269.
9. *Ibid.*
10. Bishop Grimley's Diary, s.d. 2 December 1869.
11. Letter to Bishop Leonard dated 18 October 1906.

CHAPTER VII

1. Allard, 26 and 24.
2. *Ibid.*, 139, 145, 154.

3. *Ibid.*, 12.
4. *Ibid.*, 5.
5. *Ibid.*, 26.
6. *Ibid.*, 18 and 26.
7. *Ibid.*, 22 and 86. The bishop, though not naming the gentleman who invited him to say Mass in his house, says that he was married to a Catholic, and implies that he was relatively well-off and helpful to Catholics. This fits in with what he writes elsewhere of Mr Snell (16 and 18), but of no one else mentioned in the correspondence.
8. *Ibid.*, 10.
9. *Ibid.*, 12.
10. *Ibid.*, 70.
11. *Ibid.*, 62.
12. *Ibid.*, 115.
13. *Ibid.*
14. *Collectanea S.C.P.F.*, 1392, 1465.
15. Allard, 115.
16. In this he was carrying out a decision of the Holy Office on a *dubium* sent by Bishop Griffith (*Collectanea* (Rome 1907) *S.C.P.F.*, 903). Bishop Grimley, Vicar Apostolic of Cape Town, reported to the Congregation of Propaganda that after diligent enquiry he had found that none of the sects in his vicariate set out conditions opposed to the substance of matrimony, (Autobiography, I, 44).
17. Allard, 36.
18. *Ibid.*, 10.
19. *Ibid.*, 292.
20. *Ibid.*, 299.
21. *Ibid.*, 121.
22. *Actus Administrationis in V.A. a Terra Natal Nuncupato*, 4.
23. Allard, 176.
24. *Ibid.*, 100, 101, 108, 124 125.
25. *Ibid.*, 37 and 38.
26. *Ibid.*, 204.
27. *Ibid.*, 212 and 355.
28. *Ibid.*, 282.
29. *Ibid.*, 261.
30. *Ibid.*, 283.
31. *Ibid.*, 271 and 279.
32. *Ibid.*, 26.
33. *Ibid.*, 35.
34. *Ibid.*, 53, 23 October 1852.
35. *Ibid.*, 34.
36. *Ibid.*, 35 and 68.
37. *Clartés Australes, passim.*
38. According to a letter of the late Father Leo Sormany, O.M.I., who saw some papers in the Archives of the Archbishop of Durban which have since disappeared.
39. March 1897 list of schools, Archives of the Archbishop of Durban.
40. Quoted *C.M.*, IX, 367.
41. Letter of 10 August 1876, to the Cardinal Prefect of Propaganda.
42. Letter 15 October 1877.
43. Letter, 2 July 1880, to the Cardinal Prefect of Propaganda.

44. Letters, 6 December 1883 and 9 May 1887, to the Cardinal Prefect of Propaganda.
45. Letter to the Congregation of Propaganda, 10 June 1884.
46. *Actes du Conseil*, Natal, 23 October 1888.
47. *Ibid.*, 21 August 1895.
48. *Ibid.*, July 1895.
49. *Ibid.*, 12 May 1892 and 13 January 1894.
50. *Ibid.*, 25 May 1891 and July 1895.
51. Report to the Holy Office, 27 November 1888. Draft in the Archives of the Archbishop of Durban.
52. Report of March 1897 to the Congregation of Propaganda. Draft in the Archives of the Archbishop of Durban.

Chapter VIII

1. *Kurze geschichtliche Ubersicht über das apostolische Vikariat Kimberley*, by Father F. J. Hagel, O.M.I. Much of the detail in the following pages comes from this monograph.
2. Letter of 2 July 1880.
3. E.g., letters of 1880, 2 July, and 1885, s.d., to the Cardinal Prefect of Propaganda.
4. Allard, 282 and 291.
5. Confirmed by a letter of the Congregation which Bishop Jolivet acknowledged on 10 August 1876.
6. Draft letters of 15 March and 2 July 1880, to the Congregation of Propaganda.
7. Undated draft of letter of 1885 or later, to the Congregation of Propaganda.
8. E.g. of 4 November 1879.
9. Quoted in Wilmot, *Life of Ricards*, 139.
10. Draft letter of 4 November 1879, to the Congregation of Propaganda.
11. Draft letter of 12 August 1882, to the Congregation of Propaganda.
12. Leonard, Letter-book VII, 809 v.
13. *Kurze Übersicht*, p. 18, quoting *Missiones Catholicae*, 1895.
14. Letter of 12 August 1882, to the Congregation of Propaganda.
15. *C.M.*, V, 682.
16. *Ibid.*, II, 357.
17. *Ibid.*, VII, 169.
18. *Ibid.*, VII, 235.
19. *Ibid.*, II, 327.
20. *Naboth's Vineyard*, Preface, x.
21. *Ibid.*, 41.
22. *Ibid.*, 160.
23. Bird, *Family Record*.
24. Quoted in *C.M.*, VIII, 436.
25. *Recollections*, 86 and 87.
26. *Ibid.*, 357.
27. *C.M.*, V, 164.
28. *Ibid.*, I.
29. Bird, *Family Record*, and Wilmot, *Life of Ricards*.
30. Butler, from *Naboth's Vineyard*, 90.

31. *Ibid.*, 130.
32. *Ibid.*, 143.
33. Diary, *passim.*
34. *C.M.*, XXI, 30 and 113.
35. Letter of 26 May 1864, to O'Haire, in O'Haire's *Recollections.*
36. Allard, 322 and 323.
37. Notebook, quoted in *C.M.*, VIII, 436.
38. Allard, 61.
39. *C.M.*, I, 353.
40. *Ibid.*, II, 575.
41. *Ibid.*, VIII, 467.
42. O'Haire, *Recollections*, 126.
43. Autobiography, I, s.a. 1864.
44. *Ibid.*
45. *Ibid.*, II, s.a. 1868.
46. *C.M.*, I, 343.
47. *Ibid.*, II, 505.
48. *Ibid.*, II, 505.
49. *Ibid.*, IV, 60.
50. *Ibid.*, III, 242.
51. *Ibid.*, 435.
52. *Ibid.*, III, 191*ff*, 503*ff*, 565*ff*.
53. *Ibid.*, III, 192.
54. *Ibid.*, VIII, 593.
55. *Ibid.*, V, 697.
56. *Ibid.*, III, 565*ff*.
57. *Ibid.*, VI, 365.
58. Autobiography, II, s.d. 2 July 1869.
59. Letter of 4 November 1879, from Bishop Jolivet to the Congregation of Propaganda.
60. *Naboth's Vineyard*, 161–2.
61. *C.M.*, LX, 376.
62. *Ibid.*, 410.
63. *Ibid.*, 545.
64. *Ibid.*, 170.
65. *Ibid.*, X, 693 and XI, 1.
66. *Ibid.*, XVI, 142.
67. *Ibid.*, XV, 326.
68. *Ibid.*, XVI, 375.
69. *Ibid.*, XVIII, 252.
70. *Ibid.*
71. *Ibid.*, XVII, 404.
72. *Ibid.*, XIV, 359.
73. *Ibid.*, XIV, 131.
74. *Ibid.*, XVI, 314.
75. *Ibid.*, XVI, 329.
76. *Ibid.*, XVI, 314.
77. *Ibid.*, XVI, 329.
78. *Ibid.*, XX, 2.
79. *Ibid.*, XXI, 113.

CHAPTER IX

1. *Annals of the Faith*, IV, 247*ff*.
2. O'Haire, *Recollections*, 125–134.
3. *Ibid.*, introduction, 12.
4. Autobiography, II, s.a. 1868.
5. O'Haire, *Recollections*, 140.
6. Autobiography, I, 101.
7. O'Haire, *Recollections*, 215.
8. *Ibid.*, 86.
9. Allard, 320.
10. *Ibid.*, 347, 349, 350, 351, 352.
11. *Ibid.*, 355.
11a. *Clarte's Australes*, 12
12. Allard 35.
13. *Ibid.*, 26.
14. *Clartés Australes*, 130.
15. Allard, 355.
16. *Ibid.*
17. Father Gerard to Mgr de Mazenod, 12 April 1861.
18. Allard, 355.
19. *Ibid.*
20. *Clartés Australes*, 149.
21. Allard, 355.
22. *Clartés Australes*, 2.
23. Laydevant, *Basutoland*, 10.
24. Autobiography, II, s.a. 1869.
25. *Clartés Australes*, quoting the Notebook of Father Gerard.
26. Gerard's Retreat-note of 19 March 1864.
27. Letter of Father Le Bihan to Bishop Jolivet, dated 29 June 1882, in the Archives of the Archbishop of Durban.
28. Letters of 18 and 28 July to Bishop Jolivet, *Ibid.*
29. *Basutoland*, 17.
30. *Clartés Australes*, 240 and 260.
31. Retreat note of Father Gerard, 19 March 1864, quoted in *Clartés Australes*.
32. *Clartés Australes*, 244.
33. *Clartés Australes*, 246.
34. Letter of 2 July 1882, to Bishop Jolivet in the Archives of the Archbishop of Durban.
35. Letter of Bishop Jolivet, 28 May 1888, in the Archives of the Archbishop of Durban.
36. *Basutoland*, 45.
37. Archives of the Archbishop of Durban.
38. *Clartés Australes*, 250*ff*.
39. *Basutoland*, 17–19.
39a. *Ibid.*, 11.
40. Letter to the Congregation of Propaganda in the Archives of the Archbishop of Durban.
41. *Actes du Conseil* (O.M.I.), Natal, in the Archives of the Archbishop of Durban.
42. *Ibid.*, s.a. 1888.
43. *Ibid.*, s.a. 1891.
44. *Ibid.*, s.a. 1895.

45. Report to the Congregation of Propaganda, March 1897, in the Archives of the Archbishop of Durban.
46. Letters in the Oblate archives in Rome.
47. *Missions*, December 1925, 283.
48. *Ibid.*
49. Letter to Father Augier in *Missions*, December 1896, p. 443.
50. Letter of Father Mathieu in *Missions*, September 1901.
51. Report in *Missions*, December 1925.
52. *Ibid.*
53. Letter to Father Augier in *Missions*, December 1896.
54. *Missions*, December 1925.
55. *Ibid.*, December 1896.
56. *Ibid.*, December 1925.
57. *Ibid.*
58. *Ibid.*, December 1896.
59. *Ibid.*, December 1925.
60. *Ibid.*, December 1909.
61. *Ibid.*, March 1909.

Chapter X

1. Dahm, *Mariannhill*; see list of sources.
2. In the Archives of the Archbishop of Durban. It is in somewhat stilted French, probably a translation.
3. *Der Trappist unter den Kaffern*, quoted in Dahm, *op. cit.*, 47.
4. In the Archives of the Archbishop of Durban.
5. In *Fliegende Blätter*, 1883, No. 12, quoted by Dahm, *op. cit.*, 178.
6. Dahm, *op. cit.*, 139 *ff*.
7. *Ibid.*, 150.
8. *Ibid.*, 47.
9. *Ibid.*, 57.
10. Quoted by Dahm, *op. cit.*, 59.
11. Bishop Jolivet's Letters, in the Archives of the Archbishop of Durban.
12. Dahm, *op. cit.*, 64.
13. Bishop Jolivet mentions Father Julius as one; but the vicar general apparently left them anonymous; Dahm, *op. cit.*, 68–9.
14. Dahm, *op. cit.*, 54.
15. *Ibid.*, 124–5.
16. *Mariannhill* (Detroit, 1935), 96.
17. Quoted in Dahm, *op. cit.*, 167.
18. Schimlek, *Mariannhill*, Chapters VI and IX.
19. Quoted by Dahm, *op. cit.*, 198, from the *Natal Record*.
20. Dahm, *op. cit.*, 202.
21. *Ibid.*, 191.
22. *Ibid.*, 188.
23. *Vergissmeinnicht*, 1889, cited Dahm, *op. cit.*, 173.
24. Dahm, *op. cit.*, 198*ff*.
25. Quoted Dahm, *op. cit.*, 192–3.
26. *Vergissmeinnicht*, 1889, Nos. 5–7, cited by Dahm, *op. cit.*, 173.
27. Schwemmer, quoted by Dahm, *op. cit.*, 174, and by Schimlek, *Mariannhill*, 362*ff*.
28. Preface to Bryant's Dictionary.

29. Appeal to the Holy Father dated 26 September 1916, in the Archives of the Archbishop of Durban.
30. Letter to the vicar apostolic dated 13 May 1916: *Ibid.*
31. Circulated 12 November 1914: *Ibid.*
32. Letter of Father M. Kalus dated 30 April 1915: *Ibid.*
33. Circular dated 24 April 1951: *Ibid.*
34. Circular dated 6 June, 1915: *Ibid.*
35. Preface to Bryant's Dictionary (1905 edition).
36. Letter of Father Cyprian Ballweg to the vicar apostolic, dated 29 April 1915, in the Archives of the Archbishop of Durban.
37. Letter of Father Julius Mbhele to the vicar apostolic dated 2 March 1915: *Ibid.*
38. Mariannhill, Zulu Question: *Ibid.*
39. Appeal to Rome dated 26 September 1916; copy sent to the vicar apostolic; *Ibid.*
40. Letter to Father J. B. Sauter dated 21 November 1923: *Ibid.*
41. The abbot's report of the conference: *Ibid.* For another view see *The Catholic Zulu Terminology Dispute* published in Mariannhill, 1958.
42. Letter of Abbot Wolpert to the vicar apostolic dated 16 October 1915, in the Archives of the Archbishop of Durban.
43. Letter to the Cardinal Prefect dated 31 May 1916, from a draft in the Archives of the Archbishop of Durban.
44. Letter of Bishop Delalle to the Prime Minister dated 20 May 1915: copy in the Archives of the Archbishop of Durban.
45. Letter of Abbot Wolpert to the vicar apostolic dated 15 October 1915: *Ibid.*
46. Letter to the vicar apostolic dated 2 March 1915: *Ibid.*
47. Letter to the vicar apostolic undated but apparently of 1917: *Ibid.*
48. Plea of Mathias Maphalala, Vitus Khathi and Maria Zulu dated 26 September 1916 (in Zulu and Italian): *Ibid.*
49. Vicar apostolic to Abbot Wolpert, 21 June 1916: *Ibid.*
50. Letter of Bishop Delalle, 18 November 1916: *Ibid.*
51. Letter of vicar apostolic to Father Wanger, 29 May 1916: *Ibid.*
52. Letter to Father Wanger by apostolic visitors, 16 December 1919, and to vicar apostolic, 19 December 1919 and 20 February 1920: *Ibid.*
53. Letter of Visitors to Bishop Delalle, 20 February 1920: *Ibid.*
54. Letter in Archives of Archbishop of Durban.
55. Petition of Mathias Maphalala, Vitus Khathi and Maria Zulu, original in Italian: *Ibid.* At the time it was generally recognized that the real author of the petition was Father Wanger himself; a fact later verified by Vitus Khathi (letter of Rev J. B. Sauter dated 14 August 1958, in the Archives of the Archbishop of Durban).
56. Letter of Rev J. B. Sauter, C.M.M., *ibid.*, in the Archives of the Archbishop of Durban.
57. See the dramatized account in Father Schimlek's *Mariannhill*, 170–187.
58. See the accounts, dramatized and undocumented but based on facts, given by Father Schimlek in *Medicine versus Witchcraft* and *Mariannhill*.
59. Schimlek, *Mariannhill*, 189.

CHAPTER XI

1. *C.M.*, XVI, 106.

2. *Ibid.*, I, 657.
3. *Ibid.*, VIII, 412.
4. Autobiography, II, 300.
5. *Chronicon*, s.d. 15 February, 11 April and 6 September 1890.
6. *C.M.*, XIV, 545.
7. *Ibid.*, XIV, 57 and 139.
8. *Ibid.*, I, 228.
9. *Ibid.*, XIV, 232.
10. *Ibid.*, IV, 354; XII, 28, quoting from the *Cape Times*; XIV, 375.
11. *Ibid.*, I, 343.
12. *Ibid.*, XVIII, 286.
13. *Ibid.*, XVIII, 207*ff.*
14. *Ibid.*
15. *Ibid.*, XII, 278.
16. *Ibid.*, VI, 165, quoting *The Standard and Digger News.*
17. *Ibid.*, XIV, 250; VIII, 464; XX, 4; XV, 225.
18. *Ibid.*, VIII, 46.
19. *Ibid.*, XVII, 350.
20. *Ibid.*, VIII, 467*ff.*
21. *Ibid.*, XVII, 22*ff.*
22. *Ibid.*, X, 72*ff.*
23. *Four Mysteries of Faith.*
24. *C.M.*, X, 85*ff.*
25. *Ibid.*, IV, 354*ff.*
26. *Ibid.*, V, 177.
27. *Ibid.*, VII, 531.
28. *Ibid.*, XV, 2.

CHAPTER XII

1. *C.M.*, XIII, 77.
2. *Cape Times*, 17 September 1883.
3. *C.M.*, II, 1.
4. *Ibid.*, XIII, 80.
5. *Ibid.*, X, 282.
6. *Ibid.*, XIX, 371.
7. *Ibid.*, XV, 65*ff.*
8. *Ibid.*, XV, 333.
9. *Ibid.*, XVI, 314*ff.*
10. *Ibid.*, XXI, 247.
11. " No Servile Tenure ", in *Daylight and Champaign.*
12. Autobiography, II, 183, s.a. 1869.
13. *Ibid.*, 185.
14. *Cape Times*, 17 September 1883; quoted in Autobiography (continuation), s.a. 1883.
15. Autobiography, II, s.a. 1869.
16. *Ibid.*
17. *Chronicon*, s.a. 1879 (in his own hand).
18. *C.M.*, I, 1891, 581.
19. *Ibid.*, XX, 43.
20. *Ibid.*, XXX, 301, and XXXIII, 419.
21. *Ibid.*, XXX, 230.

Chapter XIII

1. *Zambes: Mission Record*, II, 436 and VI, 378–9.
2. *C.M.*, XV, 505.
3. *Ibid.*, XXV, 516.
4. Report to the Congregation of Propaganda, No. 39 in File " Convent at Umzinto ": Archives of the Archbishop of Durban.
5. Decree of the Congregation of Propaganda dated 13 August 1911.
6. Decree of the Congregation of Religious of 26 June 1917.
7. Letter of Bishop Delalle, 15 December 1917: copy in the Archives of the Archbishop of Durban.
8. Report of Bishop Delalle in *Missions*, March 1909.

Chapter XIV

1. *C.M.*, XVII, 404.
2. *Ibid.*, XIX, 139.
3. *Ibid.*, XIX, 269.
4. *Ibid.*, XX, 2.
5. *Ibid.*, XX, 244.
6. *Ibid.*, XVIII, 382.
7. *Ibid.*, XX, 308.
8. *Ibid.* XXII, 3.
9. *Ibid.* XXII, 1.
10. *Ibid.*, XXI, 113.
11. *Ibid.*, XXIV, 425.
12. *Ibid.*, XXIV, 563.
13. *Ibid.*, XXV, 49, 102, 129, 181.
14. *Ibid.*, XXVI, 111; XXVII, 37, 88, 321.
15. *Ibid.*, XXVII, 88.
16. *Ibid.*, XXVI, 385; XXVII, 411.
17. *Ibid.*, XXVII, 168.
18. *Ibid.*, XXVII, 459, 599.
19. *Ibid.*, XXXIV, 74.
20. *Ibid.*, XXVII, 6, 36, 55, 134.
21. Letter Books in the Archives of the Archbishop of Durban.
22. Letter of 21 October 1917 in the Archives of the Archbishop of Durban.
23. *C.M.*, XXIX, 138.
24. *Ibid.*, XI, 1ff.
25. *Ibid.*, XXVII, 92.
26. *Ibid.*, XXV, 559.
27. *Ibid.*, XXVI, 326.
28. *Ibid.*, XXXIII, 557.
29. Letter of the vicar apostolic to the Cardinal Prefect of Propaganda, dated 13 December 1905, in the Archives of the Archbishop of Durban.
30. *C.M.*, XXIX, 66.
31. *Ibid.*, 337.
32. *Ibid.*, 385.
33. *Ibid.*, XXX, 1 and 193.

INDEX

Adolph, Father, disgruntled Trappist, 236-7

Advertiser and Mail, Cape Colony, 77, 81

African Missions, Fathers of the (S.M.A.), 42, 95, 140, 141, 142, 332

Albany, Cape Colony, 15, 17

Aletheia, by Bishop Ricards, 112, 113, 116-9

Alexandra township, 303

Algoa Bay, Bishop Griffith at, 28

Alice, Cape Colony, 101

Aliwal, diocese of, 331, 332; seminary at Aliwal North, 329

Allard, Bishop Marie Jean François, O.M.I., first Vicar Apostolic of Natal, arrives, 152; initial preoccupations, 152-60; missions to the Zulus, 160-2, 204-6; in Basutoland, 207-22; in the Boer Republics, 49, 170, 171, 172; resigns, 83; view of the Dutch, 183, 188; of the British, 146, 210, 291; mentioned, 35, 42, 48, 50, 137, 205, 301

Allies, T. W., 44

Alois, Father, Zulu secular priest, 256

Annals of Natal, 86

Apartheid, 339-51

Assumptionist nuns, French, at Grahamstown, 44, 102

Augenis, Bushmanland, 62

Augsburg, Bavaria, 102, 103, 105, 109, 134, 298

Augustinian Canonesses (Canonesses Regular Hospitallers of the Mercy of Jesus of the Order of St Augustine), in Natal, 166, 224, 228, 301-2

Baird, Major-General Sir David, 6, 9, 22

Bantu Education Act (1953), 339-40, 346-7

Barberton, Transvaal, 171, 174, 175

Barkly West, near Kimberley, 170

Barnabò, Cardinal Prefect of Propaganda, 74, 140, 141, 142, 156, 158

Barr, Frederick, first Editor of *The Cape Colonist*, 47

Barret, Father, O.M.I., missionary to the Zulus, 160, 205

Barry, Henry Edward, 140, 61(?)

Basutoland, prefecture of (later vicariate), 45; becomes dioceses of Maseru and Leribe, *qq.v.*, 336; Jolivet in, 163-74, *passim*; Allard in, 207-23; mentioned, 85, 104, 137, 142, 301, 321, 324, 326, 327, 329, 331, 339

Bathurst, Cape Colony, 15, 17, 29

Baudry, Father Alexander, O.M.I., second Prefect Apostolic of Basutoland, 228

Beaconsfield, near Kimberley, 170

Beaufort (Fort Beaufort; Beaufort West), 17, 18, 19, 30, 38, 140, 195, 197, 200

Bechuanas, Bechuanaland, entrusted to the O.M.I., 143, 151; in Kimberley vicariate, 174, 336; prefecture of, 331, 337; British protectorate, 321, 327; mentioned, 40, 138, 140, 142, 334

Begley, Mr, of Cape Town, 24

Bell, Colonel, 9, 25, 30

Benedict XV, Pope, 317

Benedictines, in Zululand, 225; in Transvaal, 324; Congregation of St Ottilien, 334; Cassinese Congregation, 335, *and see* Pietersburg, Abbey Nullius of; nuns, 329

Bethlehem mission, Orange Free State, 227; diocese of, 331, 336

Bethulie, Orange Free State, 170

Bird, Lt.-Colonel Christopher, 25; *also* 8, 10, 13, 24, 53, 178; John, son of, 86-7; *also* 39, 152, 153, 159, 178, 179, 180

Bloemfontein, capital of Orange Free State, metropolitan See, 331, 334, 335; Hoenderwanger's mission, 42, 48, 160, 170; schools at, 134, 171; Apostolic Delegation at, 327-8; mentioned, 39, 41, 152, 156, 163, 164, 172, 209

Blue Nuns, *see* Little Company of Mary

Bompart, Father, O.M.I., 158, 170, 171

Boshof, President, of the Orange River State, 49, 188

Botha, Louis, 190, 191, 247, 312-3, 321

Braamfontein, Transvaal, 191, 303

Brady, Rev. John, 8, 12

Brand, Sir Jan Hendrik, President of the Orange Free State, 77, 171, 188 and n.

Breecher, Mr, Lutheran missionary at Kokfontein, 64-5, 67

Bremersdorp, diocese of, 331, 335; see Swaziland

373